lonely planet

CRUISE PORTS
CARIBBEAN

A GU[illegible]YS ON SHORE

Joshua Kinser, Ray Bartlett, Paul Clammer, Alex Egerton,
Anna Kaminski, Catherine Le Nevez, Hugh McNaughtan,
Liza Prado, Andrea Schulte-Peevers, Regis St Louis,
Mara Vorhees, Luke Waterson, Karla Zimmerman

Contents

In September 2017 the Caribbean was hit by two Category 5 hurricanes (p300). While we have endeavoured to keep the information in this book as up-to-date as possible, some places may still be affected while the communities rebuild.

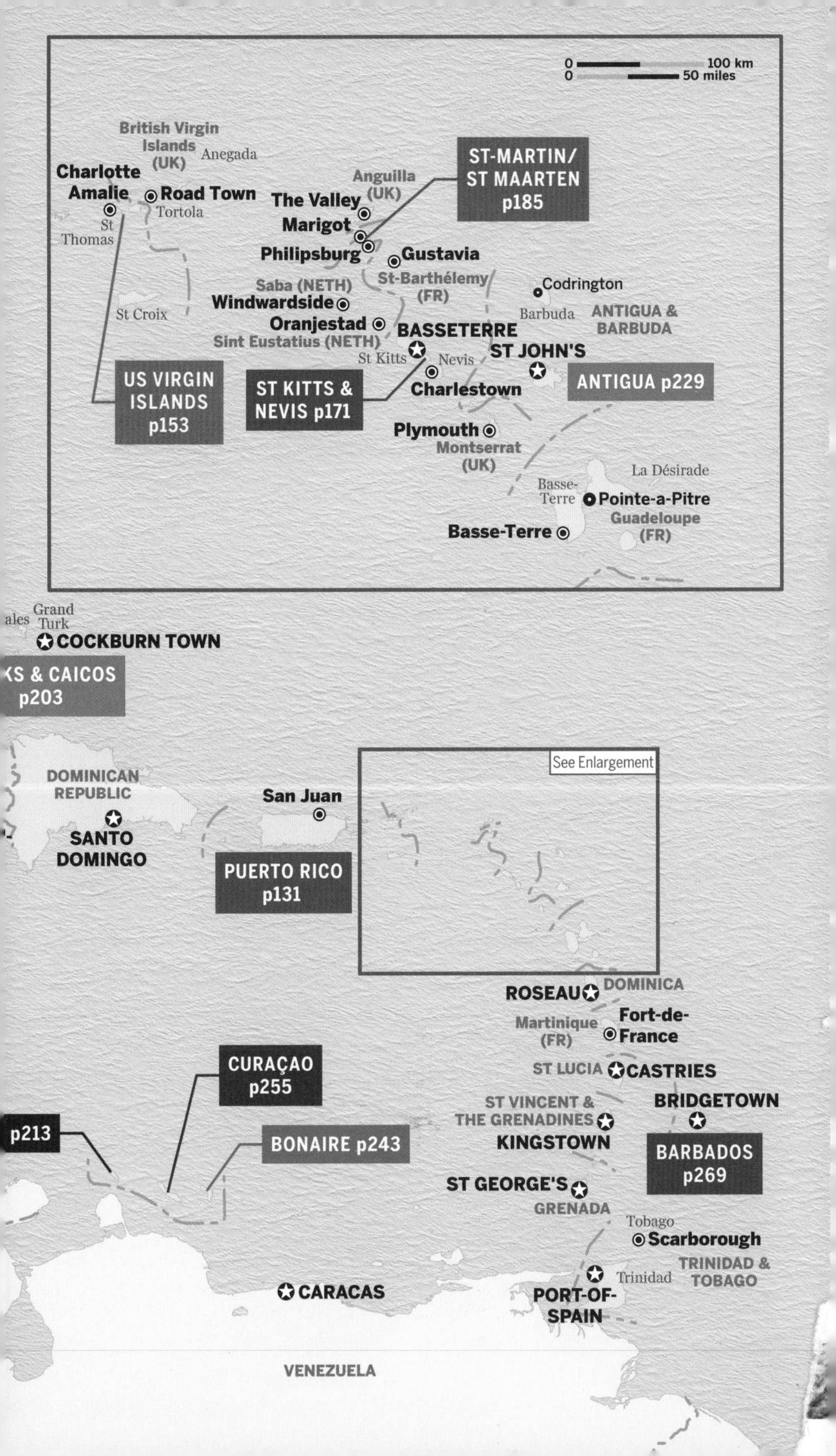

0 100 km
0 50 miles

British Virgin Islands (UK)
Anegada
Charlotte Amalie
Road Town
Tortola
St Thomas
St Croix
Anguilla (UK)
The Valley
Marigot
Philipsburg
ST-MARTIN/ ST MAARTEN p185
Gustavia
St-Barthélemy (FR)
Saba (NETH)
Windwardside
Oranjestad
Sint Eustatius (NETH)
BASSETERRE
St Kitts
Nevis
Charlestown
Codrington
Barbuda
ANTIGUA & BARBUDA
ST JOHN'S
ANTIGUA p229
US VIRGIN ISLANDS p153
ST KITTS & NEVIS p171
Plymouth
Montserrat (UK)
La Désirade
Basse-Terre
Pointe-a-Pitre
Guadeloupe (FR)
Basse-Terre

Grand Turk
ales
COCKBURN TOWN
KS & CAICOS p203
DOMINICAN REPUBLIC
SANTO DOMINGO
San Juan
PUERTO RICO p131
See Enlargement
ROSEAU
DOMINICA
Martinique (FR)
Fort-de-France
ST LUCIA
CASTRIES
CURAÇAO p255
p213
BONAIRE p243
ST VINCENT & THE GRENADINES
KINGSTOWN
BRIDGETOWN
BARBADOS p269
ST GEORGE'S
GRENADA
Tobago
Scarborough
TRINIDAD & TOBAGO
Trinidad
PORT-OF-SPAIN
CARACAS
VENEZUELA

Allure
Seas

Welcome to Caribbean Cruise Ports

From mountain peaks to shimmering reefs, spicy salsa rhythms to deep rolling reggae, pirate hideouts to sugar-sand beaches, the Caribbean is a dizzyingly diverse region to explore on a cruise ship.

Cruise the Caribbean and discover a joyous mosaic of islands beckoning paradise hunters. It's a lively and intoxicating profusion of people and places spread over 7000 islands (fewer than 10% are inhabited). But, for all they share, there's also much that makes them different. Can there be a greater contrast than the bustling capital of San Juan in Puerto Rico and the largely undeveloped hideaway of St John in the US Virgin Islands? Or between booming British-oriented St Kitts and its sleepy Dutch-affiliated neighbor Sint Eustatius, just across a narrow channel?

Set sail on azure seas and dock near dazzling white beaches and verdant forests so vivid you'll need sunglasses to avoid hurting the eyes. Dive below the waters for a color chart of darting fish and corals. Feel the sand between your toes at any one of a thousand picture-perfect beaches. Outdoor-adventure enthusiasts make a beeline for unspoilt islands such as nature-lovers' Nevis near St Kitts or the diving around Grand Cayman and Curaçao.

You can find any kind of island adventure here. You can choose to relax on the sand or the ship, party at a resort, explore a new community, hop between islands, discover wonders under the water or catch a perfect wave above, revel in a centuries-old culture (and sway to some of the world's greatest music while you're at it), and then run off to find your inner pirate...

Just about anything is possible in the Caribbean.

Cruise the Caribbean and discover a joyous mosaic of islands beckoning paradise hunters

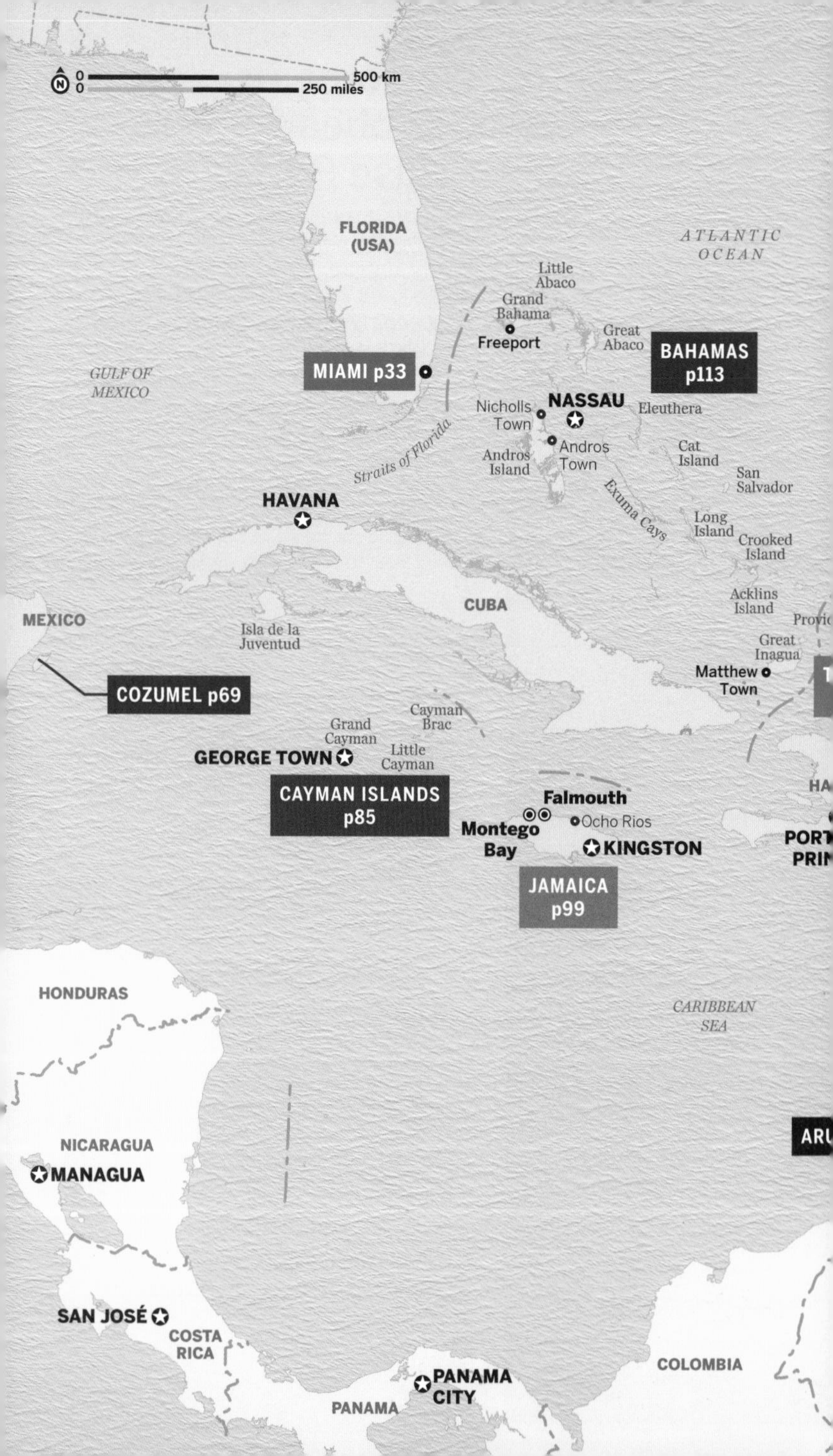

0
0
500 km
250 miles
FLORIDA (USA)
ATLANTIC OCEAN
GULF OF MEXICO
Little Abaco
Grand Bahama
Freeport
Great Abaco
BAHAMAS p113
MIAMI p33
Nicholls Town
NASSAU
Eleuthera
Andros Town
Andros Island
Straits of Florida
Cat Island
San Salvador
Exuma Cays
Long Island
Crooked Island
HAVANA
Acklins Island
CUBA
MEXICO
Isla de la Juventud
Great Inagua
Matthew Town
COZUMEL p69
Cayman Brac
Grand Cayman
Little Cayman
GEORGE TOWN
CAYMAN ISLANDS p85
Falmouth
Montego Bay
Ocho Rios
KINGSTON
JAMAICA p99
HONDURAS
CARIBBEAN SEA
NICARAGUA
MANAGUA
SAN JOSÉ
COSTA RICA
PANAMA CITY
PANAMA
COLOMBIA

Plan Your Trip
Cruise Ports Caribbean Top 12

DARRYL BROOKS/SHUTTERSTOCK ©

St-Martin/Sint Maarten

Half French, half Dutch, all Caribbean

Within walking distance of St-Martin's dock in Philipsburg are world-class beaches lined with shops, restaurants, and bars, as well as a historic district that can easily be explored with only a day in port. A ferry from the cruise port to the seafront shopping district makes St-Martin particularly accessible. Locals are exceptionally friendly, and the absence of street and beach peddlers makes the port experience a breath of fresh sea air.

1

MFFOTO/SHUTTERSTOCK ©

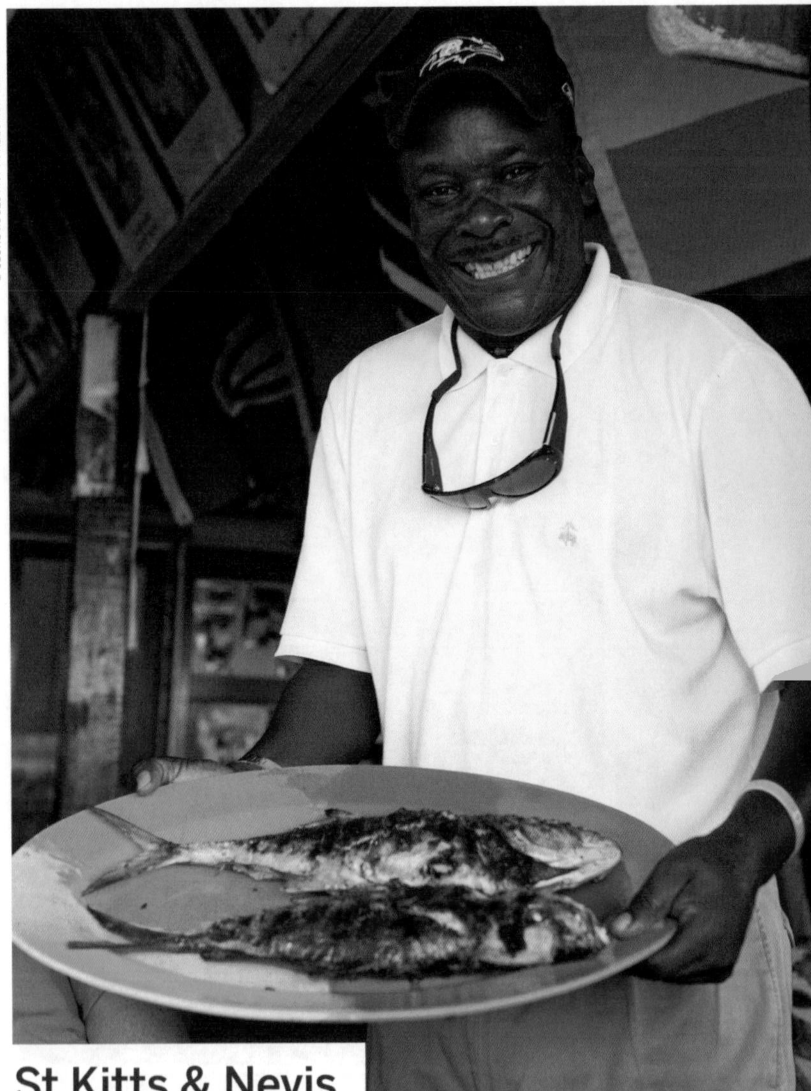

St Kitts & Nevis

Authentic Caribbean islands

Whether it's the unpretentious and honest local flavors found in the restaurants, or the vast protected swaths of tropical terrain on the islands, cruising to these two volcanic stars of the Caribbean is to sail into the very heart of the West Indies. St Kitts and Nevis are highlights of the Caribbean route: honest and down-to-earth islands without the tourist hype. Sunshine's Beach Bar & Grill, Nevis (p177)

2

GAIL JOHNSON/SHUTTERSTOCK ©

GRACECAT/SHUTTERSTOCK ©

Curaçao

Leisurely strolls and blue liqueur

This eminently walkable cruise port is lined with pastel-colored storefronts, bars, and restaurants that are sure to fill you with the Caribbean spirit, and any room left can be topped off with a cocktail made from the island's Curaçao liqueur. The Dutch, Spanish, and Caribbean history of the island can be explored by crossing the Queen Emma Bridge and trekking around Punda, the main shopping and tourism district of the island.

3

Barbados

Beautiful beaches and Bajan buffets

Barbados has some of the best beaches found along the Caribbean cruising routes. Whether you're looking to snorkel, swim, surf, or just sit in the shade of a tropical palm, the beach that you've been missing your entire life is waiting for you here. Add excellent shopping, restaurants, and historical sights all near the cruise terminal in Bridgetown and you have a recipe for cruise-port perfection that's as wonderful as the sticky pudding and popular Bajan buffets reflecting the English and Caribbean heritage of this multicultural island.

Bonaire

A scuba diver's paradise

Bonaire is a diver's paradise – so much so that it features on the license plates. Passengers looking to snorkel will love the large number of dive sites and impressive reefs that line the island's coast. The beaches are largely rock and coral, rather than the long stretches of white sand found on other Caribbean islands. Dive in with a mask and fins though and you'll find a reason to smile among the stunning coral and diverse sea life.

CHRISTOPHER KIMMEL/GETTY IMAGES ©

CORALIE MATHIEU/SHUTTERSTOCK ©

JUNIOR BRAZ/SHUTTERSTOCK ©

Aruba

White-sand beaches and stylish shopping

The long stretches of exceptionally beautiful white-sand beaches are the top Aruba attraction for cruise passengers, and just steps from the dock are upscale shops, casinos, restaurants, beach bars, and historical sights that you and your shipmates can explore. Several beaches are within walking distance of the cruise port, but beat the crowds and head north to some of the most picture-worthy stretches of sandy coast.

BLUEORANGE STUDIO/SHUTTERSTOCK ©

St Thomas & St John

Escape the crowds

While St Thomas is a wonderful port in its own right, the real pirate treasure lies off the coast on the nearby island of St John. Take the ferry to visit this mostly undeveloped and preserved island, where luxury and natural beauty are as perfectly blended as the iced piña coladas being served: a ticket for the St John island ferry is your pass to Caribbean contentment.

Grand Cayman

A touch of Euro style

Even though tourists can often overwhelm the charm of this European-influenced cruise port, the nearby sun-drenched beaches and excellent shopping within walking distance of the dock keep passengers coming back to Grand Cayman. Leave the bustle of the beach bars and busy boutiques behind and board a boat headed to one of the offshore reefs for snorkeling or diving on some of the best underwater sites in the Caribbean.

Top right: Seven Mile Beach (p88)

RUTH PETERKIN/SHUTTERSTOCK ©

STEPHEN FRINK COLLECTION / ALAMY STOCK PHOTO ©

9

Grand Turk

Highlights are beneath the surface

There's great shopping and beaches close to the port, but the real island sights are swimming and swaying in the currents below the ocean's surface. The adventurous will find diving and snorkeling bliss among the largely healthy and remarkably colorful reefs that lie just offshore. This scrubby and dry Atlantic island has some of the largest reefs in the world, so pack your mask, fins, and underwater cameras in your cruise luggage.

DENIS BURDIN/SHUTTERSTOCK ©

CLAUDE HUOT/SHUTTERSTOCK ©

ANNA HOYCHUK/SHUTTERSTOCK ©

Antigua

Great beaches and maritime history

Spend some time in the sun at one of the great beaches on the west coast of the island, such as Valley Church Beach. Then head south and visit Nelson's Dockyard for a look through the historic porthole into the maritime marvel of this well-preserved harbor that was once used by Horatio Nelson to repair and refit Royal Navy ships during the Napoleonic Wars.

10

SEAN PAVONE/SHUTTERSTOCK ©

San Juan

Explore the Old Town on foot

Spanish, American and Caribbean history and culture collide on Puerto Rico, where cruise passengers will enjoy walking the cobblestone streets of Old Town San Juan. The central location of the cruise port makes this stop a joy for passengers wanting to take in the sights on foot. El Yunque National Forest boasts lush rainforest trails, exotic wildlife and tropical botanical spectacles.

11

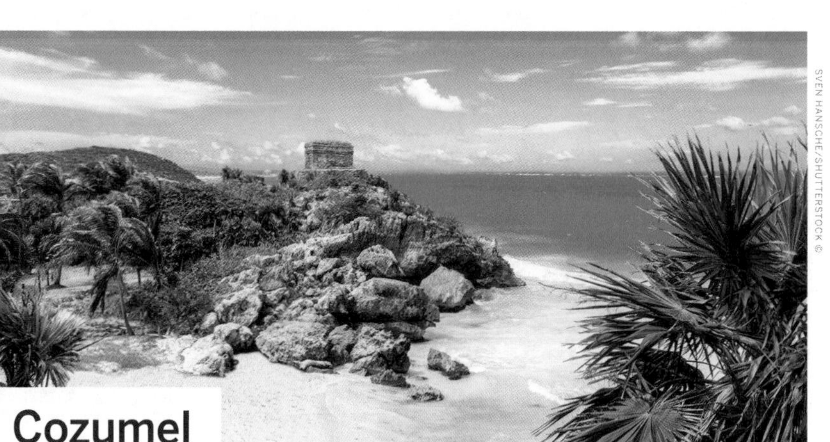

SVEN HANSCHE/SHUTTERSTOCK ©

Cozumel

A great base for the Yucatán coast

You may feel as if you've sailed back in time if you day-trip to the ancient Mayan ruins of Tulum near the island of Cozumel. The towering, iconic temples are relics of the complex civilization that once inhabited this stretch of the Mexican Riviera. A less-developed southern coast with long beaches and easy access to shopping, beach bars, and authentic as well as affordable Mexican cuisine round out the highlights of this culturally rich island.

12

Plan Your Trip
Hot Spots for...

CLAUDIO306/SHUTTERSTOCK ©

Beaches

The Caribbean has a beach for everyone, whether you're looking to snorkel, swim or just lounge in the sun with a rum punch in hand.

Barbados (p269)
Barbados is the island darling of beach lovers worldwide with excellent surfing, diving and swimming.

Carlisle Bay
Snorkel fine reefs at beaches near the port. (p272)

Aruba (p213)
White sand and long stretches of beach make it easy for cruise passengers to find a secluded spot.

Eagle Beach
Less-crowded beach with bars and cafes. (p218)

St-Martin/Sint Maarten (p185)
A beautiful beach lined with shops, restaurants, and bars is within walking distance of the cruise port.

Great Bay Beach
One of the best beaches in the Caribbean. (p188)

AMANDA NICHOLLS/SHUTTERSTOCK ©

Diving & Snorkeling

Diving and snorkeling dominate the watersports scene in the Caribbean, with most ships making at least one stop at a port with excellent reefs or wrecks offshore.

Bonaire (p243)
Choose from 90 different dive sites in the clear and well-marked waters off Bonaire.

Hilma Hooker Wreck
Explore this large 1984 wreck site and sea life. (p246)

Grand Cayman (p85)
Spotts Beach is the place for snorkeling, while a huge US Navy ship offshore is the spot for diving.

USS Kittiwake
Dive this amazing 249ft submarine rescue ship.(p91)

Grand Turk (p203)
Some 25 incredible wall dives are spread offshore at this Caribbean hot spot.

Pillory Beach Reefs
Snorkel or dive the reef walls off Pillory Beach. (p206)

Shopping

From upscale boutiques to Caribbean craft markets, there's no shortage of shopping stopovers on the Caribbean cruising circuit.

RITU MANOJ JETHANI/SHUTTERSTOCK ©

Aruba (p213)
Low duty rates and excellent shopping near the cruise port make Aruba hard to resist.

Royal Plaza Mall
Huge shopping center in a colonial building. (p225)

Curaçao (p255)
The cruise ship docks within walking distance of the shopping action in downtown Willemstad.

Rif Fort
This old fort is now a mega shopping mall. (p265)

Barbados (p269)
High-end boutiques and handmade crafts at the many shops between the cruise port and downtown.

Pelican Craft Village
Local artisans selling island arts and crafts. (p279)

History

Explore the ruins of Spanish forts, walk the historic English harbors, and discover ruins from the original island inhabitants on the culturally rich islands of the Caribbean.

PLUSONE/SHUTTERSTOCK ©

Puerto Rico (p131)
Cruise ships dock in historic San Juan, so you can explore the Spanish forts and sights on foot.

El Morro
Tour the oldest Spanish fort in the New World. (p134)

Antigua (p229)
This tropical island is steeped in English maritime history.

Nelson's Dockyard
Explore the harbor where Nelson was stationed. (p232)

Curaçao (p255)
Established by the Dutch in 1643, the historic district near the port is a Unesco World Heritage site.

Fort Amsterdam
A Dutch fort constructed in the 17th century. (p262)

Plan Your Trip
Need to Know

When to Go

High Season (Dec–Apr)

- People fleeing the northern winter arrive in droves and prices peak.
- The region's driest time.
- Can be cool in the northern Caribbean from Cuba to the Bahamas.

Shoulder (May, Jun & Nov)

- The weather is good, rains are moderate.
- Warm temperatures elsewhere reduce visitor numbers.
- Best mix of affordable rates and good weather.

Low Season (Jul–Oct)

- Hurricane season; odds of being caught are small, but tropical storms are like clockwork.
- Good for Eastern Caribbean's surf beaches, such as Barbados.

Currencies

US dollar (US$) and local currencies

Languages

English, Spanish, French, Dutch

Visas

Citizens of Canada, the EU and the US don't need visa for visits of under 90 days.

Money

The US dollar is king. Credi cards are widely accepted i most destinations. ATMs ar generally common on all bu small islands. Many give ou US dollars in addition to th local currency.

Cell Phones

Purchase a cell phone service plan from your service provider or buy a plan from the cruise company. A good option offered by many cruise companies is to purchase a phone app that allows you to text othe people on board the ship.

Time

Eastern Standard Time (ES five hours behind GMT/ UTC): Turks and Caicos, Jamaica, the Cayman Islands the Dominican Republic. Atlantic Standard Time (AST; four hours behind GMT/ UTC): all other islands.

Costs for a Day in Port

Budget: Less than US$50

- Breakfast or lunch: US$15
- Beach chair or snorkeling gear rental: US$15
- Souvenirs or two or three beverages: US$15
- Local buses: US$5

Midrange: US$50–200

- Breakfast and lunch at a popular restaurant near the coast: US$45
- Beach chair and snorkeling gear rental: US$30
- Driving or walking tour: US$40–75
- Souvenirs and beverages: US$50-75

Top End: More than US$200

- Activities and/or an excursion in a beautiful place: US$100 and up
- Breakfast and lunch at a fine-dining restaurant: US$100 per person and more
- Souvenirs and beverages: US$100 and up

Useful Websites

Lonely Planet (www.lonelyplanet.com/caribbean) Destination information, hotel bookings, traveler forum and more.
Caribbean Journal (www.caribjournal.com) Regional news and travel features.
Cruise Critic (www.cruisecritic.com) Large cruise forum, reviews and info on cruise deals.
Cruise Line (www.cruiseline.com) Ship reviews, deals and a cruise forum.

What to Pack

The Caribbean islands are casual, so bring light, comfy clothes: a bathing suit, T-shirt and shorts will be your wardrobe most of the time. However, most Caribbean people like to dress smartly when they can, so try to keep your beachwear to the beach and change into something more formal when heading to dinner. On many Caribbean islands it is frowned upon for men to walk around shirtless other than on a beach.

Opening Hours

Opening hours vary across the region, although Sunday remains sacrosanct, with businesses and offices firmly shut throughout the Caribbean in most places except very near the port area. Note that small businesses may close for a period between August and November.

Wi-Fi Access

Wi-fi is widely available throughout the Caribbean except on very small islands, and it is easy to find free internet connections at shops, especially near ports. Look for coffee shops, cafes and bars with a wi-fi symbol on the door.

Getting Around the Ports

Many islands have affordable and reliable public transportation in the form of large open-air taxis that are locally referred to as jungle taxis. They hold many passengers at a time and often cost less than US$5 per person to go anywhere on the island. Sedan-style taxis are also available on most islands, and personal shuttles for individuals, couples or large groups are often readily available near ports. For island-hopping and traversing the sea, water-taxi services with a posted schedule are available on most islands and depart from multiple locations on larger islands. Car, scooter, jeep, bike, personal water craft and Segway rentals are other options on most islands.

For more on **getting around**, see p310

Month by Month

BLUEGREEN PICTURES/ALAMY STOCK PHOTO ©

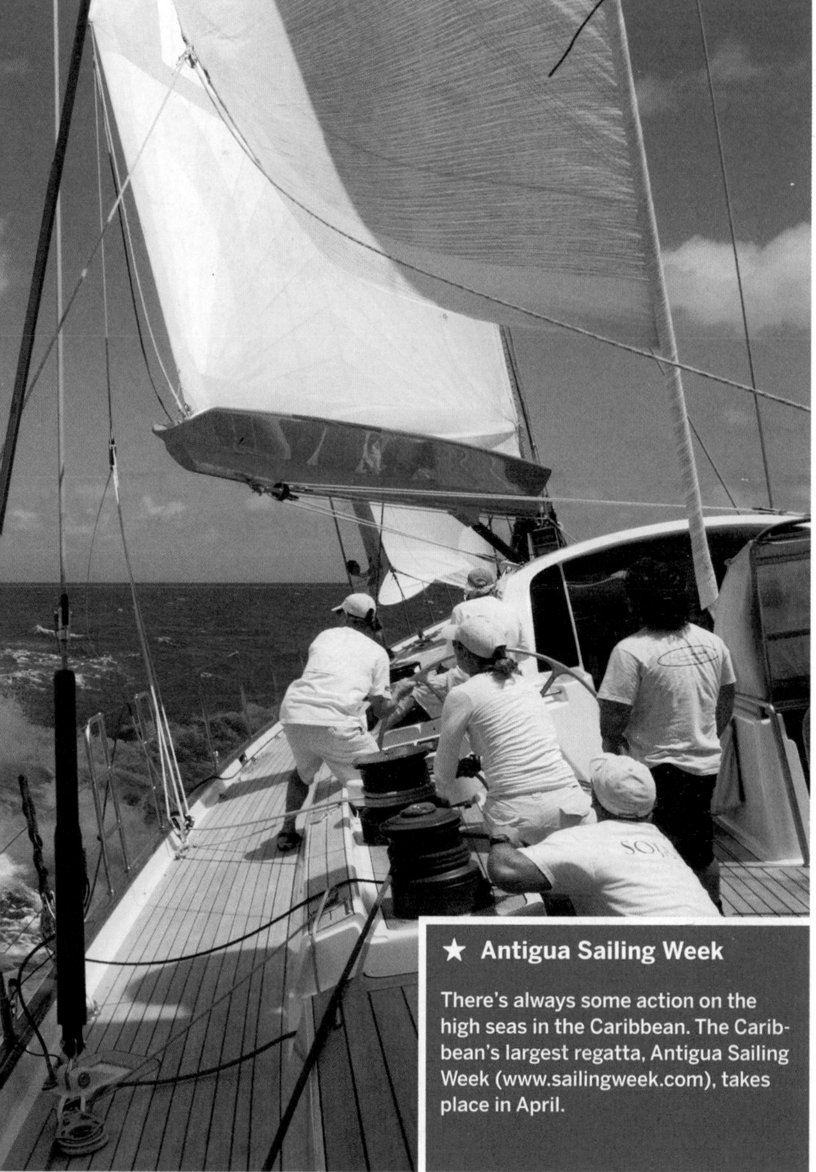

★ Antigua Sailing Week

There's always some action on the high seas in the Caribbean. The Caribbean's largest regatta, Antigua Sailing Week (www.sailingweek.com), takes place in April.

Plan Your Trip
Month by Month

BOYKOV/SHUTTERSTOCK ©

January

New Year is celebrated with gusto in the Caribbean. Resorts are full and people are partying. Weather across the region is balmy, with the odd cool day in the north.

Día de los Reyes

Across Puerto Rico, Día de los Reyes on January 6 toasts the three kings and is the highpoint of a two-month-long extravaganza of Christmas celebrations. Many towns have festivals in their plazas.

Festival San Sebastián

Puerto Rico's famous street party, Fiestas de la Calle San Sebastián, draws big crowds to Old San Juan for a week in mid-January. There are parades, dancing and much more.

February

Carnival is a huge event in many Caribbean countries, where it is tied to the Lenten calendar and celebrated with exuberance.

☆ Bob Marley Birthday Bash

Love for the sound that plays in beach bars worldwide brings fans to the Bob Marley Museum in Jamaica on Bob Marley's birthday, February 6, and kicks off Jamaica's reggae month.

ABCs of Carnival

Aruba, Bonaire and Curaçao's Carnivals all begin right after New Year and culminate with parades over the weekend before Ash Wednesday.

March

It's high season throughout the Caribbean. The late-winter influx of visitors is greeted by lovely weather.

Spring Break

In March and April, thousands of American college students descend on Montego Bay

Above: Aruba Carnival

MICHAEL DWYER / ALAMY STOCK PHOTO ©

in Jamaica for spring break. Other huge destinations are St Thomas in the US Virgin Islands and San Juan.

☆ Sint Maarten Heineken Regatta

This four-day race (www.heinekenregatta.com) has been luring sailors to the coast of St-Martin/Sint Maarten in the US Virgin Islands for more than 38 years. Live music, events and parties fill the nights after thrilling days of world-class racing.

April

Easter signals more Carnivals. High season continues but the winds of change are blowing. Temperatures are climbing in the south but the Caribbean is mostly dry.

Antigua Sailing Week

The Caribbean's largest regatta, Antigua Sailing Week (www.sailingweek.com) follows the Antigua Classic Yacht Regatta and involves a range of sailing and social events around Nelson's Dockyard and Falmouth Harbour.

★ Best Festivals

Pirate Week on Grand Cayman, April

Reggae Sumfest on Jamaica, July

Antigua Carnival, August

Junkanoo on Nassau, December

Jamaica Carnival

The Easter Carnival in Kingston brings people into the streets for music and an impressive costume parade (www.jamaica-carnival.com). Huge, as you'd expect.

Carnival

The two-week Sint Maarten Carnival, on the Dutch side, outclasses its counterpart on the French side. Activities begin in the second week after Easter.

Above: Festival San Sebastián

May

May sees the last of the Caribbean's Carnivals, as the temperatures start to rise.

Cayman Batabano

Cayman Islands' answer to Carnival is a weeklong festival of music and masquerade parades – for adults and children alike – during the first week in May.

June

June remains dry and relatively storm-free. Like May, it's not a peak time for visitors, except the savvy ones who value dry, sunny days and lower cruise rates.

☆ St Kitts Music Festival

Top-name calypso, soca, reggae, salsa, jazz and gospel performers from throughout the Caribbean pack into Basseterre's Warner Park during this three-day music festival.

July

A busy month! Summer holiday crowds start arriving, as do the very first tropical storms of the hurricane season. There's another round of Carnivals and other special events.

Crop-Over Festival

Beginning in mid-July and running until early August, the Crop-Over Festival is Barbados' top event and features fairs, activities and a parade.

Reggae Sumfest

The big mama of all reggae and dancehall festivals, held in late July in Montego Bay Jamaica, this event brings top acts together for an unforgettable party. Even if you're not attending, you're attending – the festivities tend to take over MoBay.

August

The summer high season continues and you can expect the first real storms of the hurricane season, although mostly that means heavy rains as opposed to big blows.

Anguilla Summer Festival

Anguilla's 10-day Summer Festival takes place around the first week of August and is celebrated with boat races, music, dancing and more.

Antigua Carnival

The famous Antigua Carnival (www.antiguacarnival.com) celebrates the country's emancipation from slavery during 10 days of merriment starting in late July, culminating with a grand parade on the first Tuesday in August. Calypso music, steel bands, masked merrymakers, floats and street parties all add to the excitement.

November

Hurricane season has mostly blown itself out and Christmas decorations are starting to appear.

Pirates Week

This wildly popular family-friendly extravaganza (www.piratesweekfestival.com) on Grand Cayman features a mock pirate invasion, music, dances, costumes, games and controlled mayhem.

St Kitts Carnival

Carnival is the biggest event on St Kitts. It starts in mid-November, kicking into high gear for two weeks of music, dancing and steel pan on December 26.

December

High season begins midmonth and cruise ships are often full. Rates are up and everything is open. Down backstreets Carnival prep is reaching fever pitch on many islands.

Junkanoo

The Bahamas' national festival starts in the twilight hours of Boxing Day (December 26). It's a frenzied party with marching 'shacks,' colorful costumes and music. Crowds prepare much of the year for this Carnival-like happening.

Plan Your Trip
Get Inspired

TONY MORAN/SHUTTERSTOCK ©

Read

Caribbean The epic James A Michener novel that spans 700 years of Caribbean history.

From Columbus to Castro: A History of the Caribbean Eric Williams provides a sweeping overview of the exciting and captivating history of the Caribbean.

A General History of the Pyrates Reputedly by Daniel Defoe, the famed author of *Robinson Crusoe*, this is the definitive collection of pirate history, lore and swashbuckling biographies.

Banana: The Fate of the Fruit that Changed the World Dan Koeppel explores the enormous impact of this ubiquitous fruit.

Watch

Captain Ron (1992) A hilarious comedy starring Kurt Russell about a family that hires a bumbling yacht captain to sail them around the Caribbean.

Master and Commander: The Far Side of the World (2003) A sailing adventure set during the Napoleonic Wars that will have you ready to take on the high seas.

Titanic (1997) The quintessential cruise-ship disaster movie starring Leonardo DiCaprio and Kate Winslet.

Marley (2012) A superb documentary about the life of Bob Marley.

Pirates of the Caribbean Watch any film in the franchise; get in a good mood and revel in the locations.

Listen

Tito Puente: Babarabatiri Includes the Puerto Rican salsa great's 'Ran Kan Kan'.

The Lashing Dogs A hot fungi band from Tortola.

Mongo Santamaría: Sofrito The 1976 album by the great Latin jazz percussionist known for his mastery of the rumba.

Antonio Carlos Jobim: Wave A relaxing bossa nova album that will get you in the mood to glide over the sea on your cruise vacation.

Bob Marley: Legend The most famous reggae album of all time, this best-of collection features Bob and the Wailers at their very best.

Above: Mayan dancers, Cozumel, Mexico

Plan Your Trip
Choose Your Cruise

Choosing your cruise is the first step in your cruise adventure, and certainly one of the most important decisions you'll need to make before you embark to the Caribbean. What cruise line and destinations suit your style and travel party are good places to start.

Narrow It Down

So many options! So many decisions! Things to consider:

Budget How much can you spend? Can you trade a cabin with a balcony (the most common kind these days) for a cheaper windowless room on a nicer ship for a longer voyage?

Style A mass-market, upscale or specialist cruise? Consider your budget; whether you prefer numerous formal evenings or to keep things casual; and any special interests you have.

Itinerary Where do you want to go and what ports of call appeal? Do you like the idea of days spent just at sea?

Size matters The megaships are geared for various budgets, so the important decision is how many people you want to sail with. On large ships, you can have 5000 potential new friends and the greatest range of shipboard diversions. Small ships, while sometimes exclusive and luxurious, are not always so, and usually lack the flashier amenities (such as climbing walls). Smaller ships will also call at smaller ports on less-visited islands.

Demographics Different cruise lines, and even ships within cruise lines, tend to appeal to different groups. Although cruisers in general are often slightly older, some ships have quite a party reputation; others are known for their art auctions and oldies music in the lounges. Also consider if you're looking for a family- or singles-oriented cruise.

Cruise Lines

Cruising is huge business and the major players earn billions of dollars a year. Many lines are actually brands owned by one of

RUTH PETERKIN/SHUTTERSTOCK ©

the two big operators: Carnival and Royal Caribbean control 90% of the market in the Caribbean.

There are also nontraditional cruises, where you can feel the wind at your back on large sailing ships equipped with modern technology.

★ Best Online Resources

Cruise Critic (www.cruisecritic.com)

Cruise Line (www.cruiseline.com)

Cruise Reviews (www.cruisereviews.com)

Cruise Mates (www.cruisemates.com)

USA TODAY (www.usatoday.com/travel/cruises)

Popular Cruise Lines

The following cruise lines sail large vessels on numerous itineraries in the Caribbean:

Carnival Cruise Lines (www.carnival.com) The largest cruise line in the world. Its enormous ships offer cruising on myriad Caribbean itineraries. Carnival ships have a festive atmosphere with lots of onboard activities, music, shows, and attractions for families and kids.

Celebrity Cruises (www.celebritycruises.com) An important brand of Royal Caribbean, it has huge ships that offer a more upscale experience than many other lines.

Costa Cruises (www.costacruises.com) Owned by Carnival, Costa is aimed at European travelers: bigger spas, smaller cabins and better coffee. Ships are huge, similar to Carnival's megaships.

Crystal Cruises (www.crystalcruises.com) Luxury cruise line with ships carrying about 800 passengers – small by modern standards. Attracts affluent older clients who enjoy a wide range of cultural activities and formal evenings.

Cunard Line (www.cunard.co.uk) Owned by Carnival, Cunard Line operates the huge *Queen Elizabeth*, *Queen Mary II* and *Queen Victoria*. The focus is on 'classic luxury' and the ships have limited Caribbean sailings.

Above: Cruise ships docked at Philipsburg, Sint Maarten (p185)

RUTH PETERKIN/SHUTTERSTOCK ©

Disney Cruise Line (https://disneycruise.disney.go.com) Disney's large ships are like floating theme parks, with children's programs and large staterooms that appeal to families.

Holland America (www.hollandamerica.com) Owned by Carnival, Holland America offers a traditional cruising experience, generally to older passengers.

Norwegian Cruise Line (NCL; www.ncl.com) Offers 'freestyle cruising' on large cruise ships, which means that dress codes are relaxed and dining options more flexible than on other lines. There are lots of extra-fee dining choices.

Princess Cruises (www.princess.com) Owned by Carnival, Princess has large ships that ply the Caribbean and offer a slightly older crowd a range of pampering activities while aboard.

Regent Seven Seas Cruises (www.rssc.com) Smaller ships (maximum 750 passengers) with a focus on luxury cabins and excellent food. All shore excursions are included in the price.

Royal Caribbean International (RCI; www.royalcaribbean.com) Carnival's arch rival has a huge fleet of megaships (some carry over 5600 people), aimed right at the middle of the market. It has itineraries everywhere in the Caribbean all the time and offers lots of activities for kids.

Non-Traditional Cruises

Sail Windjammer (www.sailwindjammer.com) Cruises around the Leeward Islands under sail on the three-masted *SV Mandalay*, a 236ft (72m) sailing yacht built in 1923.

Sea Cloud Cruises (www.seacloud.com) This German-American company operates luxury cruises in the Eastern Caribbean. The fleet includes the *Sea Cloud*, a four-masted 360ft (110m) ship dating from 1931, and a modern sibling. On both, the sails are set by hand.

Star Clippers (www.starclippers.com) These modern four-masted clipper ships have tall-ship designs and carry 180 passengers. Itineraries take in smaller islands of the Eastern Caribbean.

Windstar Cruises (www.windstarcruises.com) Windstar's luxury four-masted 440ft (134m) vessels have high-tech computer-operated sails and carry less than 400 passengers. The sails aren't the main means of propulsion most of the time.

EMPERORCOSAR/SHUTTERSTOCK ©

Theme Cruises

Old TV shows, science fiction, computers, musicians, (very) minor celebrities, soap operas, sports teams, nudism... What these all have in common is that they're all themes for cruises.

Cruise lines sell group space to promoters of theme cruises, but typically no theme is enough to fill an entire ship. Rather, a critical mass of people will occupy a block of cabins and have activities day and night just for them, including lectures, autograph sessions, costume balls and performances. No theme or interest is too obscure or improbable. To find one, jump online and search your phrase with 'cruise'.

LGBTI Cruises

One of the largest segments of special-interest cruises are those aimed at lesbian, bisexual, gay and transgender people. So popular are these cruises that often an entire ship will be devoted to catering for LGBTI passengers. Start by checking out the following operators:

Olivia (www.olivia.com) Organizes lesbian-only cruises.

RSVP Vacations (www.rsvpvacations.com) Good for active travelers, RSVP has trips on both large cruise ships and smaller yachts.

When to Go

High season for Caribbean cruising is the same as at resorts in the islands: mid-December to April. The largest number of ships sail at this time and prices are at their highest. At other times there are much fewer voyages but prices drop. Storms are more likely to cause itineraries to suddenly change during hurricane season from June to November.

From left: Shipboard view of Nassau, Bahamas (p113); Heavensight cruise port, Charlotte Amalie, St Thomas (p153).

Plan Your Trip
Sustainable Cruising

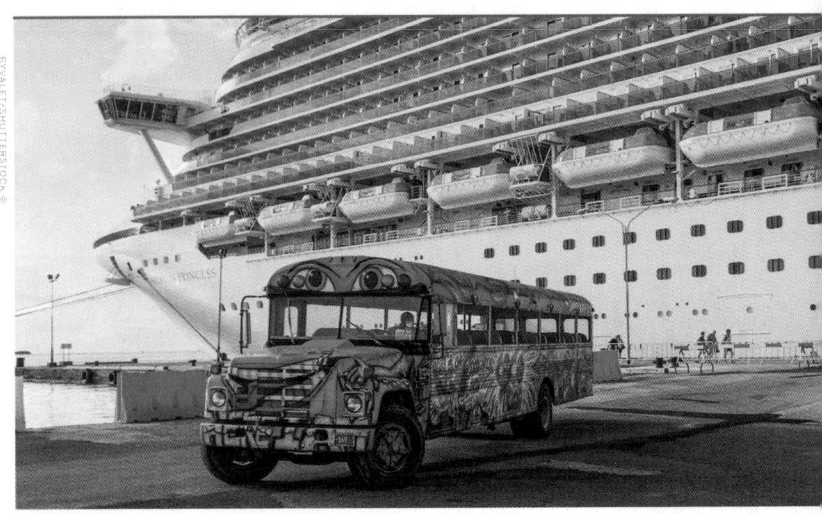

From air and water pollution to the swamping of popular destinations by hordes of tourists, traveling on cruise ships isn't without significant impacts – choose your cruise line carefully.

Environmental Issues

Although all travel comes with an environmental cost, by their very size, cruise ships have an outsized effect. Some issues:

Air pollution According to UK-based Climate Care, a carbon-offsetting company, cruise ships emit more carbon per passenger than airplanes – nearly twice as much. Most ships burn low-grade bunker fuel, which contains more sulfur and particulates than higher-quality fuel. The US and Canada are phasing in new regulations to require ships to burn cleaner fuel when they are close to land.

Water pollution Cruise ships generate enormous amounts of sewage, solid waste and gray water. While some countries and states have imposed regulations on sewage treatment, there's little regulation in the Caribbean. In 2016 Princess Cruises was fined US$40 million for illegal sewage dumping.

Cultural impact Although cruise lines generate money for their ports of call, thousands of people arriving at once can change the character of a town and seem overwhelming to locals and noncruising travelers. In Bonaire, for example, 7000 cruisers can arrive in one day – half the country's population.

What You Can Do

Email the cruise lines and ask them about their environmental policies: wastewater treatment, recycling initiatives and whether they use alternative energy sources. Knowing that customers care about these things has an impact. There are also organizations that review lines and ships on their environmental records:

Friends of the Earth (www.foe.org/cruisereportcard) Letter grades given to cruise lines for environmental and human health impacts.

STARRYVOYAGE/SHUTTERSTOCK ©

World Travel Awards (www.worldtravelawards.com) Annual awards for the 'World's Leading Green Cruise Line.'

Consume Less

Turn off the tap Fresh water is an extremely precious commodity in the Caribbean. Many islands rely on desalination plants or rainwater collected in cisterns. Keep in mind that winter – peak tourism time – is the driest time of year.

Skip bottled water If the water is safe to drink, fill a bottle to cut down on plastic.

Ride the bus Islands such as Aruba, Barbados and Grand Cayman have excellent bus networks.

Say no to plastic Try to carry your own bag for purchases and aqvoid plastic straws.

Be Ecosmart

Travel globally, shop locally Not only will buying local products buoy the local economy, it will also help to save you money. Local beer is always fresher than imported.

Avoid coral Don't touch it in the wild and don't buy it in shops or from vendors. Also avoid any souvenirs made of seashell or turtle shell. Buying goods made with any of these only encourages environmental destruction and hunting.

Don't litter Almost everything discarded on land makes its way to the sea, where it can wreak havoc on marine life. Needless to say, don't drop trash over the rails of the ship, either.

Consider the dolphins Be aware that wild dolphins are often captured to be used in enclosed swim-with-dolphins tourist attractions, a practice that has been condemned by wildlife conservationists.

★ Best for Sustainability

Aruba has set a goal of utilizing 100% renewable energy by 2020

Bonaire's protected marine park is a UNESCO World Heritage Site

Barbados utilizes solar power for water heating

From left: Oranjestad (p222), Aruba; Philipsburg market (p194), Sint Maarten

Plan Your Trip
Family Time Ashore

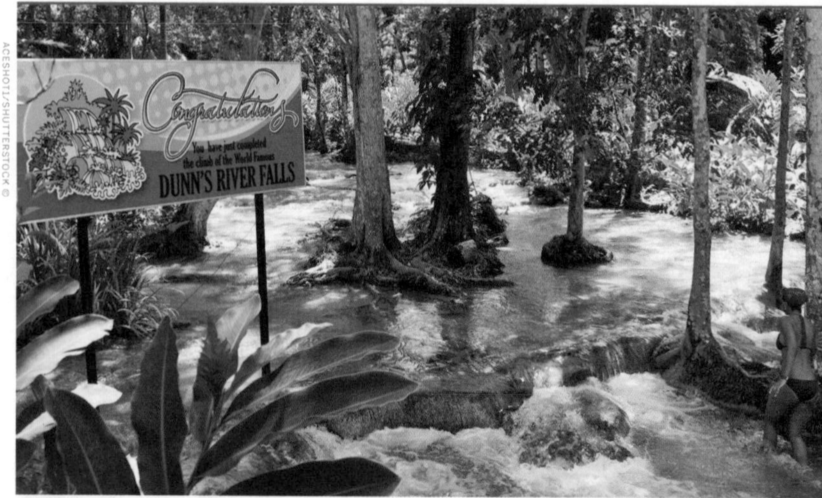

ACESHOT1/SHUTTERSTOCK ©

The Caribbean isn't just a huge playground for adults, it's one for kids too. Islands dedicated to adult pursuits, such as diving or hiking, might leave little ones out of the action, but many islands have myriad activities for children.

The Basics

- For a day in port with children bring diapers (if needed), plenty of water, swim-safety gear such as life jackets, sunscreen, hats, sunglasses, comfortable shoes for walking around the large ports, a stroller or baby backpack if the children tend to get tired after walking short distances, and snacks.
- The larger islands will have complete health facilities. They will also have large supermarkets with diapers, familiar treats from home etc.
- To help kids acclimatize to the Caribbean heat, take it easy at first and make sure they drink plenty of water. Children should wear a high-protection sunscreen and cover up whenever they're outside to avoid sunburn and heatstroke.
- Bring insect repellent formulated for children and whatever medication you normally use to treat insect bites.

Best Port Activities for Kids

Exciting Critters

Stingray City, Grand Cayman (p90) Get up close in the water with these semi-wild (but harmless) creatures.

Maho Bay, St John (p158) Lots of seagrass means enormous sea turtles nibbling close to shore.

Donkey Sanctuary, Aruba (p224) Befriend these former beasts of burden at this child-friendly centre.

RICHARD WHITCOMBE/SHUTTERSTOCK ©

Amazing Adventures

Antigua Rainforest Zip Line Tours (p237) Make like mini Tarzans and Janes while roaring on a wire through the treetops.

Dunn's River Falls, Jamaica (p102) Popular child-friendly attraction that has you swimming and climbing up a series of beautiful waterfalls.

Tanamá River Adventures, Puerto Rico (p146) Tubing and rapelling through caves on family-designed tours.

Pirates!

Faro y Parque Histórico de Arecibo, Puerto Rico (787-880-7540; Rte 655; adult/child US$12/10; 9am-6pm Mon-Fri, 10am-7pm Sat & Sun) Capture young imaginations at this pirate-themed historical amusement park.

Pirates of Nassau, Bahamas (p123) Explore a full-scale replica pirate ship at this brilliant interactive museum.

Pirates Week, Grand Cayman (p22) Mock pirate invasions and more keep scurvy dogs entertained in this popular festival.

★ Best Cruise Lines for Kids

Disney Cruise Line (https://disney-cruise.disney.go.com)

Royal Caribbean International (www.royalcaribbean.com)

Carnival (www.carnival.com)

Princess (www.princess.com)

Norwegian (www.ncl.com)

From left: Dunn's River Falls (p102), Jamaica; Scuba diver with stingrays

MIAMI

In This Chapter

Miami at a Glance

Miami has so many different facets to its diverse neighborhoods that it's hard to believe it all fits in one place. By day you can admire incredible photo-realistic murals in Wynwood, then spend the evening immersed in Afro Cuban jazz in Little Havana, followed perhaps by rooftop drinks atop the city's latest skyscraper. Crossing town you can't help feeling like you've passed into another city. In Miami Beach you can endlessly wander amid art deco masterpieces, each one bursting with personality – best followed by late-afternoon strolls along the sands, when the golden light is mesmerizing.

Miami in Two Days

Start your trip with a tour around the Miami Beach art deco district with the **Design Preservation League** (p53), and consider a visit to the **Wolfsonian-FIU** (p44) and **New World Center** (p44). On your second day, head to Downtown Miami and take in the **art museum** (p47) and **HistoryMiami** (p47), as well as the **Brickell City Centre** (p48).

Miami in Four Days

On your third day, go to Little Havana and watch the locals slap dominoes at **Máximo Gómez Park** (p49). Then go to Wynwood to peruse galleries and dine like royalty at **Alter** (p59) or **Kyu** (p58). On day four, witness the full opulent fantasy of Miami at sites such as the **Vizcaya Museum** (p51) and the **Biltmore Hotel** (p49).

North Beach
Canoe among the mangroves at Oleta River State Park, then enjoy the beautiful North Beach shoreline.

WYNWOOD WALLS

ART DECO HISTORIC DISTRICT

South Beach
Enjoy a sparkling beach, beautiful art-deco architecture and buzzing bars and restaurants.

Cruise Port

ATLANTIC OCEAN

ni
ews,
use-
rez Art
atch

Crandon Park

Key Biscayne
A tropical realm with magnificent beaches and lush nature trails with stunning views of Miami.

Bill Baggs Cape Florida State Park

South Beach Map (p46)
Downtown Miami Map (p50)

Ocean Drive and Miami Beach (p36)

0 5 km
0 2.5 miles

Little Haiti & the Upper East Side
Something of Miami's great new frontier, with new restaurants, hotels and galleries.

Wynwood & the Design District
Miami's most creative neighborhoods are justly famed for a burgeoning arts scene.

Little Havana
An atmospheric place to explore, with Latin jazz spilling out of colorful storefronts.

Coral Gables
Visit the striking Biltmore Hotel, a lush tropical garden and one of America's loveliest swimming pools.

Coconut Grove
Intriguing shops and cafes, and a walkable village-like vibe.

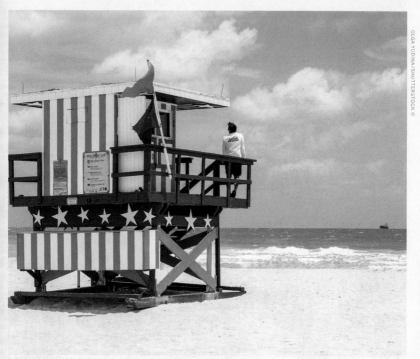

Lifeguard tower, South Beach (p44)

Arriving in Miami

Miami International Airport Taxis ($35) and shared SuperShuttle vans (about $22) run to South Beach (40 minutes). The Miami Beach Airport Express (bus 150) costs $2.65 and makes stops all along Miami Beach.

Fort Lauderdale-Hollywood International Airport GO Airport Shuttle runs shared vans to Miami (around $25). A taxi costs around $75.

Fast Facts

Currency US dollar (US$)

Language English

Money ATMs are widely available throughout Miami, including in the nearby Bayside Marketplace with waterfront shops, restaurants and bars.

Visas Not required for citizens of the US, EU or Australia.

Best for free wi-fi Each terminal at the cruise port allows passengers to access free wi-fi.

Art deco buildings, Collins Ave

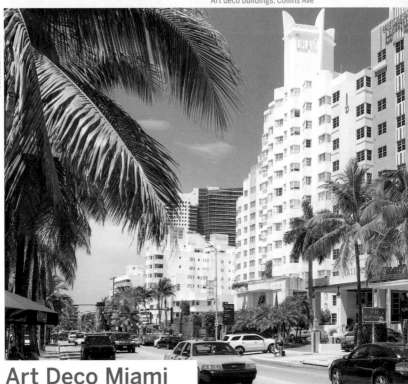

Art Deco Miami

The world-famous Art Deco Historic District of Miami Beach is pure exuberance: architecture of bold lines, whimsical tropical motifs and a color palette that evokes all the beauty of the Miami landscape. It's hard not to be captivated when strolling among these restored beauties from a bygone era.

Great For...

Don't Miss

Strolling the 700 block of Ocean Dr at night to soak up the best of the deco neon.

Background

For much of its history Miami Beach was little more than an empty landscape of swaying palm trees, scrubland and sandy shoreline. It wasn't until the early 20th century that a few entrepreneurs began to envision transforming the island into a resort. Beginning in the 1920s, a few hotels rose up that catered to an elite crowd of wealthy industrialists vacationing from the north. And then disaster struck. In 1926 a hurricane devastated much of the island and South Florida.

When it was time to rebuild, Miami Beach underwent a dramatic rebirth. As luck would have it, at exactly that moment, a bold new style of architecture – art deco – was all the talk in America. Miami Beach would become the epicenter of this groundbreaking new design movement.

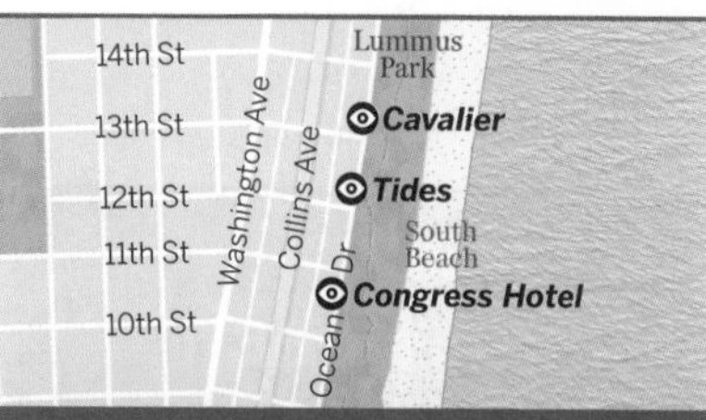

Explore Ashore

Many of the best art deco buildings can be found between 11th and 14th Sts. Miami Design Preservation League (p53) runs excellent walking tours of the deco district.

Take a Break

Have your deco-district meal at the 11th St Diner (p56), a deco masterpiece in itself.

Deco Style

The art deco building style was very much rooted in the times. The late 1920s and 1930s was an era of invention – of new automobiles, streamlined machines, radio antennae and cruise ships. Architects manifested these elements in the strong vertical and horizontal lines, at times coupled with zig-zigs or sleek curves, all of which created the illusion of movement, of the bold march into the future.

In Miami Beach, architects also incorporated local motifs such as palm trees, flamingos and tropical plants. Nautical themes also appeared, with playful representations of ocean waves, seahorses, starfish and lighthouses. The style later became known as tropical deco, with architects coming up with unique solutions to the challenges of building in a hot climate.

The Best of Ocean Drive

One stretch of Ocean Dr has a collection of some of the most striking art deco buildings in Miami Beach. Between 11th and 14th Sts, you'll see many of the classic deco elements at play in beautifully designed works – each unique and full of character. Close to 11th St, the **Congress Hotel** displays perfect symmetry in its three-story facade, with window-shading 'eyebrows' and a long marquee down the middle that's reminiscent of the grand movie palaces of the 1930s. About a block north, the **Tides** is one of the finest of the nautical themed hotels, with porthole windows over the entryway, a reception desk of Key limestone (itself imprinted with fossilized sea creatures), and curious arrows on the floor, meant to denote the ebb and flow of the tide. Near 13th St, the **Cavalier** has a whimsical seahorse theme, with stylized depictions of the sea creature; it also has palm-tree-like iconography.

Art Deco Miami Beach

Explore the architectural and aesthetic backbone of South Beach on this stroll past the colorful buildings of Miami's Art Deco Historic District.

Start Art Deco Museum
Distance 1.2 miles
Duration 2 to 3 hours

Take a Break... Lunch at the **11th St Diner** (p56), a gleaming aluminum Pullman car that was imported in 1992 from Wilkes-Barre, Pennsylvania.

Classic Photo The Post Office is a striking building with a round facade and a lighthouse-like cupola.

4 Turn left and down 14th St to Washington Ave and the **US Post Office** (p45), at 13th St. It's a curvy block of white deco in the stripped classical style. Step inside to admire the wall mural, domed ceiling and marble stamp tables.

5 Continue half a block east to the imposing **Wolfsonian-FIU** (p44), an excellent design museum.

14th St
13th St
12th St
11th St
10th St
9th St
8th St
7th St
Washington Ave
Collins Ct
Collins Ave

3 At 14th St peek inside the sun-drenched **Winter Haven Hotel** to see its fabulous terrazzo floors, made of stone chips set in mortar that's polished when dry.

2 Head north along Ocean Dr. Between 12th and 14th Sts you'll see two deco hotels: the **Carlyle** (p45), boasting modernistic styling, and the **Cardozo Hotel** (p45), featuring sleek, rounded edges.

14th St
Collins Ave
Ocean Ct
13th St
A1A
12th St
Ocean Dr
11th St
Lummus Park
South Beach
START
FINISH
Biscayne Bay

1 Start at the **Art Deco Museum** (p44) at the corner of Ocean Dr and 10th St for an exhibit on art deco style.

6 Continue walking Washington Ave, turn left on 7th St and then continue north along Collins Ave to the **Hotel of South Beach**. L Murray Dixon designed the hotel as the Tiffany Hotel, with a deco spire, in 1939.

7 Turn right on 9th St and go two blocks to Ocean Dr, where you'll spy nonstop deco beauties; the middling **Ocean's Ten** restaurant boasts an exterior designed by deco legend Henry Hohauser.

Wynwood Walls mural

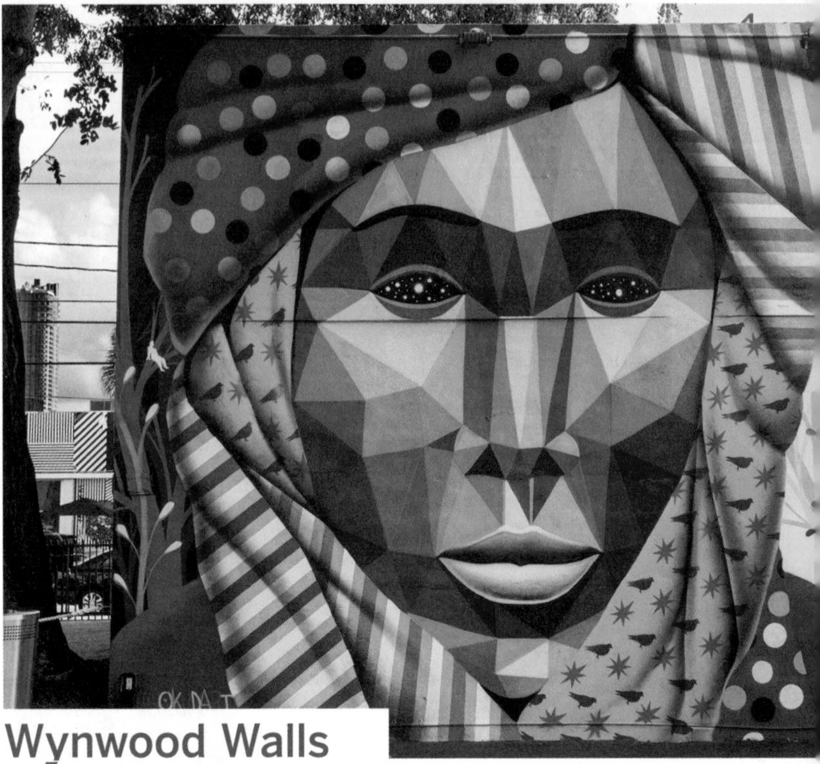

Wynwood Walls

In the midst of rusted warehouses and concrete blah, Wynwood Walls – a collection of murals and paintings laid out over an open courtyard – invariably bowls people over with its sheer color profile and unexpected location.

Great For...

Don't Miss

Wynwood Walls offers private walking tours ($25 per person) led by street artists. Book online.

Back Story

Ever since the 1970s, Wynwood had been known as little more than a district of sprawling warehouses. And then Tony Goldman arrived.

Goldman, who's credited with the revitalization of South Beach (as well as New York's SoHo district), saw enormous potential in the blighted neighborhood. Although artists were already living in the area, it remained barren and forbidding at night. Goldman began buying up properties. Once assembled, he unleashed his master plan. He would invite artists from around the world to create the biggest and boldest collection of street art ever assembled in Miami. Around the corner, he also opened the first restaurant in the neighborhood – Joeys, a pioneering Italian restaurant, which is still around today.

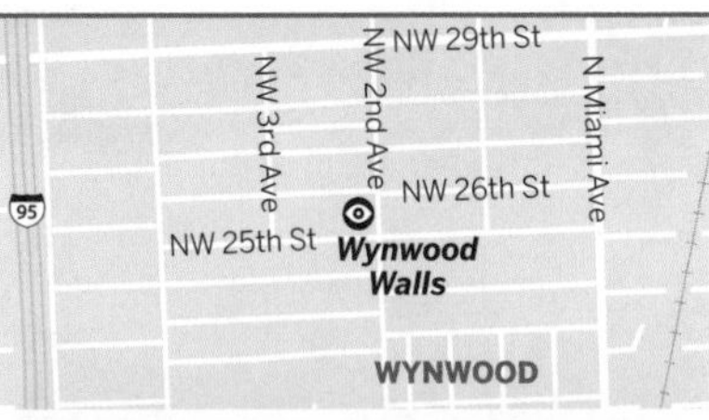

Explore Ashore

To get here, take the free Wynwood Trolley from the Adrienne Arsht Center or the Biscayne Trolley from Downtown.

★ Top Tips

- Go early in the day to beat the crowds.
- The **Wynwood Art Walk** (www.artcircuits.com; 7-10pm) FREE is held on the second Saturday of the month.

Goldman started with the warehouse complex of six buildings on 25th to 26th Sts. Using the buildings as blank canvases, his roster of artists set to work. Art-world superstar Jeffrey Deitch helped co-curate the first year's project in 2009. Artists were offered free airfares, hotel accommodations and all the supplies they needed, then given free rein to paint Goldman's 18 walls. The plan was a smash success. That year at Art Basel, thousands of visitors came to see the street murals, and the new Wynwood Walls were the talk of the town.

The Art

Since the founding of the project, more than 50 artists from 16 different countries have painted on the walls. Among the first crop of talented artists was Shepard Fairey, whose 'Obey' street tags (depicting the mug of Andre the Giant) and 'Hope' posters (with Obama's portrait) helped garner him wide-reaching acclaim. Other famous artists who've installed their work include Os Gemeos (twin brothers who hail from Brazil), French painter Invader, the Japanese artist Aiko and the Portuguese Alexandre Farto (aka Vhils), who 'carves' rather than paints – at times even using a jack-hammer to create realistic portraits on concrete walls. Unlike a lot of art in traditional galleries, the street art contains a visceral edge that explores topics like homelessness, police brutality, disenfranchisement, rampant materialism and the ever-widening chasm of inequality between the haves and the have-nots. There are also fantastical science-fiction scenes, dynamic color swaths swirling with abstract patterns, and beautiful portraits of positive people. The Dalai Lama, Aung San Suu Kyi, Martin Luther King Jr, Bob Marley and, uh, Yoda, have all graced the walls at one time or another.

Observation tower, Shark Valley

Wildlife-Watching in the Everglades

From moonlit glimpses of graceful alligators to seeing the slow, rhythmic flap of a great blue heron, the Everglades offer a majestic array of wildlife encounters.

Great For...

Don't Miss

Ranger-led tours of the Everglades, which include fascinating info on wildlife and ecosystems.

Anhinga Trail

If you do just one walk in the Everglades, make sure it's on the Anhinga Trail. Gators sun on the shoreline, razor-billed anhinga spear their prey and wading birds stalk haughtily through the reeds. You'll get a close-up view of wildlife on this short (0.8-mile) trail at the **Royal Palm Visitor Center** (☎305-242-7700; www.nps.gov/ever; State Rd 9336; ⏲9am-4:15pm). There are various overlooks, where you can sometimes see dozens of alligators piled together in the day.

Come back at night (be sure to bring a flashlight) for a view of the gators swimming along the waterways – sometimes right beside you. The park offers periodic ranger-led walks along the boardwalk at night, though you can always do it yourself. Seeing the flashlight-lit glittering eyes of

Everglades flamingo

KWADRAT/SHUTTERSTOCK ©

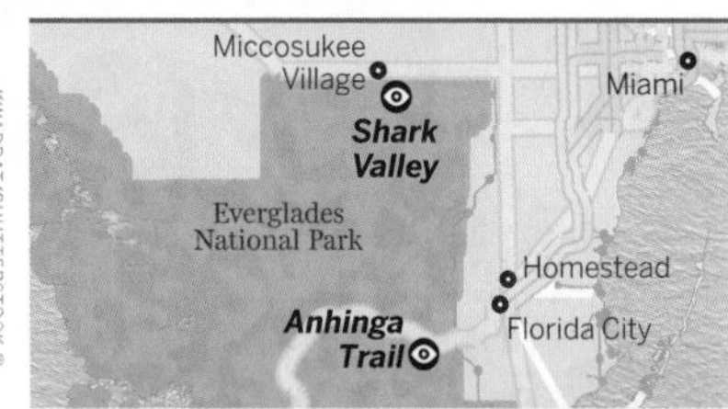

Explore Ashore

A one-week vehicle pass ($25) covers the whole Everglades National Park and allows multiple entries. It's 55 miles, or a one-hour drive, from South Beach, Miami, to the Royal Palm Visitor Center,

★ Top Tip

Wildlife is most easily seen during the dry winter months (December to April).

alligators prowling the waterways is an unforgettable experience!

Shark Valley

It sounds like it should be the headquarters for the villain in a James Bond movie, but **Shark Valley** (☎305-221-8776; www.nps.gov/ever/planyourvisit/svdirections.htm; 36000 SW 8th St, N 25°45.27.60', W 80°46.01.01'; car/cyclist/pedestrian $25/8/8; ⏰9am-5pm; P 👪) 🍃 is in fact a slice of national park heavy with informative signs and knowledgeable rangers. Found in a cypress, hardwood and riverine section of the Everglades, Shark Valley is a more traditionally jungly part of the park than the grassy fields and forest domes surrounding the Ernest Coe visitor center.

A 15-mile paved trail takes you past small creeks, tropical forest and 'borrow pits' (human-made holes that are now basking spots for gators, turtles and birdlife). The pancake-flat trail is perfect for bicycles, which can be rented at the entrance for $9 per hour. Bring water.

If you don't feel like exerting yourself, the most popular and painless way to immerse yourself in the Everglades is via the two-hour **tram tour** (☎305-221-8455; www.sharkvalleytramtours.com; adult/child under 12yr/senior $25/19/12.75; ⏰departures 9:30am, 11am, 2pm, 4pm) that runs along Shark Valley's entire 15-mile trail. If you only have time for one Everglades activity, this should be it, as guides are informative and witty, and you'll likely see gators sunning themselves on the road. Halfway along the trail is the 50ft-high Shark Valley Observation Tower, an ugly concrete tower that offers dramatic, beautiful views of the park.

Ocean Drive

Ocean Dr is the great cruising strip of Miami: an endless parade of classic cars, testosterone-sweating young men, peacock-like young women, street performers, vendors, those guys who yell unintelligible nonsense at everyone, celebrities pretending to be tourists, tourists who want to play celebrity, beautiful people, not-so-beautiful people, people people and the best ribbon of art-deco preservation on the beach. Say 'Miami.' That image in your head? It's probably Ocean Dr.

TRAVELVIEW/SHUTTERSTOCK ©

SIGHTS

Miami's major sights aren't concentrated in one neighborhood. The most frequently visited area is South Beach, which is home to a humming nightlife, beautiful beaches and art-deco hotels. But you'll find historic sites and museums in the Downtown area, art galleries in Wynwood and the Design District, old-fashioned hotels and eateries in Mid-Beach (in Miami Beach), more beaches on Key Biscayne, and peaceful neighborhood attractions in Coral Gables and Coconut Grove.

South Beach

Art Deco Museum Museum

(Map p46; www.mdpl.org/welcome-center/art-deco-museum; 1001 Ocean Dr; $5; ⏲10am-5pm Tue-Sun, to 7pm Thu) This small museum is one of the best places in town for an enlightening overview of the art-deco district. Through videos, photography, models and other displays, you'll learn about the pioneering work of Barbara Capitman, who helped save these buildings from certain destruction back in the 1970s, and her collaboration with Leonard Horowitz, the talented artist who designed the pastel color palette that become an integral part of the design visible today.

Wolfsonian-FIU Museum

(Map p46; ☎305-531-1001; www.wolfsonian.org; 1001 Washington Ave; adult/child $10/5, 6-9pm Fri free; ⏲10am-6pm Mon, Tue, Thu & Sat, to 9pm Fri, noon-6pm Sun, closed Wed) Visit this excellent design museum early in your stay to put the aesthetics of Miami Beach into context. It's one thing to see how wealth, leisure and the pursuit of beauty are revealed in Miami Beach, but it's another to understand the roots and shadings of local artistic movements. By chronicling the interior evolution of everyday life, the Wolfsonian reveals how these trends were architecturally manifested in SoBe's exterior deco.

New World Center Notable Building

(Map p46; ☎305-673-3330, tours 305-673-3331; www.newworldcenter.com; 500 17th St; tours $5; ⏲tours 4pm Tue & Thu, 1pm Fri & Sat) Designed by Frank Gehry, this performance hall rises majestically out of a manicured lawn just above Lincoln Rd. The glass-and-steel facade encases characteristically Gehry-esque sail-like shapes within that help shape the magnificent acoustics and add to the futuristic quality of the concert hall. The grounds form a 2-5-acre public park aptly known as **SoundScape Park** (www.nws.edu).

Carlyle Architecture

(Map p46; 1250 Ocean Dr) The Carlyle comes with futuristic styling, triple parapets, a *Jetsons* vibe and some cinematic cachet: *The Birdcage* was filmed here.

Cardozo Hotel Architecture

(Map p46; 1300 Ocean Dr;) The Cardozo and its neighbor, the Carlyle, were the first deco hotels saved by the Miami Design

Wolfsonian-FIU

Preservation League, and in the case of the Cardozo, we think they saved the best first. Its beautiful lines and curves evoke a classic automobile from the 1930s.

Post Office Architecture

(Map p46; 1300 Washington Ave; ⌚8am-5pm Mon-Fri, 8:30am-2pm Sat) Make it a point to mail a postcard from this 1937 deco gem of a post office, the very first South Beach renovation project tackled by preservationists in the '70s. This Depression moderne building in the 'stripped classic' style was constructed during President Roosevelt's administration and funded by the Works Progress Administration (WPA) initiative, which supported artists who were out of work during the Great Depression.

Jewish Museum of Florida-FIU Museum

(Map p46; ☎305-672-5044; www.jmof.fiu.edu; 301 Washington Ave; adult/student & senior $6/5, Sat free; ⌚10am-5pm Tue-Sun, closed Jewish holidays) Housed in a 1936 Orthodox synagogue that served Miami's first congregation, this small museum chronicles the rather large contribution Jews have made to the state of Florida. After all, it could be said that while Cubans made Miami, Jews made Miami Beach, both physically and culturally. Yet there were times when Jews were barred from the American Riviera they carved out of the sand, and this museum tells that story, along with some amusing anecdotes (like seashell Purim dresses).

North Beach

Oleta River State Park State Park

(☎305-919-1844; www.floridastateparks.org/oletariver; 3400 NE 163rd St; vehicle/pedestrian & bicycle $6/2; ⌚8am-sunset; P 👪) Tequesta people were boating the Oleta River estuary as early as 500 BC, so you're just following in a long tradition if you canoe or kayak in this park. At almost 1000 acres, this is the largest urban park in the state and one of the best places in Miami to escape the madding crowd. Boat out to the local mangrove island, watch the eagles fly by, or just chill on the pretension-free beach.

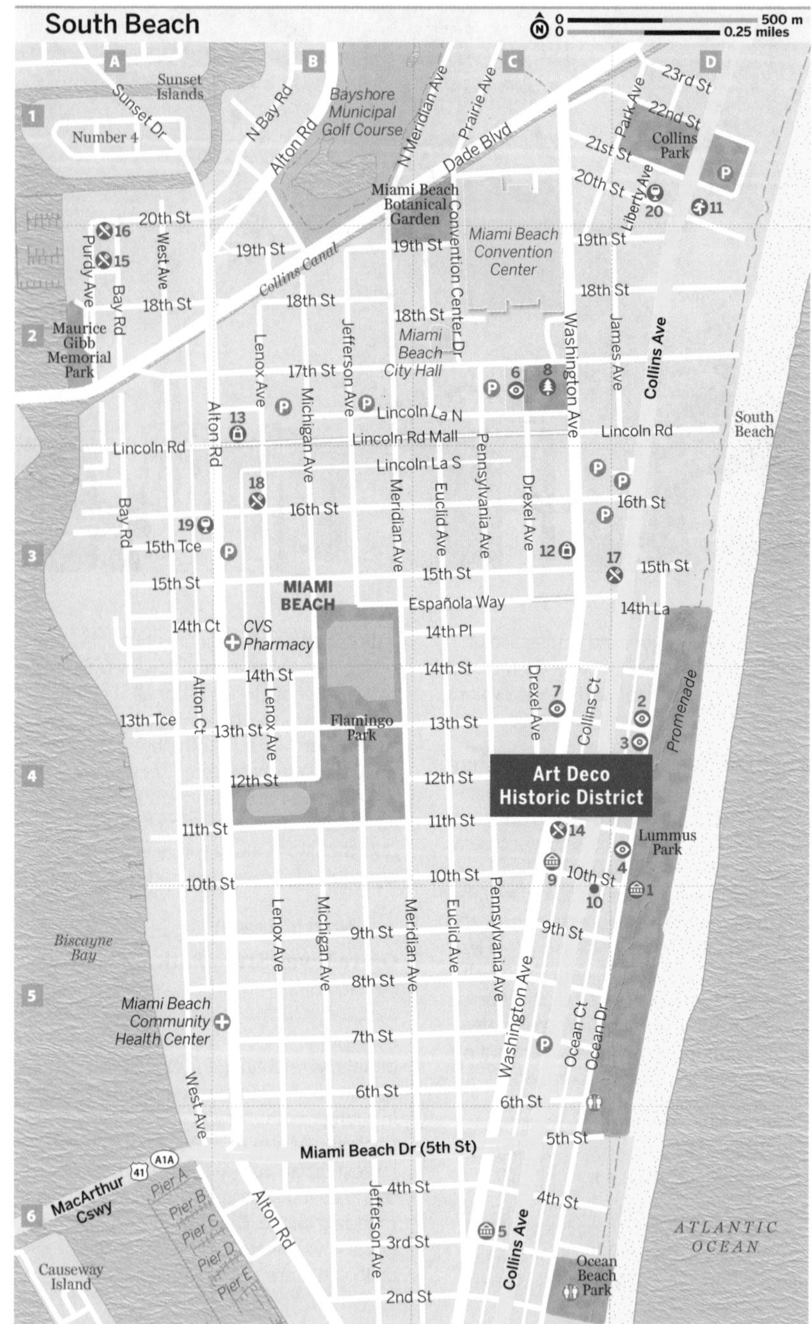

South Beach
0 500 m
0 0.25 miles
A
B
C
D
1
2
3
4
5
6
Sunset Islands
Number 4
Sunset Dr
N Bay Rd
Alton Rd
Bayshore Municipal Golf Course
N Meridian Ave
Prairie Ave
Dade Blvd
23rd St
22nd St
Park Ave
Collins Park
21st St
20th St
Liberty Ave
Miami Beach Botanical Garden
Convention Center Dr
Miami Beach Convention Center
19th St
18th St
20th St
19th St
Collins Canal
West Ave
Purdy Ave
Bay Rd
18th St
Maurice Gibb Memorial Park
Miami Beach City Hall
17th St
Lenox Ave
Jefferson Ave
Washington Ave
James Ave
Collins Ave
Michigan Ave
Lincoln La N
Lincoln Rd Mall
Lincoln Rd
Lincoln La S
Lincoln Rd
South Beach
Meridian Ave
Euclid Ave
Pennsylvania Ave
Drexel Ave
16th St
16th St
15th Tce
15th St
15th St
15th St
MIAMI BEACH
Española Way
14th La
14th Ct
CVS Pharmacy
14th Pl
14th St
14th St
Alton Ct
Promenade
13th Tce
13th St
Flamingo Park
13th St
Collins Ct
12th St
12th St
Art Deco Historic District
11th St
11th St
Lummus Park
10th St
10th St
10th St
9th St
9th St
Biscayne Bay
8th St
Miami Beach Community Health Center
7th St
Ocean Ct
Ocean Dr
6th St
6th St
5th St
Miami Beach Dr (5th St)
A1A
41
MacArthur Cswy
Pier A
Pier B
Pier C
Pier D
Pier E
4th St
4th St
3rd St
2nd St
Causeway Island
ATLANTIC OCEAN
Ocean Beach Park
1
2
3
4
5
6
7
8
9
10
11
12
13
14
15
16
17
18
19
20

South Beach

Haulover Beach Park Park

(☎305-947-3525; www.miamidade.gov; 10800 Collins Ave; per car Mon-Fri $5, Sat-Sun $7; ⊙sunrise-sunset; P) Where are all those tanned men in gold chains and Speedos going? That would be the clothing-optional beach in this 40-acre park hidden from condos, highways and prying eyes by vegetation. There's more to do here than get in the buff, though; most of the beach is 'normal' (there's even a dog park) and it is one of the nicer spots for sand in the area. The park is on Collins Ave about 4.5 miles north of 71st St.

Downtown Miami

Pérez Art Museum Miami Museum

(PAMM; Map p50; ☎305-375-3000; www.pamm.org; 1103 Biscayne Blvd; adult/seniors & students $16/12, 1st Thu & 2nd Sat of month free; ⊙10am-6pm Fri-Tue, to 9pm Thu, closed Wed; P) The Pérez can claim fine rotating exhibits that concentrate on post-WWII international art, but just as impressive are its location and exterior. This art institution inaugurated Museum Park, a patch of land that overseas the broad blue swath of Biscayne Bay. Swiss architects Herzog & de Meuron designed the structure, which integrates tropical foliage, glass and metal – a melding of tropical vitality and fresh modernism that is a nice architectural analogy for Miami itself.

HistoryMiami Museum

(Map p50; ☎305-375-1492; www.historymiami.org; 101 W Flagler St; adult/child $10/5; ⊙10am-5pm Mon-Sat, from noon Sun; ♿) South Florida – a land of escaped slaves, guerrilla Native Americans, gangsters, land grabbers, pirates, tourists, drug dealers and alligators – has a special history, and it takes a special kind of museum to capture that narrative. This highly recommended place, located in the **Miami-Dade Cultural Center**, does just that, weaving together the stories of the region's successive waves of population, from Native Americans to Nicaraguans.

Patricia & Phillip Frost Museum of Science Museum

(Map p50; ☎305-434-9600; www.frostscience.org; 1101 Biscayne Blvd; adult/child $28/20; ⊙9am-6pm; P ♿) This sprawling new Downtown museum spreads across 250,000 sq ft that includes a three-level aquarium, a 250-seat state-of-the-art planetarium and two distinct wings that delve into the wonders of science and nature. Exhibitions range from weather phenomena to creepy crawlies, feathered dinosaurs and vital-microbe displays, while Florida's fascinating Everglades and biologically rich coral reefs play starring roles.

FOTOLUMINATE LLC/SHUTTERSTOCK ©

Miami River Walk

Bayfront Park Park

(Map p50; ☎305-358-7550; www.bayfrontparkmiami.com; 301 N Biscayne Blvd) Few American parks can claim to front such a lovely stretch of turquoise (Biscayne Bay), but Miamians are lucky like that. Notable park features are two performance venues: the **Klipsch Amphitheater** (www.klipsch.com/klipsch-amphitheater-at-bayfront-park), which boasts excellent views over Biscayne Bay and is a good spot for live-music shows, while the smaller 200-seat **Tina Hills Pavilion** hosts free springtime performances (lawn seating can accommodate 800 more).

Miami Riverwalk Waterfront

(Map p50) This pedestrian walkway follows along the northern edge of the river as it bisects Downtown, and offers some peaceful vantage points of the bridges and skyscrapers dotting the urban landscape. You can start the walk at the south end of Bayfront Park and follow it under bridges and along the waterline till it ends just west of the SW 2nd Ave Bridge.

Brickell City Centre Area

(Map p50; www.brickellcitycentre.com; 701 S Miami Ave; ⏰10am-9:30pm Mon-Sat, noon-7pm Sun) One of the hottest new developments in Miami opened its doors in late 2016, after four long years of construction. The massive billion-dollar complex spreads across three city blocks, and it encompasses glittering residential towers, modernist office blocks and a soaring five-star hotel (the **EAST, Miami**). There's much to entice both Miami residents and visitors to the center, with restaurants, bars, a cinema and loads of high-end retailers (Ted Baker, All Saints, Kendra Scott).

Wynwood & the Design District

Margulies Collection at the Warehouse Gallery

(☎305-576-1051; www.margulieswarehouse.com; 591 NW 27th St; adult/student $10/5; ⏰11am-4pm Tue-Sat mid-Oct–Apr) Encompassing 45,000 sq ft, this vast not-for-profit exhibition space houses one of the best collections in Wynwood. Thought-provoking large-format installations are the focus at the Warehouse, and you'll see works by some of the leading 21st-century artists here.

Bakehouse Art Complex Gallery
(BAC; ☎305-576-2828; www.bacfl.org; 561 NW 32nd St; ⏲noon-5pm; P) FREE One of the pivotal art destinations in Wynwood, the Bakehouse has been an arts incubator since well before the creation of the Wynwood Walls. Today, this former bakery houses galleries and some 60 studios, and the range of works you can find here is quite impressive. Check the schedule for upcoming artist talks and other events.

Little Havana

Máximo Gómez Park Park
(cnr SW 8th St & SW 15th Ave; ⏲9am-6pm) Little Havana's most evocative reminder of Old Cuba is Máximo Gómez Park, or 'Domino Park,' where the sound of elderly men trash-talking over games of chess is harmonized by the quick clack-clack of slapping dominoes. The jarring backtrack, plus the heavy smell of cigars and a sunrise-bright mural of the 1994 Summit of the Americas, combine to make Máximo Gómez one of the most sensory sites in Miami (although it is admittedly one of the most tourist-heavy ones as well).

Coral Gables

Fairchild Tropical Garden Gardens
(☎305-667-1651; www.fairchildgarden.org; 10901 Old Cutler Rd; adult/child/senior $25/12/18; ⏲9:30am-4:30pm; P) If you need to escape Miami's madness, consider a green day in the country's largest tropical botanical garden. A butterfly grove, tropical plant conservatory and gentle vistas of marsh and Keys habitats, plus frequent art installations from artists like Roy Lichtenstein, are all stunning. In addition to easy-to-follow, self-guided walking tours, a free 45-minute tram tours the entire park on the hour from 10am to 3pm (till 4pm weekends).

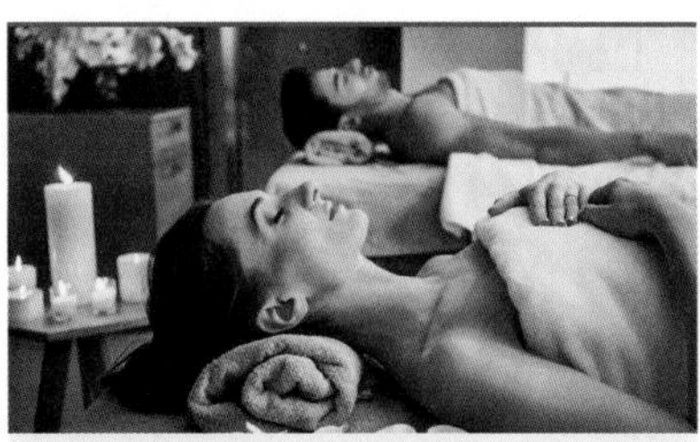

Miami Day Spas

As you may have guessed, Miami offers plenty of places to get pampered. Some of the most luxurious spas in town are found at high-end hotels, where you can expect to pay $300 to $400 for a massage and/or acupressure, and $200 for a body wrap. Some great options:

Spa at Mandarin Oriental Miami (Map p50; ☎305-913-8332; www.mandarinoriental.com; 500 Brickell Key Dr, Mandarin Oriental Miami; manicures $75, spa treatments $175-425; ⏲8:30am-9:30pm)

Carillon Miami Wellness Resort (☎866-276-2226; www.carillonhotel.com; 6801 Collins Ave, Carillon Hotel; treatments $165-300; ⏲8am-9pm)

Lapis (☎305-674-4772; www.fontainebleau.com; 4441 Collins Ave, Fontainebleau; treatments $90-350; ⏲9:30am-6:30pm Sun-Fri, to 7:30pm Sat)

Spa at the Setai (Map p46; ☎855-923-7908; www.thesetaihotel.com; 101 20th St, Setai Hotel; 1hr massage from $180; ⏲9am-9pm)

KZENON/SHUTTERSTOCK ©

Biltmore Hotel Historic Building
(☎855-311-6903; www.biltmorehotel.com; 1200 Anastasia Ave; ⏲tours 1:30pm & 2:30pm Sun; P) In the most opulent neighborhood of one of the showiest cities in the world, the Biltmore peers down her nose and says, 'hrmph.' It's one of the greatest of the grand hotels of the American Jazz Age, and if this joint were a fictional character from a novel, it'd be, without question, Jay Gatsby.

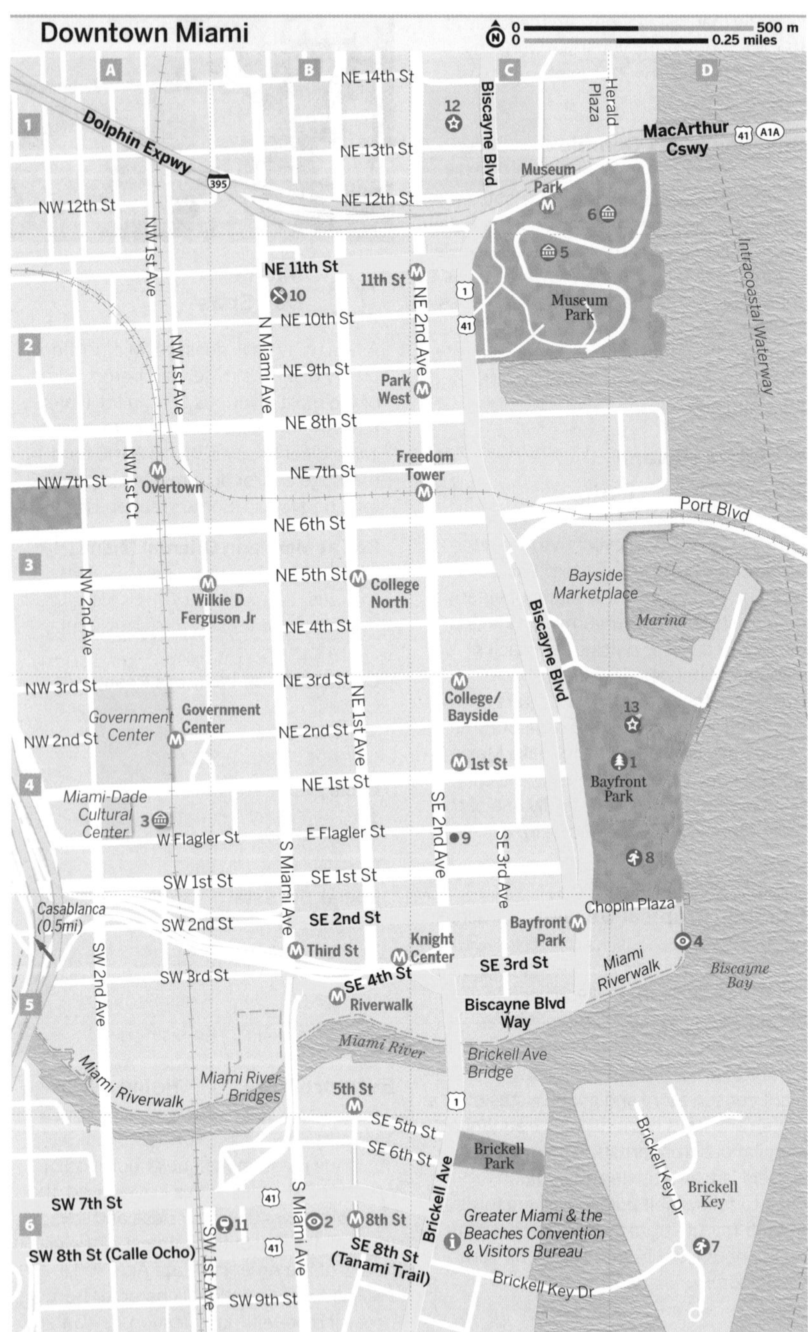
Downtown Miami
0
500 m
0
0.25 miles
A
B
C
D
1
2
3
4
5
6
NE 14th St
NE 13th St
NE 12th St
NW 12th St
Dolphin Expwy
395
Biscayne Blvd
Herald Plaza
MacArthur Cswy
41
A1A
Museum Park
12
6
5
Museum Park
Intracoastal Waterway
NE 11th St
11th St
10
NE 10th St
NE 2nd Ave
1
41
NW 1st Ave
N Miami Ave
NE 9th St
Park West
NE 8th St
Freedom Tower
NE 7th St
NW 7th St
NW 1st Ct
Overtown
Port Blvd
NE 6th St
NE 5th St
College North
Wilkie D Ferguson Jr
NE 4th St
NW 2nd Ave
Bayside Marketplace
Marina
Biscayne Blvd
NE 3rd St
NW 3rd St
College/ Bayside
Government Center
Government Center
NE 2nd St
NW 2nd St
NE 1st Ave
13
1st St
1
Bayfront Park
NE 1st St
Miami-Dade Cultural Center
3
W Flagler St
E Flagler St
SE 2nd Ave
9
SE 3rd Ave
S Miami Ave
SW 1st St
SE 1st St
8
Casablanca (0.5mi)
SW 2nd St
SE 2nd St
Chopin Plaza
Bayfront Park
Knight Center
4
Third St
SE 3rd St
Miami Riverwalk
Biscayne Bay
SW 3rd St
SE 4th St
SW 2nd Ave
Riverwalk
Biscayne Blvd Way
Miami River
Brickell Ave Bridge
Miami Riverwalk
Miami River Bridges
5th St
1
SE 5th St
Brickell Key Dr
SE 6th St
Brickell Park
Brickell Ave
Brickell Key
SW 7th St
41
S Miami Ave
11
2
8th St
Greater Miami & the Beaches Convention & Visitors Bureau
SW 8th St (Calle Ocho)
41
SE 8th St (Tanami Trail)
7
SW 1st Ave
Brickell Key Dr
SW 9th St

Downtown Miami

Sights

1 Bayfront Park D4
2 Brickell City Centre B6
3 HistoryMiami A4
4 Miami Riverwalk D5
5 Patricia & Phillip Frost Museum of Science C2
6 Pérez Art Museum Miami C1

Activities, Courses & Tours

7 Spa at Mandarin Oriental Miami D6
8 Tina Hills Pavilion D4
9 Urban Tour Host C4

Eating

10 All Day B2
Verde .... (see 6)

Drinking & Nightlife

11 Blackbird Ordinary B6

Entertainment

12 Adrienne Arsht Center for the Performing Arts C1
13 Klipsch Amphitheater D4

Al Capone had a speakeasy on site, and the Capone Suite is said to be haunted by the spirit of Fats Walsh, who was murdered here.

Lowe Art Museum Museum

(☎305-284-3535; www.miami.edu/lowe; 1301 Stanford Dr; adult/student/child $13/8/free; ⏰10am-4pm Tue-Sat, noon-4pm Sun) Your love of the Lowe, on the campus of the University of Miami, depends on your taste in art. If you're into modern and contemporary works, it's good. If you're into the art and archaeology of cultures from Asia, Africa and the South Pacific, it's great. And if you're into pre-Columbian and Mesoamerican art, it's fantastic.

Coconut Grove

Vizcaya Museum & Gardens Historic Building

(☎305-250-9133; www.vizcayamuseum.org; 3251 S Miami Ave; adult/6-12yr/student & senior $18/6/12; ⏰9:30am-4:30pm Wed-Mon; P) They call Miami the Magic City, and if it is, this Italian villa, the housing equivalent of a Fabergé egg, is its most fairy-tale residence. In 1916 industrialist James Deering started a Miami tradition by making a ton of money and building ridiculously grandiose digs. He employed a thousand people (then 10% of the local population) and stuffed his home with 15th- to 19th-century furniture, tapestries, paintings and decorative arts; today the grounds are used for rotating contemporary-art exhibitions.

Kampong Gardens

(☎305-442-7169; www.ntbg.org; 4013 Douglas Rd; adult/child $15/5; ⏰tours by appointment only 10am-3pm Mon-Sat) David Fairchild, the Indiana Jones of the botanical world and founder of Fairchild Tropical Garden, would rest at the Kampong (Malay/Indonesian for 'village') in between journeys in search of beautiful and economically viable plant life. Today this lush garden is listed on the National Register of Historic Places and the lovely grounds serve as a classroom for the National Tropical Botanical Garden. Self-guided tours (allow at least an hour) are available by appointment, as are $20 one-hour guided tours.

Little Haiti & the Upper East Side

Little Haiti Cultural Center Gallery

(☎305-960-2969; www.littlehaiticulturalcenter.com; 212 NE 59th Tce; ⏰10am-9pm Tue-Fri, 9am-4pm Sat, 11am-7pm Sun) FREE This cultural center hosts an art gallery with often thought-provoking exhibitions from Haitian painters, sculptors and multimedia artists. You can also find dance classes, drama productions and a Caribbean-themed market during special events. The building itself is quite a confection of bold tropical colors, steep A-framed roofs and lacy decorative elements. Don't miss the mural in the palm-filled courtyard.

Understand

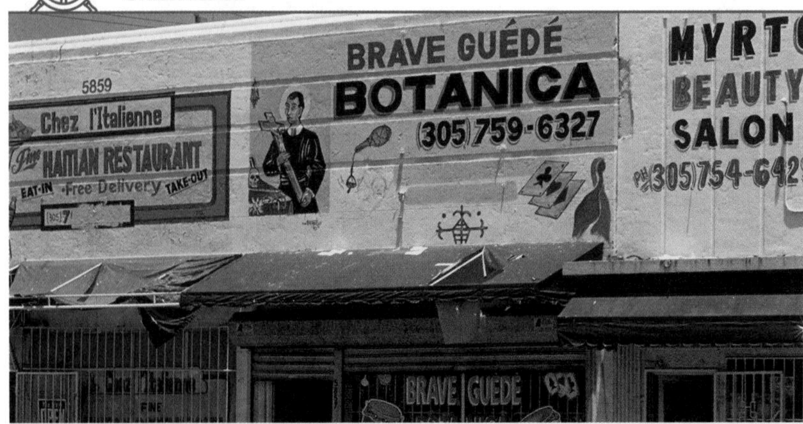

Little Haiti's Botanicas

If you pay a visit to Little Haiti, you might notice a few storefronts emblazoned with 'botanica' signs. Not to be confused with a plant store, a *botanica* is a Vodou shop. *Botanicas* are perhaps the most 'foreign' sight in Little Haiti. Storefronts promise to help in matters of love, work and, sometimes, 'immigration services'. But, trust us, there are no marriage counselors or INS guys in here. As you enter you'll probably get a funny look, but be courteous, curious and respectful and you should be welcomed.

Before you browse, forget stereotypes about pins and dolls. Like many traditional religions, Vodou recognizes supernatural forces in everyday objects, and powers that are both distinct from and part of one overarching deity. Ergo you'll see shrines to Jesus next to altars to traditional Vodou deities. Notice the large statues of what look like people; these actually represent *loa* (pronounced lwa), intermediary spirits that form a pantheon below God in the Vodou religious hierarchy. Drop a coin into a *loa* offering bowl before you leave, especially to Papa Legba, spirit of crossroads and, by our reckoning, travelers.

Key Biscayne

Bill Baggs Cape Florida State Park — State Park

(305-361-5811; www.floridastateparks.org/capeflorida; 1200 S Crandon Blvd; per car/person $8/2; 8am-sunset, lighthouse 9am-5pm; P) If you don't make it to the Florida Keys, come to this park for a taste of its unique island ecosystems. The 494-acre space is a tangled clot of tropical fauna and dark mangroves – look for the 'snorkel' roots that provide air for half-submerged mangrove trees – all interconnected by sandy trails and wooden boardwalks, and surrounded by miles of pale ocean. A concession shack rents out kayaks, bikes, in-line skates, beach chairs and umbrellas.

Crandon Park — Park

(305-361-5421; www.miamidade.gov/parks/parks; 6747 Crandon Blvd; per car weekday/

weekend $5/7; ⏰sunrise-sunset; P) This 1200-acre park boasts **Crandon Park Beach**, a glorious stretch of sand that spreads for 2 miles. Much of the park consists of a dense coastal hammock (hardwood forest) and mangrove swamps. The beach here is clean and uncluttered by tourists, faces a lovely sweep of teal goodness and is regularly named one of the best beaches in the USA. Pretty cabanas at the south end of the park can be rented by the day ($40).

ACTIVITIES

Virginia Key Outdoor Center — Outdoors

(VKOC; www.vkoc.net; 3801 Rickenbacker Causeway, Virginia Key; kayak or bike hire 1st hour $25, each additional hour $10; ⏰9am-4:30pm Mon-Fri, from 8am Sat & Sun) This highly recommended outfitter will get you out on the water in a hurry with kayaks and stand-up paddleboards, which you can put in the water just across from their office. The small mangrove-lined bay (known as Lamar Lake) has manatees, and makes for a great start to the paddle.

Venetian Pool — Swimming

(☎305-460-5306; www.coralgablesvenetian-pool.com; 2701 De Soto Blvd; adult/child Sep-May $15/10, Jun-Aug $20/15; ⏰11am-5:30pm Tue-Fri, 10am-4:30pm Sat & Sun, closed Dec-Feb;) Just imagine: it's 1923, tons of rock have been quarried for one of the most beautiful neighborhoods in Miami, but now an ugly gash sits in the middle of the village. What to do? How about pump the irregular hole full of water, mosaic and tile up the whole affair, and make it look like a Roman emperor's aquatic playground?

Yoga by the Sea — Yoga

(www.thebarnacle.org; class $15; ⏰6:30-7:45pm Mon & Wed) A lovely open-air setting for yoga is on the grass overlooking the waterfront at the Barnacle Historic State Park. Hatha yoga classes happen twice weekly in the evenings. Bring your own mat.

The Lincoln Road Experience

Lincoln Road Mall, an outdoor pedestrian thoroughfare between Alton Rd and Washington Ave, is all about seeing and being seen; there are times when Lincoln feels less like a road and more like a runway. Carl Fisher, the father of Miami Beach, envisioned the road as a Fifth Ave of the South. Morris Lapidus, one of the founders of the loopy, neo-baroque Miami Beach style, designed much of the mall, including shady overhangs, waterfall structures and traffic barriers that look like the marbles a giant might play with.

KAMIRA/SHUTTERSTOCK ©

TOURS

History Miami Tours — Tours

(www.historymiami.org; tours $30-60) Historian extraordinaire Dr Paul George leads fascinating walking tours, including culturally rich strolls through Little Haiti, Little Havana, Downtown and Coral Gables at twilight, plus the occasional boat trip to Stiltsville and Key Biscayne. Tours happen once a week or so. Get the full menu and sign up online.

Miami Design Preservation League — Walking

(MDPL; Map p46; ☎305-672-2014; www.mdpl.org; 1001 Ocean Dr; guided tours adult/student $25/20; ⏰10:30am daily & 6:30pm Thu) Tells the stories and history behind the art-deco buildings in South Beach, with a lively

Art Walks: Nightlife Meets Art

Ever-flowing (not always free) wine and beer, great art, a fun crowd and no cover charge (or velvet rope): welcome to the wondrous world where art and nightlife collide. The Wynwood and Design District Art Walks are among the best ways to experience an alternative slice of Miami culture. Just be careful, as a lot of galleries in Wynwood are separated by short drives (the Design District is more walkable). Art Walks take place on the second Saturday of each month, from 7pm to 10pm (some galleries stretch to 11pm); when it's all over, lots of folks repair to **Wood Tavern** (305-748-2828; www.woodtavernmiami.com; 2531 NW 2nd Ave; 5pm-3am Tue-Sat, 3pm-midnight Sun) or Bardot (p62). Visit www.artofmiami.com for information on participating galleries.

IMAGE COURTESY OF WYNWOOD WALLS. MARTHA COOPER ©

guide from the Miami Design Preservation League. Tours last 90 minutes. Also offers tours of Jewish Miami Beach, Gay & Lesbian Miami Beach and a once-monthly tour (first Saturday at 9:30am) of the MiMo district in the North Beach area.

Urban Tour Host Walking

(Map p50; 305-416-6868; www.miamiculturaltours.com; 25 SE 2nd Ave, Ste 1048; tours from $20) Urban Tour Host runs a program of custom tours that provide face-to-face interaction in all of Miami's neighborhoods. For something different, sign up for a Miami cultural community tour that includes Little Haiti and Little Havana, with opportunities to visit Overtown, Liberty City and Allpattah.

SHOPPING

Nomad Tribe Clothing

(305-364-5193; www.nomadtribeshop.com; 2301 NW 2nd Ave; noon-8pm) This boutique earns high marks for carrying only ethically and sustainably produced merchandise. You'll find cleverly designed jewelry from Miami-based Kathe Cuervo, Osom brand socks (made of upcycled thread), ecologically produced graphic T-shirts from Thinking MU, and THX coffee and candles among much else.

Polished Coconut Fashion & Accessories

(3444 Main Hwy; 11am-6pm Mon-Sat, noon-5pm Sun) Colorful textiles from Central and South America are transformed into lovely accessories and home decor at this eye-catching store in the heart of Coconut Grove. You'll find handbags, satchels, belts, sun hats, pillows, bedspreads and table runners made by artisans inspired by traditional indigenous designs.

Taschen Books

(Map p46; 305-538-6185; www.taschen.com; 1111 Lincoln Rd; 11am-9pm Mon-Thu, to 10pm Fri & Sat, noon-9pm Sun) An inviting and well-stocked collection of art, photography, design and coffee-table books to make your home look that much smarter. A few volumes worth browsing include David Hockney's color-rich art books, the *New Erotic Photography* (always a great conversation starter) and Sebastião Salgado's lushly photographed landscapes.

Malaquita Arts & Crafts

(www.malaquitadesign.com; 2613 NW 2nd Ave; 11am-7pm) This artfully designed store has merchandise you won't find elsewhere, including lovely handblown vases, embroidered clothing, Mesoamerican tapestries, vibrantly painted bowls, handwoven palm baskets and other fair-trade objects.

Cuban cigars

Brooklyn Vintage & Vinyl Music
(www.facebook.com/brooklynvintageand vinyl; 3454 NW 7th Ave; ⌚noon-9pm Tue-Sat) Although it opened in late 2016, this record store on the edge of Wynwood has already attracted a following. It's mostly vinyl (plus some cassettes and a few T-shirts), with around 5000 records in the inventory. Staff can give good tips for exploring new music.

Guantanamera Cigars
(www.guantanameracigars.com; 1465 SW 8th St; ⌚10:30am-8pm Sun-Thu, to midnight Fri & Sat) In a central location in Little Havana, Guantanamera sells high-quality hand-rolled cigars, plus strong Cuban coffee. It's an atmospheric shop, where you can stop for a smoke, a drink (there's a bar here) and some friendly banter. There's live music here most nights. The rocking chairs in front are a fine perch for people-watching.

Havana Collection Clothing
(☎786-717-7474; 1421 SW 8th St; ⌚10am-6pm) One of the best and most striking collections of *guayaberas* (Cuban dress shirts) in Miami can be found in this shop. Prices are high (plan on spending about $85 for shirt), but so is the quality, so you can be assured of a long-lasting product.

EATING

Miami is a major immigrant entrepôt and a sucker for food trends. Thus you get a good mix of cheap ethnic eateries and high-quality top-end cuisine here, alongside some poor-value dross in touristy zones like Miami Beach. The best new areas for dining are in Downtown, Wynwood and the Upper East Side; Coral Gables has great classic options.

South Beach

Taquiza Mexican $
(Map p46; ☎305-748-6099; www.taquiza miami.com; 1506 Collins Ave; tacos $3.50-5; ⌚8am-midnight Sun-Thu, to 2am Fri & Sat) Taquiza has acquired a stellar reputation among Miami's street-food lovers. This takeout stand with a few outdoor tables serves up delicious perfection in its steak, pork, shrimp or veggie tacos (but no fish

Bayside Marketplace

options) served on handmade blue-corn tortillas. They're small, so order a few.

11th St Diner Diner $

(Map p46; ☎305-534-6373; www.eleventhstreetdiner.com; 1065 Washington Ave; mains $10-20; ⏱7am-midnight Sun-Wed, 24hr Thu-Sat) You've seen the art-deco landmarks. Now eat in one: a Pullman-car diner trucked down from Wilkes-Barre, Pennsylvania – as sure a slice of Americana as a *Leave It to Beaver* marathon. The food is as classic as the architecture, with oven-roasted turkey, baby back ribs and mac 'n' cheese among the hits – plus breakfast at all hours.

Pubbelly Fusion $$

(Map p46; ☎305-532-7555; www.pubbellyboys.com; 1418 20th St; sharing plates $11-24, mains $19-30; ⏱6pm-midnight Tue-Thu & Sun, to 1am Fri & Sat; 🖉) Pubbelly's dining genre is hard to pinpoint, besides delicious. It skews between Asian, North American and Latin American, gleaning the best from all cuisines. Examples? Try black-truffle risotto, pork-belly dumplings or the mouthwatering kimchi fried rice with seafood. Hand-crafted cocktails wash down the dishes a treat.

Yardbird Southern US $$

(Map p46; ☎305-538-5220; www.runchickenrun.com; 1600 Lenox Ave; mains $18-38; ⏱11am-midnight Mon-Fri, from 8:30am Sat & Sun; 🖉) Yardbird has earned a diehard following for its delicious haute Southern comfort food. The kitchen churns out some nice shrimp and grits, St Louis–style pork ribs, charred okra, and biscuits with smoked brisket, but it's most famous for its supremely good plate of fried chicken, spiced watermelon and waffles with bourbon maple syrup.

North Beach

27 Restaurant Fusion $$

(☎786-476-7020; www.freehandhotels.com; 2727 Indian Creek Dr, Freehand Miami Hotel; mains $17-28; ⏱6:30pm-2am Mon-Sat, 11am-4pm & 6:30pm-2am Sun; 🖉) This new spot sits on the grounds of the very popular Broken Shaker (p61, one of Miami Beach's best-loved cocktail bars). Like the bar, the setting is amazing – akin to dining in an old tropical cottage, with worn wood floorboards, candlelit tables, and various rooms slung with artwork and curious knickknacks, plus a lovely terrace.

Cafe Prima Pasta Italian $$

(305-867-0106; www.cafeprimapasta.com; 414 71st St; mains $17-26; 5-11:30pm Mon-Sat, 4-11pm Sun) We're not sure what's better at this Argentine-Italian place: the much-touted pasta, which deserves every one of the accolades heaped on it, or the atmosphere, which captures the dignified sultriness of Buenos Aires. You can't go wrong with the small, well-curated menu, with standouts like gnocchi formaggi, baked branzino, and squid-ink linguine with seafood in a lobster sauce.

Downtown Miami

All Day Cafe $

(Map p50; www.alldaymia.com; 1035 N Miami Ave; coffee $3.50, breakfast $10-14; 7am-7pm Mon-Fri, from 9am Sat & Sun;) All Day is one of the best places in the Downtown area to linger over coffee or breakfast – no matter the hour. Slender Scandinavian-style chairs, wood-and-marble tables and the Françoise Hardy soundtrack lend an easy-going vibe to the place.

Casablanca Seafood $$

(www.casablancaseafood.com; 400 N River Dr; mains $15-34; 11am-10pm Sun-Thu, to 11pm Fri & Sat) Perched over the Miami River, Casablanca serves up some of the best seafood in town. The setting is a big draw – tables on a long wooden deck just above the water, with the odd seagull winging past. But the fresh fish is the real star here.

Verde American $$

(Map p50; 786-345-5697; www.pamm.org/dining; 1103 Biscayne Blvd, Pérez Art Museum Miami; mains $13-19; Fri-Tue 11am-5pm, to 9pm Thu, closed Wed;) Inside the Pérez Art Museum Miami (p47), Verde is a local favorite for its tasty market-fresh dishes and great setting – with outdoor seating on a terrace overlooking the bay. Crispy mahimahi tacos, pizza with squash blossoms and goat cheese, and grilled endive salads are among the temptations.

Top Five Cheap Eats

Wynwood Yard Gourmet food truck fare

Taquiza (p55) Stellar street food and tacos

El Nuevo Siglo (p59) Luscious Latin Amiercan bites at killer prices

Chef Creole (p61) Caribbean shack food in Little Haiti

Coral Bagels (p59) Buzzing deli serving fresh bagels

NEHOPHOTO/SHUTTERSTOCK ©

Wynwood & the Design District

Panther Coffee Cafe $

(305-677-3952; www.panthercoffee.com; 2390 NW 2nd Ave; coffees $3-6; 7am-9pm Mon-Sat, from 8am Sun;) Miami's best independent coffee shop specializes in single-origin, small-batch roasts, fired up to perfection. Aside from sipping on a zesty brewed-to-order Chemex-made coffee (or a creamy latte), you can enjoy microbrews, wines and sweet treats. The front patio is a great spot for people-watching.

Wynwood Yard Food Trucks $

(www.thewynwoodyard.com; 56 NW 29th St; mains $7-14; noon-11pm Tue-Thu, to 1am Fri-Sun;) On a once-vacant lot, the Wynwood Yard is something of an urban oasis for those who want to enjoy a bit of

Understand

Miami Food Specialties

Cuban Sandwich

The traditional Cuban sandwich, also known as a *sandwich mixto,* is not some slapdash creation. It's a craft best left to the experts – but here's some insight into how they do it. Correct bread is crucial – it should be Cuban white bread: fresh, soft and easy to press. The insides (both sides) should be buttered and layered (in the following order) with sliced pickles, slices of roast Cuban pork, ham (preferably sweet-cured ham) and baby Swiss cheese. Then it all gets pressed in a hot *plancha* (sandwich press) until the cheese melts.

Arepas

The greatness of a city can be measured by many yardsticks. The arts. Civic involvement. Infrastructure. What you eat when you're plowed at 3am. In Miami, the answer is often enough *arepas,* delicious South American corn cakes that can be stuffed (Venezuelan-style) or topped (Colombian-style) with any manner of deliciousness; generally, you can't go wrong with cheese.

Stone Crabs

The first reusable crustacean: only one claw is taken from a stone crab – the rest is tossed back in the sea (the claw regrows in 12 to 18 months, and crabs plucked again are called 'retreads'). The claws are so perishable that they're always cooked before selling. For straight-out-of-the ocean freshness, try them in Everglades City.

Cuban sandwich HANS GEEL/SHUTTERSTOCK ©

casual open-air eating and drinking. Around a dozen different food trucks park here, offering gourmet mac 'n' cheese, cruelty-free salads, meaty schnitzel plates, zesty tacos, desserts and more. There's also a bar, and often live music.

Kyu Fusion **$$**

(☎786-577-0150; www.kyumiami.com; 251 NW 25th St; sharing plates $17-38; ⏰noon-11:30pm Mon-Sat, 11am-10:30pm Sun, bar till 1am Fri & Sat; 🍷) 🌿 One of the best new restaurants in Wynwood, Kyu has been dazzling locals and food critics alike with its creative Asian-inspired dishes, most of which are cooked up over the open flames of a wood-fired grill. The buzzing industrial space is warmed up via artful lighting and wood accents (tables and chairs, plus shelves of firewood for the grill).

Alter Modern American **$$$**
(305-573-5996; www.altermiami.com; 223 NW 23rd St; 5-/7-course set menu $69/89; 7-11pm Tue-Sun) This new spot, which has garnered much praise from food critics, brings creative high-end cooking to Wynwood courtesy of its award-winning young chef Brad Kilgore. The changing menu showcases Florida's high-quality ingredients from sea and land in seasonally inspired dishes with Asian and European accents.

Little Havana

El Nuevo Siglo Latin American **$**
(1305 SW 8th St; mains $8-12; 7am-8pm) Hidden inside a supermarket of the same name, El Nuevo Siglo draws foodie-minded locals who come for delicious cooking at excellent prices – never mind the unfussy ambience. Grab a seat at the shiny black countertop and nibble on roast meats, fried yucca, tangy Cuban sandwiches, grilled snapper with rice, beans and plantains, and other daily specials.

El Carajo Spanish **$$**
(305-856-2424; www.el-carajo.com; 2465 SW 17th Avenue; tapas $5-15; noon-10pm Mon-Wed, to 11pm Thu-Sat, 11am-10pm Sun;) Pass the Pennzoil please. We know it is cool to tuck restaurants into unassuming spots, but the Citgo station on SW 17th Ave? Really? Really. Walk past the motor oil into a Granadan wine cellar and try not to act too fazed. The food is absolutely incredible.

Doce Provisions Modern American **$$**
(786-452-0161; www.doceprovisions.com; 541 SW 12th Ave; mains $11-25; noon-3:30pm & 5-10pm Mon-Thu, noon-3:30pm & 5-11pm Fri, noon-11pm Sat, 11am-9pm Sun) For a break from old-school Latin eateries, stop in at Doce Provisions, which has more of a Wynwood vibe than a Little Havana one. The stylish industrial interior sets the stage for dining on creative American fare – rock shrimp mac 'n' cheese, fried chicken with sweet plantain waffle, short rib burgers and truffle fries – plus local microbrews.

Coral Gables

Threefold Cafe **$$**
(305-704-8007; 141 Giralda Ave; mains $13-19; 8am-4:30pm;) Coral Gables' most talked-about cafe is a buzzing, Aussie-run charmer that serves up perfectly pulled espressos (and a good flat white), along with creative breakfast and lunch fare. Start the morning with waffles and berry compote, smashed avocado toast topped with feta, or a slow-roasted leg of lamb with fried eggs.

Frenchie's Diner French **$$**
(305-442-4554; www.frenchiesdiner.com; 2618 Galiano St; mains lunch $14-24, dinner $24-34; 11am-3pm & 6-10pm Tue-Sat) Tucked down a side street, it's easy to miss this place. Inside, Frenchie's channels an old-time American diner vibe, with black-and-white checkered floors, a big chalkboard menu, and a smattering of old prints and mirrors on the wall. The cooking, on the other hand, is a showcase for French bistro classics.

Coconut Grove

Last Carrot Vegetarian **$**
(305-445-0805; 3133 Grand Ave; mains $6-8; 10:30am-6pm Mon-Sat, 11am-4:30pm Sun;) Going strong since the 1970s, the Last Carrot serves up fresh juices, delicious pita sandwiches, avocado melts, veggie burgers and rather famous spinach pies, all amid old-Grove neighborliness. The Carrot's endurance next to massive CocoWalk is testament to the quality of its good-for-your-body food served in a good-for-your-soul setting.

Coral Bagels Deli **$**
(305-854-0336; 2750 SW 26th Ave; mains $7-11; 6:30am-3pm Mon-Fri, 7am-4pm Sat &

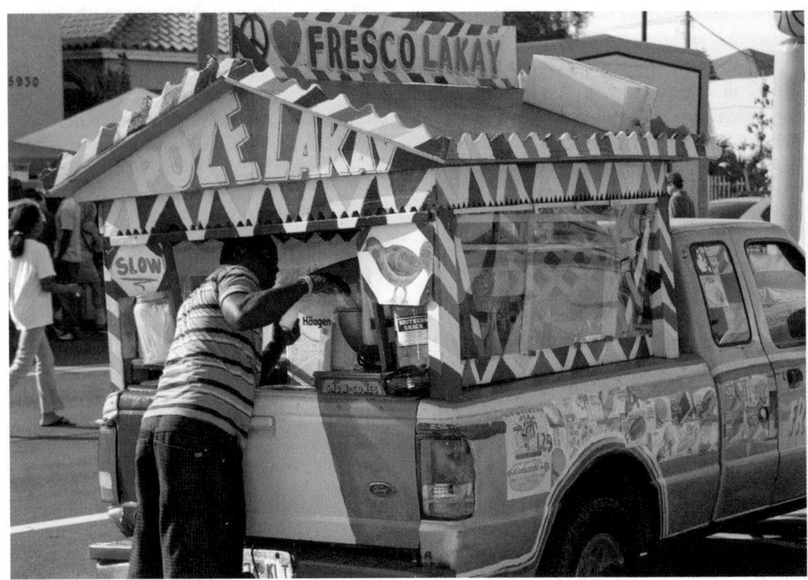

Food truck, Little Haiti

Sun; P) Although it's out of the way (one mile north of Coconut Grove's epicenter), this is a great place to start the day. The buzzing little deli serves proper bagels, rich omelets and decadent potato pancakes with apple sauce and sour cream. You'll be hard pressed to spend double digits, and you'll leave satisfied.

Boho Mediterranean **$$**

(305-549-8614; 3433 Main Hwy; mains $19-26, pizzas $12-17; noon-11pm Mon-Fri, from 10am Sat & Sun) This Greek-run charmer is helping to lead the culinary renaissance in Coconut Grove, serving up fantastic Mediterranean dishes, including tender marinated octopus, creamy risotto, thin-crust pizzas drizzled with truffle oil and zesty quinoa and beet salads. The setting invites long, leisurely meals with its jungle-like wallpaper, big picture windows and easygoing vibe.

Spillover Modern American **$$**

(305-456-5723; www.spillovermiami.com; 2911 Grand Ave; mains $13-25; 11:30am-10pm Sun-Tue, to 11pm Wed-Sat;) Tucked down a pedestrian strip near the CocoWalk, the Spillover serves up locally sourced seafood and creative bistro fare in an enticing vintage setting (cast-iron stools and recycled doors around the bar, suspenders-wearing staff, brassy jazz playing overhead). Come for crab cakes, buffalo shrimp tacos, spear-caught fish and chips, or a melt-in-your-mouth lobster Reuben.

Little Haiti & the Upper East Side

Phuc Yea Vietnamese **$**

(305-602-3710; www.phucyea.com; 7100 Biscayne Blvd; 6pm-midnight Tue-Sat, 11:30am-3:30pm & 6-9pm Sun) Not unlike its cheeky name, Phuc Yea pushes boundaries with its bold and deliciously executed Vietnamese cooking – served up in a graffiti-smeared and hip-hop loving setting. You too can heed the call to get 'Phuc'd up!' (undoubtedly a good thing since 'phuc' means 'blessings and prosperity') by indulging in lobster summer rolls, fish curry, spicy chicken wings and other great sharing plates.

Chef Creole Haitian $

(☎305-754-2223; www.chefcreole.com; 200 NW 54th St; mains $7-20; ⏰11am-10pm Mon-Sat) When you need Caribbean food on the cheap, head to the edge of Little Haiti and this excellent takeout shack. Order up fried conch, oxtail or fish, ladle rice and beans on the side, and you'll be full for a week. Enjoy the food on nearby picnic benches while Haitian music blasts out of tinny speakers – as island an experience as they come.

Mina's Mediterranean $$

(☎786-391-0300; www.minasmiami.com; 749 NE 79th St; mains $16-30, sharing plates $6-16; ⏰5-10pm Tue-Thu, to 11pm Fri, noon-11pm Sat, 11am-9pm Sun; 🍷) Soaring ceilings, vintage travel posters and a friendly vibe set the stage for a memorable meal at Mina's. The Mediterranean menu is great for sharing, with creamy hummus, refreshing dolmas, spanakopita (spinach-filled pastries) and toothsome fried calamari among the great starters.

 DRINKING & NIGHTLIFE

Too many people assume Miami's nightlife is all about being wealthy and attractive and/or phony. Disavow yourself of this notion, which only describes a small slice of the scene in South Beach. Miami has an intense variety of bars to pick from that range from grotty dives to beautiful – but still laid-back – lounges and nightclubs.

Blackbird Ordinary Bar

(Map p50; ☎305-671-3307; www.blackbird ordinary.com; 729 SW 1st Ave; ⏰3pm-5am Mon-Fri, 5pm-5am Sat & Sun) Far from ordinary, the Blackbird is an excellent bar, with great cocktails (the London Sparrow, with gin, cayenne, lemon juice and passion fruit, goes down well) and an enormous courtyard. The only thing 'ordinary' about the place is the sense that all are welcome for a fun and pretension-free night out.

Sweet Liberty Bar

(Map p46; www.mysweetliberty.com; 237 20th St; ⏰4pm-5am Mon-Sat, from noon Sun) A much-loved local haunt near Collins Park, Sweet Liberty has all the right ingredients for a fun night out: friendly, easygoing bartenders who whip up excellent cocktails (try a mint julep), great happy-hour specials (including 75¢ oysters) and a relaxed, pretension-free crowd. The space is huge, with flickering candles, a long wooden bar and the odd band adding to the cheer.

Broken Shaker Bar

(☎305-531-2727; www.freehandhotels.com; 2727 Indian Creek Dr, Freehand Miami; ⏰6pm-3am Mon-Fri, 2pm-3am Sat & Sun) Craft cocktails are having their moment in Miami, and if mixology is in the spotlight, you can bet Broken Shaker is sharing the glare. Expert bartenders run this spot, located in the back of the Freehand Miami hotel which takes up one closet-sized indoor niche and a sprawling plant-filled courtyard of excellent drinks and beautiful people.

The Full Moon Drum Circle

If there's a full moon, check out the beach between 79th and 85th Sts – a big, boisterous drum circle is held here that doubles as a full-moon party. The beat tends to start between 8:30pm and 9:30pm, and can run well into the wee hours. That said, drinking (and the consumption of other substances) is technically illegal on the beach, and police have broken up the event before. Still, it tends to be a pretty fun party that shouldn't be missed if you're in the area and want to see an incredible moonset.

Fire spinning, Miami Beach MAY NEUMAN//SHUTTERSTOCK ©

Bodega Cocktail Bar
(Map p46; ☎305-704-2145; www.bodegasouthbeach.com; 1220 16th St; ⊙noon-5am) Bodega looks like your average hipster Mexican joint – serving up delicious tacos ($3 to $5) from a converted Airstream trailer to a party-minded crowd. But there's actually a bar hidden behind that blue porta potty door on the right. Head inside (or join the long line on weekends) to take in a bit of old-school glam in a sprawling drinking den.

Wynwood Brewing Company Microbrewery
(☎305-982-8732; www.wynwoodbrewing.com; 565 NW 24th St; ⊙noon-10pm Sun & Mon, to midnight Tue-Sat) The beer scene has grown in leaps and bounds in Miami, but this warmly lit spot, which was the first craft brewery in Wynwood, is still the best. The family-owned 15-barrel brewhouse has friendly and knowledgeable staff, excellent year-round brews (including a blonde ale, a robust porter and a top-notch IPA) and seasonal beers, and there's always a food truck parked outside.

Bardot Club
(☎305-576-5570; www.bardotmiami.com; 3456 N Miami Ave; ⊙8pm-3am Tue & Wed, to 5am Thu-Sat) You really should see the interior of Bardot before you leave the city. It's all sexy French vintage posters and furniture (plus a pool table) seemingly plucked from a private club that serves millionaires by day, and becomes a scene of decadent excess by night. The entrance is in a parking lot behind the building.

Ball & Chain Bar
(www.ballandchainmiami.com; 1513 SW 8th Street; ⊙noon-midnight Mon-Wed, to 3am Thu-Sat, 2-10pm Sun) The Ball & Chain has survived several incarnations over the years. Back in 1935, when 8th St was more Jewish than Latino, it was the sort of jazz joint Billie Holiday would croon in. That iteration closed in 1957, but the new Ball & Chain is still dedicated to music and good times – Latin music and tropical cocktails.

ENTERTAINMENT

Adrienne Arsht Center for the Performing Arts Performing Arts
(Map p50; ☎305-949-6722; www.arshtcenter.org; 1300 Biscayne Blvd; ⊙box office 10am-6pm Mon-Fri, & 2hr before performances) This magnificent venue manages to both humble and enthrall visitors. Today the Arsht is where the biggest cultural acts in Miami come to perform; a show here is a must-see on any Miami trip. There's an Adrienne Arsht Center stop on the Metromover.

Cubaocho Live Performance
(☎305-285-5880; www.cubaocho.com; 1465 SW 8th St; ⊙11am-10pm Tue-Thu, to 3am Fri & Sat) Jewel of the Little Havana Art District, Cubaocho is renowned for its concerts, with excellent bands from across the Spanish-speaking world. It's also a community center, art gallery and research outpost for all things Cuban. The interior resembles an old Havana cigar bar, yet the walls are decked out in artwork that references both the classical past of Cuban art and its avant-garde future.

New World Symphony Classical Music
(NWS; Map p46; ☎305-673-3330; www.nws.edu; 500 17th St) Housed in the New World Center (p44) – a funky explosion of cubist lines and geometric curves, fresh white against the blue Miami sky – the acclaimed New World Symphony holds performances from October to May. The deservedly heralded NWS serves as a three- to four-year preparatory program for talented musicians from prestigious music schools.

Tower Theater Cinema
(☎305-237-2463; www.towertheatermiami.com; 1508 SW 8th St) This renovated 1926 landmark theater has a proud deco facade and a handsomely renovated interior, thanks to support from the Miami-Dade Community College. In its heyday, it was the center of Little Havana social life, and via the films it showed served as a bridge between immigrant society and American pop culture.

Cubaocho, Little Havana

Today it frequently shows independent and Spanish-language films (sometimes both).

INFORMATION

Greater Miami & the Beaches Convention & Visitors Bureau (Map p50; ☎305-539-3000; www.miamiandbeaches.com; 701 Brickell Ave, 27th fl; ⊙8:30am-6pm Mon-Fri) Offers loads of info on Miami and keeps up to date with the latest events and cultural offerings.

MEDICAL SERVICES

Coral Gables Hospital (☎305-445-8461; 3100 Douglas Rd, Coral Gables) A community-based facility with many bilingual doctors.

CVS Pharmacy This chain has many 24-hour pharmacies, including one in **South Beach** (Map p46; ☎305-538-1571; 1421 Alton Rd, South Beach; ⊙24hr).

Miami Beach Community Health Center (Stanley C Meyers Center; Map p46; ☎305-538-8835; www.miamibeachhealth.org; 710 Alton Rd, South Beach; ⊙7am-5pm Mon-Fri) Walk-in clinic with long lines.

Mount Sinai Medical Center (☎305-674-2121, emergency room 305-674-2200; www.msmc.com; 4300 Alton Rd; ⊙24hr) The area's best emergency room. Be aware that you must eventually pay, and fees are high.

GETTING THERE & AWAY

The majority of travelers come to Miami by air, although it's feasible to arrive by car, bus or even train. Miami is a major international airline hub, with flights to many cities across the USA, Latin America and Europe. Most flights come into Miami International Airport (MIA), although many are also directed to Fort Lauderdale-Hollywood International Airport (FLL).

AIR

Located 6 miles west of Downtown, the busy **Miami International Airport** (MIA; ☎305-876-7000; www.miami-airport.com; 2100 NW 42nd Ave) has three terminals and serves over 40 million passengers each year. Around 60 airlines fly into Miami. The airport is open 24 hours and is laid out in a horseshoe design. There are left-luggage facilities on two concourses at MIA,

Biking on the Florida coast

between B and C, and on G; prices vary according to bag size.

Around 26 miles north of Downtown Miami, **Fort Lauderdale-Hollywood International Airport** (FLL; ☎866-435-9355; www.broward.org/airport; 320 Terminal Dr) is also a viable gateway airport to the Florida region.

CAR & MOTORCYCLE

Driving to Florida is easy; there are no international borders or entry issues. Incorporating Florida into a larger USA road trip is very common, and having a car while in Miami can be very handy.

GETTING AROUND

TO/FROM THE AIRPORT

From Miami International Airport, taxis charge a flat rate, which varies depending on where you're heading. It's $22 to Downtown, Coconut Grove or Coral Gables; $35 to South Beach; and $44 to Key Biscayne. Count on 40 minutes to South Beach in average traffic, and about 25 minutes to Downtown.

Metro buses leave from Miami Airport Station (connected by electric rail to the airport) and run throughout the city; fares are $2.25. The Miami Beach Airport Express (Bus 150) costs $2.65 and makes stops all along Miami Beach, from 41st to the southern tip. You can also take the **SuperShuttle** (☎305-871-8210; www.supershuttle.com) shared-van service, which will cost about $22 to South Beach. Be sure to reserve a seat the day before.

From Fort Lauderdale-Hollywood International Airport, count on at least 45 minutes from the airport to Downtown by taxi, and at least an hour for the ride to South Beach. Prices are metered. Expect to pay about $75 to South Beach and $65 to Downtown. Alternatively, a shared van service is available from the airport with **GO Airport Shuttle** (☎800-244-8252; www.go-airportshuttle.com). Prices are around $25 to South Beach.

BICYCLE

Citi Bike (☎305-532-9494; www.citibikemiami.com; 30min/1hr/2hr/4hr/1-day rental $4.50/6.50/10/18/24) is a bike-share program where you can borrow a bike from scores of kiosks spread around Miami and Miami Beach.

Miami is flat, but traffic can be horrendous (abundant and fast-moving), and there isn't much cycling culture (or respect for cyclists) just yet. Free paper maps of the bike network are available at some kiosks, or you can find one online. There's also a handy smartphone app that shows you where the nearest stations are.

For longer rides, clunky Citi Bikes are not ideal (no helmet, no lock and only three gears).

Other rental outfits:

Bike & Roll (Map p46; ☎305-604-0001; www.bikemiami.com; 210 10th St; hire per 2hr/4hr/day from $10/18/24, tours $40; ⌚9am-7pm) Also does bike tours.

Brickell Bikes (☎305-373-3633; www.brickell-bikes.com; 70 SW 12th St; bike hire 4/8 hr $20/25; ⌚10am-7pm Mon-Fri, to 6pm Sat)

BUS

Miami's local bus system is called **Metrobus** (☎305-891-3131; www.miamidade.gov/transit/routes.asp; tickets $2.25), and though it has an extensive route system, service can be pretty spotty. Each bus route has a different schedule and routes generally run from about 5:30am to 11pm, though some are 24 hours. Rides cost $2.25 and must be paid in exact change (coins or a combination of bills and coins) or with an Easy Card (available for purchase from Metrorail stations and some shops and pharmacies). An easy-to-read route map is available online. Note that if you have to transfer buses, you'll have to pay the fare each time if paying in cash. With an Easy Card, transfers are free.

CAR & MOTORCYCLE

If you drive around Miami, there are a few things to know. Miami Beach is linked to the mainland by four causeways built over Biscayne Bay. They are, from south to north: the MacArthur (the extension of US Hwy 41 and Hwy A1A); Venetian ($1.75 toll); Julia Tuttle and John F Kennedy. There's also a $1.75 toll over the Rickenbacker Causeway to Key Biscayne. The tolls are automated, so ask about hiring a Sunpass if you're renting a vehicle.

The most important north–south highway is I-95, which ends at US Hwy 1 south of Downtown Miami. US Hwy 1, which runs from Key West all the way north to Maine, hugs the coastline. It's called Dixie Hwy south of Downtown Miami and Biscayne Blvd north of Downtown Miami. The Palmetto Expressway (Hwy 826) makes a rough loop around the city and spurs off below SW 40th St to the Don Shula Expressway (Hwy 874, a toll road). Florida's Turnpike Extension makes the most western outer loop around the city. Hwy A1A becomes Collins Ave in Miami Beach.

MIAMI TROLLEYS

A new free bus service has hit the streets of Miami, Miami Beach, Coconut Grove, Little Havana and Coral Gables, among other locations. The Trolley (www.miamigov.com/trolley) is actually a hybrid-electric bus disguised as an orange and green trolley. There are numerous routes, though they're made for getting around neighborhoods and not *between* them.

The most useful services for travelers are the following:

Biscayne Travels along Biscayne Blvd; handy for transport from Brickell to Downtown and up to the edge of Wynwood.

Brickell Connects Brickell area (south of the Miami River in the Downtown area) with the Vizcaya Museum & Gardens.

Coral Way Goes from Downtown (near the Freedom Tower) to downtown Coral Gables.

Wynwood Zigzags through town, from the Adrienne Arsht Center for the Performing Arts up through Wynwood along NW 2nd Ave to 29th St.

SLS Brickell Hotel

Where to Stay

In general, prices are quite high in Miami, with top South Beach hotels priced similarly to high-end options in NYC or LA. You'll save money by looking in neighborhoods outside of Miami Beach and Downtown.

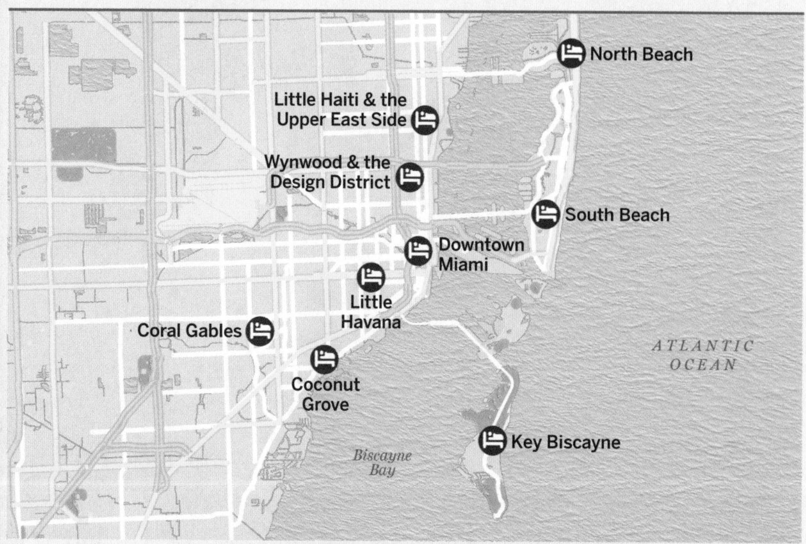

Neighborhood	Atmosphere
South Beach	Lovely architecture, great restaurants and bars, and the beach on your doorstep; prices are high, and it can feel very touristy.
North Beach	Peaceful beachfront and limited development make for a fine setting; prices here are generally high.
Downtown Miami	Great views over Biscayne Bay, good dining and shopping.
Wynwood & the Design District	Top-notch art galleries, shops, restaurants and bars; options are extremely limited here.
Little Haiti & the Upper East Side	Fascinating architecture from the MiMo (Miami Modern) period, good restaurants and bars, more local feel.
Coconut Grove	Laid-back local feel, with nice choice of eateries.
Coral Gables	Generally excellent value and a local atmosphere; good cafes.
Little Havana	Local vibe; delicious Latin cooking at your fingertips; very few options, limited nightlife.
Key Biscayne	Beautiful beaches and proximity to nature and outdoor activities; limited accommodation options and not many restaurants.

COZUMEL

Diving off Cozumel (p76)

In This Chapter

Cozumel at a Glance

At first glance, Cozumel – a small island located about 12 miles off the mainland from Playa del Carmen – is just another cheesy island destination. But leave the hotel zone behind and you'll see an island of quiet cool and genuine authenticity. Garages still have shrines to the Virgin, there's a spirited Caribbean energy, and of course there are some exciting things to do, such as diving some of the best reefs in the world. Cruise ships dock at Punta Langosta and Puerta Maya ports. Punta Langosta is in the heart of San Miguel, the most developed area on the island, while Puerta Maya is about 3 miles further south.

With a Day in Port

- Spend the day at the ancient Mayan ruins of Tulum and the beautiful cliff-side beach nearby. (p72)
- Dive or snorkel one of the many impressive reefs such as the Santa Rosa Wall or Palancar Reef. (p76)
- Hire a driver to take you on a tour of the coastal road and explore the less visited southern end of the island. (p74)

Best Places for...

Coffee El Coffee Cozumel (p81)

Cocktails La Cocay (p81)

Local cuisine La Choza (p80)

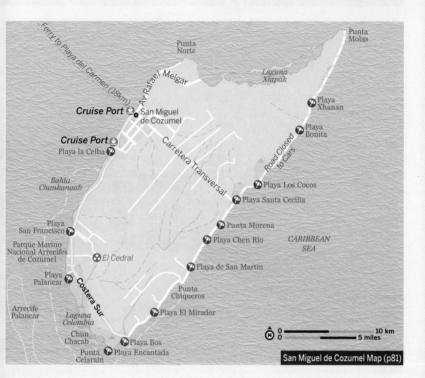

San Miguel de Cozumel Map (p81)

Getting from the Port

Ships dock at Punta Langosta and Puerta Maya.

Taxis It's a short ride to San Miguel from both cruise ports (from M$35).

Walking From Punta Langosta, walk the flat pathway to downtown San Miguel.

Accessibility The wide seaside sidewalk in San Miguel is wheelchair friendly, but there isn't much shade. Wear a large-brimmed hat or bring an umbrella.

Fast Facts

Currency Mexican Peso (M$), US dollar (US$) at some businesses

Languages Spanish, English

Money ATMs are common, and passengers can exchange US dollars for local currency at the exchange counter near the cruise ports.

Visas Not required for citizens of the US, EU or Australia.

Best for free wi-fi Jeanie's restaurant (p80).

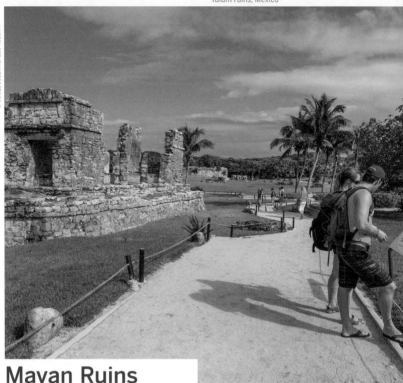

Tulum ruins, Mexico

Mayan Ruins at Tulum

The ruins of Tulum preside over a rugged coastline, a strip of brilliant beach and green-and-turquoise waters that'll leave you floored.

Great For...

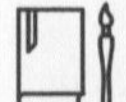

Don't Miss

Swimming in the clear water and relaxing at the beach below the cliffs.

Most archaeologists believe that Tulum was occupied during the late post-Classic period (AD 1200–1521) and that it was an important port town during its heyday. The Maya sailed up and down this coast, maintaining trading routes all the way down into Belize. When Juan de Grijalva sailed past in 1518, he was amazed by the sight of the walled city, its buildings painted a gleaming red, blue and yellow and a ceremonial fire flaming atop its seaside watchtower.

To get to Tulum from Punta Langosta, take a ferry from the Playa del Carmen ferry terminal. A taxi or van to Tulum is easy to find near the ferry terminal once in Playa Del Carmen.

Exploring the Ruins

Once inside, head east toward the **Casa del Cenote**, named for the small pool at its

Sculpture detail on the Temple of Frescoes

Explore Ashore

Allow five hours (seven hours is ideal) for Tulum: three hours travel time (a 45-minute ferry ride followed by a 45-minute taxi ride), giving you two hours to explore the site and nearby beach.

Need to Know

www.inah.gob.mx; Hwy 307 Km 230; M$70, parking M$100, tours from M$700; ⏲8am-5pm

southern base. From the cenote, walk south toward the bluff holding the **Templo del Dios del Viento** (Temple of the Wind God), which provides the best views of El Castillo juxtaposed with the sea below.

Next, head west to **Estructura 25**, which has some interesting columns on its raised platform and, above the main doorway (on the south side), a beautiful stucco frieze of the Descending God. Also known as the Diving God, this upside-down, part-human figure appears elsewhere at Tulum, as well as at several other east-coast sites and Cobá. It may be related to the Maya's reverence for bees (and honey), perhaps a stylized representation of a bee sipping nectar from a flower. South of Estructura 25 is El Palacio, notable for its X-figure ornamentation. From here, head east back toward the water and skirt the outside edge of the central temple complex (keeping it to your right). Heading inland again on the south side, you can enter the complex through a corbeled archway past the restored **Templo de la Estela** (Temple of the Stela). Stela 1, now in the British Museum, was found here. It was inscribed with the Maya date corresponding to AD 564. At first this confused archaeologists, who believed Tulum had been settled several hundred years later than this date. It's now thought that Stela 1 was brought to Tulum from Tankah, a settlement 4km to the north dating from the Classic period.

At the heart of the complex you can admire Tulum's tallest building, a watchtower appropriately named **El Castillo** (The Castle) by the Spaniards. Note the Descending God in the middle of its facade, and the Toltec-style 'Kukulcánes' (plumed serpents) at the corners, echoing those at Chichén Itzá. South of the Castillo you'll find steps leading down to a crowded beach.

Driving the Coastal Road

Drive south on the Coastal Road to escape the tourist crowds of San Miguel de Cozumel and to relax on less-developed beaches.

Great For...

Don't Miss

Playa Palancar Beach Park, a free beach with beach-chair rentals and snorkeling offshore.

The route encompassing Playa Palancar and Parque Punta Sur will take you south from San Miguel, then counterclockwise around the island.

Access to many of Cozumel's best stretches of beach has become limited. Resorts and residential developments with gated roads create the most difficulties. Pay-for-use beach clubs occupy some other prime spots, but you can park and walk through or around them and enjoy adjacent parts of the beach without obligation. Sitting under their umbrellas or otherwise using the facilities requires you to fork out some money, either a straight fee or a *consumo mínimo* (minimum consumption of food and drink), which can add up in some places. It's not always strictly applied, especially when business is slow.

Explore Ashore

Rent a car (scooters are popular but not recommended) at one of the reputable car rental shops or hire a tour guide with transportation. The drive can be done in two hours but five hours is recommended to allow time to stop for a swim at beaches.

Need to Know

There are some places along the way to stop for food and drink, but it's good to bring water all the same.

Playa Palancar

About 17km south of town, **Palancar** (Carretera Costera Sur Km 19; snorkel-gear rental M$130) is a great beach to visit during the week when the crowds thin out. It has a beach club renting snorkel gear and there's a restaurant. Near the beach, Arrecife Palancar (Palancar Reef) has some excellent diving and snorkeling.

Parque Punta Sur

For the price of admission to this **park** (987-872-40-14; www.cozumelparks.com; Carretera Costera Sur Km 27; adult/child 3-11yr US$14/8; 9am-4pm Mon-Sat), you can visit a lighthouse, a small nautical museum and a Maya ruin. About 10 minutes away by car is an observation tower where you can see migratory birds and possibly crocodiles. The park area offers a beach with a shallow reef, a restaurant and three midday boat tours to Laguna Colombia. You'll need your own vehicle or a taxi (M$300 one way)

East Coast

The eastern shoreline is the wildest part of the island and presents some beautiful seascapes and many small blowholes (there's a bunch around Km 30.5). Swimming is dangerous on most of the east coast because of riptides and undertows. At Playa Chen Río, just past El Pescador restaurant at Km 42, there's a saltwater pool.

At Punta Chiqueros, at Km 37, a restaurant rents bodyboards and longboards. As you travel along the coast, consider stopping at one of several restaurant-bars with great lookout points, such as **Freedom in Paradise** (www.bobmarleybar.com; Carretera Coastal Oriente Km 29.5; 10am-5:30pm) or **Coconuts Bar & Grill** (www.coconutscozumel.com; Carretera Coastal Oriente Km 43.5; 10am-7pm).

Diving & Snorkeling

Cozumel offers an impressive number of excellent reefs and wrecks to dive and snorkel. The best sites are found in the Cozumel Reefs National Marine Park.

Great For...

Don't Miss

The Santa Rosa Wall, a drift dive along a steep coral wall bursting with sea life and color.

Diving

Cozumel and its surrounding reefs are among the world's most popular diving spots.

The sites have fantastic year-round visibility (commonly 30m or more) and a jaw-dropping variety of marine life that includes spotted eagle rays, moray eels, groupers, barracudas, turtles, sharks, brain coral and some huge sponges. The island can have strong currents (sometimes around 3 knots), making drift dives the standard, especially along the many walls. Even when diving or snorkeling from the beach you should evaluate conditions and plan your route, selecting an exit point down-current beforehand, then staying alert for shifts in currents. Always keep an eye out (and your ears open) for boat

BLUE-SEA.CZ/SHUTTERSTOCK ©

Explore Ashore

Most two-tank dive trips require five hours total. Single tank dives usually take 2½ hours total. Consider a one-tank dive or half-day snorkel tour and spend the first half of the day relaxing on a beach near the departure place of your tour.

Need to Know

It's easy to find a reputable dive shop where you can set up dive and snorkel tours in advance of your cruise.

traffic as well. It's best not to snorkel alone away from the beach area.

If you encounter a decompression emergency, head immediately to the hyperbaric chamber at **Cozumel International Clinic** (987-872-14-30; Calle 5 Sur, btwn Avs Melgar & 5 Sur; 24hr).

If diving and snorkeling are your primary goals, you may want to time your trip for March to May, as the chance of hurricanes is minimal. Severe weather can increase turbidity and prevent the boats from leaving, among other hassles.

Snorkeling

The best snorkeling sites are reached by boat. Most snorkeling-only outfits in downtown San Miguel go to one of three stretches of reef nearby, all accessible from the beach. If you go with a dive outfit instead, you can often get to better spots, such as Palancar Reef or the adjacent Colombia Shallows, near the island's southern end.

You can save on boat fares (and see fewer fish) by walking into the gentle surf north of San Miguel. One good spot is a beach club next to Hotel Playa Azul, 4km north of the turnoff to the airport; its *palapas* offer shade, and it has a swimming area with a sheltering wharf and a small artificial reef.

But your best option for snorkeling is heading out on a diving boat with Deep Blue (p78), which will take you to three of the best snorkeling sites on the island.

Santa Rosa Wall

This is the biggest of the famous sites. The wall is so large most people are able to see only a third of it on one tank. Regardless of where you're dropped, expect to find enormous overhangs and tunnels covered with corals and sponges. Stoplight parrotfish, black grouper and barracuda hang out here. The minimum depth is 30ft, with an average closer to 95ft, so carry a flashlight with you.

Punta Sur Reef

Unforgettable for its coral caverns, each of which is named, this reef is for very experienced divers only. Butterfly fish, angelfish and whip corals abound at the reef.

Colombia Shallows

Colombia Shallows lends itself equally well to snorkeling and diving. Because it's a shallow dive (maximum depth 30ft, average 6ft to 13ft), its massive coral buttresses covered with sponges and other resplendent life forms are well illuminated.

Palancar Gardens

This dive consists of a strip reef about 95ft wide and very long, riddled with fissures and tunnels. The major features here are enormous stovepipe sponges and vivid yellow tube sponges, and you can always find damselfish, parrotfish and angelfish around you.

Dive Operators

There are scores of dive operators on Cozumel. All limit the size of their groups to six or eight divers, and the good ones take pains to match up divers of similar skill levels. Some offer snorkeling and deep-sea fishing trips as well as diving instruction.

Prices are usually quoted in US dollars. In general expect to pay anywhere between US$80 and US$100 for a two-tank dive (equipment included) or an introductory 'resort' course. PADI open-water certification costs US$350 to US$420. Multiple-dive packages and discounts for groups or those paying in cash can bring rates down significantly.

Deep Blue Diving

(☎987-872-56-53; www.deepbluecozumel.com; Calle Salas 200; 2-tank dives with/without equipment US$100/80, snorkeling incl gear US$60; ⏲7am-9pm) This PADI and National Association of Underwater Instructors (NAUI) operation has knowledgeable staff, state-of-the-art gear and fast boats that give you a chance to get more dives out of a day. A snorkeling outing visits three sites.

Aldora Divers Diving

(☎987-872-33-97; www.aldora.com; Calle 5 Sur 37; 1-/2-tank dives incl equipment US$55/95, 3-tank shark-cave dives US$200; ⏲7am-3pm & 6-8pm) One of the best dive shops in Cozumel, Aldora will take divers to the windward side of the island when weather is bad on the western side. It also does full-day excursions to caves with sleeping sharks; these trips include a stop at a lagoon with Maya ruins. Any lionfish (an invasive species) caught are quickly turned into tasty ceviche.

Cozumel's waters boast excellent visibility and a jaw-dropping array of marine life from spotted eagle rays, moray eels, groupers, barracudas, turtles and sharks, to brain coral and huge sponges.

San Miguel de Cozumel

SIGHTS

Museo de la Isla de Cozumel Museum

(987-872-14-34; www.cozumelparks.com; Av Melgar s/n; M$60; 9am-4pm Mon-Sat) The Museo de la Isla de Cozumel presents a clear and detailed picture of the island's flora, fauna, geography, geology and ancient Maya history. Thoughtful and detailed signs in English and Spanish accompany the exhibits. It's a good place to learn about coral before hitting the water, and it's one not to miss before you leave the island.

El Cedral Archaeological Site

(24hr) FREE This Maya ruin, a fertility temple, is the oldest on the island. It's the size of a small house and has no ornamentation. El Cedral is thought to have been an important ceremonial site; the small church standing next to the tiny ruin today is evidence that the site still has religious significance for locals. The village of El Cedral is 3km west of Carretera Costera Sur near Km 17.

EATING

Cheapest of Cozumel's many eating places are the market *loncherías* (lunch stalls) next to the **Mercado Municipal** (Calle Salas s/n, btwn Avs 20 & 25 Sur; snacks & mains M$25-80; 8am-5pm).

Taquería El Sitio Tacos $

(Calle 2 Norte; tacos & tortas M$12-37; 7:30am-12:30pm) For something quick, cheap and tasty, head over to El Sitio for breaded shrimp and fish tacos or a *huevo con chaya torta* (egg and tree spinach sandwich). The folding chairs and cement floor aren't fancy, but the food is good.

Camarón Dorado Seafood $

(www.facebook.com/camaron.dorado; cnr Av Juárez & Calle 105 Sur; tortas M$33-38, tacos M$17-28; 7am-3pm Tue-Sun;) If you're headed to the windward side of the island or just want to see a different aspect of Cozumel, drop by the Camarón Dorado for a bite, assuming you're early enough. Be warned: these items are highly addictive. It's 2.5km southeast of the ferry terminal.

Cocina Económica Las Palmas Mexican $

(cnr Calle 3 Sur & Av 25 Sur; mains M$65-130, set menu M$65; 9am-7pm Mon-Sat;) This place really packs 'em in at lunchtime. And though it gets hotter than Hades, you'll love the Maya favorites such as *poc-chuc* (grilled pork; M$65) or the *pechuga rellena* (stuffed chicken breast; M$70). Mighty tasty!

La Choza Mexican $$

(987-872-09-58; Av 10 Sur 216; breakfast M$52-70, lunch & dinner M$96-180, set menu M$115; 7am-10pm;) An excellent and popular restaurant with a garden in back that offers regional Mexican cuisine, with classics like chicken in *mole poblano* (a sauce of chilies, fruits, nuts, spices and chocolate). All mains come with soup. La Choza also offers a *comida corrida* (set menu) for the lunch crowd. The coffee is brewed with cinnamon. Yum!

Burritos Gorditos Fast Food $$

(www.facebook.com/burritosgorditos; Av 5 Norte s/n; burritos US$5-8; 9am-3pm Mon-Sat) This friendly little burrito joint prepares the typical vegetarian, chicken and beef variety, or you can experiment with Yucatán-inspired *cochinita* (slow-cooked pork) or apple-cinnamon-flavored burritos. Plan on coming hungry because these are *grande*.

Jeanie's Mexican $$

(987-878-46-47; www.jeaniescozumel.com; Av Melgar 790; breakfasts M$79-110, mains M$110-230; 7am-10pm;) The views of the water are great from the outdoor patio here. Jeanie's serves waffles, plus hash-brown potatoes, eggs, sandwiches and other tidbits like vegetarian fajitas. Frozen coffees beat the midday heat. Between 5pm and 7pm they do a lovely happy hour, too!

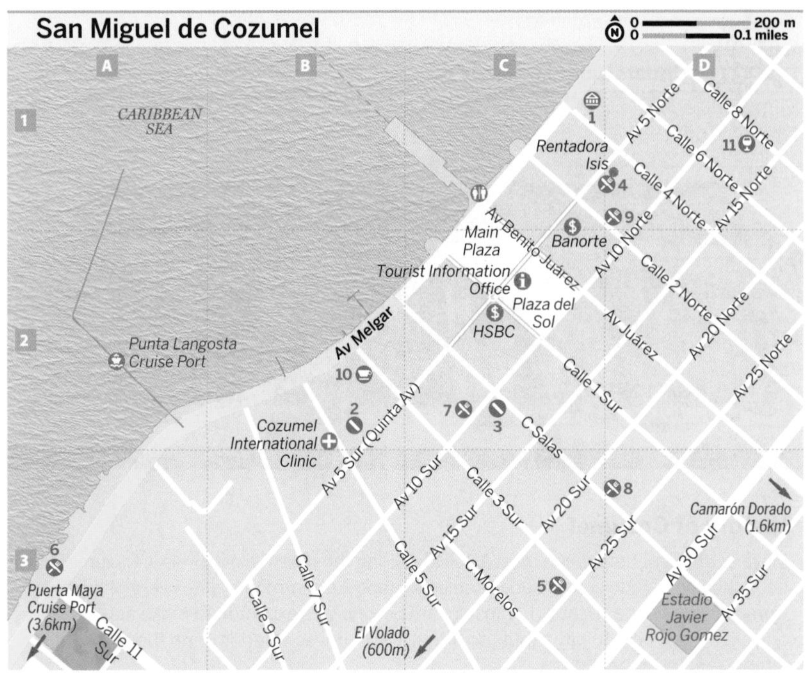

San Miguel de Cozumel

Sights
1 Museo de la Isla de Cozumel........C1

Activities, Courses & Tours
2 Aldora Divers........B2
3 Deep Blue........C2

Eating
4 Burritos Gorditos........D1
5 Cocina Económica Las Palmas........C3
6 Jeanie's........A3
7 La Choza........C2
8 Mercado Municipal........D3
9 Taquería El Sitio........D1

Drinking & Nightlife
10 El Coffee Cozumel........B2
11 La Cocay........D1

DRINKING & NIGHTLIFE

El Coffee Cozumel Cafe

(cnr Calle 3 Sur & Av Melgar; mains M$63-89; 7am-11pm) A tempting array of fresh-baked goods and organic coffee from the Mexican highlands make this place popular with locals and visitors alike. Pies are baked fresh daily, and they make a mean iced latte if you need to beat the heat.

La Cocay Bar

(987-872-55-33; www.lacocay.com; Calle 8 Norte 208; 5:30-11pm;) A great place for an after-dinner drink, La Cocay has a good wine list and serves Mexican craft beers. Unlike most places in Yucatán, here you can actually order a Negroni and they'll say 'Coming right up.'

Understand

History of Cozumel

Maya settlement here dates from AD 300. During the post-Classic period, Cozumel flourished as a trade center and, more importantly, a ceremonial site. Every Maya woman living on the Yucatán Peninsula and beyond was expected to make at least one pilgrimage here to pay tribute to Ixchel, the goddess of fertility and the moon, at a temple erected in her honor.

At the time of the first Spanish contact with Cozumel in 1518, there were at least 32 Maya building groups on the island. According to Spanish chronicler Diego de Landa, a year later Hernán Cortés sacked one of the Maya centers but left the others intact. Smallpox introduced by the Spanish wiped out half the 8000 Maya and, of the survivors, only about 200 escaped genocidal attacks by conquistadors in the late 1540s.

The island remained virtually deserted until 1848 when indigenous people fleeing the Caste War began to resettle Cozumel. At the beginning of the 20th century the island's population grew, thanks to the craze for chewing gum (locals harvested the gum base, chicle). After the demise of chicle, Cozumel's economy remained strong owing to the construction of a US air base here during WWII.

When the US military departed, the island fell into an economic slump, and many people moved away. It wasn't until the 1960s that Cozumel started to gain fame as a popular diving destination with tourism really starting to take off in the early 1980s.

Ancient Tulum ruins near Cozumel TONY PRISOVSKY/SHUTTERSTOCK ©

El Volado Bar
(cnr Av 20 Sur & Calle 15 Sur; 6:30pm-2am Tue & Wed, 7:30pm-3am Thu-Sun) If you're in port for the night, this two-story Mexican pub is a good spot to brush up on your Spanish, as locals outnumber the tourists most of the time.

INFORMATION

MONEY

ATMs are best way to get quick cash.

Banorte (Av 5 Norte s/n, btwn Av Juárez & Calle 2 Norte; 9am-5pm Mon-Fri, to 2pm Sat)

Streetscape, San Miguel de Cozumel

HSBC (cnr Av 5 Sur & Calle 1 Sur; 9am-5pm Mon-Fri)

TOURIST INFORMATION

Tourist Information Office (987-869-02-11; 2nd fl, Av 5 Sur s/n, Plaza del Sol; 8am-3pm Mon-Fri) Pick up maps and travel brochures here.

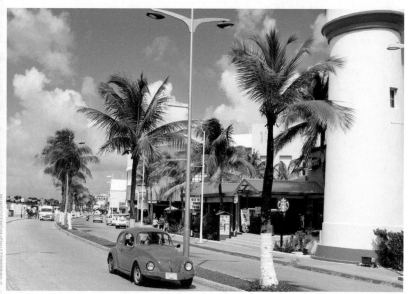

GETTING AROUND

San Miguel's sights and restaurants are easily accessed on foot.

CAR

A car is the best way to get to the island's further reaches, and you'll get plenty of offers to rent one. All rental contracts should automatically include liability insurance *(daños a terceros)*. Rates start at around M$500 per day all-inclusive, though you'll pay more during late December and January.

Rentadora Isis (987-872-33-67; www.rentadoraisis.com.mx; Av 5 Norte, btwn Calles 2 Norte & 4 Norte; scooter/car per day incl liability insurance US$20/35; 8am-6:30pm) A fairly no-nonsense, family-run place with cars ranging from looking in great shape to total clunkers; it rents convertible Volkswagen Beetles and Golfs with little seasonal variation in prices.

TAXI

As in some other towns on the Yucatán Peninsula, the taxi syndicate on Cozumel wields a good bit of power. Fares are around M$35 (in town), M$80 (to the Zona Hotelera) and M$1000 for a day trip around the island. Fares are posted just outside the ferry terminal.

Seven Mile Beach (p88)

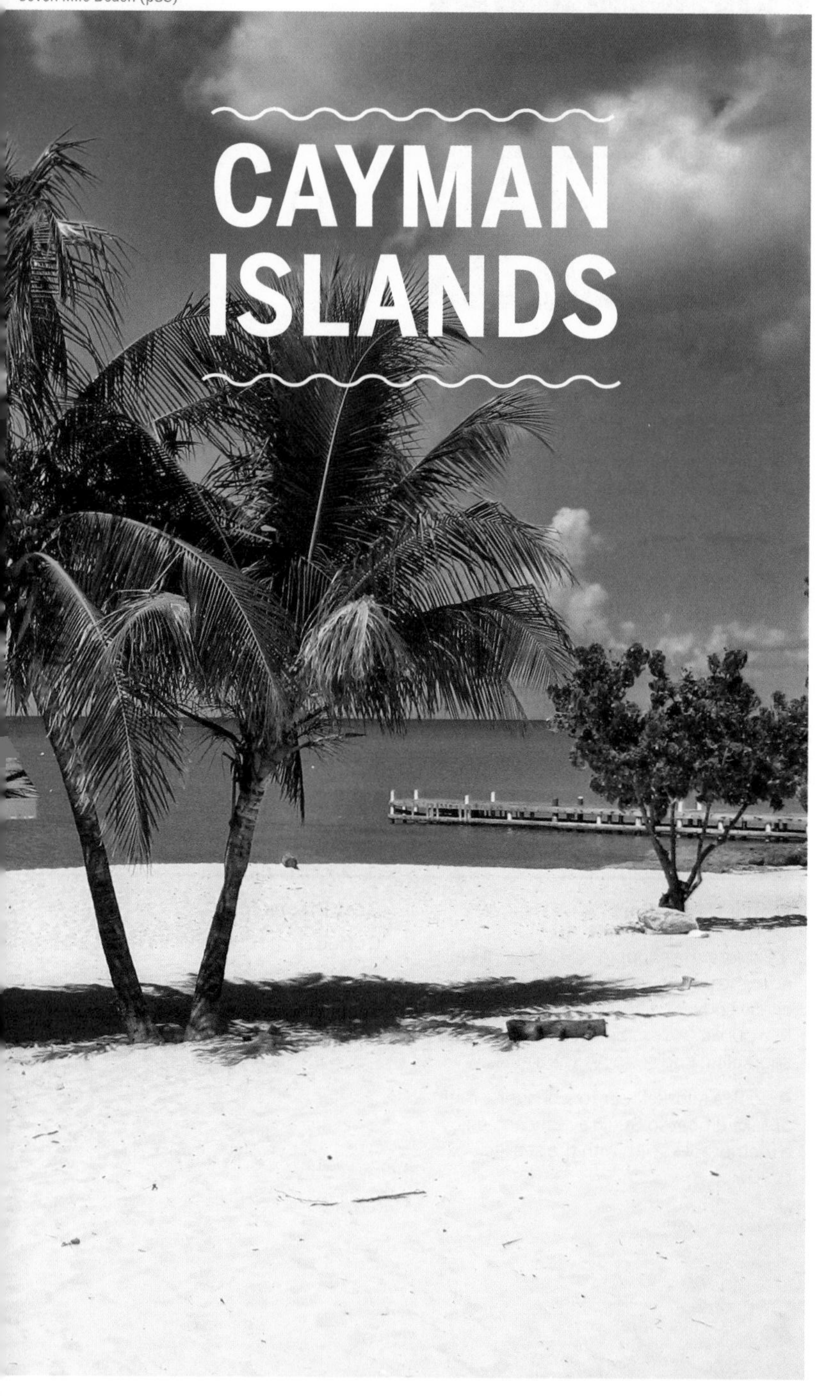

In This Chapter

Cayman Islands at a Glance

George Town, on Grand Cayman, is the supremely wealthy but surprisingly modest capital of the Cayman Islands. While undoubtedly cosmopolitan, it is tiny, tidy and pleasantly tropical – though it can feel overrun by tourists at times. George Town is a draw for dining, shopping and a few historic sights, but you'll likely spend most of your time somewhere north of here, exploring beaches and enjoying underwater activities.

With a Day in Port

- Explore the shopping in George Town near the port if you're looking to purchase souvenirs, then take a quick taxi to a public-access beach for swimming, snorkeling and sunning. (p95)
- Book a snorkel tour to a beautiful reef or take a boat to Stingray City and enjoy a memorable swim with the sea life. (p90)

Best Places for...

Coffee Bread & Chocolate (p96)

Cocktails Calico Jack's (p89)

Local cuisine Cayman Cabana (p96)

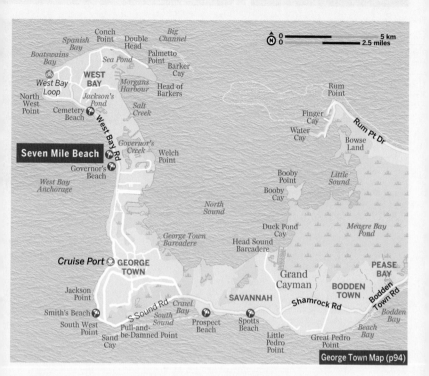

Conch Point
Spanish Bay
Big Channel
Double Head
Boatswains Bay
Palmetto Point
Sea Pond
Barker Cay
WEST BAY
West Bay Loop
Morgans Harbour
Head of Barkers
North West Point
Jackson's Pond
Salt Creek
Cemetery Beach
West Bay Rd
Governor's Creek
Seven Mile Beach
Welch Point
Governor's Beach
West Bay Anchorage
North Sound
George Town Barcadere
Cruise Port
GEORGE TOWN
Jackson Point
Smith's Beach
S Sound Rd
South Sound
Crawl Bay
South West Point
Pull-and-be-Damned Point
Sand Cay
Prospect Beach
Spotts Beach
SAVANNAH
Little Pedro Point
Rum Point
Finger Cay
Water Cay
Rum Pt Dr
Bowse Land
Booby Point
Little Sound
Booby Cay
Duck Pond Cay
Meagre Bay Pond
Head Sound Barcadere
Grand Cayman
BODDEN TOWN
PEASE BAY
Shamrock Rd
Bodden Town Rd
Bodden Bay
Beach Bay
Great Pedro Point
0 5 km
0 2.5 miles

George Town Map (p94)

Getting from the Port

The George Town port exits directly into the most developed area of George Town. Taxis and tour van operators are easy to find around the cruise port.

Fast Facts

Currency Caymans Island dollar (CI$), US dollar is widely accepted

Languages English

Money ATMs widespread.

Visas Not required for citizens of the US, EU or Australia.

Best for free wi-fi Daily Grind cafe, a short walk from the port.

Seven Mile Beach

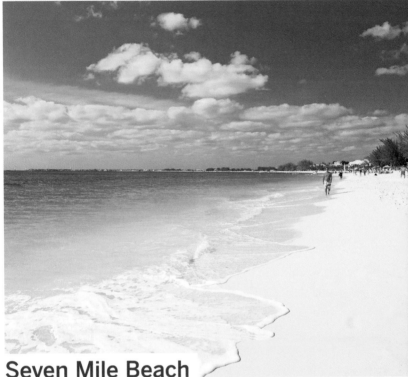

RUTH PETERKIN/SHUTTERSTOCK ©

Seven Mile Beach

The focal point of Cayman's tourism industry is Seven Mile Beach, a gorgeous stretch of unbroken white sand, which offers unlimited opportunities for swimming, sunbathing and sunset viewing.

Great For...

Don't Miss

Snorkeling the clear, warm water off Seven Mile Beach.

Although it's really only about 5.5 miles long, this stunning strand of beach has flawless white sand and crystal blue waters – just as pretty as a postcard. It is lined with resorts and vacation properties, but the beach itself is public. The main public beach access point – just south of the Kimpton – has a big parking lot, a playground, beach volleyball and lounge-chair rental, with beach bars and plenty of other diversions nearby. It's crowded but a lot of fun.

Governor's Beach

Tucked in between resorts, the tree-shaded parking lot opens onto a sweet section of Seven Mile Beach that is rarely crowded. There's a reason they call it Governor's Beach: this quiet stretch of sand fronts the governor's mansion.

SOBRIGHT7/SHUTTERSTOCK ©

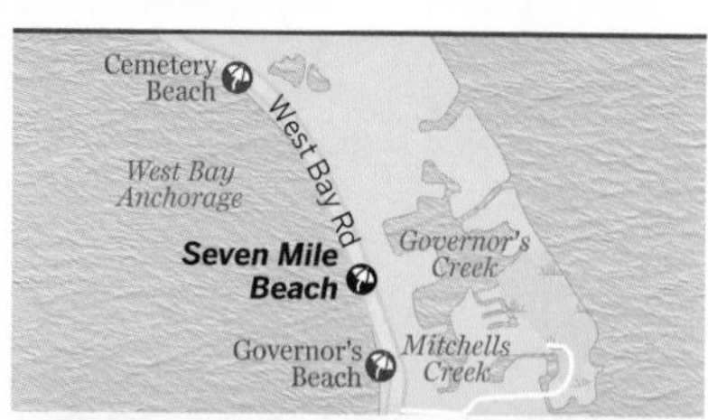

Explore Ashore

Seven Mile Beach is 2.6 miles from the cruise port. It's possible to walk by following the narrow, paved path that hugs close to the road and follows along the seafront. A taxi or van is easy to find near the port.

Need to Know

You'll often find a quiet stretch away from the crowds if you walk a bit out of town and explore the public beach access points.

Cemetery Beach

Ask a local where they like to spend a sunny day, and they will likely direct you to this gorgeous strip of sand at the northern end of Seven Mile Beach. It's rarely crowded – not because it's haunted, but because there are no big resorts in the area.

Take a Break

There are numerous cafes, bars and clubs along Seven Mile Beach so you won't have to look far for some refreshment.

Calico Jack's Beach Bar

(West Bay Rd; 9am-1am Sun-Fri, to midnight Sat) 'Calico Jack' Rackham was an English pirate who marauded around these parts in the 18th century. Nowadays, he lends his name (not to mention his mug) to this classic beach bar – a place for locals, tourists, and everybody who likes to dance, drink and let loose on the sand. It's high-energy fun, especially during infamous full-moon parties.

Tiki Beach Beach Bar

(www.tikibeachcayman.net; West Bay Rd; 11am-10pm) There are lots of good times to be had at Tiki Beach. Rent snorkel gear, ride a waverunner or challenge your friends to a game of beach volleyball. Or sidle up to the bar for cocktails, dinner or dancing under the stars. Or...all of the above. This place is popular with visitors so it's often busy.

Snorkelers at Stingray City

JO ANN SNOVER/SHUTTERSTOCK ©

Snorkeling with Wildlife

Grand Cayman offers plenty of opportunities to get up close and personal with the stunning local marine life without necessarily needing a diving license.

Great For...

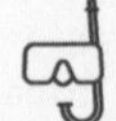

Don't Miss

Spotts Beach, where you have a higher probability than other beaches of seeing marine life.

Spotts Beach

This pretty little public beach is the favorite feeding spot for sea turtles, who come to chow down on sea grass. Don your mask and snorkel and swim with them, but please don't touch, chase or otherwise harass these gentle creatures. You can often spot them from the pier. Snorkeling with sea turtles in the wild is a wonderful alternative to the contrived turtle encounters at the Turtle Center. The beach is about 4 miles west of Bodden Town. Take the 20-minute taxi ride southeast to Shamrock Rd and look for the Spotts Public Beach sign.

Stingray City

This stretch of sandy seafloor in the North Sound is a meeting place for southern stingrays. As soon as you enter the water you'll be swarmed by these prehistoric

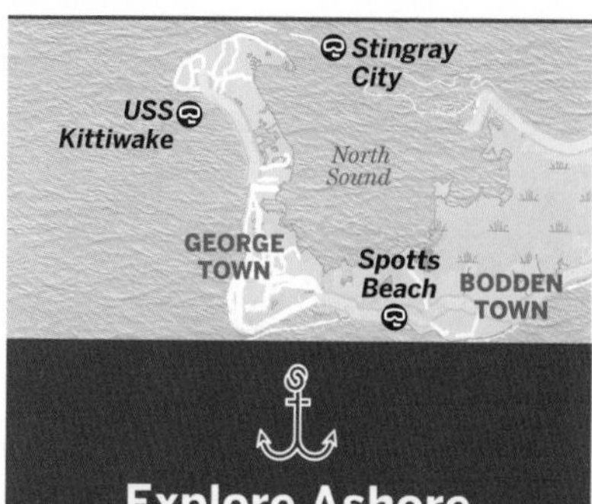

Explore Ashore

Allow 40 minutes for the round trip from the cruise port to Spotts Beach. A minimum of three hours total is suggested. Allow four hours total including transportation for a single-tank dive on the USS *Kittiwake*, and allow four hours total including transportation for a visit to Stingray City

Need to Know

Taxis and vans are readily available near the cruise port; it's around US$10 per person to Spotts Beach. Tours to Stingray City include transportation and boat ride from the port and cost $40 to $50. A one-tank diving trip on the USS *Kittiwake* includes transportation and boat ride from the port and costs $80 to $120 including government entry fee.

creatures. Lots of tour operators take clients here, including Captain Marvin's Watersports (p92). Dive shops lead trips to a nearby, slightly deeper site (14ft), so divers are underwater while stroking and feeding the animals.

Studies have shown that the stingrays have both unusual growth (since they have an unbalanced diet) and have oddball schedules (normally they are nocturnal). It's not the wildest wildlife you'll ever meet, but it's a rare opportunity to get up-close and personal with a stingray. Stingray City is only reached via boat, and many tour operators near the cruise port offer tours here. Captain Marvin's check-in is at the Waterfront Center on North Church St, 300ft to the north and across the street from the cruise port.

USS Kittiwake

Cayman's top requested dive site, this 249ft US Navy **submarine rescue ship** (www.facebook.com/kittiwakecayman). The wreck was sunk deliberately to create an artificial reef and dive site: ample entries and exits allow divers to swim through and explore the many rooms, peek through windows, sit at a table in the mess hall or take a turn at the steering wheel.

Lying between 15ft and 64ft below the surface, the wreck is clearly visible to snorkelers and free divers, making it a popular spot even if you don't dive.

Cycling the Island

Cycling is always a fantastic way to explore a new place, and Grand Cayman is no exception. **West Bay Loop** (☎939-0911; www.westbayloop.com; Northwest Point Rd; tour US$70, rental per day US$40-60) is a popular route/tour, while **Eco Rides** (www.ecoridescayman.ky; per person US$70-100; ⏰7:30am Tue-Sun) offers informative tours of the East End. Alternatively, rent a bike from Cayman Auto Rentals (p97) and go it alone.

ERIC LAUDONIEN/SHUTTERSTOCK ©

George Town

SIGHTS

Cayman National Museum Museum

(www.museum.ky; cnr Harbour Dr & Shedden Rd; adult/child US$8/3; ⏰9am-5pm Mon-Fri, 10am-2pm Sat) The centerpiece of this small museum is the engaging audiovisual presentation that offers an overview of the island's heritage. Natural and cultural history are the focus of exhibits, including one on animals that have become extinct. Housed in George Town's oldest building, the museum also displays two rooms of the Old Gaol, with recently discovered prisoners' graffiti on the walls.

National Gallery of the Cayman Islands Gallery

(www.nationalgallery.org.ky; Esterley Tibbetts Hwyn; ⏰10am-5pm Mon-Sat) FREE This small but delightful museum offers a wonderful break from the sand and sun. The ground floor houses rotating exhibits, while the 2nd floor shows off the national collection of Caribbean and Caymanian works. The impressive quarters include a lovely sculpture garden and a small gift shop.

ACTIVITIES & TOURS

Blue Water Excursions Fishing, Snorkeling

(☎925-8738; www.bluewaterexcursions.com; Yacht Dr, Cayman Islands Yacht Club; ⏰half-day excursion US$550-700) Local fisherman Captain Richard Orr is at the helm of his 32ft vessel, *Trouble Maker.* Private snorkeling excursions make two snorkel stops, plus Stingray City. Alternatively, spend some time in the deep sea, reeling in your dinner.

Captain Marvin's Watersports Snorkeling

(☎945-6975; www.captainmarvins.com; N Church St; tours adult/child US$45/30; ⏰tours 10am & 2:30pm Mon-Fri, 9am & 1pm Sat & Sun) Apparently, Captain Marvin originated this now standard tour to Stingray City, which includes two or three snorkel stops after the main attraction. Price includes transportation from Seven Mile Beach.

Divers Down Diving

(☎945-1611; www.diversdown.net; 69 N Church St, George Town; 2-tank dive US$105) Caters to cruise-ship passengers, with three boat dives per day. Also offers trips to the USS *Kittiwake* and Stingray City, as well as various training packages.

Sea Elements Boating, Kayaking

(☎936-8687; www.caymanseaelements.com; tours adult/child from US$35/25) Excellent, informative tours focus on the island's natural wonders, including Bio Bay swimming (among the bioluminescence), mangrove tours by boat or kayak, and custom trips to Stingray City. Tours depart from the Cayman Island Yacht Club in Governor's Bay. Transportation is provided.

Understand

Cayman Iguanas

Endemic to Grand Cayman, the blue iguana is quite a spectacle, at up to 3ft in length and often with a brilliant azure hide. The creature is sometimes called a 'blue dragon' for its exotic appearance. As recently as 2002 there were fewer than a dozen left in the wild. Now their numbers are resurgent (around 750 at last count) thanks to the **Blue Iguana Recovery Program** (www.blueiguana.ky; Queen Elizabeth II Botanic Park; tours adult/child incl park US$30/20; ⏲tours 11am Mon-Sat), which breeds iguanas and protects habitat.

On Cayman Brac and Little Cayman, the resident star is the Sister Islands rock iguana, recognizable by its distinctive black feet, which contrast with its lighter gray or green body. Endemic to the Sister Islands, the species is critically endangered, especially on Cayman Brac, where there are less than 100 individuals. Little Cayman is home to some 1500 rock iguanas.

Sadly, the most common species of iguana in Cayman is the invasive green iguana. These rapacious reptiles (now numbering nearly half a million) are decimating local vegetation and competing for resources with the local species. In recent years, scientists have found hatchlings that they believe are a cross-breed between rock and green iguanas, which could prove to be devastating for the native species.

MAYLAT/SHUTTERSTOCK ©

Atlantis Adventures Submarine Tours

(☎949-7700; www.caymanislandssubmarines.com; 30 S Church St; adult/child Seaworld Observatory US$39/19, Atlantis submarine US$89/59) It's possible to visit the underwater world without even mussing up your hair. The Seaworld Observatory was specially designed for the shallow reefs around Grand Cayman, offering a front-row view of two shipwrecks and one fish feeding. The *Atlantis XI* submarine descends to depths up to 100ft, with options to go by day or by night.

Red Sail Sports Snorkeling

(☎945-0178; www.redsailcayman.com; ⏲8am-6pm) Runs snorkel tours to the USS *Kittiwake*. Allow 15 minutes for a taxi ride from the cruise port to Red Sail Sports, located north of the port, about 1.2 miles east of Seven Mile Beach on Turnberry Dr.

George Town
0 500 m
0 0.25 miles
A
B
C
D
1
2
3
4
5
6
Esterley Tibbets Hwy
6
Lawrence Blvd
W Bay Rd
2
Courts Rd
Esterley Tibbets Hwy
N Church St
Eastern Ave
Bodden Rd
CARIBBEAN SEA
Nixon Rd
Rock Hole Rd
Cayman Auto Rentals
5
10
11
School Rd
8
Mary St
4
Soundway
N Sound Way
Cruise Port
9
12
Department of Tourism
1
Shedden Rd
3
GEORGE TOWN
S Church St
7
Elgin Ave
Crewe Rd
Pure Art (1.5km); National Trust (1.6km)

George Town

Sights
1 Cayman National Museum........................A6
2 National Gallery of the Cayman Islands........................B2

Activities, Courses & Tours
3 Atlantis Adventures........................A6
4 Captain Marvin's Watersports........................A5
5 Divers Down........................A5

Shopping
6 Camana Bay........................B1
7 Cayman Craft Market........................A6
8 Tortuga Rum Co........................D5

Eating
9 Bread & Chocolate........................B6
10 Cayman Cabana........................A5
11 Greenhouse........................B5
12 Singh's Roti Shop & Bar........................B6

SHOPPING

The malls clustered around the waterfront carry the usual tourist consumer goods, such as watches, jewelry and more watches. There are more international, upscale shops across the island at Camana Bay. For more artistic souvenirs, visit the Cayman Craft Market (also catering to cruise-ship passengers) or the treasure trove at Pure.

Tortuga Rum Co Food

(www.tortugarumcakes.com; North Sound Way; 10am-5pm Mon-Fri) Some 10,000 addictive rum cakes are made here daily. Sure, you can buy them all over the island – and the region – but those at the factory are freshest.

Pure Art Arts & Crafts

(www.pureart.ky; cnr S Church St & Denham Thompson Way; 9am-6pm Mon-Thu, to 5pm Fri & Sat) About 1.5 miles south of the center, this traditional Caymanian house is packed with arts and crafts – a perfect stop for creative souvenirs, most of which are locally made.

Cayman Craft Market Arts & Crafts

(www.craftmarket.ky; cnr S Church St & Boilers Rd; 8:30am-3pm Mon-Fri) This local handicraft market is a good place to pick up conch shells, Caymanite jewelry and other handmade products. Local food products are also on sale.

Camana Bay Mall

(www.camanabay.com; 10 Market St; 10am-5:30pm Mon-Fri, 10am-2pm Sat) Courtesy of the ubiquitous Dart development group, this vast upscale mall and multi-use development has transformed the North Sound side of Seven Mile Beach. There's plenty of shops, restaurants, fountains and movie theaters – plus a 75ft observation tower to see where Dart might place its next development.

That's Cayman, Bub

If there's one thing that gets the dander up of locals (in a polite way of course), it's hearing their nation referred to as 'the Caymans'. Don't ask why: they don't know any more than a resident of San Francisco shudders at hearing 'Frisco' – it's nails on a chalkboard. Preferred terms for the entire country are 'Cayman' or 'Cayman Islands'. As a pair, Cayman Brac and Little Cayman are known as the 'Sister Islands' and the individual islands are called by their correct names.

George Town, Grand Cayman

EATING

There are worthwhile restaurants clustered around downtown George Town and strung out along West Bay Rd. Day-trippers will want to move beyond the immediate zone of the cruise-ship tender dock. Within walking distance, there's a range of restaurants serving excellent local fare.

Singh's Roti Shop & Bar Caribbean $

(www.singhsroti.ky; cnr Doctor Roy's Dr & Shedden Rd; mains US$8-11; 9am-10pm Sun-Thu, to midnight Fri & Sat) In a city where dinner often means a three-figure check, this cheerful hole-in-the-wall is a great place for some tongue-searing roti (curry filling, often potatoes and chicken, rolled inside flat bread). Definitely one of George Town's best bargains.

Bread & Chocolate Vegan $

(www.cafe.ky; cnr Dr Roys Dr & Edward St; mains US$10-16; 8am-4pm Mon-Fri, 9am-2pm Sat & Sun;) 'Bread & Chocolate' refers to the signature French toast, which is stuffed with chocolate hazelnut butter and bananas, dipped in coconut batter and topped with fresh fruit. If you can resist that, you might be tempted by the other breakfast and lunch offerings, which range from delicious to decadent. The entire menu is animal-free from beet burger to BLT.

Greenhouse Vegetarian $

(www.greenhousecayman.com; 72 N Church St; mains US$12-15; 8am-4pm Mon-Sat;) Here's your perfect downtown lunch stop, with fresh, creative combinations of toppings and stuffings for sandwiches, salads and pizzas. Health-conscious eaters will be in heaven. Dietary restrictions pose no challenge here, as the menu is rife with gluten-free, paleo and veg-friendly options.

Cayman Cabana Caribbean $$

(949-3080; www.caymancabanarestaurant.com; 53 N Church St; mains US$16-25, farm-to-table dinner US$75; 9am-10pm Mon-Sat) Anytime is a good time to sit on the seaside deck, sip cocktails and dine on burgers, sandwiches and Caymanian specialties.

You'll find out what they mean when they promise to 'love ya like cook food.' On Thursday nights, Cabana takes the concept of 'local cuisine' to a whole new level, offering a farm-to-table feast that will delight your senses (reservations required).

Eats Cafe Diner **$$**
(www.eats.ky; Cayman Falls Center, West Bay Rd, Seven Mile Beach; breakfast US$8-12, sandwiches US$12-16, mains US$16-30; ⏲6:30am-11pm) No matter what you're in the mood for, you're likely to find it on the mile-long menu at Eats Cafe. The old-fashioned diner has seating in big booths, nostalgic posters on the wall and sports on the multiple screens. Also on-site: Legendz sports bar and Yoshi sushi bar.

 INFORMATION

Cayman Islands Tourism Association (www.cita.ky; 1320 West Bay Rd, Seven Mile Beach; ⏲9am-4pm Mon-Fri) Operates a useful office near Seven Mile Beach.

Department of Tourism (www.caymanislands.ky; Harbour Dr) Located at the North Terminal cruise-ship dock at George Town harbor; open when cruise ships are in port.

National Trust (www.nationaltrust.org.ky; 558 S Church St; ⏲9am-5pm Mon-Fri, 10am-4pm Sat) The main office; has a wealth of information.

 GETTING AROUND

Historic George Town is compact and pleasantly walkable, but Seven Mile Beach sprawls out for nearly 7 miles to the north, so it's useful to have a rental car – try **Cayman Auto Rentals** (☎949-1013; www.caymanautorentals.com.ky; N Church St), which rents not only cars but also scooters and bicycles (US$19 to US$25 per day). That said, many tour companies offer transportation from this area to the major attractions.

Peoples & Cultures

For centuries, the Cayman Islands had been left to simmer undisturbed in their own juices as the rest of the world rushed headlong into modernity. As recently as 50 years ago (aside from a few adventurers and fishing nuts) there were few tourists. Electric power was provided solely by noisy generators, and most islanders did without it. What has occurred between then and now constitutes a Caymanian cultural revolution, with the advent of large-scale tourism and big-business banking.

Historically, the population is an amalgamation of British, Jamaican and African peoples, but contemporary Cayman has become even more multifaceted. Nowadays, North America is well represented, as are Europe, South America and Southeast Asia. This large influx of expatriate workers – representing more than 80 countries – means that Caymanians make up just half of the population in their own country.

Pirate Week, George Town, Grand Cayman
MEUNIERD/SHUTTERSTOCK ©

The George Town bus depot serves as the dispatch point for color-coded minibuses to all districts of Grand Cayman. Buses run every day from 6am to 11pm and to 1am on Friday. Bus stops are few and far between: flag down a bus from any point along the route.

Street musicians, Falmouth (p106)

JAMAICA

In This Chapter

Jamaica at a Glance

Falmouth is the busiest of Jamaica's cruise ports, but many ships also dock at Ocho Rios and Montego Bay, also on the north coast. Falmouth is a bustling Jamaican town with a limestone-bricked, English-style church and market traders selling roasted yam and sugarcane under the pretty gingerbread verandas of Harbour Lane. The Ocho Rios port is within walking distance of the downtown shopping district, close to beaches, rainforests and waterfalls in the surrounding lush mountain landscape. Cruise ships docking at Montego Bay put passengers close to the shopping, restaurants and bars along the Hip Strip and provide easy access to beautiful beaches.

With a Day in Port

- Shop in Falmouth for Blue Mountain Coffee and Jamaica kitsch, then take a taxi to a nearby beach. Burwood Public Beach and Duncan Bay Beach are nearby to the east of the port. (p106)
- For an all-day adventure, take a taxi to Dunn's River Falls, a beautiful waterfall and tropical garden with a small beach that's very popular. (p102)

Best Places for...

Coffee Tropical Bliss Oasis (p107)

Street food Water Square (p106)

Local cuisine Donna's (p107)

Getting from the Port

Falmouth cruise port is closed to the local public, with only locals who work in the port area and shops allowed access. To get out of the port district of Falmouth, you'll need to navigate through the shops and the taxi square at the southwest end of the cruise port.

Fast Facts

Currency Jamaican dollar (J$), US dollar is widely accepted.

Language English, Patois.

Money ATMs widespread.

Visas Not required for citizens of the US, EU or Australia.

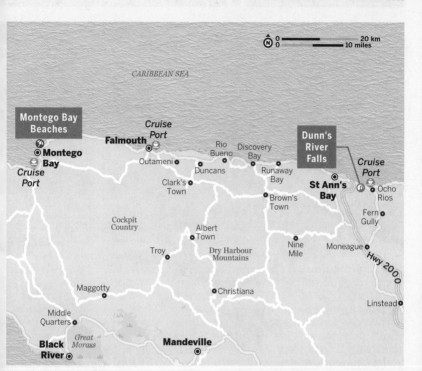

Best for free wi-fi Maragaritaville (Falmouth), Island Village shopping center (Ocho Rios), Hard Rock Cafe (Montego Bay).

Dunn's River Falls

These famous falls, 70km east of Falmouth, are Jamaica's top-grossing tourist attraction. While it's hard to avoid crowds, the falls are a highlight for the multitiered cascades and stunning setting.

Great For...

Don't Miss

Hiking up the falls – bring water sandals or shoes with excellent grip.

Cruise passengers will need at minimum six hours in port; the falls are best visited from either Falmouth or Ocho Rios ports – passengers docking at Montego Bay are best staying close and enjoying its world-class beach resorts.

Climbing the Falls

Great throngs of people can sometimes make it seem more like a theme park than a natural wonder, but this doesn't make the climb up the falls any less exhilarating. You clamber up great tiers of limestone that step down 180m in a series of beautiful cascades and pools. The water is refreshingly cool, with everything shaded by tall rainforest.

Guides can help with the climb (tip expected), but aren't strictly necessary; although the current is strong in places,

Explore Ashore

A route taxi (J$2000) from Falmouth to Dunn's River Falls takes around one hour each way. Allow six hours for this adventure, with two hours at the falls and extra time to eat and make it back aboard before the ship's horn blows.

Need to Know

974-2857; www.dunnsriverfallsja.com; adult/child US$20/12; 8:30am-4pm Sat-Tue, 7am-4pm Wed-Fri

the ascent is easily achieved by most able-bodied people. Swimwear is essential. There are changing rooms, and you can rent lockers (J$500) and buy jelly shoes from vendors.

Save money and pack your own water shoes or sandals in your cruise luggage. If climbing the falls is out of your comfort zone, the small beach at the base of the falls and the surrounding tropical garden paths are well worth exploring.

Tours

Cool Runnings Cruise

(974-2446; www.coolrunningscatamarans.com; 1 Marvins Park, Ocho Rios) Specializes in catamaran cruises, including: the Dunn's River Falls Cruise (US$86), which includes an hour's snorkeling and entry to the falls; the charming Sunset Dinner Cruise (US$75), with drinks and buffet dinner; and the adults-only Wet & Wild Cruise. Prices include pick-up from your hotel.

Wilderness Tours Tours

(382-4029; www.wildernessatvtours.com; tours per person US$75-105; 9am & 1pm Mon-Sat) Two all-terrain-vehicle tours into the mountains and through the forest, the more expensive one including Dunn's River Falls.

Take a Break

Lion's Den Jamaican $

(848-4413; A3; meals J$450-1700; 8am-4pm Mon-Sat) West of Ocho Rios near the entrance to the falls, the Lion's Den is worth a stop for its decent Jamaican fare and unique decor.

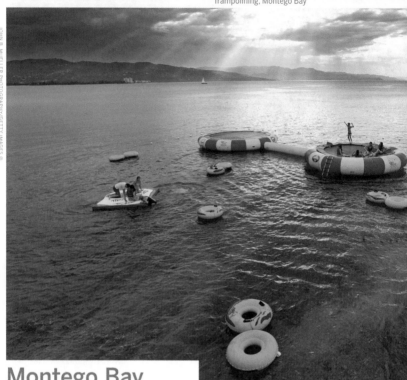

Trampolining, Montego Bay

JOHN B. MUELLER PHOTOGRAPHY/GETTY IMAGES ©

Montego Bay Beaches

Surrounded by beautiful beaches, most of them a short taxi ride away, the Montego Bay (MoBay) port is best enjoyed by beach lovers who prefer to spend the day soaking up the sun and sipping cold drinks in the shade of palm trees.

Great For...

Don't Miss

Doctor's Cave Beach – a beautiful beach with plenty of amenities and activities.

Doctor's Cave Beach

It may sound like a rocky hole inhabited by lab-coated troglodytes, but this is actually Montego Bay's most famous **beach** (876-952-2566; www.doctorscavebathingclub.com; adult/child US$6/3; 8:30am-sunset) and the one with the most facilities. A pretty arc of sugary sand fronts a deep-blue gem studded with floating dive platforms and speckled with tourists sighing happily. Er, lots of tourists – and a fair few Jamaicans as well. The upside is an admission charge keeps out the beach hustlers, though it doesn't ensure that the beach is kept clean.

Founded as a bathing club in 1906, Doctor's Cave earned its name when English chiropractor Sir Herbert Barker claimed the waters here had healing properties. People flocked to Montego Bay,

kick-starting a tourism evolution that would culminate in the appearance of *Homo margaritavillus* decades later. There are lots of facilities on hand including a restaurant, a grill bar, an internet cafe and water sports, and lots of things to rent (beach chairs, towels, snorkeling gear).

Dead End Beach

A meet-the-locals affair just north of Montego Bay's Gloucester Ave, this narrow **strip** (Kent Ave) is also known as Buccaneer Beach. The lack of space promotes togetherness; at high tide it's pretty accurate to drop the 'beach' from 'dead end.' There are no facilities here, but the lack of crowds makes the sunsets over the bay all the more gorgeous.

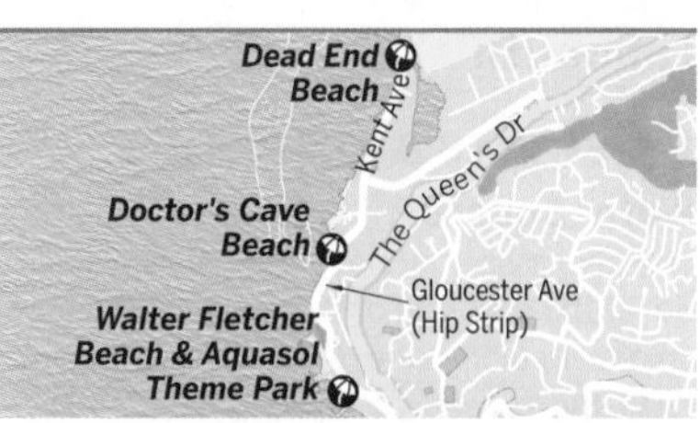

Explore Ashore

A taxi ride to Doctor's Cave Beach from the cruise port will take about 20 minutes each way. Plan to spend a total of at least four hours, leaving plenty of time to relax on the beach and walk the Hip Strip, stopping for jerk chicken and the requisite Red Stripe lager or a coconut-and-banana smoothie.

Need to Know

Most of the best beaches near the port require a day pass (around US$6 for the day).

Walter Fletcher Beach & Aquasol Theme Park

While the theme-park moniker is pushing it (the kid-orientated facilities consist of some blow-up water slides and a go-cart circuit), this place on **Walter Fletcher Beach** (979-9447; Gloucester Ave; adult/child US$6/5; 10am-10pm;), with its food stalls and local crowds, offers a decent spot to relax in a chilled-out local environment.

The beach is sandy and relatively clean and the water is safe for swimming, with some limited snorkeling possibilities. Food and drink comes courtesy of the on-site deck-bar with things heating up at sunset especially at weekends. Look out for billboards advertising sporadic live-music events.

Falmouth

SIGHTS & ACTIVITIES

Water Square Square

The best place to orient yourself is Water Sq, at the east end of Duke St. Named for an old circular stone reservoir dating from 1798, the square (actually a triangle) has a fountain topped by an old waterwheel. Back in the day this fountain pumped fresh water (before New York City had any such luxury). In the evening, the square really comes to life, with people limin' under the coconut trees, blaring reggae and delicious smells wafting from stalls.

Courthouse Notable Building

(Seaboard St) One block east of Water Sq is Seaboard St and the grandiose Georgian courthouse in Palladian style, fronted by a double curling staircase and Doric columns, with cannons to the side. The current building, dating from 1926, is a replica of the original 1815 structure that was destroyed by fire. The town council presides here.

Falmouth Heritage Walks Historical

(☎407-2245; www.falmouthheritagewalks.com; ⊙on cruise ship days & by reservation) This excellent outfit consists of a knowledgeable guide offering three ways of exploring history-rich Falmouth. The Heritage Walking Tour (adult/child US$25/15) is an interesting two-hour look at Falmouth's handsome Tropical-Georgian architecture. The Food Tour (US$45/25) combines snippets of culture with tastings of street food, while the Jewish Tour (US$15/10) visits Falmouth's Jewish cemetery with gravestones etched in Hebrew.

EATING

Water Square Street Food $

(Water Sq; mains from J$300; ⊙6-9pm) If you're in port for the evening, head here for, hands down, the best local street food. On one side, jerk chicken is cooked up in oil drums; there's also a good stall serving stewed chicken and other home-cooked food. An old guy cooks up the best jerk pork for miles around, while another specialises

Understand

Beware Scammers!

The cruise ports in Jamaica have earned a rather notorious reputation due to the high number of robberies and scams, as well as the constant barrage of overly-aggressive street vendors. Here are two common scams:

Hair-braiding scam The most popular Jamaican deception comes in the form of a hair braid. The number of annoying hair braiders is about equal to the number of Red Stripes found in the country. The hair braiders will ask cruise passengers if they would like their hair braided, often misleading the cruise passenger by offering the service for US$5. Most passengers assume the price is for all of their hair to be braided, but the price is actually per braid. The hair braider often braids about 20 braids and then demands US$100, usually rather aggressively. Most passengers reluctantly pay.

Carved coconut scam Don't even make eye contact with the Jamaicans carrying coconuts near the cruise port. These shysters ask passengers if they would like their name carved on a coconut. Most of them tell the passengers that the coconut is free, a welcome gift on behalf of the Jamaican people. The trickster will then ask for the passenger's name, carve it on the coconut, and then aggressively demand around US$20. Welcome to Jamaica. If asked, say 'No,' politely but firmly then briskly walk away.

Ocho Rios, Jamaica

in *escoveich* fish (fried, with a spicy, pickled sauce) and *festival* (deep-fried dough dumpling).

Donna's Jamaican $
(☎617-5175; Market St, cnr Duke St; mains J$600-1000; ⏰7:30am-9:30pm) Divided into a casual, canteen-style dining area and a takeout section, this restaurant gets packed at lunchtimes as locals stop by for their fried chicken, curry goat and oxtail fix. Good for hearty Jamaican breakfasts involving callaloo and ackee.

Tropical Bliss Oasis Cafe $
(Albert George Market; snacks J$170-500; ⏰9am-5pm Mon-Sat; 📶) Enjoy a moment or two of bliss with a fruit smoothie and sandwich at this pleasant perch in Albert George Market.

GETTING AROUND

Falmouth is very compact and easily navigable on foot.

Buses, minibuses and route taxis arrive and depart on opposite sides of Water Sq for Martha Brae (J$120, 15 to 20 minutes), Montego Bay (J$200, 45 minutes), Albert Town (1½ hours, J$250) and Ocho Rios (J$350, 80 minutes).

Knutsford Express (☎971-1822; www.knutsfordexpress.com) stops in Glistening Waters, 2km east of Falmouth, from where you can flag down a route taxi (J$70) to bring you into town. If the planned prettification of the town center goes ahead, all transportation will be moved way south along Market St.

Ocho Rios

Ocho Rios is a former fishing village on a wide bay that was developed for tourism in the mid-1980s. Cruise ships dock frequently (up to three a day) at the central pier that commands the town's focus, giving 'Ochi' a slightly 'packaged' feel, spiced up by the entreaties of 'guides' and souvenir sellers. The hassle quotient is relatively minor, however, and the town has a relaxed vibe when there's no ship in dock.

Tourism has endowed the town with a great eating scene, lively nightlife and a plethora of guiding companies offering everything from scuba diving to zip-line tours. Throw in some of Jamaica's best waterfalls, and Ocho Rios makes an excellent base for exploring the north coast.

SHOPPING

Wassi Art Arts & Crafts

(☎974-5044; Bougainvillea Dr; ⏰9am-5pm Mon-Sat, 10am-4pm Sun) Family-owned Wassi Art employs more than 50 artists to make its colorful, richly decorated terra-cotta pottery. Free tours are offered, detailing the entire process including clay processing, painting and firing. Pots start from US$5 and go all the way up to hundreds of dollars.

Wassi Art is in the Great Pond District, signed from Milford Rd (the A3), from where it's a convoluted (but signed) drive.

Olde Craft Market Arts & Crafts

(Main St; ⏰9am-5pm) This market features fair-quality ceramics and art, as well as the usual T-shirts with chirpy Jamaican slogans and Rasta tams with fake dreadlocks attached.

EATING & DRINKING

Ocho Rios Jerk Centre Jerk $

(☎974-2549; 16 Da Costa Dr; meals J$550-1000; ⏰11am-midnight) The liveliest jerk joint in town serves excellent jerk pork, chicken and conch, as well as barbecue ribs. There are daily specials, the best being curry goat (J$550) and goat-head soup. Grab a Red Stripe and watch sports on the big-screen TV while you're waiting for your food. There are DJs on Friday nights.

Devon House I-Scream Ice Cream $

(Island Village; per scoop J$200; ⏰hours vary) Serves some of the best ice cream on the island. The shop tends to shut earlier if there's no cruise ship in dock.

Island Coffees Coffee

(Island Village; ⏰9am-9pm; 📶) Small but cheery modern coffee shop, serving excellent coffee (Blue Mountain, of course) and other hot drinks, smoothies and a host of sandwiches and wraps (from J$500), plus suitably sweet and sticky cakes (J$250).

Souvenirs for sale, Ocho Rios

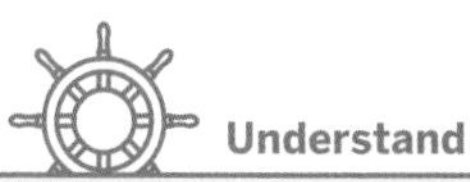

Christmas Rebellion

The weeklong Christmas Rebellion, which began on Kensington Estate on December 27, 1831, and engulfed much of the Montego Bay region, was the most serious slave revolt to rock colonial Jamaica. Its impact and the public outcry over the terrible retribution that followed were catalysts for the British parliament passing the Abolition Act in 1834.

The instigator of the revolt was Samuel Sharpe (1801–32), the slave of a Montego Bay solicitor. Sharpe acted as a deacon of Montego Bay's Burchell Baptist Church and became a 'Daddy' (leader) of the church. He used his pulpit as a forum to encourage passive rebellion. In 1831 Sharpe counseled fellow slaves to refuse to work during the Christmas holidays. Word of the secret, passive rebellion spread throughout St James and neighboring parishes. Inevitably word leaked out, and warships and extra troops were sent to Montego Bay.

The rebellion turned into a violent conflict when the Kensington Estate was set on fire. Soon plantations and great houses throughout northwest Jamaica were ablaze, and Sharpe's noble plan was usurped by wholesale violence. Fourteen colonialists were murdered before authorities suppressed the revolt. Swift and cruel retribution followed.

As part of the colonialists' punishments, more than a thousand slaves were killed. Day after day for six weeks following the revolt's suppression, magistrates of the Montego Bay Courthouse handed down death sentences to scores of slaves, who were hanged two at a time on the Parade – among them 'Daddy' Sam Sharpe. He was later named a national hero and the Parade was renamed Sam Sharp Sq.

INFORMATION

Tourist Information (974-7705; Shop 3, Ocean Village Plaza, Main St; 9am-5pm Mon-Thu, to 4pm Fri) Represents the Jamaica Tourist Board, with helpful, knowledgeable staff. It also operates an **information booth** on Main St, open when cruise ships are in port.

GETTING AROUND

Minibuses and route taxis ply Main St and the coast road, costing J$100 for short hauls.

BUS

Buses, minibuses and route taxis arrive at and depart from Ocho Rios' **Transportation Center** (Evelyn St). During daylight hours there are frequent departures – fewer on Sundays – for destinations along the north coast. There is no set schedule: they depart when full. A bus to Montego Bay (90 minutes) will cost at least J$500.

Knutsford Express (www.knutsfordexpress.com; Island Village) has scheduled departures on comfortable air-con coaches to Montego Bay and Falmouth from its depot at Island Village. Arrive 15 minutes prior to departure to register your ticket. The fare to/from Montego Bay is approximately J$1950.

TAXI

JUTA (974-2292) is the main taxi agency catering to tourists. A licensed taxi to Montego Bay will cost about US$120.

Montego Bay

Montego Bay has two distinct faces: there's the smooth tourist countenance that grins contentedly from the pages of a thousand glossy Caribbean brochures, and there's MoBay proper, a pretty gritty city, second only to Kingston in terms of status and chaos. Most of the big all-inclusive resorts

Falmouth cruise port

are located well outside the urban core in the fancy suburb of Ironshore. Stay in the city, however, and you're faced with an entirely different proposition – a riot of cacophonous car horns and bustling humanity that offers an unscripted and uncensored slice of Jamaican life, warts and all.

The Hip Strip (aka Gloucester Ave), with its midrange hotels and ubiquitous souvenir shops flogging Bob Marley T-shirts, acts as a kind of decompression chamber between MoBay's two halves. You won't find many hipsters here, but in among the hustlers and smoky jerk restaurants there's a detectable Jamaican rhythm to the action on the street.

SIGHTS

Sam Sharpe Square Square

(Fort St) This bustling cobbled square is named for Samuel Sharpe (1801–32), national hero and leader of the 1831 Christmas Rebellion; it is also where he was hanged in its aftermath. At the square's northwest corner is the **National Heroes' Monument**. Nearby is the **Cage**, a tiny brick building built in 1806 as a lockup for vagrants and other miscreants.

SHOPPING

Aside from the Gallery of West Indian Art, MoBay's shopping scene is, frankly, underwhelming. Out of the typical souvenirs on offer, the items actually produced in Jamaica are: Blue Mountain coffee, rum, bamboo trinkets, woven baskets and lacquered wooden carvings of Rasta heads and animals. The rest is mass-produced in China and Indonesia; sellers lie about their items' origins.

Gallery of West Indian Art Art

(952-4547; www.galleryofwestindianart.com; 11 Fairfield Rd; 10am-5pm Mon-Fri) In the suburb of Catherine Hall, this is the best quality gallery in town. It sells genuinely original arts and crafts from around the Caribbean including Cuban, Haitian and Jamaican canvases, hand-painted wooden animals, masks and handmade jewelry. Most of the work here is for sale. Call ahead.

Harbour Street Craft Market Gifts & Souvenirs

(Harbour St; ⏲7am-7pm) The largest selection of typical Jamaican souvenirs in MoBay – coconut-palm baskets, woven hats, towels and clothing in Rasta colours, wood carvings and art – is found at this market, which extends for three blocks between Barnett and Market Sts.

EATING

Pork Pit Jerk $

(☎952-1046; 27 Gloucester Ave; mains J$500-800; ⏲11am-11pm; 📶) At this glorified food shack on the Hip Strip, a half-roasted chef slaves over a blackened barbecue fashioned from pimento wood sticks laid over smoking hot coals. His meat-cooking travails send a delicious aroma wafting down Gloucester Ave and provide a perfect advert for the Pork Pit's obligatory jerk pork (and jerk chicken). Eat it under the 300-year-old cotton tree.

Nyam 'n' Jam Jamaican $

(☎952-1922; 17 Harbour St; mains J$500-1000; ⏲8am-11pm) On the cusp of the craft market, you can retreat to check out this truly authentic Jamaican dining experience. Settle down for snapper with a spicy sauce; jerk or brown stew chicken; curried goat; or oxtail with rice and peas. There's a round-the-clock branch at the City Centre Mall, too.

INFORMATION

Banks on Sam Sharpe Sq and in the Baywest Shopping Center all have 24-hour ATMs. Flanking the Doctor's Cave Beach Club are ATMs operated by National Commercial Bank and **Scotiabank** (Gloucester Ave). The cruise-ship terminal is served by a branch of National Commercial Bank in the Montego Freeport Shopping Centre.

GETTING AROUND

You can walk between any place along Gloucester Ave and downtown (it's about 2.5km from Kent Ave to Sam Sharpe Sq). You'll need transportation for anywhere further.

BUS

Comfortable **Knutsford Express** (☎876-971-1822; www.knutsfordexpress.com; ⏲4am-9:30pm) buses run from their own terminal next to Pier One near downtown MoBay. Book tickets more than 24 hours in advance for a small discount. Be at the bus station 30 minutes before departure to register your ticket. There are nine daily services to Falmouth (35 minutes; J$850).

TAXI

Jamaica Union of Travelers Association (JUTA; ☎876-952-0813) has taxi stands on Gloucester Ave at the Gloucestershire and Coral Cliff Hotels and at Doctor's Cave Beach Hotel, downtown at the junction of Market and Strand Sts, and by the bus station. Identify JUTA members by the red plates and JTB decal emblazoned on their vehicles.

At last visit, certified fares from the airport for up to four passengers: Falmouth (US$60) and Ocho Rios (US$120).

BAHAMAS

Musician, Junkanoo Festival (p22)

In This Chapter

Bahamas at a Glance

Renowned as a maritime playground for sun-starved Americans, the Bahamas are so much more than sun and sand. Stretched between the depths of the North Atlantic and Florida's eastern coast, this stunning string of more than 700 islands and 2400 cays, most uninhabited, is fringed by spectacular coral and fathomless ocean trenches. From the grit and bustle of funky Nassau to the vast mangroves of Andros, there's an astonishing array of beaches, reefs, forests and historic towns to be discovered.

With a Day in Port

Cruise ships dock at Nassau on New Providence and Freeport on Grand Bahama.

Nassau Explore the shops and historic buildings downtown before hitting Junkanoo Beach. For a full-day adventure, visit Paradise Island. (p116)

Freeport Spend an hour or so walking the straw market, then visit Taino Beach. For a full-day adventure, take a diving or snorkeling tour. (p126)

Best Places for...

Coffee Starbucks near the cruise port (Nassau)

Cocktails Khyla's Island Philosophy (p126; Nassau), Margaritaville Sandbar (p129; Freeport)

Local cuisine Fish Fry (p125; Nassau), Billy Joe's on the Beach (p128; Freeport)

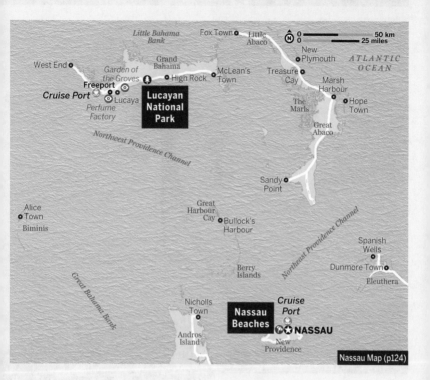

Getting from the Port

Nassau The port is conveniently located in downtown Nassau. A pleasant, paved walkway leads west to Junkanoo Beach, 1km away. A water-taxi terminal for boats to Paradise Island and Atlantis resort is steps from the cruise port.

Freeport The port is in an industrial shipping center with little to enjoy for the cruise passenger. Take a land taxi to one of the popular nearby beaches, and avoid walking on your own near the port at night.

Fast Facts

Currency Bahamian dollar, US Dollar is widely accepted

Language English,

Money ATMs are found across the island, including at Rawson Square directly across from the cruise port.

Visas Not required for citizens of the US, EU or Australia.

Best for free wi-fi Starbucks (Charlotte St, ⌚7am-7pm) near the Nassau cruise port.

Cable Beach

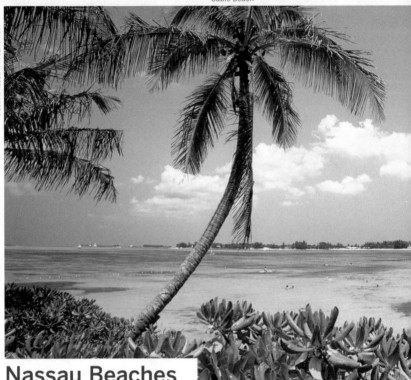

Nassau Beaches

Nassau's beaches deliver the tropical beauty and Caribbean-blue water that passengers love. The close proximity of world-class beaches to the cruise port have helped Nassau become the most visited cruise port in the Caribbean.

Great For...

Don't Miss

Junkanoo Beach, a short walk or taxi ride from the cruise port.

Junkanoo Beach

Between downtown Nassau and Araway Cay, Junkanoo is popular with locals and visitors alike, with beach-shack bars, volleyball nets, sky-juice vendors and friendly Bahamians in ample supply. The beach is spacious with shade under the palms that line the seaside road. Swimming is excellent, the gradual drop off making it easy to wade in the waves. Snorkeling isn't fantastic, but you can still see plenty of tropical fish swimming in the beautiful waters near shore. The cruise-ship pier is visible from the beach, and it's fun to watch the cruise ships arrive and sail away as you sit in a comfortable lounger and look over the Caribbean Sea, perhaps with a cold drink in your hand and your feet in the warm sand.

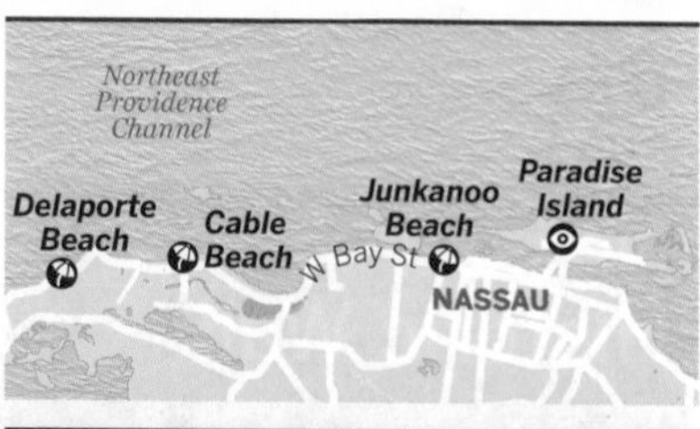

Explore Ashore

Walk the paved seaside path to Junkanoo Beach (20 minutes) or take a short taxi ride (1km). Allow at least three hours total. For Paradise Island and Atlantis, take the water taxi from the terminal near the cruise port (BS$8 return, 40 minutes each way). Allow at least four hours.

Take a Break

Enjoy free and fast wi-fi at **Starbucks** (Charlotte St, 7am-7pm) near the cruise terminal.

Junkanoo Beach Club (242-373-8018; www.junkanoobeachfreeport.com; Jolly Roger Dr, Taino Beach; BS$3; 10am-6pm;) offers snorkeling, kayaking, jet-skiing and paddle-boarding, and has a restaurant, changing facilities and (free) beach chairs, wi-fi and paddleboats.

Paradise Island

Privileged Paradise Island – linked to Nassau by two great arcs that may as well be bridges to another world – is unashamedly built for profit and pleasure. Its landscape is mostly artificial: vast hotels straight from the covers of fantasy paperbacks, hangar-sized casinos, ersatz 'villages' in which to shop and eat, and the lushest lawns you'll see anywhere in the Bahamas. As well as a number of beaches, the island is home to the Atlantis megaresort and water park.

Cable Beach

New Providence's biggest and most popular beach has three curving miles of white sand and sparkling turquoise sea, just west of downtown Nassau. Named for the undersea telegraphic cable that came ashore here in 1892, Cable Beach is lined with resorts, hotels and casinos. It's often packed with vacationing families, spring breakers, water-sports operators and roving souvenir vendors. If you want a beach chair, pay a day-use fee at one of the hotels for use of its facilities.

Delaporte Beach

Delaporte is a little quieter than the resort-backed Cable Beach to the east, while offering the same sand and the same sea.

Nassau Historic Walk

The cruise port is in the heart of Nassau's Historic District. The relatively safe and well-policed business district, as well as the high number of interesting historic buildings and museums within a short distance of one another makes this port a good choice for a walking tour. If your feet aren't up for a day of walking, consider hiring a taxi or a van.

Start Nassau Straw Market (across from the cruise port)
Distance 1.7km
Duration 4 hours (minimum)

2 Find your inner pirate at the **Pirates of Nassau** (p123) museum.

6 Take a break from the heat and enjoy the **National Art Gallery of the Bahamas** (p123), before heading back to the Straw Market for more shopping or lunch.

5 Have a cigar at **Graycliff Cigar Co** (p122) and watch the craftsmen hand roll cigars on site.

N 0 200 m
0 0.1 miles

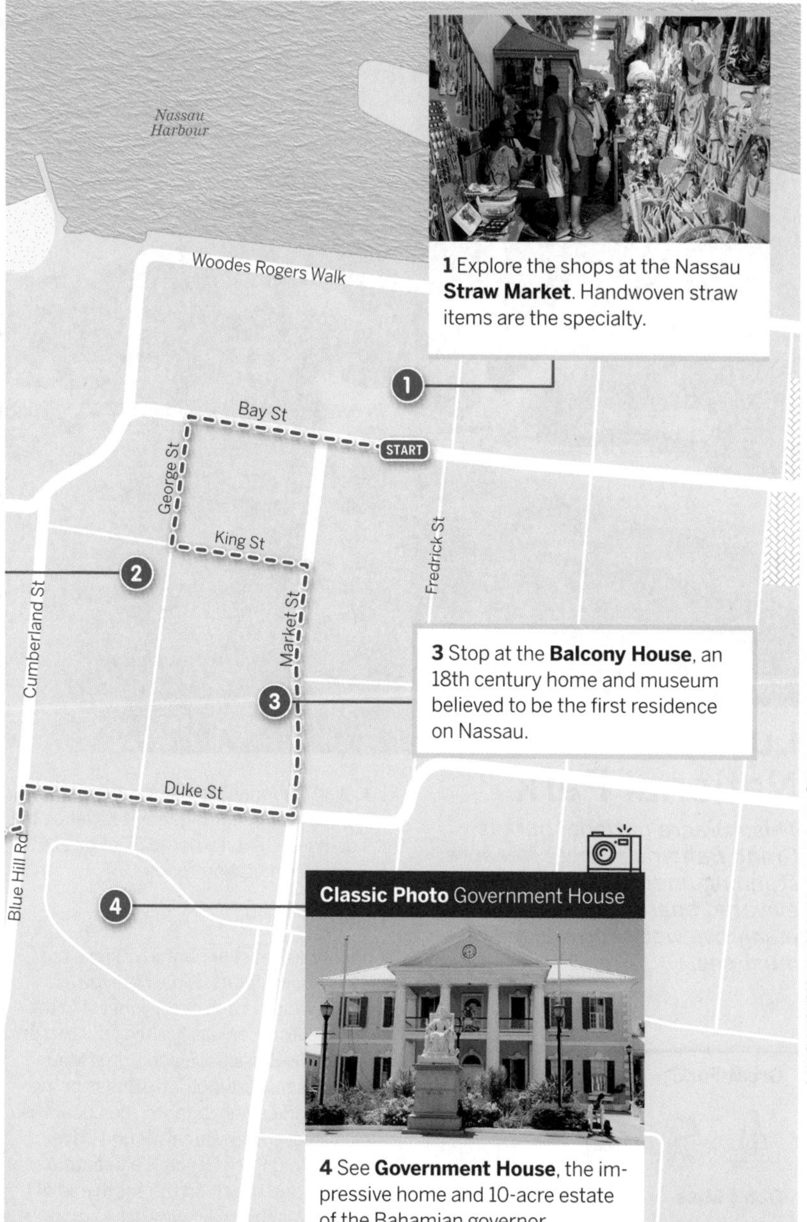

1 Explore the shops at the Nassau **Straw Market**. Handwoven straw items are the specialty.

3 Stop at the **Balcony House**, an 18th century home and museum believed to be the first residence on Nassau.

4 See **Government House**, the impressive home and 10-acre estate of the Bahamian governor.

Kayaking the mangrove trails

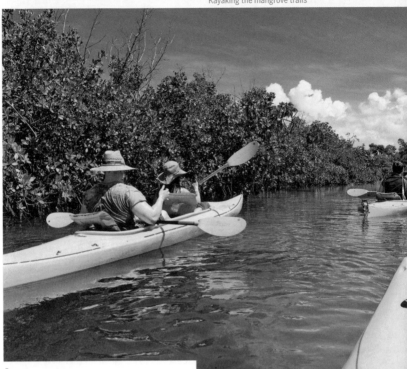

HEMIS/ALAMY ©

Lucayan National Park

This 40-acre national park is Grand Bahama's finest treasure: stunning underwater caves and elevated boardwalks through mangrove wetlands make this a must-see.

Great For...

Don't Miss

Exploring Ben's Cave and beautiful Gold Rock Beach

Lucayan National Park is remote and requires some pre-arrangement to get to, but it's unique in that it's home to all six of the Bahamas' vegetation zones.

Caves

About 40km east of Ranfurly Circle, the park is known for its underwater cave system, which is one of the longest in the world. Visitors can easily check out two of the caves – Ben's Cave and Burial Mound Cave – via a short footpath. Bones of the island's earliest inhabitants, the Lucayans, were discovered in Burial Mound Cave in 1986. Gold Rock Beach is a beautiful and secluded beach on the south end of the park. It's the beach you see in many of the ads for the Bahamas, and one you

iba diver, Ben's Cave

IMAGE SOURCE/ALAMY ©

Explore Ashore

To get to Lucayan from Freeport, rent a car or set up a tour in advance of your cruise through one of the many local tour operators. The drive takes around 45 minutes each way. Allow a minimum of four hours in total.

Need to Know

Admission to Lucayan is US$5 per person (www.bahamas.com/vendor/lucayan-national-park).

don't want to miss if you're a beach lover. It has excellent snorkeling and swimming. Horseback rides and kayak rentals are also available for purchase from the onsite national park vendor. Unfortunately, much of the park and trails are not wheelchair accessible.

Mangrove Trails

Mangrove trails spill out onto the secluded and beautiful Gold Rock Beach, definitely worth a stop if you're out this way. You'll see more raccoons and seabirds than people, but watch your food at the picnic area near the beach – the raccoons are unabashed (but harmless) beggars. Gold Rock Beach is an excellent picnic area, secluded and beautiful.

Tours

Bahamas EcoVentures (242-352-9323; www.bahamasecoventures.com; Wed, Fri & Sun) Organizes fascinating 40-minute walks through the pristine mangroves of the park (BS$15 per person). If you don't fancy the stroll, there's a four-hour airboat tour to Hawksbill Creek, with a guide to point out blue holes (underwater sea caves), turtles, sharks and bonefish.

Smiling Pat's Adventures (242-533-2946;www.smilingpat.com;by appointment) The ever-cheerful Pat earns top ratings for her energetic bus tours, which include a culture-oriented West End tour (BS$75) that ends in a trip to her grandmother's bakery, and a beach tour (BS$75) that hits Lucayan National Park and the filming location of *Pirates of the Caribbean II* and *III*.

Nassau

Nassau is the gritty, vivacious alter ego to the relaxed character of most of the Bahamas. The country's only city, it teems with haring jitneys, bawling straw-goods vendors, rum-happy locals and sun-seeking tourists. Whether you come to shop, eat, party or sight-see, Nassau is *the* place for a dose of urban excitement.

SIGHTS

Downtown Nassau and Bay St largely consist of modern commercial buildings dedicated to tourism, although some historic buildings remain. Other sights are dotted throughout Nassau, in walkable proximity to each other, especially to the landward side of Bay St.

Graycliff Cigar Co Factory

(☎242-302-9150; www.graycliff.com; Graycliff Hotel & Restaurant, West Hill St; ⏰9am-5pm) FREE Wandering into this cigar factory is

Understand

Essential Food & Drink

Conch Roasted, cracked (fried), chopped into salads or dipped in dough and fried into fritters, this chewy sea snail is ubiquitous in the Bahamas. Think calamari. Starchy side dishes like peas 'n' rice (rice with beans), mac 'n' cheese and potato salad round out the menu.

Boil fish A breakfast dish of grouper stewed with lime juice, onions and potatoes. Usually served with johnnycake, a sweetish type of flat cornbread.

Spiny Caribbean lobster The Bahamas' native lobster, often served sautéed with onions and pepper, minced and even curried.

Souse A thick stew of chicken, sheep's head, pig's trotter or other 'leftover' meats.

Guava duff Boiled pastry filled with sweet guava paste and topped off with rum or cream sauce.

Beer Wash everything down with a cold Kalik or Sands beer.

Rum cocktails Try goombay smash or a Bahama mama.

Switcher A refreshing lime-based drink, sometimes available as an alcoholic version.

Sky Juice Gin and coconut milk.

Conch fritters MEVZUP/SHUTTERSTOCK ©

Graycliff Cigar Co

like falling into 1920s Cuba. In a narrow, smoke-yellowed room with old-fashioned mosaic floors, up to 16 *torcedores* (cigar rollers) are busy at work, their fingers a blur as they roll hand-dried tobacco leaves into premium stogies. Cigar-rolling lessons (BS$75) and demonstrations paired with rum tastings (BS$150) are available Monday to Saturday.

Pirates of Nassau Museum

(☎242-356-3759; www.piratesofnassau.com; cnr King & George Sts; adult/child BS$13/6.50; ⏲9am-6pm Mon-Sat, to 12:30pm Sun; 👪) Don't even try to ignore the pirate pacing outside the museum: like any seafaring ruffian worth his peg leg, he had you in his sights the moment you turned the corner. But that's OK – with its scale replica of the pirate ship *Revenge*, animatronic pirates and accessible exhibits on everything from marooning to pirate Hall-of-Famers, this museum provides the right mix of entertainment and history for kids and parents alike. There's a great gift shop, Plunder, next door.

National Art Gallery of the Bahamas Museum

(☎242-358-5800; www.nagb.org.bs; cnr West & West Hill Sts; adult/child BS$5/free; ⏲10am-4pm Tue-Sat, from noon Sun) If you're jangled by the chaos of Bay St, you'll find a welcome oasis inside the stately 1860s-era Villa Doyle: a grand art museum that's one of the gems in the Bahamian crown. The permanent collection focuses on modern and contemporary Bahamian artists, from renowned sculptor Antonius Roberts to folk painter Wellington Bridgewater. There are also pieces by artists of the wider Caribbean, and temporary exhibits on ecological, cultural and historical themes relevant to the islands.

ACTIVITIES

Seaworld Explorer Boating

(☎242-356-2548; www.seaworldtours.com; Bay St; adult/child BS$45/25; 👪) A connecting boat whisks passengers out to this window-lined, 45-passenger semisubmarine beyond Nassau Harbour. From there it takes a diverting 90-minute excursion

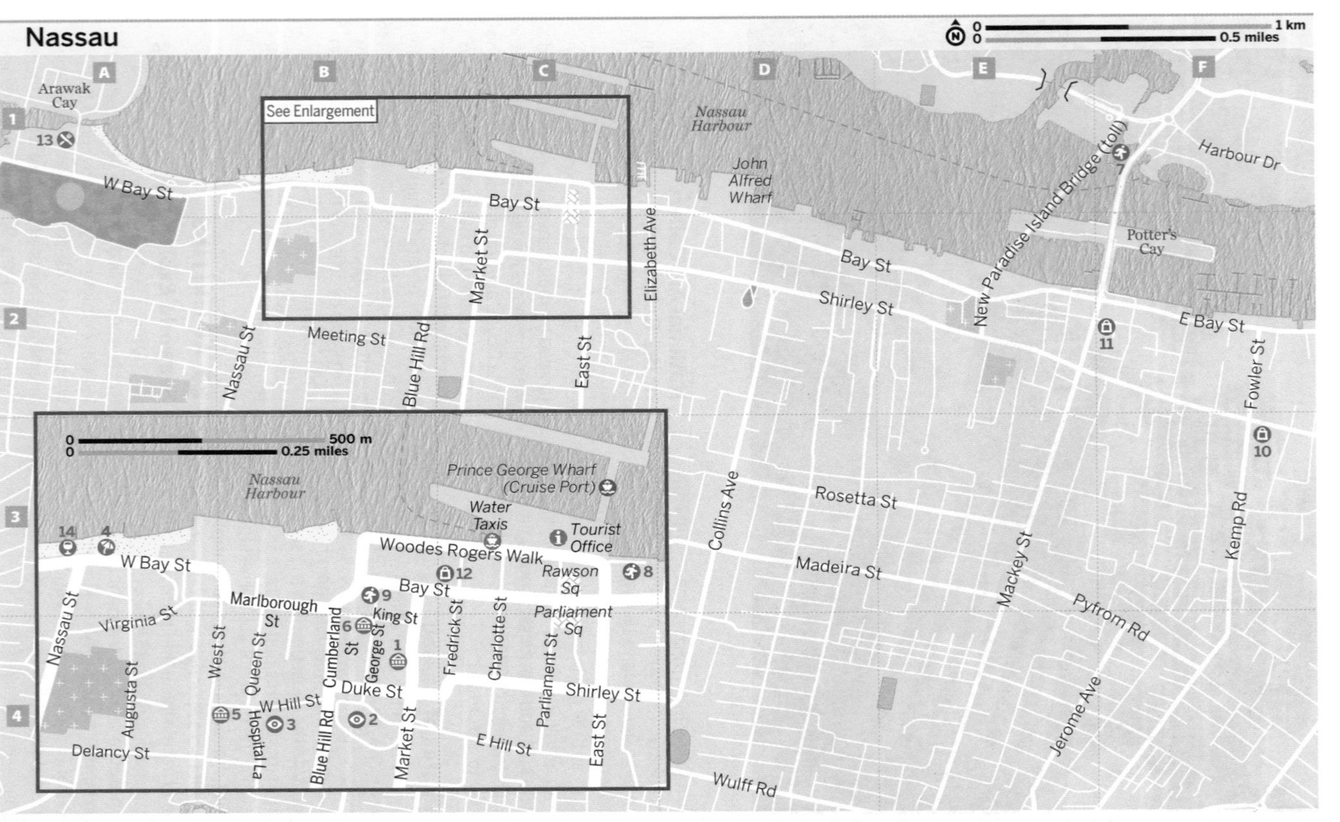
Nassau
0 1 km
0 0.5 miles
Arawak Cay
See Enlargement
Nassau Harbour
John Alfred Wharf
Harbour Dr
Potter's Cay
New Paradise Island Bridge (toll)
W Bay St
Bay St
Market St
Elizabeth Ave
Shirley St
E Bay St
Fowler St
Meeting St
Nassau St
Blue Hill Rd
East St
Collins Ave
Rosetta St
Madeira St
Mackey St
Kemp Rd
Pyfrom Rd
Jerome Ave
Wulff Rd
0 500 m
0 0.25 miles
Prince George Wharf (Cruise Port)
Water Taxis
Tourist Office
Woodes Rogers Walk
Rawson Sq
Parliament Sq
Marlborough St
Virginia St
King St
Fredrick St
Charlotte St
Parliament St
Cumberland St
George St
West St
Queen St
Augusta St
Duke St
W Hill St
Hospital La
E Hill St
Delancy St

Nassau

Sights

1 Balcony House Museum B4
2 Government House B4
3 Graycliff Cigar Co B4
4 Junkanoo Beach A3
5 National Art Gallery of the Bahamas B4
6 Pirates of Nassau B4

Activities, Courses & Tours

7 Flying Cloud Catamaran Cruises & Snorkeling Tours F1
8 Seaworld Explorer C3
9 Tru Bahamian Food Tours B3

Shopping

10 Bahama Art & Handicraft F3
11 Bahama Handprints F2
Plunder! .... (see 6)
12 Straw Market C3

Eating

13 Fish Fry A1

Drinking & Nightlife

14 Khyla's Island Philosophy A3

through the fish-filled coral reefs of the **Sea Gardens Marine Park**, off the north shore of Paradise Island.

Flying Cloud Catamaran Cruises & Snorkeling Tours Cruise

(☎242-394-5067; www.flyingcloud.info) These fast-flying 17m catamarans whisk you away for half- and full-day snorkel adventures (BS$70/95), or for sunset dinner cruises (BS$70). Departures are from the Paradise Island ferry terminal, and free transport can be provided to and from your hotel.

TOURS

Tru Bahamian Food Tours Food

(☎242-601-1725; www.trubahamianfoodtours.com; cnr George & Bay Sts; adult/child BS$75/53; ⏲8am-9pm Mon-Sat, to 6pm Sun) This outfit's Bites of Nassau tour is a 3½-hour excursion around the best of Bahamian food, stopping off at six local kitchens to meet the chefs and sample the good stuff. Tours meet near George and Bay Sts, or you can book a customized cooking class.

SHOPPING

Visitors flock to Bay St for duty-free liquor, jewelry, perfume and cigars, but savings are not guaranteed; check prices at home before your trip. Most stores close at night and on Sunday, even when the cruise ships are in port. Bahamian-made products are sold at booths throughout Festival Place at Prince George Wharf.

Bahama Handprints Clothing

(☎242-394-4111; www.bahamahandprints.com; Island Traders' Bldg, Ernest St; ⏲10am-4pm Mon-Fri, 9am-2pm Sat) Actually on Ernest St, just behind the main Island Traders' Building, this boutique and factory outlet sells lovely, handmade interior-design fabric, clothes, accessories and furnishings. It's possible to tour the factory by arrangement.

Bahama Art & Handicraft Arts & Crafts

(☎242-394-7892; East Shirley St; ⏲8:30am-4:30pm Tue-Sat) If you're interested in picking up traditional Bahamian handicrafts from around the islands, this shop makes it easy. The paintings, jewelry, driftwood sculptures, handmade baskets and other pieces are the work of many different producers from across the archipelago.

EATING & DRINKING

Fish Fry Bahamian $

(☎242-425-7275; Arawak Cay, off West Bay St; mains BS$12-22; ⏲7am-midnight) The colorful village of conch stands, bars, jerk joints and seafood restaurants at Arawak Cay, known collectively as the 'Fish Fry', is one of Nassau's great experiences. Come for conch salad, fried chicken wings, fritters, blackened snapper, 'sky juice' (a high-octane libation of coconut water and gin), rake 'n' scrape bands, reggae DJs, Junkanoo dances and friendly chatter.

Khyla's Island Philosophy Bar
(242-544-0721; Junkanoo Beach, West Bay Dr; 11am-6pm) This tiny charismatic beach bar exemplifies all that is convivial and distinctive about Nassau, with an ebullient proprietress (Khyla), ever-welcoming locals and good tunes on the laptop. Sadly gutted by fire in 2016, Island Philosophy still opened the next day, dispensing beers and basic mixes along with life wisdom from its small beachside deck. Try the signature ginger switcher (BS$10).

 INFORMATION

MONEY

Banks are clustered around Rawson Sq and Bay St. ATMs dispensing US and Bahamian dollars are found throughout Nassau and at banks such as the Royal Bank of Canada and Scotiabank.

TOURIST INFORMATION

Tourist Office (242-323-3182, 242-322-7680; www.bahamas.com; Welcome Centre, Festival Pl, Prince George Wharf; 8am-11pm) In addition to picking up the usual pamphlets, maps and advice, you can join 45-minute guided walking tours of historic Nassau from this office, leaving at 10am, 11:30am, 1pm, 2:30pm and 3:45pm Monday to Saturday (BS$10 per person).

 GETTING AROUND

Minibuses, known locally as 'jitneys,' are Nassau's only public transport. The route number and principal stops are painted on the front of each bus, and a single fare within Nassau – paid as you get off – is only BS$1.25 (BS$2 will get you to Love Beach, or BS$2.50 to just outside the airport). To catch one, flag it down from the roadside, then simply sing out 'bus stop' when you want to get off.

Water taxis (242-363-1030; 9am-6pm) connect Prince George Wharf and Paradise Island every 30 minutes from 8am to 6pm. One way/return fares are BS$4/8.

Freeport

Freeport, Grand Bahama's only urban settlement, was built seemingly overnight in the 1950s to serve as a duty-free tourist

Marketplace, Bahamas

MOMO PRODUCTIONS/GETTY IMAGES ©

destination for Rat Pack–era pleasure-seekers. Half a century and several major hurricanes later, it's now an uninspiring grid of banks, strip malls and government buildings, with little appeal for travelers.

Lucaya, a modern coastal suburb of Freeport, is where most of the vacation action takes place. Its tidy – some might say antiseptic – strip of shops and restaurants which visitors will find safe and walkable. On warm nights, when the music is thumping at the Port Lucaya Marketplace bandstand, this is the place to be.

SIGHTS & ACTIVITIES

Garden of the Groves Gardens

(242-373-5668; www.thegardenofthegroves.com; cnr Midshipman Rd & Magellan Dr; adult/child BS$16.50/11; 9am-4pm) This 12-acre botanical garden is a lush tropical refuge on an island that's otherwise mostly scrub pine and asphalt. A walking trail meanders through groves of tamarind and java plum trees, past cascading (artificial) waterfalls, a placid lagoon and a tiny 19th-century hilltop chapel. The spiritually minded will enjoy a meditative stroll through the limestone labyrinth, a replica of the one at Chartres Cathedral in France. Kids will dig the raccoon habitat, where trapped specimens of the invasive critter come to retire.

Perfume Factory Factory

(242-352-9391; www.perfumefactory.com; International Bazaar, East Mall Dr; 9am-5pm Mon-Fri, 11am-3pm Sat) FREE Also known as Fragrance of the Bahamas, this company occupies a three-story pink Bahamian house at the rear of the **International Bazaar** (some shops daily, others only for cruise-ship tours). Free tours (during the week) reveal some secrets of production, and you can pick up a bottle of the ever-popular Pink Pearl (frangipani-based, with a pink conch-shell 'pearl' inside) or blend your own signature sniff.

Bahamian Culture

Contemporary Bahamian culture still revolves around family, church and the sea, but the proximity of North America and the arrival of cable TV has had a profound influence on contemporary life and material values.

In Nassau and Freeport, most working people are employed in banking, tourism or government work and live a nine-to-five lifestyle.

The citizens inhabiting the islands outside of New Providence and Grand Bahama, called the Out Islands or Family Islands, are a bit more neighborly and traditional. Thus the practice of Obeah (a form of African-based ritual magic), bush medicine, and folkloric songs and tales still infuse their daily lives. Though tourism is bringing change to the Out Islands, many people still live simple lives centered on fishing, catching conch and lobster, and raising corn, bananas and other crops.

MOMO PRODUCTIONS/GETTY IMAGES ©

Ocean Motion Water Sports

(242-373-9603; www.oceanmotionwatersportsbahamas.com; Lucaya Beach) On the beach in front of Our Lucaya Beach & Golf Resort, this large outfit offers parasailing (BS$80 per person), snorkeling (adult/child BS$55/25), boat tours (BS$30 per person) and more.

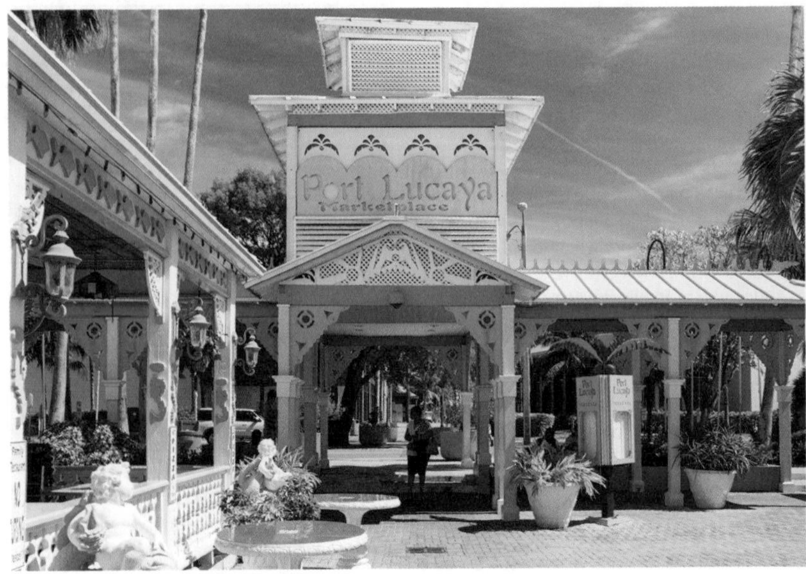

Port Lucaya Marketplace, Freeport

TOURS

Reef Tours Water Sports

(☎242-373-5880; www.reeftoursfreeport.com; Port Lucaya Marketplace, Lucaya; 👪) Introducing visitors to the delights of the Grand Bahamas since 1978, Reef Tours offers a wine-and-cheese-fueled Enchanted Evening Sail (BS$40), a glass-bottomed-boat tour (adult/child BS$30/18), a snorkel and fish-feeding trip (adult/child BS$40/20) and more. It's great value compared to many Bahamian tourist operations.

Paradise Watersports Cruise

(☎242-373-4001;www.the-bahamas-watersports.com) Paradise runs 1½-hour tours on its glass-bottomed boat (adult/child BS$30/18), taking in the reef, shipwrecks and more. It also takes deep-sea fishing and snokeling tours (BS$130/65 per person) and rents out waverunners (BS$70 per 30 minutes). Just call to arrange your fun.

EATING & DRINKING

Billy Joe's on the Beach Bahamian $

(☎305-735-8267; Lucaya Beach; mains BS$13-15; ⏰10am-5:30pm) Tucking into a bowl of Billy Joe's conch salad as you wiggle your bare feet in the sand is a quintessential Grand Bahama experience. This venerable waterfront conch shack was here long before the Grand Lucaya complex took over the beach, and it's still the place to go for cold Kalik and conch cooked any way you like it.

Geneva's Place Bahamian $

(☎242-352-5085; cnr East Mall Dr & Kipling Lane; mains BS$14-16; ⏰7am-10pm) You'll hardly spot a non-Bahamian face in this huge, fluorescent-lit dining room, popular with locals for traditional breakfasts such as pig's feet souse and sardines and grits. Lunch means cracked conch or minced turbot, while dinner features massive portions of fish, chicken or steak.

Margaritaville Sandbar Bar
(242-373-4525; www.sandbarbahamas.com; Churchill Beach, Mather Town; 11:30am-midnight;) It's a little tricky to find (ask a local), but this funky little beach shack is an under-the-radar classic. It's the best place on Grand Bahama for NFL addicts to get their Sunday fix, and closing time depends entirely on how lively things get.

INFORMATION

Grand Bahama Island Tourism Board (242-352-8356; www.grandbahamavacations.com)

Port Lucaya Marketplace Tourist Office (242-373-8988; www.bahamas.com; Port Lucaya Marketplace, Sea Horse Rd; 9am-5pm)

GETTING AROUND

It is not recommended to walk around the area of Freeport right outside the port. The Freeport cruise terminal is in an industrialized area with high crime, and it is important to especially avoid visiting this area at night when cruise passengers become targets for robberies. Take a taxi from the cruise terminal to one of the popular beaches or to the town of Freeport, 20-minutes away. Lucayan National Park is quite compact and it's easy to get around on foot. However, getting to the park can prove to be quite difficult from the cruise port. It is best to arrange a tour from one of the reputable tour companies before embarking on your cruise.

A handful of private minibuses operate as 'public buses' on assigned routes from the bus depot at Winn Dixie Plaza in Freeport, traveling as far afield as West End and McLean's Town. Buses are frequent and depart when the driver decides he has enough passengers. In Lucaya, the main bus stop is on Seahorse Dr, 400m west of the Port Lucaya Marketplace.

The Bahamian Beat

The Bahamas rock to the soul-riveting sounds of calypso, soca, reggae and its own distinctive music, which echoes African rhythms and synthesizes Caribbean calypso, soca and English folk songs into its own goombay beat.

Goombay – the name comes from an African word for 'rhythm' – derives its melody from a guitar, piano or horn instrument, accompanied by any combination of goatskin goombay drums, maracas, rhythm sticks, rattles, conch-shell horns, fifes, flutes and cowbells, to add a *kalik-kalik-kalik* sound.

Rake 'n' scrape is the Bahamas' down-home, working-class music, usually featuring a guitar, an accordion, shakers made from the pods of poinciana trees, and other makeshift instruments, such as a saw played with a screwdriver.

Fares from Freetown include Port Lucaya Marketplace (BS$1.25), East End (BS$8, twice daily) and West End (BS$4, twice daily). Though drivers are meant to stick to their circuit, they'll often function as impromptu taxis, taking you wherever you want for a fee. Just ask.

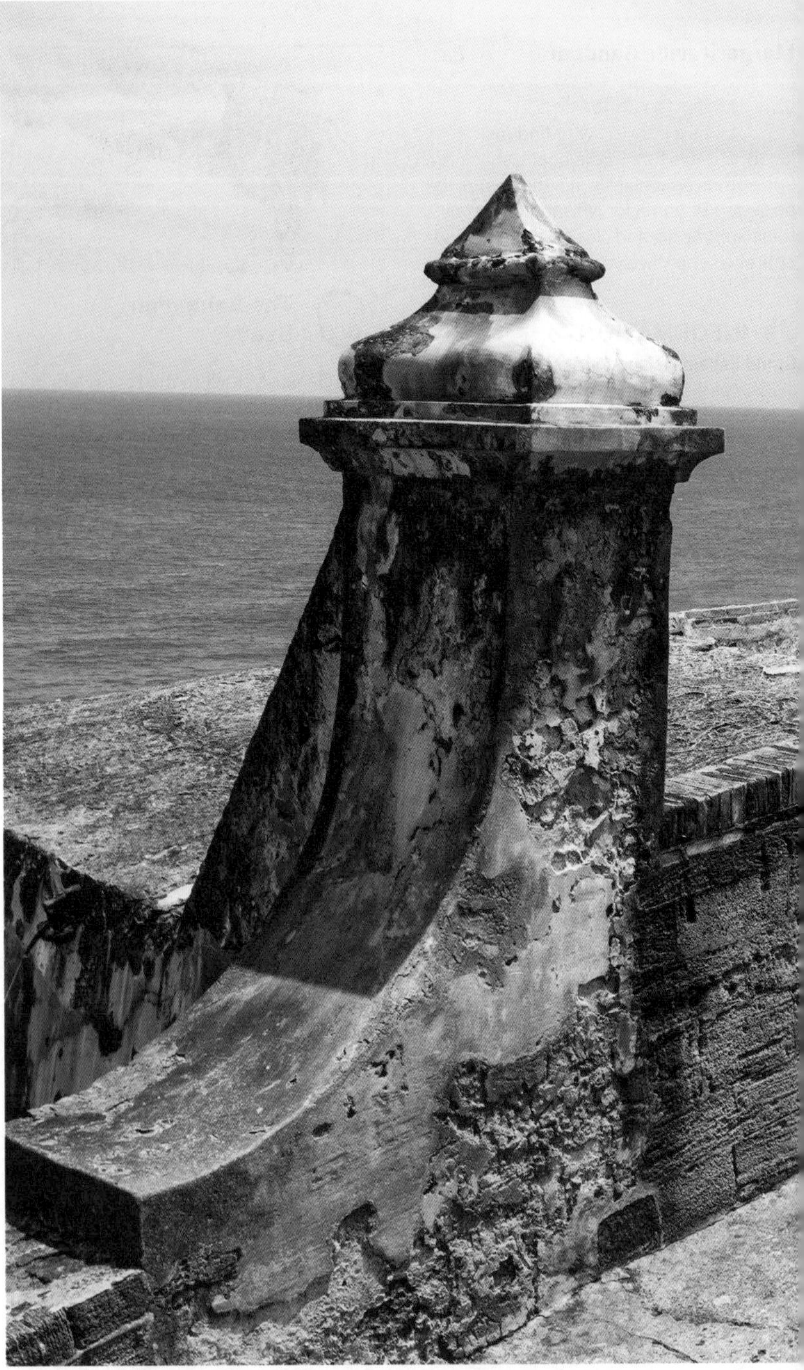

JOEL CARILLET/GETTY IMAGES ©

El Morro (p134), San Juan

PUERTO RICO

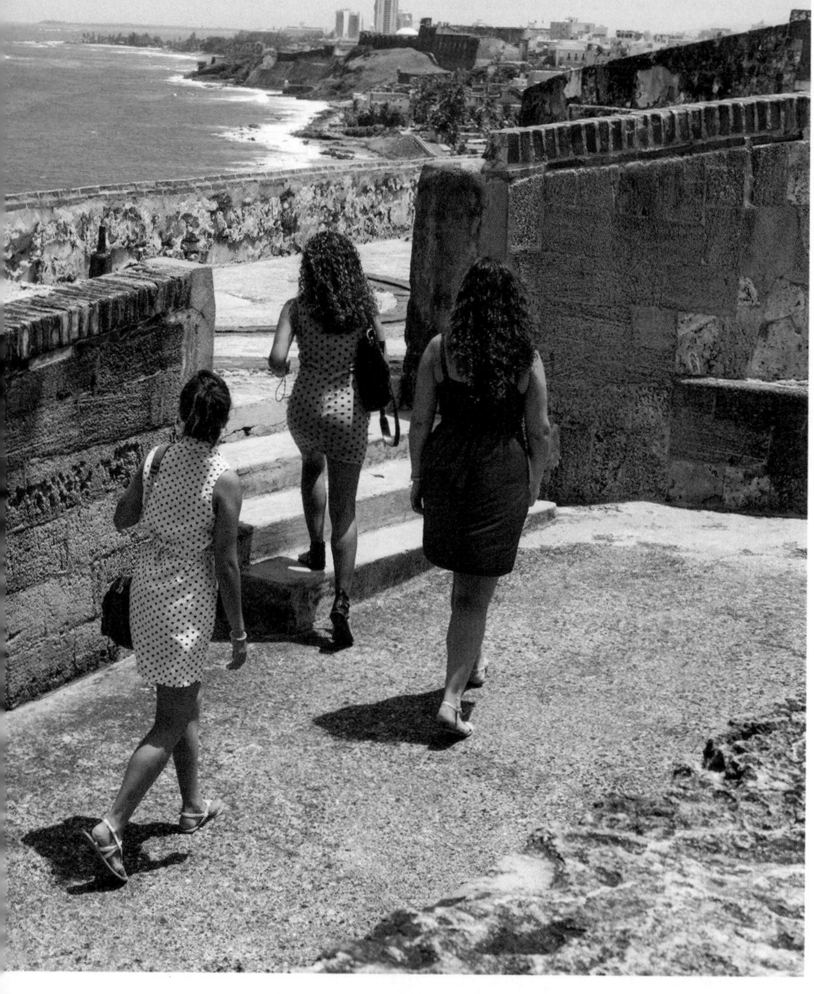

In This Chapter

Puerto Rico at a Glance

Established in 1521, Puerto Rico's capital San Juan is the second-oldest European-founded settlement in the Americas. Shoehorned onto a tiny islet that guards the entrance to San Juan harbor, the Old Town was inaugurated almost a century before the* Mayflower *laid anchor in present-day Massachusetts: today it juxtaposes historical authenticity with pulsating modern energy. Beyond its timeworn 15ft-thick walls, San Juan is far more than a collection of well-polished colonial-era artifacts – it's also a mosaic of ever-evolving neighborhoods such as Santurce, which has a raw vitality fueled by street art, superb restaurants and a bar scene that takes over the streets at night.

With a Day in Port

- Explore the beautiful, colorful, and historic Old Town district (two hours; p140).
- Take a pleasant stroll along the Paseo de la Princesa to El Morro, an amazing 16th century fortress. (p134)
- Head to El Yunque National Forest. (p136)

Best Places for...

Coffee Café Cola'o (p148)

Dancing Nuyorican Cafe (p149)

Local cuisine Cafe Puerto Rico (p148)

Ice cream Señor Paleta (p147)

Puerto Rico was dealt a double blow in September 2017 when hurricanes Irma and Maria (p142) swept through. While we have endeavoured to keep the information in this chapter as up-to-date as possible, some places may still be affected while the community rebuilds.

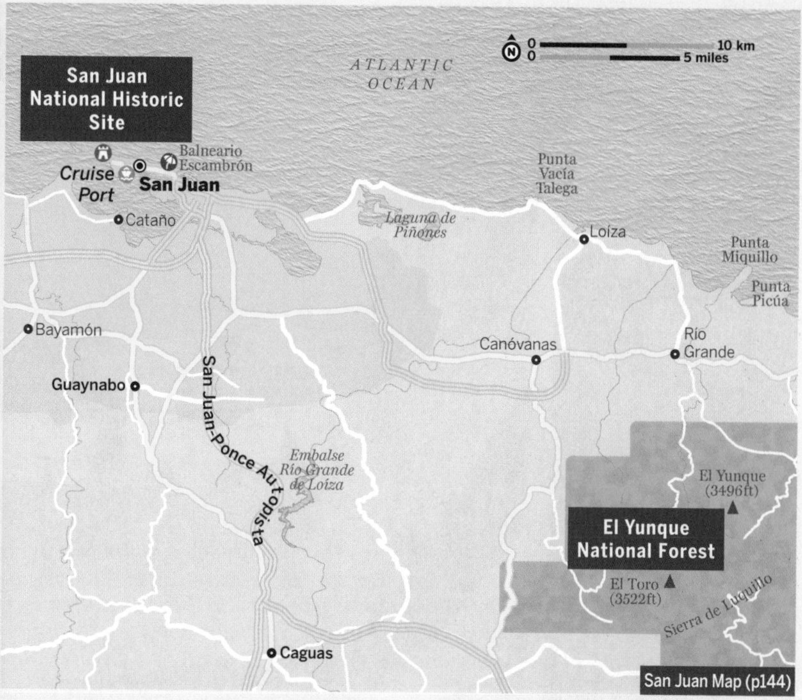

San Juan Map (p144)

Getting from the Port

Most ships dock at the piers along Calle La Marina just a short walk from Old San Juan.

Transportation Taxis within Old San Juan cost US$7. A free trolley service links many sights in Old San Juan. All routes pass by Pier 4 of the cruise-ship terminal along Calle La Marina.

Accessibility The cobblestone streets are uneven, and can be slippery in wet weather.

Fast Facts

Currency US dollar (US$)

Languages Spanish, English

Money ATMs are common; banks are open Monday to Friday.

Visas Not required for citizens of the US, EU or Australia.

Best for free wi-fi Old San Juan library and many cafes.

Fuerte San Cristóbal

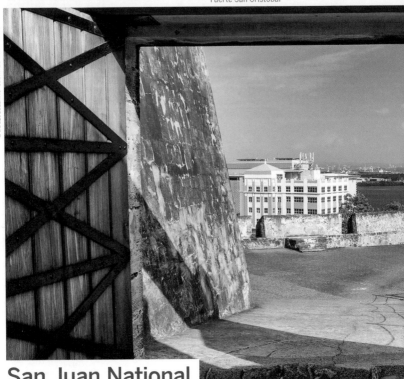

San Juan National Historic Site

A visit to the two megastars of the San Juan National Historic Site, El Morro and Fuerte San Cristóbal, can be made even more rewarding with a just bit of planning.

Great For...

Don't Miss

Hour-long free guided tours roam the tunnels at Fuerte San Cristóbal every weekend.

El Morro

The star of Old San Juan, **El Morro** (Fuerte San Felipe del Morro; ☎787-729-7423; www.nps.gov/saju; 501 Norzagaray, adult/child US$5/free; ⏰9am-6pm; 🚌Fort) juts aggressively over bold headlands, glowering across the Atlantic at would-be conquerors. The 140ft-high walls date back to 1539 and El Morro is said to be the oldest Spanish fort in the New World. Displays document the construction of the fort, which took almost 200 years, as well as El Morro's role in rebuffing attacks on the island by the British, the Dutch and, later, the US military. A short film providing a historical overview of the fort is screened every 15 minutes.

The gray castellated lighthouse on the 6th floor has been in operation since 1846, making it the island's oldest light station still in use today. After suffering severe

Explore Ashore

Take the free trolley or grab a taxi from the port (faster, but $7 each way). Walk the Paseo de la Princesa to El Morro and then stop by Fuerte San Cristóbal before returning to the cruise port (one hour of walking, three hours total).

Need to Know

Free tours of the fort run Saturday (English) and Sunday (Spanish) at 10:30am and 12:30pm; arrive at least half an hour beforehand to sign up.

damage during a US Navy bombardment during the 1898 Spanish-American War, the original lighthouse was rebuilt in 1906 with unique Spanish-Moorish features.

At a minimum, try to make the climb up the ramparts to the sentries' walks along the Santa Barbara Bastion and Austria Half-Bastion for the expansive views (consider wearing comfortable shoes as there are many steep stairs).

On weekends, the fields leading up to the fort are alive with picnickers, lovers and kite flyers. The scene becomes a kind of impromptu festival with food vendors' carts on the perimeter.

Fuerte San Cristóbal

San Juan's second major fort is Fuerte San Cristóbal, one of the largest military installations the Spanish built in the Americas. In its day, San Cristóbal covered 27 acres with a maze of six interconnected forts protecting a central core with 150ft walls, moats, booby-trapped bridges and tunnels. The fort has a fascinating museum, a store, military archives, a reproduction of military barracks, and stunning views.

The fort was constructed to defend Old San Juan against land attacks from the east via Puerta de Tierra. Construction began in 1634 in response to an attack by the Dutch a decade previously, though the main period of enlargement occurred between 1765 and 1783.

Seven acres were lopped off the fort in 1897 to ease congestion in the Old Town and the following year the Spanish marked Puerto Rico's entry into the Spanish-American War by firing at the battleship USS *Yale* from its cannon battery. The fort became a National Historic Site in 1949 and part of the Unesco World Heritage Site in 1983.

El Yunque National Forest

Lush forests, verdant hills and crashing waterfalls attract visitors to El Yunque, the only tropical rainforest in the US National Forest System. It's a place to embark on hikes through the oxygen-rich mist and gawk at Jurassic-sized ferns.

Great For...

Don't Miss

Hiking the lush, rainforest trails with spectacular ocean views.

One of Puerto Rico's crown jewels, El Yunque National Forest boasts nearly 29,000 acres of lush mountainous terrain, with waterfalls dotting the landscape, rushing rivers and gurgling brooks, bromeliads clinging to towering trees, and bamboo groves opening to spectacular ocean views.

El Yunque (named after the Taíno god, Yúcahu) has 22 miles of trails, some short and paved, others long, steep and barely there. Almost all gain some elevation; one of the toughest is to El Yunque's peak, El Toro, almost 3605ft above sea level. Both casual and experienced hikers are sure to find rewarding trails.

The park was closed for a period in late 2017 following extensive damage caused by Hurricane Maria.

DAVID BOROK/SHUTTERSTOCK ©

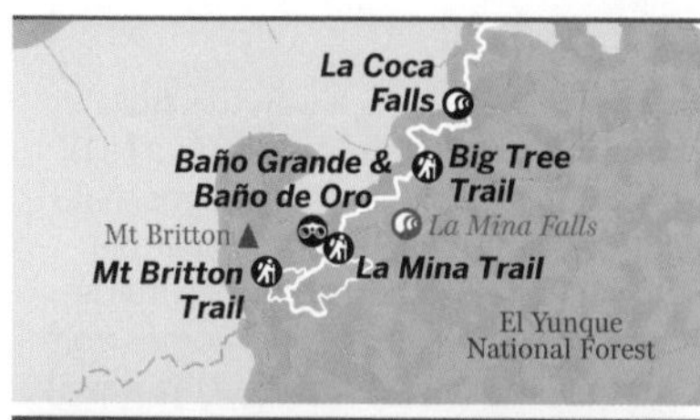

Explore Ashore

There are *públicos* (public vans) running between San Juan and Fajardo, the main access point for the national park, but to penetrate further into the countryside, a car is necessary. It is easy to organize a tour. The drive from San Juan to Fajardo takes around 75–90 minutes.

Need to Know

(787-888-1880; www.fs.usda.gov/elyunque; Northern Entrance, Km 4, Hwy 191; adult/child $4/free; 7:30am-6pm)

La Coca Falls

The first spectacular natural feature you see as Hwy 191 climbs south toward the forest peaks is an 85ft cascade as the stream tumbles from a precipice to the right of the highway onto boulder formations.

Baño Grande & Baño de Oro

Baño Grande, a former swimming hole built during the Depression by the Civilian Conservation Corps, lies across Hwy 191 from the Palo Colorado Information Center. About 50yd up the road, Baño de Oro is another former swimming hole that is now a popular spot for photo opportunities. This water hole takes its name from the Río Baño de Oro, which feeds the pool. The Spaniards gave the river the name 'bath of gold' because they mined it for gold during the 16th century.

La Mina Trail

The forest's newest trail was opened in 1992 as an extension of the Big Tree Trail, though it can also be done in isolation from its starting point at the Palo Colorado Information Center. The trail heads downhill through palo colorado forest to La Mina Falls and an old mine tunnel. Mostly paved, it's an easy though often slippery 0.6-mile walk down, and a steep hike back up. The payoff are the falls, which drop 35ft into a perfect natural swimming pool. Take your bathing suit to cool off after the intense walk. It can be confusing to find the trailhead; signage is lacking and there are several paths that dead-end at picnic sites. If in doubt, follow the sound of the river and stay on the paved path.

Big Tree Trail

About half an hour each way, this trail through tabonuco forest to La Mina Falls contains bilingual interpretive signs that highlight sights such as a 300-year-old ausubo tree. This short 0.86-mile trail is moderately difficult; its name comes from the size of the vegetation along the way. It's probably the most popular trail in the park; combine it with La Mina Trail.

Mt Britton Trail

If you are short on time and want to feel as if you have really 'summited,' take the 0.8-mile (45-minute) climb up through the palma sierra forest into the cloud forest that surrounds this peak.

The trail is a continuous climb on paved surfaces to the evocative stone Mt Britton Tower, built in the 1930s by the Civilian Conservation Corps. When not shrouded by clouds, the panoramic views extend over the forest to the Atlantic Ocean and the Caribbean.

The trailhead is on a dirt track, which veers off Hwy 191 for half a kilometer at the latter's endpoint at Km 13.

El Yunque Trail

On a clear day, never-ending views extending to Vieques and Culebra reward hikers who tackle the almost 1500ft of elevation gain on this 2.4km trail. This is the main event for most hikers, taking you to the top of El Yunque (3496ft) in 1½ hours or longer. It starts opposite the Palo Colorado Information Center.

Yokahú Tower

This 65ft, Moorish-looking stone tower was built as a lookout in 1962. It's the first good place for vistas of the islands to the east, but there are better vantage points higher up on the mountain. The tower often gets crowded with tour groups. Pass it by unless you have extra time.

Tour Operators

AdvenTours (☎787-530-8311; www.adventourspr.com; tours per person from US$75; ⏰1-8pm Mon-Fri, tour schedules vary) offers a huge range of excursions including birdwatching tours and night hikes in El Yunque National Forest to spot nocturnal animals and bioluminescent fungi. You can custom-design trips and arrange for pick up in San Juan.

Hiking Safety

It's a good idea to check in at the visitors center for the latest weather update before heading out for a trek. El Yunque's weather reflects its wet ecosystem: sudden surges of light rain can occur anytime during the year in this dense rainforest, so throw on some protective gear and get on with your day. During hurricane season El Yunque can get drenched; some trails might be closed due to mudslides and streams swell enormously.

DANITA DELIMONT STOCK/AGEFOTOSTOCK ©

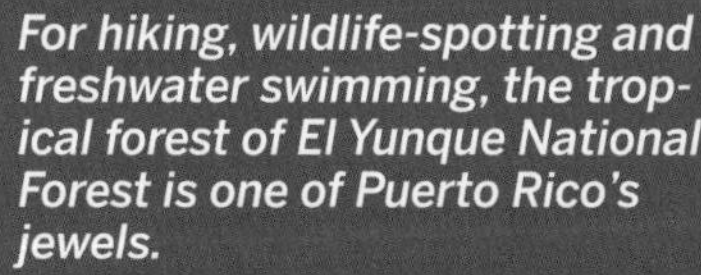

For hiking, wildlife-spotting and freshwater swimming, the tropical forest of El Yunque National Forest is one of Puerto Rico's jewels.

LEFT: INFINITE_EYE/SHUTTERSTOCK ©; RIGHT: JASON PATRICK ROSS/SHUTTERSTOCK ©

Hiking and canyoning in El Yunque National Forest.

Old San Juan Historic Walk

Cruise ships dock right in the heart of the historic district of San Juan, making this an excellent port to explore on foot.

Start Café Cola'o
Distance 2.75 miles
Duration 3 to 4 hours

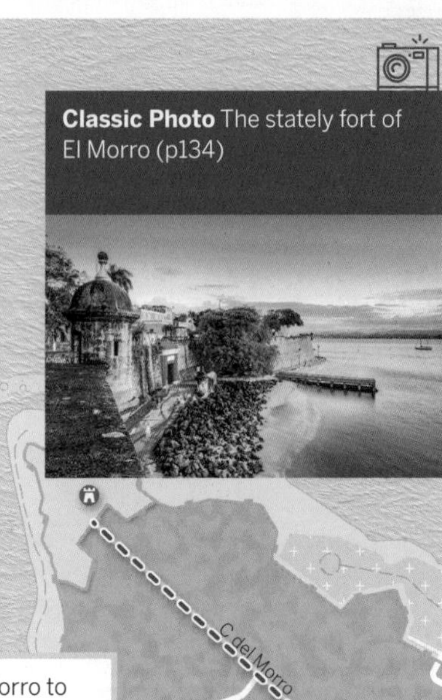

Classic Photo The stately fort of El Morro (p134)

7 Head down Calle del Morro to the **Casa Blanca** (p142), the ancestral home for 250 years of the descendants of Juan Ponce de León and the oldest permanent residence in the Americas. End at the Plaza de San José, with its statue of Juan Ponce de León.

Bahía de San Juan

4 Pass through the gate and turn right onto leafy Caleta de San Juan up the slope to the beautiful **Plazuela Las Monjas**. On the north side of the plaza is Hotel El Convento and to the east lies the Catedral de San Juan (pictured).

3 In the 17th and 18th centuries, Spanish ships once anchored in the cove just off these ramparts to unload colonists and supplies, all of which entered the city through a tall red portal known as **Puerta de San Juan**.

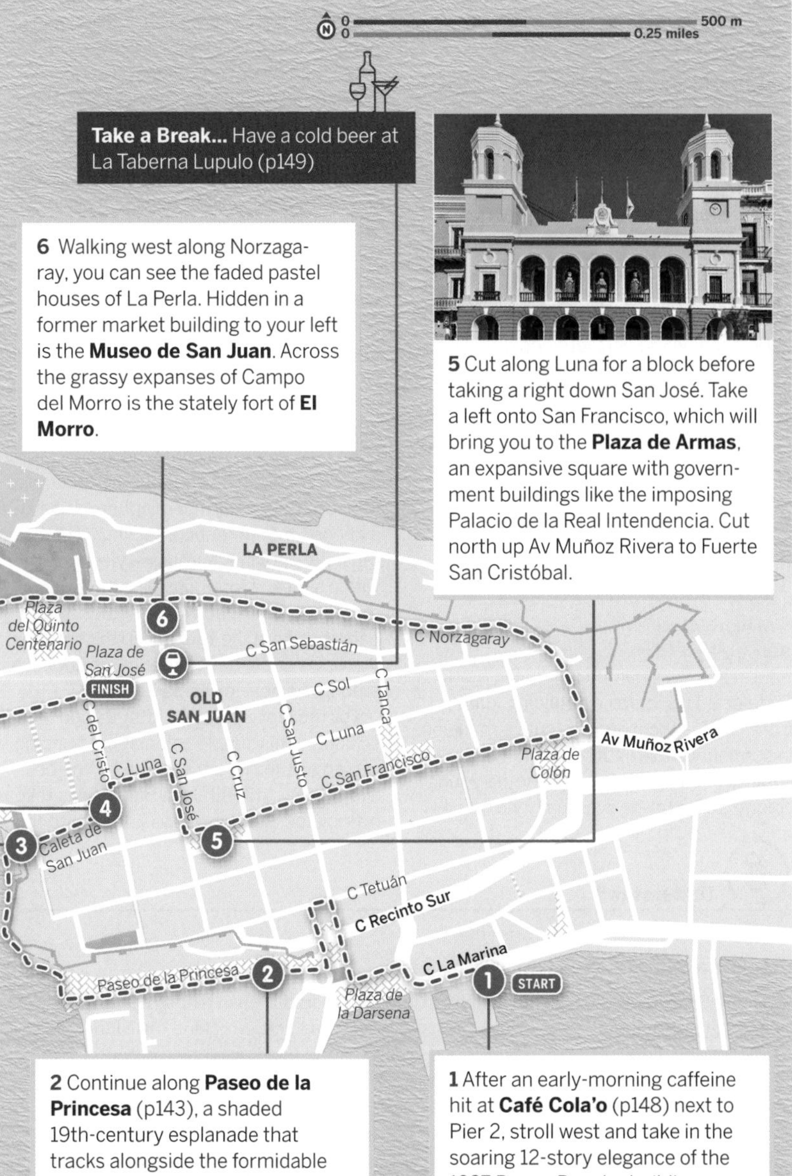

Take a Break... Have a cold beer at La Taberna Lupulo (p149)

6 Walking west along Norzagaray, you can see the faded pastel houses of La Perla. Hidden in a former market building to your left is the **Museo de San Juan**. Across the grassy expanses of Campo del Morro is the stately fort of **El Morro**.

5 Cut along Luna for a block before taking a right down San José. Take a left onto San Francisco, which will bring you to the **Plaza de Armas**, an expansive square with government buildings like the imposing Palacio de la Real Intendencia. Cut north up Av Muñoz Rivera to Fuerte San Cristóbal.

2 Continue along **Paseo de la Princesa** (p143), a shaded 19th-century esplanade that tracks alongside the formidable old city walls to the brink of the Bahía de San Juan.

1 After an early-morning caffeine hit at **Café Cola'o** (p148) next to Pier 2, stroll west and take in the soaring 12-story elegance of the 1937 Banco Popular building, an art-deco gem at the corner of San Justo and Tetuán.

San Juan

SIGHTS

Balneario Escambrón Beach

(off Av Muñoz Rivera, Puerta de Tierra; parking US$5; 8:30am-6pm; D53, T3, T5, T21) A sheltered arc of raked sand, decent surf breaks, plenty of local action and a 17th-century Spanish fort shimmering in the distance are the hallmarks of this fine beach only a stone's throw from Old San Juan and the busy tourist strip of Condado. Best of all, it's often uncrowded.

Perched on the northern end of the slither of land that is Puerta de Tierra, it abuts majestic Parque del Tercer Milenio. This palm-fringed yet rugged beach just might be one of the best municipal options offered anywhere. There are lifeguards, restrooms, gear rental stands and snack bars, along with a large parking lot.

La Fortaleza Historic Site

(El Palacio de Santa Catalina; 787-721-7000; www.fortaleza.gobierno.pr; Calle Recinto, Old San Juan; suggested donation US$3; tours 9am-3:30pm Mon-Fri) Guarded iron gates mark La Fortaleza. This imposing building, dating from 1533, is the oldest executive mansion in continuous use in the western hemisphere. The original fortress for the young colony, La Fortaleza eventually yielded its military preeminence to the city's newer and larger forts and was remodeled and expanded to domicile island governors for more than three centuries. You can take a 30-minute guided tour that includes the mansion's Moorish gardens, the dungeon and the chapel.

Tour schedules change daily; call on the day you wish to visit to reserve a place, or stop by the Tour Guides Office near the west end of Calle Forteleza.

Casa Blanca Historic Building

(White House; 787-725-1454; Calle San Sebastián, Old San Juan; entrance US$3; 8am-noon & 1-4pm Wed-Sun) First constructed in 1521 as a residence for Puerto Rico's pioneering governor, Juan Ponce de León (who died before he could move in), Casa Blanca is the oldest continuously occupied house in the western hemisphere. Today it's a historic monument containing a sparse museum and an Alhambra-style garden with a series of fountains. The interior rooms are furnished with antiques and paintings from the 16th and 17th centuries; the views of the bay from the 2nd floor are among the best in Old San Juan.

For the first 250 years after its construction, this simple colonial-era building served as the ancestral home for the de León family. In 1783 Casa Blanca was taken over by the Spanish military, then with the

Understand

Hurricanes Maria & Irma

In early September 2017, Puerto Rico anxiously prepared for two catastrophic hurricanes that threatened its shores. Hurricane Irma came first, wrecking the islands of Culebra and Vieques and causing serious damage and flooding along the country's northeastern coast. Just a week later, Hurricane Maria made a more direct impact, becoming the strongest hurricane to hit Puerto Rico in 89 years.

Maria left the island with massive destruction and serious flooding; its delicate electrical grid crumpled and thousands were left without power or water. Tourism is very important to Puerto Rico's economy, but the extent of the damage makes it hard to predict when the island will be back open for business; before you travel, check advice from state travel entities for information on any restrictions or significant closures.

Raíces Fountain, Paseo de la Princesa

change of Puerto Rico's political status in 1898, it provided a base for US military commanders until 1966.

Cuartel de Ballajá Notable Building

(☎787-721-3737; www.ballaja.com; cnr Norzagaray & Calle del Morro, Old San Juan; ⊙9am-noon & 1-4pm Tue-Sat, noon-5pm Sun) FREE Built in 1854 as a military barracks, the *cuartel* is an impressive three-story edifice with large gates on two ends, ample balconies, a series of arches and a protected central courtyard that served as a plaza and covers a reservoir. It was the last building constructed by the Spaniards in the New World. Facilities once included officers' quarters, warehouses, kitchens, dining rooms, prison cells and stables. A small but jam-packed exhibit outlines the history of the building; Spanish signage only.

Today the edifice houses several administrative offices, a dance studio, a music school, a cafe (p148) and the first-rate **Museo de las Américas** (Museum of the Americas; ☎787-724-5052; www.museolasamericas.org; adult/child US$6/4; ⊙9am-noon & 1-4pm Tue-Fri, 10am-5pm Sat, noon-5pm Sun).

Paseo de la Princesa Waterfront

(Walkway of the Princess; Old San Juan) Evoking a distinctly European feeling, the Paseo de la Princesa is a 19th-century esplanade just outside the city walls. Lined with antique streetlamps, trees, statues, benches, food vendors' carts and street entertainers, this romantic walkway ends at the magnificent **Raíces Fountain** (Roots Fountain), a stunning sculpture and water feature that depicts the island's eclectic Taíno, African and Spanish heritage. Festivals and fairs are often held here, including the weekend **artisans fair** (⊙noon-8pm Fri-Sun).

Plaza de Colón Square

(Columbus Plaza; cnr San Francisco & Tetuán, Old San Juan) Tracing its roots back more than a century to the 400-year anniversary of Columbus' first expedition, the Plaza de Colón is dominated by its towering statue of Columbus atop a pillar. Ringed with tall trees and outdoor cafes, the plaza sees a lot of action. The city wall at this end of Old San Juan was torn down in 1897 and the plaza stands on the site of one of the city's original gated entries, Puerta Santiago.

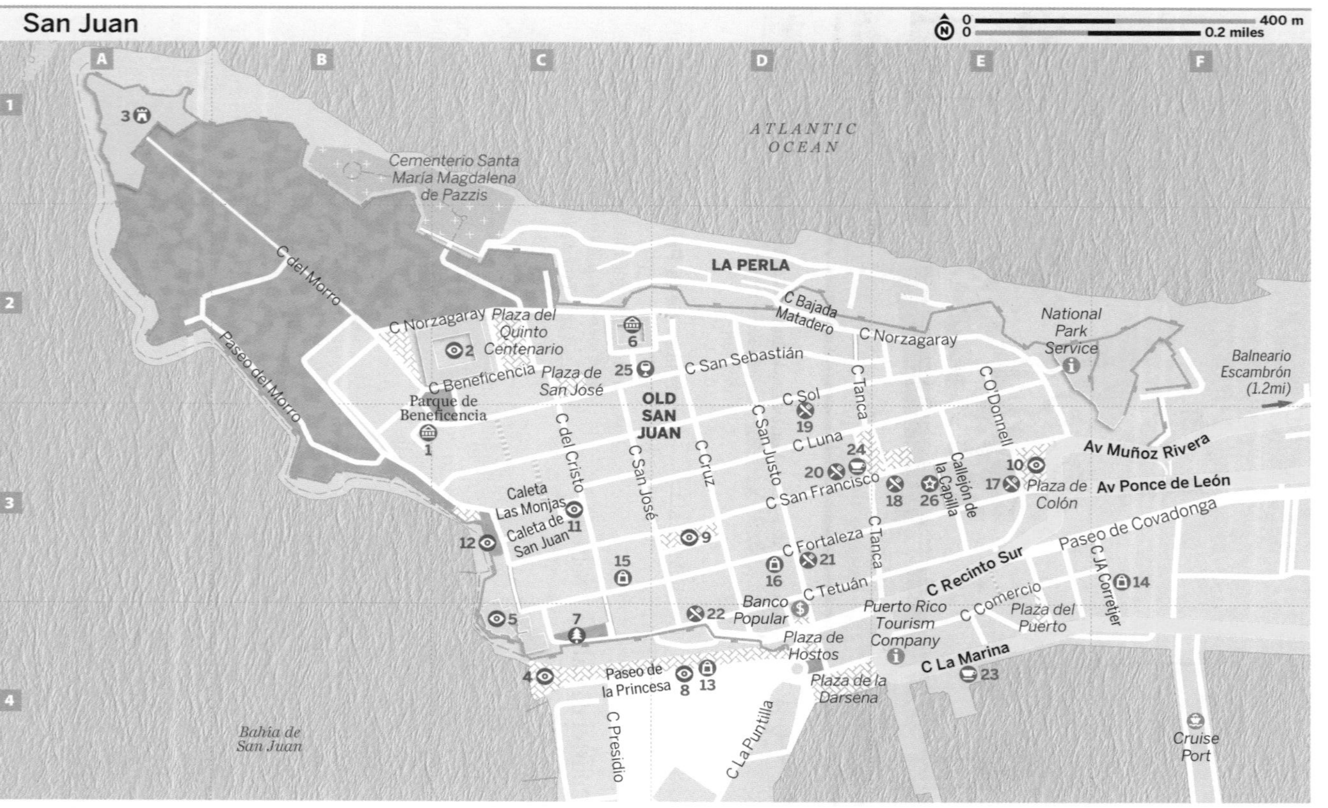
San Juan
0 400 m
0 0.2 miles
A B C D E F
1 2 3 4
ATLANTIC OCEAN
Cementerio Santa María Magdalena de Pazzis
LA PERLA
C del Morro
Paseo del Morro
C Norzagaray
Plaza del Quinto Centenario
C Beneficencia
Plaza de San José
Parque de Beneficencia
OLD SAN JUAN
C San Sebastián
C Bajada Matadero
National Park Service
Balneario Escambrón (1.2mi)
C Sol
C Tanca
C O'Donnell
C Luna
C del Cristo
C San José
C Cruz
C San Justo
C San Francisco
Callejón de la Capilla
Av Muñoz Rivera
Av Ponce de León
Plaza de Colón
Caleta Las Monjas
Caleta de San Juan
C Fortaleza
Paseo de Covadonga
C Recinto Sur
C JA Corretjer
C Tetuán
C Comercio
Banco Popular
Puerto Rico Tourism Company
Plaza del Puerto
Plaza de Hostos
C La Marina
Paseo de la Princesa
Plaza de la Darsena
Bahía de San Juan
C Presidio
C La Puntilla
Cruise Port
1 2 3 4 5 6 7 8 9 10 11 12 13 14 15 16 17 18 19 20 21 22 23 24 25 26

San Juan

Parque de las Palomas Park
(Pigeon Park; cnr Calle del Cristo & Tetuán, Old San Juan) On the southern end of Calle del Cristo, Parque de las Palomas is in a tree-shaded cobblestone courtyard on the top of the city wall, with brilliant views of Bahía de San Juan and the crisscrossing water traffic.

Paloma means 'dove' or 'pigeon' and it's the latter you'll encounter in the hundreds. With a lot more class than their often-scrabbling-about urban brethren, these pigeons fly in and out of dovecote-like holes in the wall and offer up a chorus of coos when at rest. Some folks come to the park just to feed them; small children come to chase them. Buy birdseed from a vendor by the gate.

ACTIVITIES

The glittering azure waters are an obvious draw for outdoor fun in San Juan. Beaches that open to the Atlantic are great for kitesurfing and surfing, while the reefs draw snorkelers and divers. The city's glassy lagoons and waterways are perfect for kayaking and paddleboarding. On land you can get out and about in the nearby green hills and mangrove forests.

Velauno Water Sports
(787-470-9099; www.velauno.com; 860 Av Ashford, Condado; 1hr paddleboard & kayak rental from US$25, tours from US$55; 9am-5pm) Velauno offers stand-up paddleboarding classes and rentals. It also has single and double kayak rentals and tours.

Pine Grove Surf Club Water Sports
(787-361-5531; www.pinegrovesurfclub.com; tours/lessons from US$35/45; 7am-6pm) Owned and operated by the friendly Nogales brothers, this operation offers fun surf lessons on Pine Grove beach, paddle-boarding tours in the lagoons of Piñones and snorkeling excursions off gorgeous Balneario Escambrón.

15 Knots Kitesurfing
(787-215-5667; www.15knots.com; Beach House Hotel, 4851 Av Isla Verde, Isla Verde; rental per hour from US$50, lessons from US$295; 10am-6pm) The often-gusty conditions off San Juan's beaches make the waters prime kitesurfing territory. This recommended outfit offers rentals and lessons.

Scuba Dogs Diving, Snorkeling
(787-783-6377; www.scubadogs.net; Parque del Tercer Milenio, Puerta de Tierra; dives from US$75; 9am-7pm Mon-Sat) This large, long-running outfit has been a tireless supporter of the offshore coral wonderland that is **Escambrón Marine Park** (off Av Muñoz Rivera, Puerta de Tierra; D53, T3, T5, T21). The Dogs offer gear rental, an array of shore and boat dive trips, plus training. Its shop is in Parque del Tercer Milenio.

Tanamá River Adventures Adventure Sports
(787-462-4121; www.tanamariveradventures.com; Hwy 111; tours US$65-100) Hiking, canyoning, caving, cave tubing...you name it, and if it utilizes the karst- and river-riddled terrain of Puerto Rico's Central Mountains, this outfit obliges.

TOURS

Excursiones Eco Tours
(787-565-0089; www.excursioneseco.com; walking/boat tours from $15/45) This community-oriented tour company offers various guided trips to lesser visited areas of San Juan, including boat tours through the city's lagoons and excursions into squatter communities and other economically underserved neighborhoods. Tours include historical background, flora and fauna details, and information about the current struggles faced in the city. Approximately 85% of all proceeds go directly to the guides themselves.

Old San Juan Farmers Market

Stop by this **market** (www.mercadoagricolanatural.com; Museo de San Juan, 150 Norzagaray, Old San Juan; snacks from US$2; 8am-1pm Sat; ; Fort, El Morro) in the courtyard of the Museo de San Juan to pick up some organic local produce or coffee, nibble on homemade chocolate, bread or cheese, peruse the handcrafted gifts or tuck into an inexpensive brunch.

Flavors of San Juan Food & Drink
(787-964-2447; www.sanjuanfoodtours.com; adult/child US$80/70) If eating your way around the Old Town is your style, Flavors of San Juan conducts three-hour walking tours that give you a tasty dose of the local cuisine. Rum tastings and a primer on prepping the popular dish *mofongo* folded in too.

SHOPPING

Popular Puerto Rican souvenirs include *santos* crafts, domino sets, *vejigante* masks, cigars, rum and coffee. The best arts and crafts shopping is in Old San Juan, though most of the schlocky T-shirt shops are there too. San Francisco and Fortaleza are packed cheek-by-jowl with shops while Calle del Cristo is home to many of the old city's more chic establishments.

Puerto Rican Art & Crafts Arts & Crafts
(787-725-5596; www.puertoricanart-crafts.com; 204 Fortaleza, Old San Juan; 10am-6pm Mon-Sat, noon-5pm Sun; City Hall) A large shop specializing in Puerto Rican folk art, paintings and jewelry. Items come from artist workshops found throughout the island. The prices are on the high end, but so is the quality.

Olé Clothing
(787-724-2445; www.olepuertorico.com; 105 Fortaleza, Old San Juan; 10am-6:30pm Mon-Sat; City Hall) Although it's beloved by tourists, this old-school hat shop is no tourist trap. As he has for generations, Guillermo Cristian Jeffs will custom-fit you

Güiro (musical instruments) for sale

for a truly authentic handwoven Panama hat (from $60).

Cigarros Antillas Cigars
(787-725-5481; Juan A Corretjer, Old San Juan; 9am-5pm; City Hall, Fort) Cigar fans should stop by the open storefront of Cigarros Antillas to see workers roll by hand. The shop specializes in medium cigars, sold in a variety of styles. Find it near Old San Juan's bus terminal.

EATING

Señor Paleta Ice Cream $
(787-724-2337; 153 Tetúan, Old San Juan; paletas US$3.50-5; 10:30am-6pm Tue, to 8:30pm Wed-Sun) Hole-in-the-wall selling artisanal *paletas* (popsicles) made from fresh fruits, nuts and other tasty treats. Flavors range from coconut, melon and *guanabana* (soursop fruit) to cheesecake, amaretto and pumpkin spice. Look for the sidewalk queue that grows longer as the day becomes hotter. The cool relief is well worth the wait.

La Bombonera Puerto Rican $
(787-705-3370; 259 San Francisco, Old San Juan; mains US$5-17; 7:30am-5pm Tue-Sun; ; City Hall, El Morro) This historic diner shines with a recent renovation including Tiffany stained-glass windows, marble-top tables and a gleaming bronze coffee machine. Even the waitstaff is gussied up in bow ties and bolero jackets. *Mallorcas* (a type of sweet bread), pastries and steaming cups of coffee are the favorites.

Manolín Puerto Rican $
(787-723-9743; www.cafemanolinoldsanjuan.com; 251 San Justo, Old San Juan; mains US$5-12; 6am-4:30pm Mon-Fri, 7am-4:30pm Sat, 8am-5pm Sun; ; City Hall, El Morro) Elbow in with the local office workers at this snaking grill and fill up on excellent *mofongo* (mashed plantains) and *churrasco a la parrilla* (skirt steak). Other all-star local fare on the menu includes garlic shrimp, pork chops and the delectable pistachio pudding. Breakfasts, especially the fluffy omelets, are worth crawling out of bed for – just get there by 10:30am.

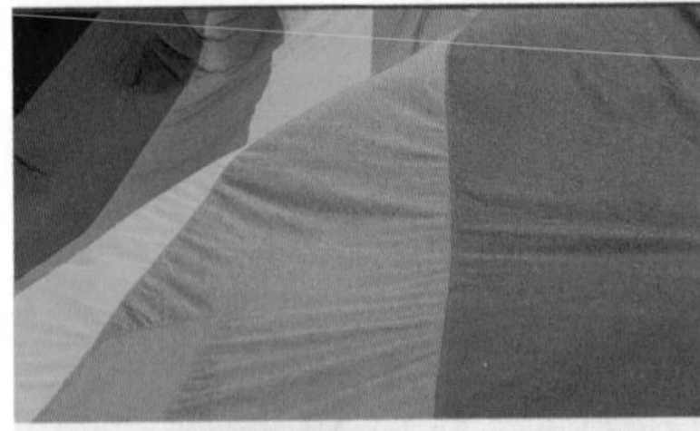

LGBTIQ San Juan

Considered to be the most gay-friendly destination in the Caribbean, San Juan has long buried its stereotypical macho image and replaced it with a culture known for its tolerance and openness.

Condado is an especially gay-friendly neighborhood. The beach at the end of Calle Vendig is a gay hangout and there are several popular cafes and restaurants nearby. For clubbing and cruising, edgy Santurce is where it's at, with new places opening all the time.

The annual **Puerto Rico Queer Filmfest** (www.puertoricoqueerfilmfest.com) takes place in mid-November; Pride events are held in early June.

Café Puerto Rico Puerto Rican **$$**

(☎787-724-2281; Plaza Colón, 208 O'Donnell, Old San Juan; mains US$12-24; ⏰11:30am-3:30pm & 5:30-10:45pm Mon-Sat, noon-9pm Sun; ❄🍷👪; 🚌Fort) An old-school restaurant with wood paneling and landscape art, Café Puerto Rico is where locals send you for *mofongo*. In this town, that's saying something. Available in yucca, green or sweet plantain, the *mofongo* comes sculpted into a bowl and stuffed with your choice of protein. The chicken in creamy garlic sauce is a fave.

El Jibarito Puerto Rican **$$**

(☎787-725-8375; www.eljibarito1977.com; 280 Sol, Old San Juan; mains US$10-27; ⏰10:30am-9pm; ❄👪) Welcome to the neighborhood, *hermano*. El Jibarito is the kind of mom-and-pop place you just know will serve a good and garlicky *mofongo* or *arroz con habichuelas* (rice and beans). Which it does. A favorite of local families and visitors, the meals are simple but hearty.

DRINKING & NIGHTLIFE

Finca Cialitos Coffee

(☎939-207-9998; www.fincacialitos.com; 267 San Francisco, Old San Juan; snacks from US$3; ⏰7:30am-4:30pm Tue-Fri, 8am-5pm Sat & Sun) Your best cup of San Juan Joe is at this cavernous yet cozy find. Beans for the brews here come from the family's coffee estate in the nearby lush hills and are roasted on-site. Friendly baristas, freshly baked pastries, simple sandwiches and comfy chairs.

Don Ruiz Coffee Shop Coffee

(☎787-723-1462; www.donruizstore.com; Cuartel de Ballajá, cnr Norzagaray & Calle del Morro, Old San Juan; snacks US$4-7; ⏰7:30am-6pm Mon-Fri, to 7pm Sat, 10:30am-6:30pm Sun) Among the many treasures inside the Cuartel de Ballajá is this fine little cafe which roasts its own coffee beans and specializes in a variety of brewing and pour-over methods. Sit outside in the historic courtyard or inside among the rich smells.

Café Cola'o Coffee

(☎787-725-4139; www.prcafecolao.com; Pier 2, Av La Marina, Old San Juan; snacks from US$3; ⏰6:30am-6pm Mon-Fri, 9am-7pm Sat & Sun; 🚌City Hall, El Morro) Café Cola'o is known for the outstanding handpicked coffee it serves from various small farms in Puerto Rico's Central Mountains. Ask baristas for recommendations – they have an encyclopedic knowledge of all things java. Pair your caffeine fix with a hot panino.

La Placita de Santurce Street Party

(Calle Dos Hermanos, Santurce; ⏰5pm-late Thu-Sat; 🚌T3, T5) Santurce's famous market – La Placita – is known as the hub of San Juan's hottest nightlife scenes. Especially good on Thursday and Friday nights, the historic market plaza and its surrounding streets host what becomes a veritable street party: people meeting up, drinking, eating and, as soon as the salsa band warms up, dancing until the wee hours.

La Taberna Lupulo Bar

(787-721-3772;150 San Sebastián,Old San Juan; noon-2am Sun-Thu, to 4am Fri & Sat) This beautiful old corner bar has been updated with Puerto Rico's best selection of microbrews. The lineup on the 50 taps is ever-changing and includes some of America's best and most unusual brews.

ENTERTAINMENT

Nuyorican Café Live Music

(787-977-1276; www.nuyoricancafepr.com; 312 San Francisco, Old San Juan; cover US$5; 8pm-late) If you have an evening in port and want to catch some sizzling salsa music, you'll find it at the Nuyorican Café. San Juan's hottest nightspot – stuffed into an alley off Fortaleza, opposite a nameless drinking hole – is a congenial hub of live Latino sounds and hip-gyrating locals. Six-piece salsa bands usually get hopping around 11pm.

INFORMATION

DANGERS & ANNOYANCES

Safety-wise, San Juan is comparable with any big city in mainland USA. Though you'll hear stories of muggings and thefts, the worst most visitors will face is tripping up on uneven sidewalks. Take all the usual precautions and you'll minimize any risk of trouble.

Never leave your belongings unguarded on the beach, don't leave your car unlocked and don't wander around after dark in deserted inner-city areas or on unpoliced beaches. Also hold off from wearing flashy jewelry or watches. Areas to avoid at night include Puerta de Tierra, parts of Santurce (especially around Calle Loíza) and the Plaza del Mercado in Río Piedras.

Old San Juan is relatively safe and well policed. However, the enclave of La Perla just outside the north wall is known for its drug-related crimes and can be unsafe at any time.

Plate of *mofongo*

MONEY

ATMs are found everywhere, most associated with full-service banks.

Banco Popular (www.popular.com; 206 Tetuán, Old San Juan; 8am-4pm Mon-Fri) Full-service locations and ATMs are found in most neighborhoods.

TOURIST INFORMATION

National Park Service (NPS; 787-729-6777; www.nps.gov; Fuerte San Cristóbal, 501 Norzagaray, Old San Juan; 9am-6pm) Oversees the San Juan National Historic Site, which includes the stunning El Morro and San Cristóbal forts.

Puerto Rico Tourism Company (PRTC; 800-223-6530, 787-721-2400; www.seepuertorico.com; 9am-5pm Mon-Fri, 10am-1pm Sat & Sun) Distributes information in English and Spanish near the cruise-ship terminal in **Old San Juan** (800-866-7827, 787-722-1709; Edificio Ochoa, 500 Tanca, Old San Juan; 8am-4pm Mon-Fri, 9am-5pm Sat; City Hall, Fort, El Morro).

GETTING AROUND

BICYCLE

With its unpredictable road conditions and drivers, San Juan can be a tough place to cycle. However, cyclists can navigate a pleasant and safe cross-city route by following the shoreline from Old San Juan through Condado and Isla Verde as far as Piñones (the last part is on a designated bike lane).

San Juan Bike Rentals (787-554-2453; www.sanjuanbikerental.com; rentals per day US$30; 7am-6pm Mon-Fri, 9am-4pm Sat) Rents a variety of well-maintained bikes, including mountain, road, hybrid and cruisers. All come with helmet, lock and bar bag. Free delivery and pick-up in metro San Juan.

PÚBLICOS

While there's no island-wide bus system, *públicos* (public vans) offer an alternative option, providing an inexpensive though often time-consuming link between San Juan and other major towns like Fajardo, Ponce or Mayagüez.

Público, San Juan

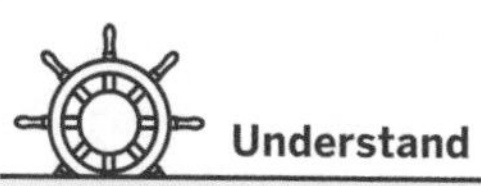

Understand

Fear & Loathing in San Juan

Long before *Fear and Loathing in Las Vegas* and the sharp, stylized prose that gave birth to 'Gonzo' journalism, US writer Hunter S Thompson earned a meager living in 1960 as a scribe for a fledgling Puerto Rican English-language weekly called *El Sportivo*, based in San Juan. It was a wild time in the city, with Americans flooding in from revolutionary Cuba. Thompson plunged into both this wild scene and innumerable bottles of rum, and was at the center of all the mayhem, until he decamped nine months later.

The essence of the era was later to emerge rather dramatically in his seminal book, *The Rum Diary*. Published in 1998 (nearly 40 years after it was written), the novel is a thinly veiled account of Thompson's alcohol-fuelled journalistic exploits as seen through the eyes of Paul Kemp, a struggling freelance writer caught in a Caribbean boomtown that was battling against an incoming tide of rich American tourists.

Hailed today – at least by Thompson fans – as a modern classic, the book was made into a 2011 movie starring Johnny Depp.

In San Juan, *público* centers include LMM international airport and the **Terminal de Carros Públicos** (787-294-2412; cnr Arzuaga & Vallejo) in Río Piedras. Vans leave once they're full and make frequent stops, dropping off and picking up passengers along the way. Service runs Monday through Saturday. Cash only.

TAXI

Taxi fares are set in the main tourism zones. From Old San Juan, trips to Condado, Ocean Park or Isla Grande Airport cost $12, and $19 to Isla Verde and Luis Muñoz Marín International Airport. Journeys within Old San Juan cost $7.

Outside of the major tourist areas, cab drivers are supposed to use meters, but that rarely happens. Insist on it, or establish a price from the start. Here's the math: meter rates are $1.75 initially and $1.90 per mile or part thereof, though the minimum fare is $3. You'll also pay a $2 gas surcharge per trip plus $1 for each piece of luggage. There's a $1 reservation charge; add a $1 surcharge between 10pm and 6am. And if there's more than five passengers, $2 per person is added. Taxis line up at the eastern end of Calle Fortaleza in Old San Juan; in other places you will likely need to call one. Try **Metro Taxi** (787-725-2870; 24hr) or **Rochdale Radio Taxi** (787-721-1900; www.taxiprrochdale.com; 24hr).

A growing alternative is to use drive share services like **Uber** (www.uber.com), a private car service offered by freelance drivers. Fares are cheaper than taxis and the service reliable; all fares are paid by credit card, using an app. In San Juan, the only places these drivers can't pick up passengers are the airports and hotels. They can drop off anywhere.

TROLLEY

A useful, if painfully slow, free **trolley service** (Fort/Green line 9am-6pm daily, El Morro/Blue & City Hall/Red lines 7am-7pm Mon-Fri, 9am-7pm Sat & Sun) links more than two dozen sights in Old San Juan. The three routes are served by buses styled like open-air trolleys, allowing you to hop on and off at the 26 stops. All routes pass by Pier 4 of the cruise-ship terminal along Calle La Marina. The trolley was suspended following hurricanes Maria and Irma and may be running on a limited schedule; check in advance.

/SHUTTERSTOCK ©

Charlotte Amalie (p164), St Thomas

US VIRGIN ISLANDS

In This Chapter

US Virgin Islands at a Glance

Most visitors arrive at the US Virgin Islands via St Thomas, and the place knows how to strike a first impression. Jungly cliffs poke high in the sky, red-hipped roofs blossom over the hills, all lapped by the turquoise yacht-dotted sea. St Thomas is the most commercialized of the Virgins, with big resorts galore, but it's also a fine island to sharpen your knife and fork, and kayak through mangrove lagoons.

With a Day in Port

- Take a ferry or catamaran to St John for a day of hiking and snorkeling. (p156)
- Enjoy sun and swimming at one of St Thomas' excellent beaches. (p160)
- Explore the chic stores at the Yacht Haven Grande marina, then take a gondola up to Paradise Point. (p164)

Best Places for...

Coffee MBW Cafe & Bakery (p167)

Local cuisine Cuzzin's Caribbean Restaurant & Bar (p167)

Cocktails Greenhouse (p168)

Ice cream Famous Delite Dairy Bar (p167)

St Thomas and St John were hit hard by hurricanes Irma and Maria (p300) in September 2017. While we have endeavoured to keep the information in this chapter as up-to-date as possible, some places may be affected while the community rebuilds.

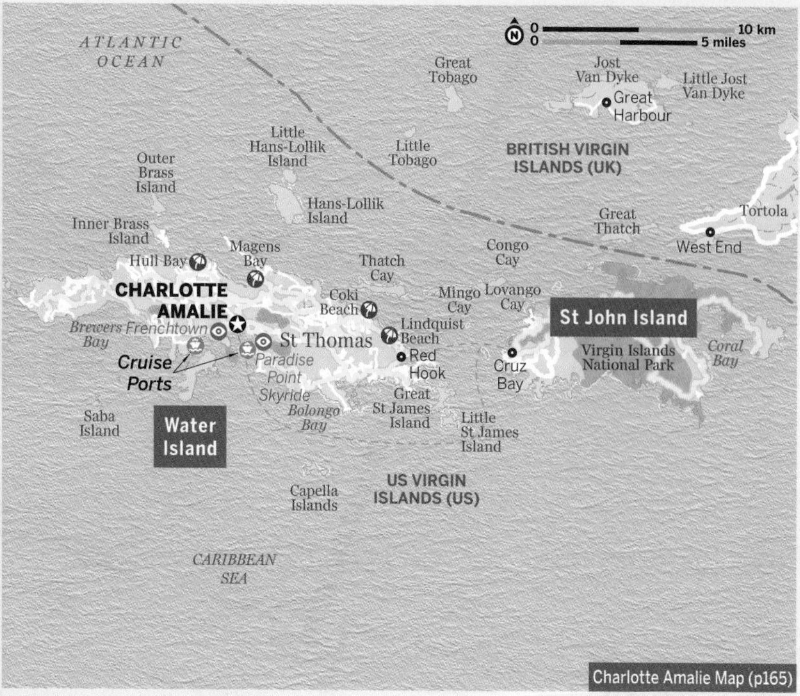

Charlotte Amalie Map (p165)

Getting from the Port

Most ships dock at the Havensight cruise port, about 2 miles east of downtown Charlotte Amalie. Another cruise port is located at Crown Bay, 2 miles west of Charlotte Amalie.

Safari taxis Open-air taxis with several rows of bench seating are the most popular way to get around St Thomas and usually cost about US$5 each way for anywhere in the Charlotte Amalie area.

Fast Facts

Currency US dollar (US$)

Languages English, French, Spanish

Money ATMs are common; most banks are open Monday to Friday.

Visas Not required for citizens of the US, EU or Australia.

Best for free wi-fi The Barefoot Buddha (p167).

Caneel Bay

St John Island

Two-thirds of St John is a protected national park, with gnarled trees and spiky cacti spilling over its edges. Hiking trails wind past petroglyphs and sugar-mill ruins, and several drop onto beaches prime for swimming with turtles and spotted eagle rays.

Great For...

Don't Miss

Hiking the forested trails in Virgins Island National Park to Honeymoon Beach and Caneel Bay Resort.

If you're looking to get a break from the crowds, take a ferry to this less-populated island with a relaxed local culture and more upscale development in general. The coast is dotted with little strips of secluded, beautiful, palm-lined beaches, many of them with fabulous snorkeling right offshore.

Hiking

Virgin Islands National Park maintains 20 trails, and any reasonably fit hiker can walk them safely without a local guide. For detailed information, go to the park website (www.nps.gov/viis), then click Plan Your Visit. The **Friends of the Park Store** (☎340-779-8700; www.friendsvinp.org; Mongoose Junction; ⏰9am-6pm) sells a terrific, more detailed map for US$3.

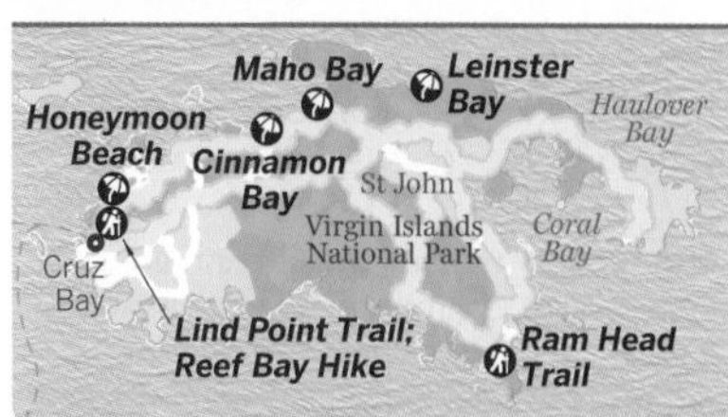

Explore Ashore

Water taxis (round-trip adult/child US$14/2) from Charlotte Amalie and Red Hook transport passengers to St John. The ferry takes 20 minutes each way; allow at least four hours total. On St John most taxis are multipassenger vans that cost US$5 to US$12 to take you anywhere on the island.

Need to Know

All ferries arrive in Cruz Bay; boats from St Thomas glide into the main ferry dock. The website www.seestjohn.com is an excellent resource, with detailed hiking-trail directions and beach guides.

If you prefer guided jaunts, the park sponsors several free ones, including birding expeditions and shore hikes, but its best-known offering is the **Reef Bay Hike** (340-693-7275; www.friendsvinp.org/hike; per person US$40; 9am-3pm Mon & Thu year-round, plus Tue & Fri Dec-Apr). Rangers lead the 3-mile downhill trek through tropical forests that takes in petroglyphs and plantation ruins and ends with a swim at Reef Bay's beach. The tour fee covers a taxi from the park's visitors center to the trailhead (about 5 miles from Cruz Bay) and a boat ride back. Book online or at the Friends of the Park Store.

One of the most accessible trails that you can tackle on your own is the **Lind Point Trail**. It departs from behind the national park visitors center and moseys for 1.1 miles through cactus and dry forest, past the occasional donkey and bananaquit, to Honeymoon Beach. A 0.4-mile upper track goes to Lind Battery, once a British gun emplacement, 160ft above the sea. The lower track goes directly to the beach. If you don't want to hike back, you can walk onward to the Caneel Bay Resort and catch a taxi.

These other favorite trails are each less than 3 miles round-trip; all have identifying signs at the trailheads:

Ram Head Rocky, uphill slog to a worth-every-drop-of-sweat clifftop view.

Leinster Bay Goes from the Annaberg sugar-mill ruins to fantastic snorkeling at Waterlemon Cay.

Cinnamon Bay () Easy loop trail that swings through tropical forest and mill ruins.

Snorkeling

The north shore is home to the island's best snorkeling spots. Our top three:

Leinster Bay Adjoins the old Annaberg sugar mill ruins. From the plantation's lot, follow the trail along the water for 25 minutes. The best snorkeling is at the bay's east end, offshore at Watermelon Cay, where turtles, spotted eagle rays, barracudas and nurse sharks swim. Be aware that the current can be strong. There are no amenities and usually few people out here.

Maho Bay The water is shallow and less choppy here than elsewhere (also good for kids) and it's a decent bet you'll see green sea turtles in the early morning or late afternoon, and maybe a stingray or two. There's a parking lot and changing room, but no other facilities. Maho can get crowded, but never overwhelmingly so.

Honeymoon Beach This beach is a mile's hike from the park visitors center along the Lind Point Trail. The handsome, white-sand strand is often empty and quiet – except on days when charter boats arrive between midmorning and midafternoon. A hut on-site sells snacks and rents chairs, hammocks, kayaks and other water-sports gear. Snorkeling is good off the west side, where tropical fish and turtles swarm over the coral reef.

Diving & Snorkeling Tours

Explore the colorful reefs and Caribbean sea life with a day of diving and snorkeling. Tours are available aboard power boats to get you out to those offshore dive spots in a hurry, or you can choose from a variety of sailboats and catamarans.

Don't Feed the Animals!

Whether you are hiking or driving on St John, it won't be long before you have a close encounter with the island's odd menagerie of feral animals. Hundreds of goats, donkeys, pigs and cats roam the island, descendants of domestic animals abandoned to the jungle eons ago. White-tailed deer and mongooses have also multiplied in unexpected numbers.

Often you'll see donkeys on Centerline Rd, where they'll come right up to your car and stick their snout in any open window.

Do not feed the animals and don't approach them for petting or taking a snapshot; they are all capable of aggression if provoked.

Cruz Bay Watersports Diving

(☎888-756-0631; www.cruzbaywatersports.com; 300a Chocolate Hole; 2-tank dive US$135; ⏰8am-6pm) Although damaged by Hurricane Irma, this company should be up and running for daily dives and snorkel trips around St John. It also offers sunset cruises and sailing jaunts to the British Virgin Island's Baths and Jost Van Dyke.

Low Key Watersports Diving

(☎340-693-8999; www.divelowkey.com; One Bay St; 2-tank dive US$125; ⏰8:30am-8pm Mon-Sat, to 6pm Sun) This is a great dive-training facility and has some of the most experienced instructors on the islands. It offers wreck dives to the RMS *Rhone,* as well as night dives and dive packages. It also has day-sail trips that go to either the Baths or Jost Van Dyke.

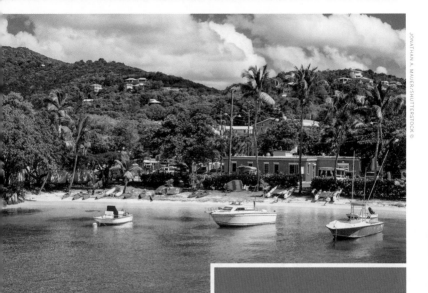

Away from most of the cruise crowds, St John is a peaceful island destination with national park hiking, beautiful beaches, watersports and a relaxed local culture

Clockwise from left: Scuba diving off St John; Cruz Bay; Sea turtle in St John harbor.

JONATHAN A. MAUER/SHUTTERSTOCK ©

LEFT: LEVENT KONUK/SHUTTERSTOCK ©, RIGHT: SHERRY CONKLIN/SHUTTERSTOCK ©

Magens Bay

/SHUTTERSTOCK ©

St Thomas' Best Beaches

Whether it's a secluded sandy strip tucked among palms and undeveloped coastline, or a sun-drenched stretch filled with visitors enjoying a party atmosphere, with more than 40 beaches St Thomas has the beach of your island dreams.

Great For...

Don't Miss

Walking the shore and swimming in the crystal-clear water at Lindquist Beach.

Lindquist Beach

Part of protected Smith Bay Park, this narrow **strand** (adult/child US$5/free) is a beauty all right: calm, true-blue water laps the soft white sand, while several cays shimmer in the distance. Hollywood has filmed several commercials here. There is a lifeguard, picnic tables and a bathhouse with showers, but no other amenities. It's low-key and lovely for a swim. Parking costs US$2 (cash only).

Magens Bay

The sugary mile that fringes heart-shaped **Magens Bay** (www.magensbayauthority.com; adult/child US$5/2; 8am-5pm;), 3 miles north of Charlotte Amalie, makes almost every travel publication's list of beautiful

Entrance to Coki Point Beach

/SHUTTERSTOCK ©

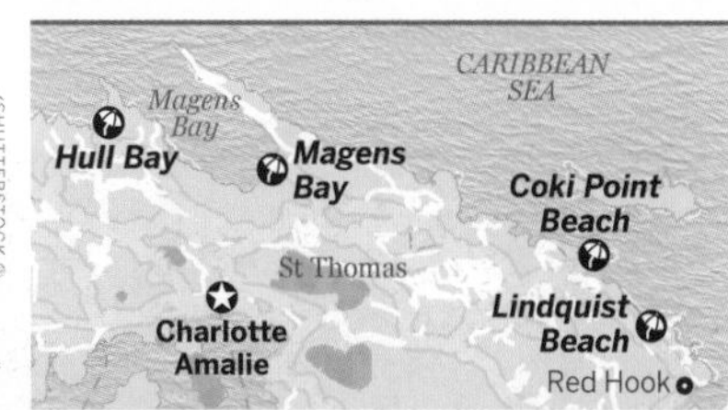

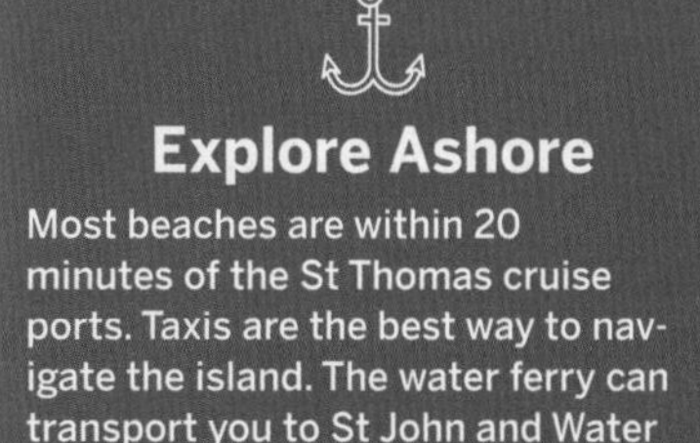

Explore Ashore

Most beaches are within 20 minutes of the St Thomas cruise ports. Taxis are the best way to navigate the island. The water ferry can transport you to St John and Water Island, where you'll find less crowded beaches.

Take a Break

Try the authentic Caribbean food at **De'Coal Pot**, a small restaurant just a short walk across Smith Bay Road from Lindquist Beach.

beaches. The seas here are calm, the bay broad and the surrounding green hills dramatic, and tourists mob the place to soak it all up. The beach has lifeguards, picnic tables, changing facilities, a taxi stand, food vendors and water-sports operators renting kayaks, paddleboards and paddleboats (US$20 to US$30 per hour).

A taxi from Charlotte Amalie costs US$10 per person. Parking costs US$2.

Coki Point Beach

Coki is on a protected cove at the entrance to Coral World Ocean Park. The snorkeling is excellent with lots of fish action, and you can dive from the shore with gear from the on-site dive shop. The narrow beach gets crowded with locals and tourists enjoying the eateries, hair-braiding vendors and loud music. A festive scene results. However, Coki is the one beach on St Thomas with touts – as soon as you arrive someone will quickly become your 'friend'.

Hull Bay

On the north coast and just west of Magens Bay, Hull Bay is usually a gem of solitude when Magens is overrun. The shady strand lies at the base of a steep valley and has a fun restaurant-bar but no other facilities. It's a locals' beach: fishers anchor their small boats here and dogs lope around. Hull Bay is also the island's surfing beach; the restaurant rents a couple of surfboards (US$35 per day). It's off the beaten path, so you'll need a car to get here.

Honeymoon Beach

Water Island

Water Island – sometimes called the 'Fourth Virgin' – floats spitting distance from Charlotte Amalie's trafficky bustle. But with only about 100 residents and very few cars or shops, it feels far more remote.

Great For...

Don't Miss

The excellent snorkeling right offshore.

Honeymoon Beach

The most popular site on the island is Honeymoon Beach, a half-mile stretch of bliss and the perfect chill spot if you're looking to escape the more crowded beaches on the mainland. It offers fine swimming and snorkeling in calm, shallow water. A couple of beach bars sell drinks, sandwiches and fish tacos, and one rents snorkel gear and kayaks. With the cruise ship in port, you'll have plenty of company but it's worth braving the crowds. Honeymoon is a 10-minute walk from the ferry dock. Follow the road uphill from the landing; when the road forks, go right and down the hill to the sand.

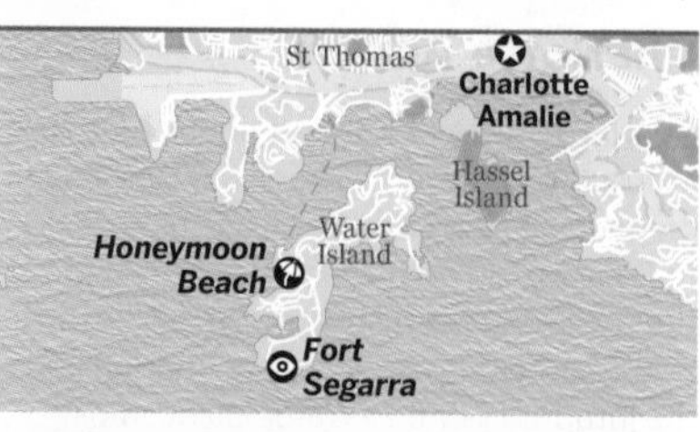

Explore Ashore

Take the Water Island Ferry from Crown Bay Marina to Water Island (10 minutes, adult/child US$14/2 round-trip). Honeymoon Beach is a short walk from the ferry dock at Water Island.

Need to Know

The ferry departs roughly every hour from outside Tickle's Dockside Pub.

Fort Segarra

WWII history buffs will love visiting this underground fort on the southern tip of the island. Explore the underground tunnels and rooms, and climb to the top of the fort and enjoy the panoramic views of the island from the observation deck.

Getting Around the Island

The entire island is only 2.5 miles tip to tip, and most people traverse it by foot, bike, or golf cart. Golf carts are available to rent at Phillips Landing, where the ferry from St Thomas docks.

Take a Break

Dinghy's Beach Bar & Grill (340-227-5525, Honeymoon Beach; wi-fi) is a welcoming tiki bar on Honeymoon Beach, where you can relax on a sunlounger with a cocktail or choose from a menu of burgers, wraps, tacos or quesadillas. You can also rent snorkeling gear, stand-up paddleboards and kayaks. Free wi-fi.

The smallest of the US Virgin Islands, Water Island was hit especially hard by Hurricane Irma in September 2017. Much of the vegetation and many homes were flattened by winds in excess of 150mph. But at the time of writing, locals were busy rebuilding, cleaning up the beaches, and the Water Island ferry was operating.

Charlotte Amalie

Charlotte Amalie stretches about 2.5 miles around St Thomas Harbor from Havensight on the east side (where cruise ships dock) to Frenchtown on the west side. Around the peninsula from Frenchtown lies Crown Bay, another cruise-ship-filled marina and the jump-off point to Water Island. Most visitors beeline to the historic downtown district, filled with duty-free shops and good local restaurants.

SIGHTS

Paradise Point Skyride Cable Car
(340-774-9809; www.ridetheview.com; adult/child US$21/10.50; 9am-5pm) Gondolas whisk visitors 700ft up Flag Hill to a scenic outlook. The ride takes seven minutes. At the top a restaurant, bar, gallery of shops and a short nature trail await. The chocolatey Bushwacker is the drink of choice while view-gaping. The tramway's base station is across the street from the Havensight cruise-ship dock and mall.

99 Steps Viewpoint
These stairs lead from Kongens Gade up into a canopy of trees at Blackbeard's Castle's foot. The steps, of which there are actually 103 (though you'll be too out of breath to count), were constructed using ship-ballast brick in the mid-18th century. The view at the top impresses. If you can, explore in the cool of the morning.

Blackbeard's Castle Historic Site
(www.blackbeardscastle.com; US$12; 9am-2pm by request) Set atop Government Hill, this five-story masonry watchtower was said to be the lookout post of pirate Edward Teach, alias Blackbeard, in the 18th century. Actually, historians don't lend much credence to the tale. What's known for certain is that colonial Danes built the tower as a military installation in 1678. You can climb up for good harbor views. It's only open on days cruise-ship groups request it.

Emancipation Garden Park
(Tolbod Gade) Emancipation Garden is where the emancipation proclamation was

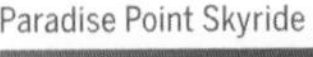
Paradise Point Skyride

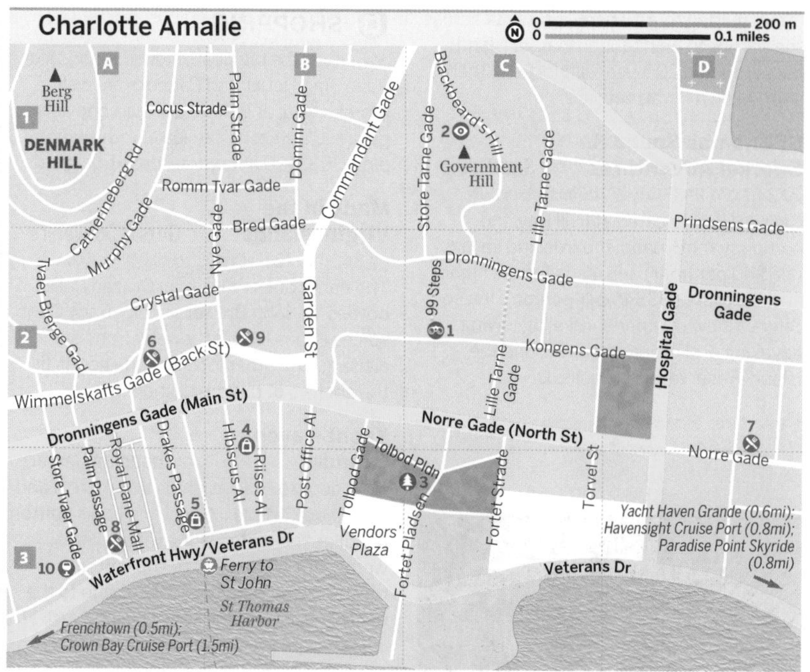

Charlotte Amalie

Sights
1 99 Steps C2
2 Blackbeard's Castle C1
3 Emancipation Garden C3

Shopping
4 AH Riise B2
5 Made in the Virgin Islands A3

Eating
6 Cuzzin's Caribbean Restaurant & Bar A2
7 Daylight Bakery & Diamond Barrel D2
8 Gladys' Cafe A3
9 MBW Cafe & Bakery B2

Drinking & Nightlife
10 Greenhouse A3

read after slaves were freed on St Croix in 1848. Carnival celebrations and concerts take place here, but mostly folks kick back under trees with a fruit smoothie from the Vendors' Plaza next door.

Frenchtown Area

The island's 'Frenchies,' aka Huguenots who immigrated to St Thomas from St-Barthélemy during the mid-19th century, populated this community of brightly painted frame houses on the harbor's western side. Nowadays the fishers' neighborhood has several good restaurants that overlook the water.

To get here from town, take a taxi (US$4 per person) or walk west on Waterfront Hwy past the Seaplane Terminal and turn left just past the post office. It's about a 1-mile jaunt from Emancipation Garden.

ACTIVITIES & TOURS

Virgin Islands Ecotours Kayaking

(340-779-2155; www.viecotours.com; Frenchtown; 3hr tour US$89) The Frenchtown outpost of the local adventure company offers guided tours where you kayak across the harbor to uninhabited Hassel Island, hike around a 200-year-old fort and then snorkel on a coral reef.

St Thomas Scuba & Snorkel Adventures Snorkeling

(☎340-474-9332; www.stthomasadventures.com; Hull Bay) Located at Hull Bay, the company rents paddleboards and kayaks (US$30 per hour) and leads terrific night snorkel tours (US$45 per person). It also offers a slew of other snorkeling, diving, kayaking and hiking jaunts around the island. Reservations required.

SHOPPING

Jewelry is the big deal in town. Brands like Rolex, Tag Heuer and Pandora are well represented, and there are diamond sellers galore. US citizens can leave with a whopping US$1600 in tax-free, duty-free goods.

Made in the Virgin Islands Gifts & Souvenirs

(☎340-776-7822; Drakes Passage; ⊙10am-4pm) The name doesn't lie: mini Cruzan Rum bottles, St John Brewers beer, Sunny Carib spices (from Tortola), jewelry from island artisans and other locally made goods fill the shelves of this small shop.

Yacht Haven Grande Shopping Center

Next door to Havensight is this marina and chic shop complex. Gucci and Louis Vuitton headline the roster, along with several waterfront bistros where you can sip cosmos and watch megayachts drift in to the dock. A **farmers market** (⊙10am-2pm, 1st & 3rd Sun) with produce and crafts sets up on the grounds every other Sunday.

AH Riise Mall

(☎340-777-2222; www.ahriise.com; 37 Main St) This is the famous mall that most visitors beeline to, where you can buy everything from watches and jewels to tobacco and liquor.

EATING

Daylight Bakery & Diamond Barrel Caribbean $

(☎340-776-1414; 18 Norre Gade; items US$2-5; ⊙6am-6pm Mon-Sat) It's mostly locals who visit this friendly spot at downtown's edge. If you can get past the guava tarts, sugar cakes and dum bread (flour sweetened with coconut and baked in a 'dum' oven), pans of okra, fish stew, fungi (semihard cornmeal pudding) and more island dishes await. Point to your choice behind the glass case, and servers heap it into a styrofoam clamshell.

Music of the USVI

Reggae and calypso tunes blast from USVI vehicles and emanate from shops, restaurants and beach bars. *Quelbe* and fungi (*foon*-ghee, also an island food made of cornmeal) are two types of folk music. *Quelbe* blends jigs, quadrilles, military fife and African drum music with lyrics (often biting satire) from slave field songs. Fungi uses homemade percussion such as washboards, ribbed gourds and conch shells to accompany a singer. The best time to experience island music is during the 'jump up' parades and competitions associated with major festivals such as Carnival on St Thomas and St John, or at St Croix' Cruzan Christmas Fiesta.

CATHLEEN A CLAPPER/SHUTTERSTOCK ©

ELIJAH LOVKOFF/SHUTTERSTOCK ©

Charlotte Amalie shopping district

MBW Cafe & Bakery Cafe $

(☎340-715-2767; www.mbwcafeandbakery.com; Back St; sandwiches US$6-13; ⏰7am-4pm) MBW stands for My Brother's Workshop, a nonprofit group that helps at-risk youth learn a trade. At the cheery cafe, teens bake the wares and run the place. The egg-filled breakfast sandwiches are a good deal, and the muffins and cake slices appease sugar addicts. Lots of locals hang out at the tables in back of the cafe.

Barefoot Buddha Cafe $

(☎340-777-3668; www.barefootbuddhavi.com; 9715 Estate Thomas; breakfast US$4-11, sandwiches US$8-11; ⏰7am-6pm Mon-Sat, 8am-3pm Sun; 📶🌶) The island's yoga-philes hang out at yin-yang decorated wood tables, tucking into healthy specials such as the blackened tofu wrap and the everyday list of toasted sandwiches (go for the hummus and rosemary goat's cheese). The Buddha is also popular for breakfast, thanks to the long list of organic coffee drinks and egg sandwiches. It's near Havensight's cruise dock.

Famous Delite Dairy Bar Ice Cream $

(☎340-777-6050; www.facebook.com/famousdelite; milkshakes US$5.50-7; ⏰12:30-6:30pm Mon, from 10:30am Tue-Sat, from 11:30am Sun; 👪) A 15-minute (uphill) walk from Magens Bay, Famous Delite whips up awesome milkshakes. Adults can get their creamy goodness spiked with booze.

Cuzzin's Caribbean Restaurant & Bar Caribbean $$

(☎340-777-4711; 7 Back St; mains US$13-22; ⏰11am-4:30pm Mon-Sat) With exposed-brick walls, burnished wood furnishings and red-clothed tables, classy-but-casual Cuzzin's is a favorite stop for West Indian cuisine. Try the conch (a local shellfish) curried, buttered or Creole-style, or the catch of the day alongside fungi, fried plantains and a rum-laden cocktail.

Gladys' Cafe Caribbean $$

(☎340-774-6604; www.gladyscafe.com; 5600 Royal Dane Mall; mains US$13-22; ⏰7am-5pm Mon-Sat, 8am-3pm Sun) With the stereo blaring beside her, Gladys belts out Tina Turner

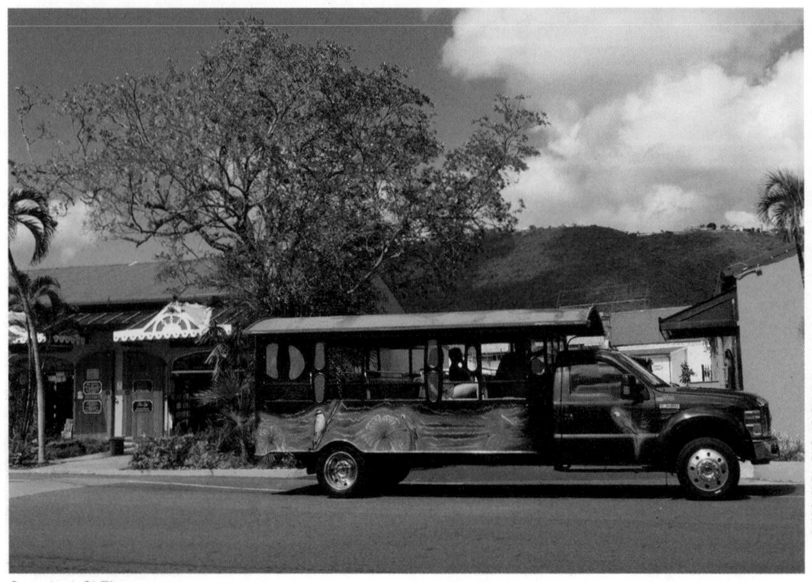

Open taxi, St Thomas

tunes while serving some of the best West Indian food around. Locals and tourists pile in for her callaloo, fungi, Ole Wife (triggerfish), fried plantains and sweet potatoes. Gladys' homemade hot sauces (for sale at the front) make a fine souvenir.

DRINKING & NIGHTLIFE

Frenchtown Brewing Microbrewery

(☎340-642-2800; www.frenchtownbrewing.com; Frenchtown; ⏰5:30-7:30pm Wed & Fri, 1-5pm Sat) The brewery is indeed micro: it's only open a few days per week, it only brews a couple of beers and they're only on tap here. Beer buffs will want to seek it out for the Belgian-style Frenchie Farmhouse Saison and Hop Alley IPA. Tours are available; call to make an appointment if you want to visit outside regular hours.

Greenhouse Pub

(☎340-774-7998; www.thegreenhouserestaurant.com; Waterfront Hwy; mains US$12-29; ⏰11am-9pm; 📶) Cavernous, open-air Greenhouse overlooks the harbor and rocks hard during happy hour (4:30pm to 7pm, when drinks are two for the price of one). The cuisine is predictable American pub fare, but the menu is extensive, with burgers, pizzas and seafood. When everything else downtown closes by 5pm, Greenhouse is the one reliable place still open.

INFORMATION

There is no official tourist office downtown, but the free *St Thomas/St John This Week* magazine has maps and everything else you'll need.

Crime is an issue on St Thomas. It is best to avoid straying too far outside the tourist business district of Charlotte Amalie if exploring on foot in town.

Understand

Environmental Issues Facing the US Virgin Islands

The US Virgin Islands have long suffered from environmental problems, including deforestation, soil erosion, mangrove destruction and a lack of freshwater. During the 18th century, logging operations denuded many of the islands to make room for plantations. The demise of the agricultural economy in the late 19th century allowed the islands to reforest, and in recent years locals (especially on St John) have begun several forest-conservation projects.

But population growth and rapid urbanization continue to pose grave threats. If not for the desalination plants (which make freshwater out of seawater) the islands couldn't support even a quarter of their population, let alone visitors. When a hurricane strikes, power and desalination facilities shut down. Islanders with enough foresight and money keep rainwater cisterns for such emergencies, but folks without suffer.

Rising sea temperatures are another topic of concern, as they impact local reefs and cause coral bleaching. In 2005, a particularly 'hot' period killed about half of the USVI's coral. Another widespread bleaching event occurred in 2010.

Prior years of overfishing have put conch in a precarious situation. Currently, conch fishing is not allowed from July through October so stocks can replenish.

 GETTING AROUND

BOAT

The **Marine Terminal** (Waterfront Hwy) is a 10-minute walk west of downtown. It's a hub for ferries to Tortola and Virgin Gorda. A ferry to St John departs downtown at the foot of Raadets Gade at 10am, 1pm and 5:30pm daily (cash only).

BUS

'Dollar' buses (aka 'safaris'; US$2) mosey along Waterfront Hwy. To get on, wave your hand to flag them down. To get off, press the buzzer when you reach your destination.

TAXI

Taxis will take you to the shopping in downtown Charlotte Amelie (US$5) from the cruise ports, or to the Water Ferry at Red Hook (US$10).

Taxis huddle around the Vendors' Plaza. The following are the set, per-person rates from downtown: Frenchtown (US$4), Havensight (US$6), Magens Bay (US$10), Red Hook (US$13).

MARIDAV/SHUTTERSTOCK ©

View from Brimstone Hill Fortress National Park (p174)

ST KITTS & NEVIS

In This Chapter

St Kitts & Nevis at a Glance

Near perfect packages – that's how you might think of St Kitts and Nevis. The two-island nation combines beaches with beauteous mountains, activities to engage your body and rich history to engage your mind. The local culture is mellow, friendly and infused with a pulsing soca beat. But if the pair offer much that's similar, they differ in the details. St Kitts is larger and feels that way, from bustling Basseterre and mighty Brimstone Hill Fortress to the party strip and resorts of Frigate Bay. Across the Narrows, tranquil Nevis is a neater package, anchored by a single volcanic mountain buttressed by a handful of beaches and a tiny colonial capital, Charlestown.

With a Day in Port

- Ride the ferry to Nevis for a day of adventure and secluded beaches. (p176)
- Explore historic Brimstone Hill Fort, then swim at Cockleshell Beach. (p174)
- Ride the St Kitts Scenic Railway that loops the coast of St Kitts. (p178)

Best Places for...

Coffee Cafe des Arts (p183)

Cocktails Sunshine's Beach Bar & Grill (p177)

Local cuisine El Fredo's (p181)

St Kitts and Nevis were damaged by Hurricane Maria and Irma (p300) in September 2017. While we have endeavoured to keep the information in this chapter as up-to-date as possible, some places may still be affected while the community rebuilds.

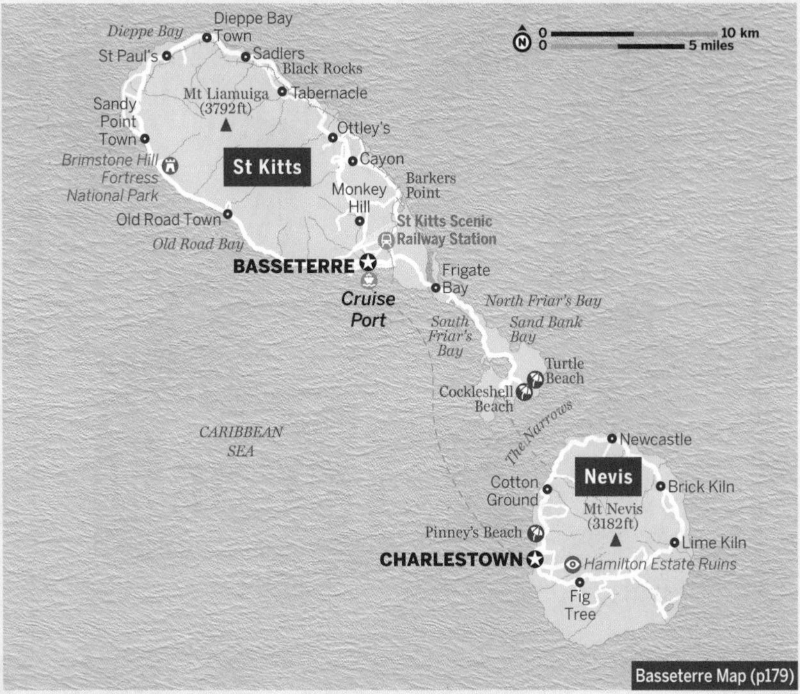

Dieppe Bay
Dieppe Bay Town
St Paul's
Sadlers
Black Rocks
Tabernacle
Mt Liamuiga (3792ft)
Sandy Point Town
Ottley's
Brimstone Hill Fortress National Park
St Kitts
Cayon
Monkey Hill
Barkers Point
Old Road Town
St Kitts Scenic Railway Station
Old Road Bay
BASSETERRE
Cruise Port
Frigate Bay
North Friar's Bay
South Friar's Bay
Sand Bank Bay
Turtle Beach
Cockleshell Beach
The Narrows
CARIBBEAN SEA
Newcastle
Nevis
Cotton Ground
Brick Kiln
Mt Nevis (3182ft)
Pinney's Beach
Lime Kiln
CHARLESTOWN
Hamilton Estate Ruins
Fig Tree
0 10 km
0 5 miles

Basseterre Map (p179)

Getting from the Port

Cruise ships dock at the terminal on the south end of St Kitts in Basseterre. Shops, restaurants, and bars are just a short walk from the ship, but taxis are readily available and cost US$5 per person to get anywhere within Basseterre.

The ferry terminal with departures to Nevis is within walking distance of the cruise port, less than a quarter mile.

Fast Facts

Currency East Caribbean dollar (EC$), US dollar (US$) is widely accepted

Language English

Money ATMs are common; most banks are open Monday to Friday.

Visas Not required for citizens of the US, EU or Australia.

Best for free wi-fi Most coffee shops and restaurants near the cruise port offer wi-fi with a purchase.

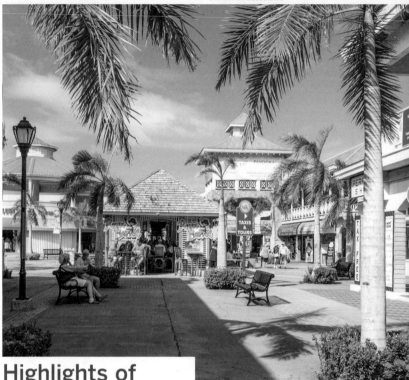

Downtown Basseterre

Highlights of St Kitts

St Kitts definitely has a beat, and it's not just the one blasting from the many minibuses hauling folks hither and yon. Highlights include exploring bustling Basseterre, the Unesco-recognized Brimstone Hill Fortress National Park and nearby beaches.

Great For...

Don't Miss

Visiting Brimstone Hill Fortress and walking Turtle Beach on Cockleshell Bay.

Explore the shopping district at the foot of Port Zante docks or learn a thing or two at historic Brimstone Hill. Of St Kitts' beaches, Cockleshell Beach is the most popular.

Cockleshell Beach

Enjoy great views of Nevis across the Narrows on this pretty but often busy crescent of white powdery sand with calm and shallow waters and several bars, restaurants and water-sports concessionaires.

Brimstone Hill Fortress National Park

Even if you're not a fan of military anything, this massive **hilltop compound** (☎869-465-2609; www.brimstonehillfortress.org; adult/child US$10/5, audio guide US$5; ⏰9:30am-5:30pm) with its citadels, bastions, barracks and ramparts will likely leave

Brimstone Hill Fortress National Park

JASON PATRICK ROSS/SHUTTERSTOCK ©

CARIBBEAN SEA
St Kitts
Brimstone Hill Fortress National Park
Basseterre
Cockleshell Beach
Turtle Beach
Nevis

a lasting impression. The British began construction in 1690 and, using slave labor, kept refining it for about a century. In 1999 it became a Unesco World Heritage site.

Start by watching the 10-minute video on the history of the island and the construction of the fortress, then wander up to polygonal Fort George to stand on the gun deck, take in the views and imagine the cannons firing all the way out to sea. One floor below are exhibits on the construction of the fortress, life at the fort, slavery, punishment and other topics, along with a re-created barrack room. For a more in-depth experience, pick up an audio guide at the ticket gate. The fortress sits at the end of a steep 0.75-mile-long road. Catch a taxi at the port and take the 35-minute ride north to the fort. A two-hour taxi tour will cost US$50 round-trip for up to four passengers.

Explore Ashore

Taxis (US$4 to US$30 for most popular destinations from the cruise port, one-way for up to four passengers) can be hired at the end of the cruise-ship dock and will take you anywhere in St Kitts.

Need to Know

Safari-taxi tours, readily available from Port Zante, cost US$30 to US$80. A one-hour tour will take you around half of the island, visiting sights in Basseterre, Caribelle Batik and Brimstone Hill.

Basseterre

On the southwestern coast of St Kitts, Basseterre has long been an important commercial hub in the Caribbean. The town is laid out in a simple grid pattern, making it easy to navigate, and most sights are within walking distance of the cruise docks. Passengers interested in shopping will want to visit the Circus, the town's main tourist shopping center.

Diving

Explore the colorful reef wall dives at Monkey Shoals, Black Coral Reef, and Green Point Reef. Nevis has a stunning swim-through dive at Devil's Canyon and reef dives at Clyde's Reef and the Ledge. Or submerge for a wreck dive at the famous M/V *River Taw*, a 144-foot tanker.

Pinney's Beach

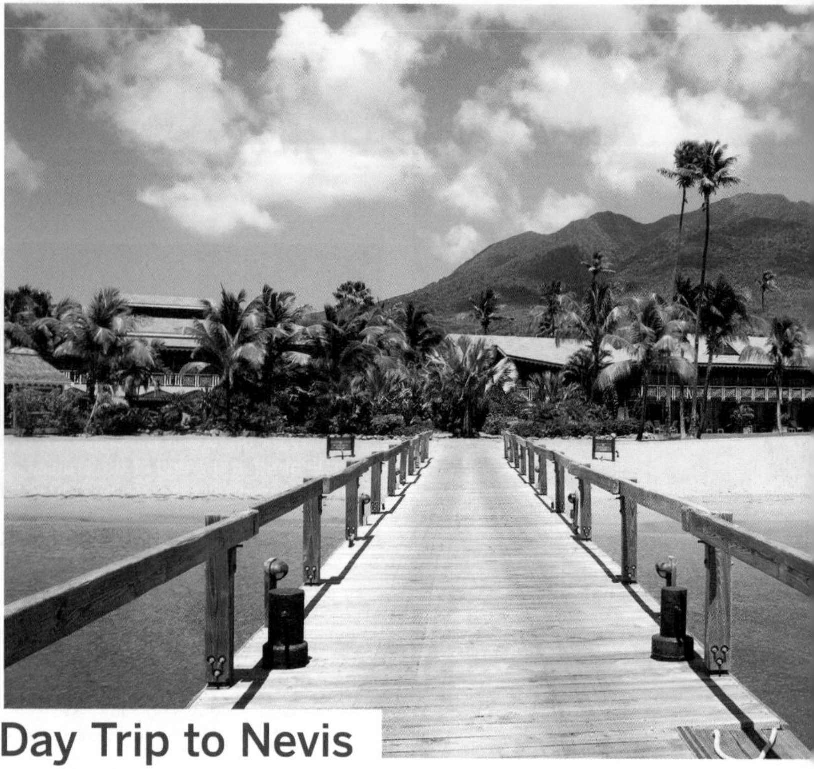

Day Trip to Nevis

Coin-shaped Nevis (nay-vis) is sprinkled with rustic charm and infused with a keen historical awareness and appreciation. Many visitors come here just for the day but wish they could stay longer. The ferry ride from St Kitts deters some travelers from venturing to the neighboring island, but the trip is well worth the time.

Great For...

Don't Miss

Soaking up the sun and local culture on Pinneys Beach.

Nevis offers respite from the tourist crowds as well as access to beautiful, secluded beaches and miles of hiking trails through lush rainforest on the slopes of Nevis Peak, the conical volcano that gives the island its shape.

Breakfast with a View

After the ferry journey to Nevis, you can grab a taxi and head to the swanky **Four Seasons Resort** (☎869-469-1111; www.fourseasons.com/nevis; Pinney's Beach) for a wonderful breakfast on its open-air terrace with a remarkable view of Pinney's Beach and the Caribbean Sea beyond. The food is as good as the view. Try the splendid breakfast buffet with tropical fruits, juices, and pastries, or indulge in the Caribbean flavors that accompany island delights like Belgian waffles with whipped cream and piña-colada

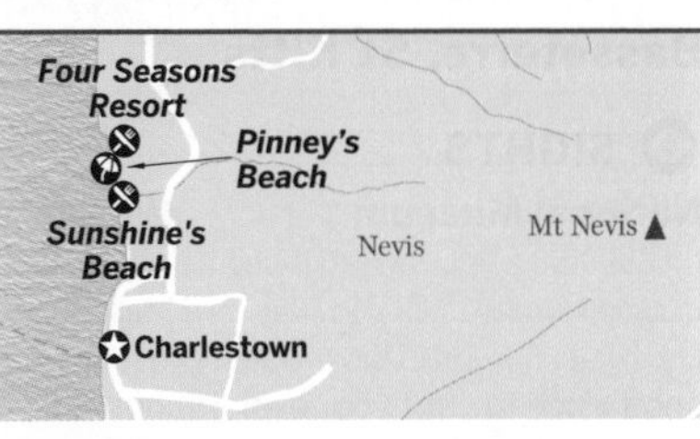

Explore Ashore

Take the ferry (one-way adult/child US$10/5, 45 minutes) from Basseterre on St Kitts to Charlestown on Nevis. Nevis is small enough that you can walk everywhere, but taxis are available from the ferry port.

Need to Know

Allow five hours for a trip to Nevis, which includes breakfast at the Four Seasons and about two hours on Pinney's Beach with drinks at Sunshine's.

sauce or island curry scrambled eggs with mango chutney.

Pinney's Beach

This 3-mile-long stretch of tan sand along the west coast has decent snorkeling right offshore. The northern end is punctuated by the Four Seasons resort and several beach bars, but quiet patches abound. Walk to the southern end of the beach and get on island time at Sunshine's, a relaxed beachfront restaurant and bar serving some of the best drinks and food on the island. Sundays are busiest.

Lunch at Sunshine's

The legendary rum-and-reggae joint **Sunshine's Beach Bar & Grill** (869-469-5817; www.sunshinesnevis.com; Pinney's Beach; mains lunch US$8-15, dinner US$15-30; 11am-late) has been getting people in a party mood for decades. A cold Carib goes well with its 'secret sauce'–marinated grilled ribs and chicken, but the signature 'Killer Bee' rum punch demands your respect: its 'sting' has been documented by hundreds of photos decorating the walls. The beach and Caribbean Sea is just steps away, so bring your swim gear, towel, and sunscreen for a full day of tropical fun.

Charlestown

The tiny island capital (p182) is worth a visit for its colonial history and brightly colored buildings. Learn about the island's past at the Museums of Nevis History, the Horatio Nelson Museum or the site of Bath Hotel – said to be the first hotel in the Caribbean.

Basseterre, St Kitts

SIGHTS

National Museum Museum

(☎869-466-2744; www.stkittsheritage.com; Bay Rd; adult/under 12yr EC$8/free; ⊙9:15am-5pm Mon-Fri, to 1pm Sat) This modest museum is a good place to start your explorations of St Kitts. Displays deal with colonial and sugar history, the road to independence, and local lifestyle and traditions. It's housed in the 1894 Old Treasury Building, a stately pile built from hand-cut volcanic limestone.

Independence Square Square

Locals 'lime' and exchange gossip on this grassy patch anchored by a circular fountain crowned by three topless nymphs.

The Discovery of St Kitts

The island known today as St Kitts was called Liamuiga (Fertile Island) by the Caribs, who arrived around AD 1300 and chased out the peaceable agrarian bands who'd been in the area for hundreds of years. When Columbus sighted the island on his second voyage to the New World, in 1493, he named it St Christopher after his patron saint, later shortened to 'St Kitts'.

Columbus used the Spanish word for 'snow' (*nieve*), to name Nevis, presumably because the clouds shrouding its mountain reminded him of a snow-capped peak. Caribs knew the island as Oualie (Land of Beautiful Waters).

Once called Pall Mall Sq, it was used in the 1790s for slave auctions and is bordered by a few 18th-century Georgian buildings and the dignified cathedral.

Immaculate Conception Cathedral Church

(Independence Sq; ⊙hours vary) This hulking gray-stone house of worship has a barrel-vaulted wooden ceiling evoking a ship's hull. Sunlight filters through elaborate stained-glass windows above an altar made of multihued marble.

St George's Anglican Church Church

(☎869-465-2167; www.facebook.com/stgeorgewithstbarnabasstkitts; Cayon St; ⊙hours vary) In a small park behind a fence, this red-roofed church has a stormy history. French Jesuits built the first one in 1670, but it was destroyed by fire, an earthquake and a hurricane, and rebuilt three times, the last time in 1869. The tower can be climbed and the cemetery has some fancy epitaphs.

Circus Square

The focus of town is the Circus, a roundabout inspired by London's Piccadilly Circus. Anchored by a green clock tower, the Victorian-style Berkeley Memorial Clock, it is surrounded by quaint buildings housing shops and banks. The terrace of the Ballahoo restaurant is a great vantage point for people-watching.

ACTIVITIES & TOURS

St Kitts Scenic Railway Rail

(☎869-465-7263; www.stkittsscenicrailway.com; Needsmust train station; adult/child from US$89/44.50; ⊙Dec-Apr) This cheerfully painted historic train previously transported sugarcane from the plantations to the factory in Basseterre. Today, it takes tourists along 18 miles of the original tracks, followed by a 12-mile bus ride. The upper deck is great for sightseeing and the lower deck has air-con. The entire trip takes three hours. The terminal is near the airport.

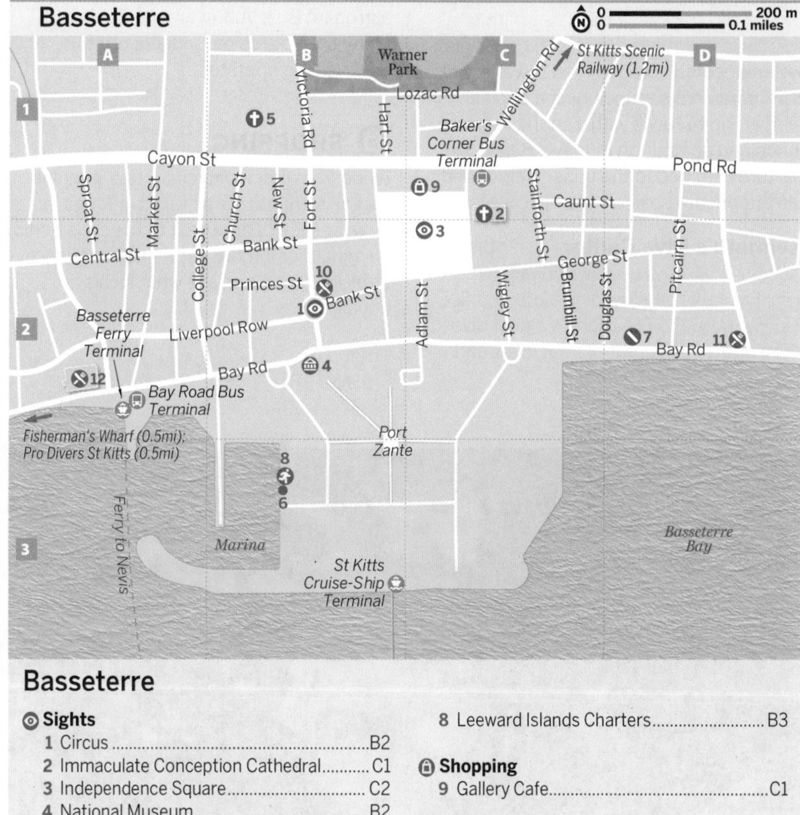

Basseterre

Sights

1 Circus ... B2
2 Immaculate Conception Cathedral ... C1
3 Independence Square ... C2
4 National Museum ... B2
5 St George's Anglican Church ... B1

Activities, Courses & Tours

6 Blue Water Safaris ... B3
7 Kenneth's Dive Center ... D2
8 Leeward Islands Charters ... B3

Shopping

9 Gallery Cafe ... C1

Eating

10 Ballahoo ... B2
11 El Fredo's ... D2
12 Farmers' Market ... A2

Pro Divers St Kitts Diving
(869-660-3483; www.prodiversstkitts.com; Fisherman's Wharf, Fort Thomas Rd; 2-tank dive incl gear US$115; closed 3 weeks Aug) Owner Austin and his team have explored every nook and cranny of the Kittitian underwater world, and offer the gamut of underwater experiences for novice to veteran divers as well as all levels of certification courses. Rates include all gear and transportation.

Leeward Islands Charters Boating
(869-465-7474; www.leewardislandscharterssstkitts.com) This class act offers a range of options, including a three-hour Sail and Snorkel trip for US$45 (Nevis departures US$62); a full day of sailing, snorkeling, drinks and beach barbecue for US$87; and two-hour sunset cruises for US$50. Boats leave from Port Zante Marina on St Kitts or the Four Seasons pier on Nevis.

Blue Water Safaris Boating
(☎869-466-4933; www.bluewatersafaris.com; Port Zante Marina; full-day cruise US$95) This well-respected company runs a variety of catamaran cruises, including a popular all-day trip to Nevis with a snorkeling stop, lunch and an hour on Pinney's Beach. Departures are tied to the cruise-ship schedule but private charters are also available.

Kenneth's Dive Center Diving
(☎869-465-2670; www.kennethdivecenter.com; Bay Rd; 2-tank dive from US$110; ⊙office 8am-5pm Mon-Fri) The island's oldest dive shop offers the gamut of boat dives and PADI certification courses, and has counted astronaut Buzz Aldrin among its clients. Many cruise-ship passengers use this experienced operator.

SHOPPING

Aside from liquor and cigarettes, genuine bargains are as rare as tulips in Tonga in duty-free Port Zante next to the cruise-ship terminal. For a more authentic experience, stroll into town and see what locals are buying.

Understand

Wild Vervet Monkeys

You'll see them on the beach, the trail and the golf course – packs of wild vervet monkeys brought from Africa to St Kitts and Nevis by French settlers in the 17th century. Since then, they have flourished, outnumbering humans two to one. They may look cute and are even used in promoting the islands to tourists, but to local farmers they're a nightmare because of their ravenous appetite for fruit and vegetable crops.

In order to get the problem under control, a nonprofit company called Arnova Sustainable Future has partnered with the Department of Agriculture to set up feeding stations on the upper slopes to curb the incentive to come down from the mountain to forage for food at lower-lying farms. Other planned measures include a spay and neuter program as well as taste, smell and hearing aversions.

Meanwhile, according to the Animal Rights Foundation of Florida, another way to decimate the Kittitian monkey population is by trapping and selling the animals to medical research and testing laboratories worldwide. Two such facilities on St Kitts also use local monkeys in their research.

Batik workshop, St Kitts

Gallery Cafe Gallery
(869-765-5994; www.facebook.com/TheGalleryCafeOnTheSquare; 10 N Independence Sq; 9am-4pm Mon-Sat) This gallery in an attractive 18th-century colonial cottage showcases paintings, pottery, jewelry and other crafts by local artists.

EATING

Central Basseterre brims with small local eateries that get flooded at lunchtime and often sell out by 2pm. Food trucks and street-food stalls set up around Port Zante, especially on cruise-ship days.

El Fredo's Caribbean $
(869-466-8871; www.facebook.com/ElFredosRestaurantandBar; cnr Bay & Sanddown Rds; mains EC$20-35; 11am-4pm Mon-Sat) Every day, there are some Kittitian faves cooking in the kitchen of this local lunchtime hot spot, be it creole snapper and garlic shrimp or more challenging pigtail soup and goat stew, all paired with a potpourri of provisions. The setting is classic Caribbean cool but the homemade sauce is hot!

Farmers' Market Market $
(Bay Rd; Mon, Wed & Sat mornings) Bag great pictures and bargain-priced fresh produce and fish at Basseterre's tin-roofed market, which is busiest on Saturday morning.

Fisherman's Wharf Seafood $$
(869-466-5535; www.fishermanswharfstkitts.com; Fort Thomas Rd; mains EC$40-115; 6:30-9:30pm Mon-Sat; P) Enjoy sweeping views of sparkling Basseterre from your table on the deck of this breezy alfresco dining spot, where an open charcoal fire tickles fresh snapper, lobster and other piscine delights to juicy perfection. All produce and seafood are sourced locally.

Ballahoo Caribbean $$
(869-465-4197; www.ballahoo.net; Circus; mains EC$29-65; 8am-3pm Mon-Wed, to 9pm Thu-Sat) From its 1st-floor perch, Ballahoo has great people-watching from terrace tables overlooking the Circus roundabout. It's a dependably good hangout no matter where the hands of the clock, with menu standouts including conch chowder and oven-roasted lamb.

GETTING AROUND

Buses heading up the west coast as far as St Paul's leave from the **Bay Road bus terminal** (Bay Rd) next to the ferry terminal, while buses heading east as far Saddlers leave from **Baker's Corner bus terminal** (Cayon St).

Charlestown, Nevis

Nevis' toy-town-sized capital has narrow streets that are steeped in colonial history and lined with both brightly painted gingerbread Victorians and Georgian stone buildings. It's well worth strolling up and down the main street with its banks, businesses, tourist office, bars and restaurants. At night the town all but shuts down.

SIGHTS

Museum of Nevis History Museum

(Hamilton House; 869-469-5786; www.nevisheritage.org; Main St; adult/child US$5/2; 8:30am-4pm Mon-Fri, 9am-noon Sat) American statesman Alexander Hamilton (1757–1804) was many things in his short life: soldier, lawyer, author of the *Federalist Papers*, US founding father, the country's first Secretary of the Treasury and, finally, the victim of a fatal duel with his political nemesis Aaron Burr. He was also born – scandalously out of wedlock – in or near the restored 1840 stone building that today contains a modest museum that chronicles his rags-to-riches career.

Horatio Nelson Museum Museum

(869-469-0408; www.nevisheritage.org; Building Hill Rd; adult/child US$5/2; 9am-4pm Mon-Fri, to noon Sat) This small museum trains its focus on Horatio Nelson, the British naval commander who married a local widow, Fanny Nisbet, in 1787 and met his demise at the Battle of Trafalgar in 1805. An endearing collection of maps, paintings, documents, busts, and memorabilia help tell his story.

Hamilton Estate Ruins Historic Site

(24hr) FREE Enjoy views of Charlestown from this romantically ruined sugar estate, which is being reclaimed by the jungle. Wander among the foundations of the Great House, the windmill, the boiling house and the chimney. It's hard to find, so ask for directions at the tourist office or go with a guide.

Jewish Cemetery Cemetery

(cnr Government Rd & Jew St; 24hr) FREE This modest cemetery is all that's left of the Jewish legacy that has its roots in the early 18th century when scores of Jews arrived on Nevis' shores after being expelled by the Portuguese from Brazil. They brought with them knowledge about the cultivation of sugarcane and thus changed the local economy forever. The oldest gravestone dates to 1674.

Bath Hotel Historic Site

Built in 1778, this venerable structure lays claim to the title of 'first hotel in the Caribbean' and was the hub of Nevisian social life through the 19th century. A who's who of politicians, crowned heads and the merely moneyed were drawn by its lavish gardens, fanciful dining rooms and hot thermal springs. It now houses government offices.

EATING & DRINKING

A good selection of local eateries awaits in Charlestown in the day time. Most places shut down after dark when the Chinese takeaways are pretty much your only option.

Wilma's Diner Caribbean $

(869-663-8010; www.facebook.com/Wilmasdiner; Main St; mains lunch EC$47, dinner US$40; 11am-3pm Mon-Sat) The gracious Wilma is a wizard in the kitchen and dishes out a daily-changing menu of hearty local fare like barbecue pork ribs or stewed chicken in her quaint and green-trimmed cottage next to the police station. A more fanciful three-course dinner is available by reservation only. Call at least one day ahead.

Understand

Geography, Flora & Fauna

Both islands have grassy coastal areas, a consequence of deforestation for sugar production. Forests tend to be second-growth or vestiges of the large rainforests that once covered much of the islands.

Away from developed areas, the climate allows a huge array of beautiful plants to thrive, especially on Nevis. Flowers such as plumeria, hibiscus and chains-of-love are common along roadsides and in gardens.

Nevis is fairly circular and the entire island benefits from runoff from Nevis Peak. St Kitts' shape resembles a tadpole. The main body is irrigated by water from the mountain ranges. However, this is of little value to the geographically isolated, arid southeast peninsula, which is covered with sparse, desertlike cacti and yucca.

Aside from the vervet monkey, another ubiquitous creature is the mongoose, imported from Jamaica by plantation owners to rid their sugarcane fields of snakes. Both islands provide plenty of avian life for birdwatchers.

Reefs around the two islands face the same threats as elsewhere in the region. On St Kitts, some of the best reefs ring the southeast peninsula.

Cafe des Arts Cafe $

(☎869-667-8768; www.facebook.com/thecafedesarts; Bayfront, Samuel Hunkins Blvd; sandwiches EC$20-40; ⏰8:15am-2pm or later Mon-Sat Nov-May; P 📶) Infused with charming boho flair and set in a little banana-tree–shaded park by the sea, this colorful outdoor cafe does brisk business with its cooked breakfasts and freshly made sandwiches, salads and quiches. Locals roll in on Tuesdays after 6pm for the ritual burger bonanza.

Octagon Bar Caribbean

(☎869-469-0673; Samuel Hunkins Blvd; dishes EC$8-18; ⏰11am-8pm; 📶) For a big dose of local color, belly up to this outdoor bar on the waterfront or order one of its cheap, simple lunches (salt fish, johnnycakes, chicken stew etc) and chow down amid trippy mermaid and dolphin murals on the shaded patio.

Baie de Marigot

ST-MARTIN/ SINT MAARTEN

In This Chapter

St-Martin/Sint Maarten at a Glance

The world's smallest area of land divided into two nations, this half-French, half-Dutch island's fascinating cultural mix incorporates a rich African heritage and 120 different nationalities speaking 80-plus languages, giving rise to some of the finest cuisine in the Caribbean. A major cruise-ship port and air hub, St-Martin/Sint Maarten boasts 37 white-sand, palm-fringed beaches, from busy stretches lined with pumping bars to tranquil hidden bays and coves. Water sports from snorkeling and diving to jet skiing abound, along with land-based adventures like hiking and treetop ziplining.

With a Day in Port

- Walk to Great Bay Beach and bask in the sun with drink service direct to your sun lounger. (p188)
- Explore the shopping in Philipsburg, then take a taxi to Orient Beach to beat the crowds. (p192)

Best Places for...

Coffee La Croissanterie (p201)

Cocktails Ocean Lounge Restaurant & Bar (p198)

Local cuisine Enoch's Place (p201)

St-Martin/Sint Maarten suffered severe damage during Hurricane Irma (p100) in September 2017. While we have endeavoured to keep the information in this chapter as up-to-date as possible, some places may still be affected while the community rebuilds.

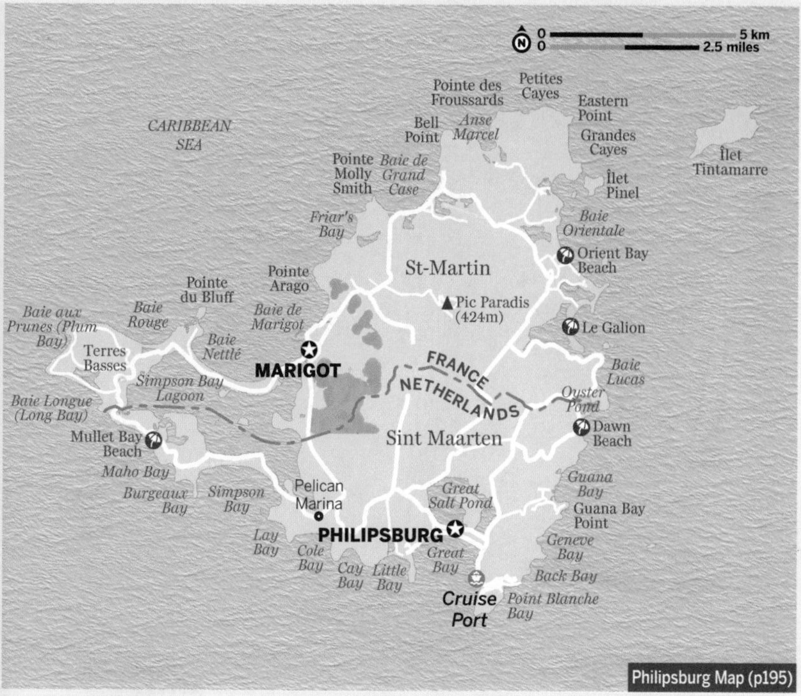

0 5 km
0 2.5 miles
CARIBBEAN SEA
Pointe des Froussards
Petites Cayes
Eastern Point
Bell Point
Anse Marcel
Grandes Cayes
Îlet Tintamarre
Pointe Molly Smith
Baie de Grand Case
Îlet Pinel
Friar's Bay
Baie Orientale
Orient Bay Beach
St-Martin
Pointe du Bluff
Pointe Arago
Pic Paradis (424m)
Baie aux Prunes (Plum Bay)
Baie Rouge
Baie de Marigot
Le Galion
Terres Basses
Baie Nettlé
MARIGOT
FRANCE
NETHERLANDS
Baie Lucas
Simpson Bay Lagoon
Oyster Pond
Baie Longue (Long Bay)
Dawn Beach
Mullet Bay Beach
Sint Maarten
Maho Bay
Guana Bay
Burgeaux Bay
Simpson Bay
Pelican Marina
Great Salt Pond
Guana Bay Point
Lay Bay
PHILIPSBURG
Geneve Bay
Cole Bay
Cay Bay
Little Bay
Great Bay
Back Bay
Cruise Port
Point Blanche Bay

Philipsburg Map (p195)

Getting from the Port

Ships dock in Philipsburg, just a short walk from shops, cafes and the excellent Great Bay Beach. Taxis can drop you off at the beach or take you anywhere in Philipsburg for US$5 to US$10. You can also purchase a water taxi all-day pass for US$7, and ride the fast boats back and forth between Great Bay Beach and your ship.

Fast Facts

Currency Sint Maarten – Netherlands Antilles guilder (NAf); St-Martin – euros (€); US dollar (US$) widely accepted

Language English, Dutch, French

Money ATMs are common; most banks are open Monday to Friday.

Visas Not required for citizens of the US, EU or Australia.

Best for free wi-fi The Greenhouse (p198) and Ocean Lounge Restaurant (p198) offer wi-fi with a purchase.

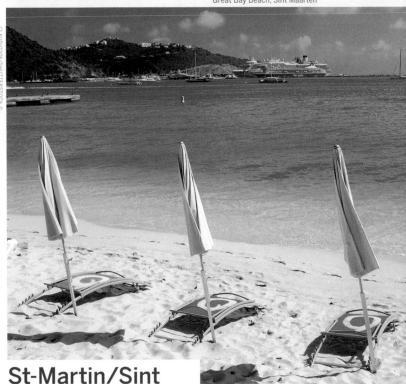

Great Bay Beach, Sint Maarten

St-Martin/Sint Maarten Beaches

The island is known for its beautiful beaches, and with one a short walk from the ship (Great Bay Beach) it's easy to have a little fun in the sun.

Great For...

Don't Miss

The southern end of Orient Bay Beach for an escape from the crowds.

Great Bay Beach

One of the best beaches in the Caribbean and conveniently within a short walk of the cruise port, Great Bay Beach has everything you need: chairs for rent, drink and snack service right to your lounger, good swimming, watersport rentals. Shops, restaurants, and bars line the seaside boardwalk, a wide pedestrian walkway that's easily accessible by wheelchair. It's easy to make a day of sipping cocktails with intermittent excursions to seek shade and souvenirs in the nearby storefronts. Make sure to sample some of the excellent cuisine at some of the finest French restaurants this side of the Atlantic. The city is kept exceptionally clean, especially the areas closest to the beach, and the French/Dutch influence is evident, making you feel as if you're wandering the mazelike

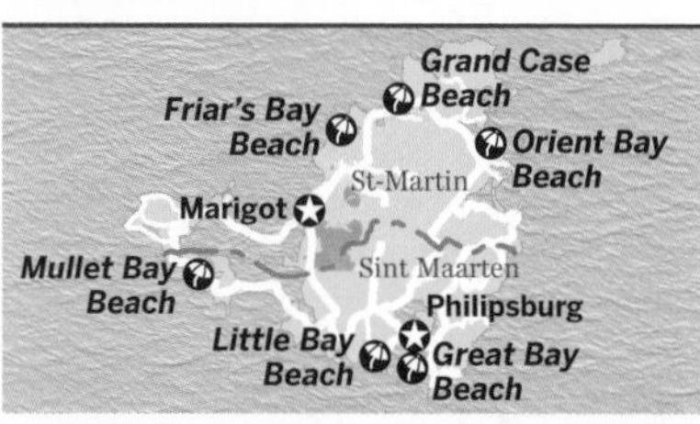

Explore Ashore

Great Bay Beach is within walking distance of the cruise port. A taxi to Orient Bay Beach takes 25 minutes and costs around US$20 for two people. Allow at least three hours for Great Bay Beach and four hours for Orient Bay Beach. A two-tank dive will require a minimum of four hours for transportation and diving time.

Need to Know

You can rent two chairs and a beach umbrella on Great Bay Beach for around US$10.

cityscape of some colorful, coastal village in Southern France. The beach is can get crowded when cruise ships are in port so if you're looking for a bit of solitude, head to Orient Bay Beach, Grand Case, Friar's Bay, or one of the many smaller beaches on the island.

Mullet Bay

Mullet Bay is not only home to the island's only **golf course** (545-2801; www.thetowersatmulletbay.com; Rhine Rd; green fees/cart/club rental US$40/40/30; sunrise-sunset), it's also the best spot to catch a wave. This local surf spot often has strong riptides, so use caution when swimming. The wide, sandy beach is lined with palm trees and close to several snack and beach bars.

Neighboring Maho Beach is popular, but since a beach goer was injured by a jet-engine blast of a plane taking-off from the adjacent airport, we don't recommend it.

Grand Case

Grand Case is a mile-long beach of white sand that curves along the coastline. Nearby is a shopping and dining district known for excellent Caribbean and French restaurants and shops. The water is calm and great for swimming, and there is good snorkeling off the shore along the reefs. Beach bars and shops are just a short walk from the shore, but it may be hard to leave the beach chair with the beautiful views of Creole Rock.

Little Bay Beach

Just south of Great Bay Beach ittle Bay Beach is a small slice of Caribbean beach heaven that is intimate and convenient to beach bars, restaurants, and watersport rentals.

Friar's Bay Beach

Friar's Bay Beach is north of Marigot and one of the best beaches on the island for swimming. The calm water makes it an excellent choice for cruisers traveling with children. The palm-lined beach was hit hard by Hurricane Irma, but the beach reopened quickly. Unfortunately, the beach bars and restaurants here were destroyed in the storm. One thing that hasn't changed is this beach's amazing view of the nearby island of Anguilla.

Orient Bay Beach

Snorkel-friendly reefs protect 5.5km of inviting white-sand beach at Orient Beach Bay, and while this sandy strand has become a busy resort area filled with beach bars, restaurants, resort and water-sports operators, its southern end is quieter and a favorite spot for nudists.

Diving & Snorkeling St-Martin

The island offers an excellent array of dive and snorkel sites that accommodate beginners to advanced divers. The best dive sites include the wrecks of the HMS Proselyte, a 32-gun Royal Navy frigate, and the Carib Cargo where you can swim with stingrays and other aquatic life as you explore the wreckage. There's excellent reef snorkeling at Mullet Bay, Friar's Bay, and Simpson's Bay. Boat tours will often take snorkelers to the Anse Marcel Reef or Creole Rock.

THIERRY DEHOVE/SHUTTERSTOCK ©

Life's a beach on St-Martin/Sint Maarten with a string of beautiful stretches of golden sand and plenty of watersports.

LEFT: THIERRY DEHOVE/SHUTTERSTOCK ©; RIGHT: RARESORZATA/GETTY IMAGES ©

Clockwise from left: Windsurfing off St-Martin/Sint Maarten; Grand Case Beach, St-Martin; Sugarcane juice

Philipsburg Historic Walk

Explore historic and charming Philipsburg and discover the French, Dutch and Caribbean cultural influences that make this easily accessible cruise port one of the most popular and well-loved along the Caribbean cruising routes.

Start cruise ship port
Distance 2.1km (1.3-miles)
Duration 3 hours

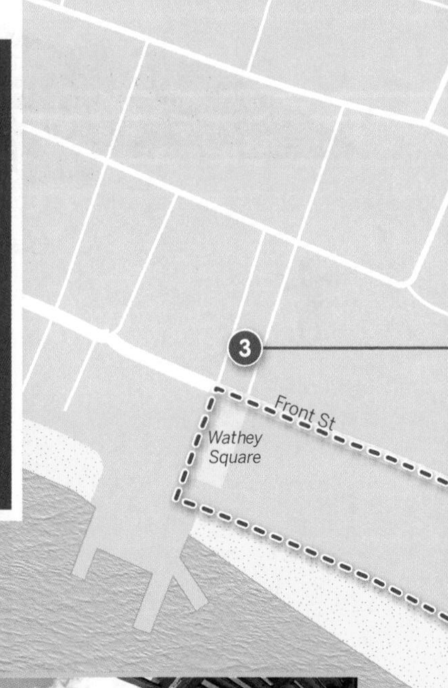

2 Continue to Great Bay Beach and grab a beach lounger or walk the Boardwalk in search of beach bars, restaurants and shops. Try **Ocean Lounge** (p114) for cocktails with a beach view.

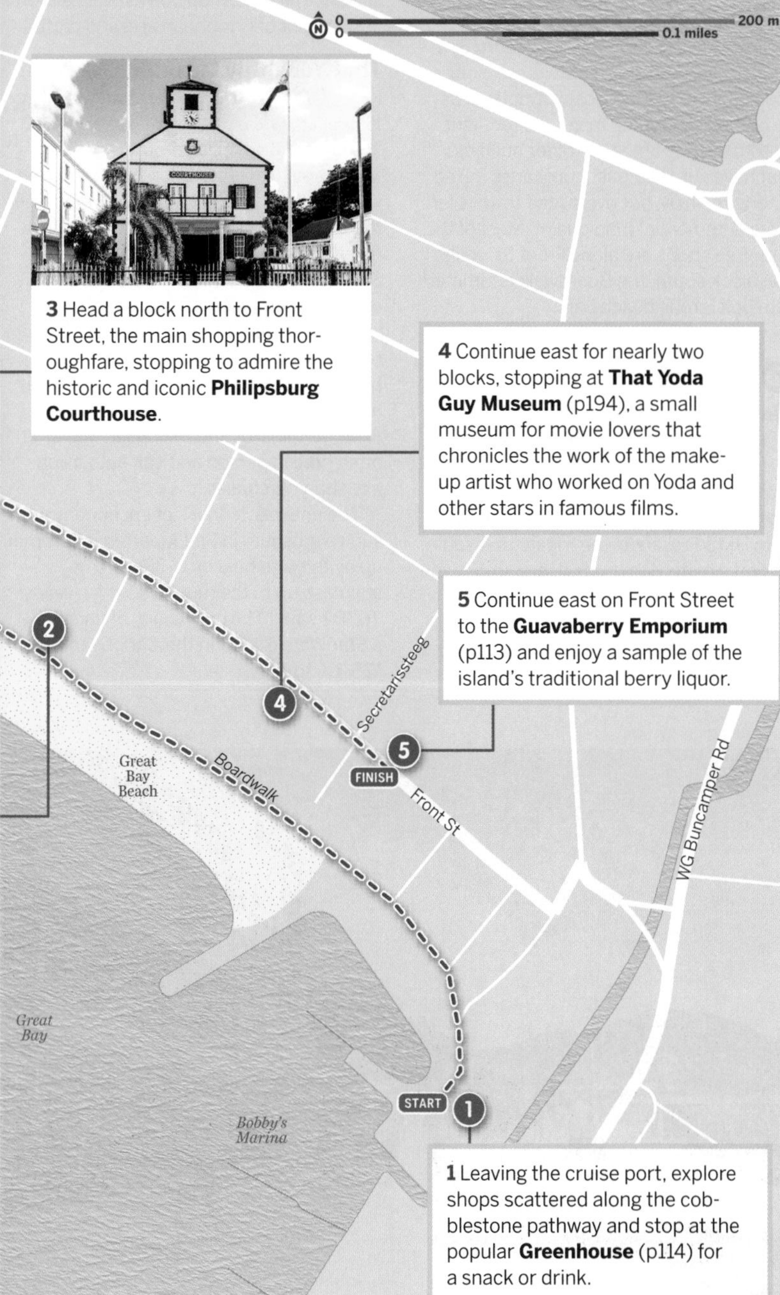

3 Head a block north to Front Street, the main shopping thoroughfare, stopping to admire the historic and iconic **Philipsburg Courthouse**.

4 Continue east for nearly two blocks, stopping at **That Yoda Guy Museum** (p194), a small museum for movie lovers that chronicles the work of the make-up artist who worked on Yoda and other stars in famous films.

5 Continue east on Front Street to the **Guavaberry Emporium** (p113) and enjoy a sample of the island's traditional berry liquor.

1 Leaving the cruise port, explore shops scattered along the cobblestone pathway and stop at the popular **Greenhouse** (p114) for a snack or drink.

Philipsburg, Sint Maarten

Philipsburg, the capital of St-Martin/Sint Maarten's Dutch side, sprawls out along a wide arcing bay that mostly functions as an outdoor shopping mall (and red-light district). There are some older buildings that have survived past hurricanes mixed among the new, but overall the town is far more commercial than quaint. Most of the duty-free shops are along Front St, while one block south, the Boardwalk is jammed with boisterous beach bars.

SIGHTS

Sint Maarten Museum Museum

(542-4917; www.museumsintmaarten.org; 7 Front St; by donation; 10am-4pm Mon-Fri) Arawak pottery shards, plantation-era artifacts, period photos and a few items from HMS *Proselyte*, the frigate that sank off Fort Amsterdam in 1801, are among the displays at this island history museum, along with exhibits covering 1995's devastating Hurricane Luis, the salt industry and slavery. The little shop downstairs sells an assortment of Caribbean arts and crafts.

That Yoda Guy Museum Museum

(542-4009; www.netdwellers.com/mo/ygme; 19 Front St; US$12; 10:30am-4pm Mon & Sat, 9:15am-5pm Tue-Fri, plus 10:30am-4pm Sun when cruise ships in port) Run by Nick Malley, who helped create Yoda of *Star Wars* fame, this 1st-floor museum starts with a short film about the creator and his work on *Star Wars*. It then winds though an exhibit of movie memorabilia including photos, Han Solo frozen in carbonite, a functioning robotic Yoda puppet, scripts, posters, storyboards, and items from other films Malley has worked on including *Men In Black*, *Alien*, *Terminator* and *Hellraiser*. Malley is often here in person and can autograph gift-shop purchases.

The unexpectedness of encountering such a museum in Sint Maarten is summed up by the sign held by C-3PO on the staircase up to the museum, which reads: 'R2-D2 says "The probability of finding a *Star Wars* exhibit in the Caribbean is 125,316 to 1".'

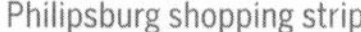

Philipsburg shopping strip

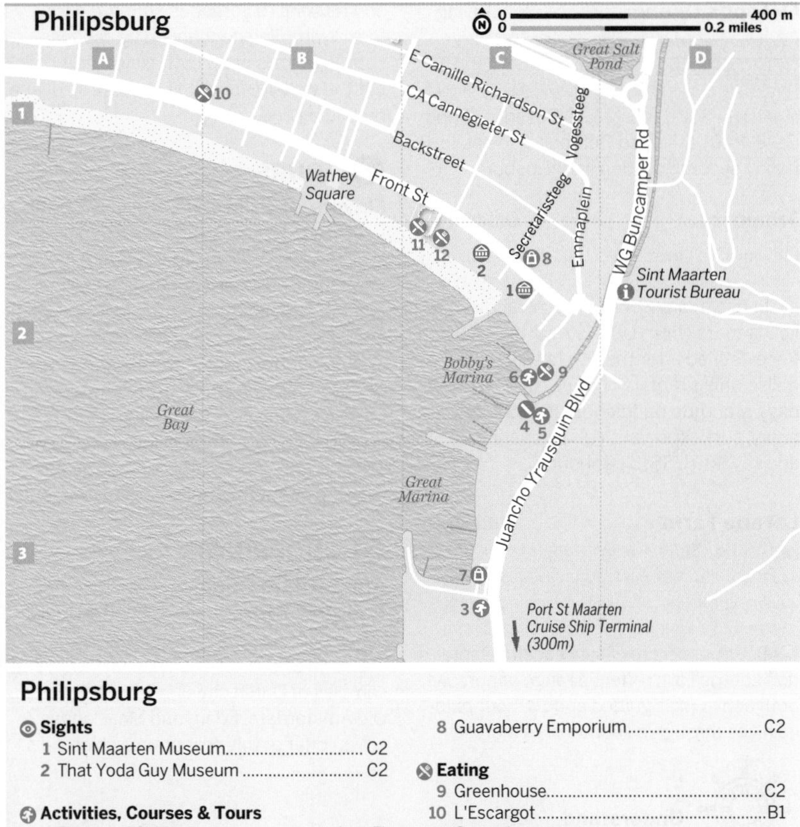

Philipsburg

Sights
1 Sint Maarten Museum C2
2 That Yoda Guy Museum C2

Activities, Courses & Tours
Flavors of St Martin .... (see 7)
3 Johnny's Scooter Rental C3
4 Octopus Diving C2
5 Sea Trek Diving C2
6 Trisport C2

Shopping
7 Amsterdam Cheese & Liquor Store C3
8 Guavaberry Emporium C2

Eating
9 Greenhouse C2
10 L'Escargot B1
11 Ocean Lounge Restaurant & Bar C2
12 Taloula Mango's C2

Drinking & Nightlife
Blue Bitch Bar .... (see 12)

ACTIVITIES

Sea Trek Diving Water Sports

(☎520-2346; www.seatrekstmaarten.com; Bobby's Marina; sea trek per person US$109; ⏲by reservation) Experience dazzling marine life without scuba diving on a 'sea trek': a 30-minute guided walk along the sea floor at a depth of around 6m wearing a full-head helmet hooked up to an air hose so you can breath normally. A water taxi whisks you to Little Bay, where there are natural and artificial reefs including a sunken helicopter.

The helmet lets you wear glasses and keeps your hair dry. Put on your swimsuit before arriving at the departure point as there are no changing facilities. Kids must be aged eight or over.

Octopus Diving Diving

(in St-Martin 0590-29-11-27; www.octopusdiving.com; Bobby's Marina; 2-tank dive US$99, snorkeling excursion US$55, snorkeling gear rental per day US$10; 7am-5pm) Based in Grand Case, PADI-affiliated Octopus also has this handy second location in Philipsburg.

Trisport Outdoors

(588-6009; www.trisportsxm.com; Bobby's Marina; 10am-5pm Mon-Sat) This versatile outfit has a range of bike, kayak and snorkeling tours (from US$49) and an 'Amazing Race' (styled after the TV show; US$75). It also offers rentals of bikes (US$25 per day), stand-up paddleboards (US$25, per hour), surf-ski kayaks (US$25 per hour) and kayaks (US$15 per hour).

Loterie Farm Outdoors

(0590-87-86-16; www.loteriefarm.com; 103 Rte de Pic Paradis; self-guided/guided hikes €5/25, adult high-ropes course €40-60, child low-ropes course €25, swimming pool €25, cabanas from €200; 9am-5pm Tue-Sun) Peaceful plantation Loterie Farm offers a range of pursuits, both active (self-guided and 1½-hour guided hikes through a section of rainforest) and relaxing (a gorgeous spring-fed free-form swimming pool ringed by cabanas. Loterie Farm is open for business but check out the website for detail of post-Hurricane rebuilding and pricing.

TOURS

Flavors of St Martin Food & Drink

(in Puerto Rico +787-964-2447; www.stmartinfoodtours.com; adult/child US$120/90) A 4½-hour tour by air-conditioned bus is a fantastic way to discover the French, Dutch and Caribbean flavors of this multicultural island. Tours meet at the Amsterdam Cheese & Liquor Store, starting with a cheese tasting, before heading off to sample sizzling barbecue fare, local rum, seafood and Sint Maarten–made gelato, learning about the island's history en route.

SHOPPING

Amsterdam Cheese & Liquor Store Food & Drinks

(581-5408; 26 Juancho Yrausquin Blvd; 8:30am-5:30pm Mon-Sat, 11am-4pm Sun) Free samples of Dutch cheeses including Gouda, Old Amsterdam, Edam and Maaslander are on offer at this emporium, which sells

Understand

Early History of the Island

For a thousand years, St-Martin/Sint Maarten was sparsely populated by the Arawaks and later the fiercer Caribs. They named the island Soualiga after the brackish salt ponds that made it difficult to settle.

Columbus sailed past on November 11, 1493, which happened to be the feast day of Saint Martin of Tours, after whom he named the island Isla de San Martin. But it was the Dutch who were the first to take advantage of the island, which was a nice stopping-off point between the Netherlands and their colonies in Brazil and New Amsterdam (New York City). After a few abortive attempts by the Spanish to regain the island, now found to be brimming with lucrative salt deposits, the French and Dutch ended up fighting for control of it.

As legend has it, the Dutch and the French decided to partition St-Martin/Sint Maarten from a march originating in Oyster Pond. The French walked northward, the Dutch south. While the French quenched their thirst with wine, the Dutch brought along *jenever* (Dutch gin). Halfway through, the Dutchmen stopped to sleep off the ill effects, effectively giving the French a greater piece of the pie.

Understand

People of St-Martin/Sint Maarten

St-Martin/Sint Maarten is a melting pot of ethnicities like no other place in the Caribbean. The island culture has its roots largely in African, French and Dutch influences, though scores of more recent immigrants – including many from the Dominican Republic, Haiti and China – have added their own elements to this multicultural society. Today, the island claims 120 different nationalities speaking over 80 different languages, although French dominates St-Martin and English dominates Sint Maarten.

St-Martin/Sint Maarten has adapted to tourism better than any other island nearby. You'll rarely meet someone who was actually born on the island. As the smallest area of land in the world divided into two nations, each side functions symbiotically while attracting tourists in very different ways. The French side embraces its European roots and seeks to re-create a certain amount of 'Old World' atmosphere. Home to the cruise-ship port, the Dutch side is much more built up with solid hurricane-resistant concrete high-rises, and a constant hum of low-lying debauchery that accompanies the dozens of gentlemen's clubs, casinos and beach bars, although it also offers a huge range of water-sports activities along its coast.

Front Street, Philipsburg CHARLES O. CECIL/ALAMY ©

cheeses in varying sizes (vacuum packed on request) alongside *jenever* (Dutch gin), spicy *speculaas* cookies, tulips, delftware and Texel wine. Get your car-park ticket stamped upon purchase for free parking.

Guavaberry Emporium Drinks
(www.guavaberry.com; 8 Front St; ⏲9:30am-5:30pm) Located inside an original Dutch West Indies town house built in the late 1700s, this emporium produces the official liqueur of St-Martin/Sint Maarten. It's made from rum, cane sugar and wild guavaberries from the island's interior, and has a bittersweet spiced flavor. There are free tastings and bottles for sale.

EATING & DRINKING

Greenhouse Brasserie $$
(☎542-2941; www.thegreenhouserestaurant.com; Kanal Steeg; sandwiches US$12-16, mains US$20-36; ⏰11am-9pm; 📶) A favorite with cruise-ship passengers, this Philipsburg landmark has specials including all-you-can-eat ribs on Monday and Thursday nights, and barbecue lobster nights on Tuesday and Friday. At other times, it serves burgers, sandwiches, salads, steaks and seafood. Its happy hour, from 4:30pm to 7pm, has two-for-one drinks as well as half-price bar snacks.

Taloula Mango's Brasserie $$
(☎542-1645; www.taloulamango.com; Boardwalk; burgers US$10-27, mains US$22-44.90; ⏰11am-9:30pm) One of the busiest beach-side eateries, Taloula Mango's is a hit with cruise-ship passengers for its burgers and grills such as baby back ribs, barbecued jerk chicken, sirloin steak and grilled mahi mahi. Upstairs is the equally jam-packed **Blue Bitch Bar** (www.bluebitchbar.com;; ⏰11am-11pm).

Ocean Lounge Restaurant & Bar Seafood, International $$$
(☎542-2572; www.hhbh.com; Holland House Beach Hotel, Boardwalk; mains US$16-38, whole lobster US$65, seafood platter for 2 US$115; ⏰kitchen 7am-10pm, bar to midnight) With a breezy terrace opening onto the seafront, the restaurant and bar at the Holland House Beach Hotel is a popular place for a sunset beverage or all-out meal of fish, gourmet burgers or grilled whole lobster. Seafood platters come with grilled lobster, sashimi tuna, king crab, oysters and shrimp.

L'Escargot French $$$
(☎542-2483; www.lescargotrestaurant.com; 96 Front St; snail menus US$11-15, mains US$25-45; ⏰11:30am-3pm & 6-10:30pm) An enchanting traditional Creole cottage painted a rainbow of vivid colors, this charmer is even more inviting inside with sepia lighting, embroidered tablecloths and Édith Piaf recordings playing in the background. House-specialty escargots (snails) are served in the shell with garlic and parsley butter or baked in mushroom caps.

L'Escargot, Philipsburg

Understand

Landscape & Wildlife

The west side of the island is more water than land, dominated by the expansive Simpson Bay Lagoon, which is one of the largest landlocked bodies of water in the Caribbean and has moorings for a large array of boats.

Birdwatching is excellent here, with over 100 different species of bird recorded. Of them, some 60 migratory species include herons, egrets, stilts, pelicans and laughing gulls, which frequent the island's salt ponds. Frigatebirds can be spotted along the coast, and hummingbirds and yellow-breasted banana quits in gardens. Dragonflies and butterflies are prevalent all over the island.

The only native mammals are bats, of which there are eight species. There are also mongooses, racoons, iguanas, geckos, tortoises, sea turtles and several species of tree frog. The waters on the entire Dutch side, from Cupecoy Bay to Oyster Pond, are protected by Sint Maarten Marine Park. Much of the French side is part of the protected nature reserve Réserve Naturelle de St-Martin.

Monarch butterfly DRAASIPOS0323/GETTY IMAGES ©

INFORMATION

Sint Maarten Tourist Bureau (☎542-2337; www.visitstmaarten.com; Vineyard Office Park, 33 WG Buncamper Rd; ⏰9am-5pm Mon-Fri) Limited tourist information.

GETTING AROUND

Philipsburg is home to the **Port St Maarten** (www.portstmaarten.com; Juancho Yrausquin Blvd) cruise-ship terminal, where you'll find taxis and car-rental companies, as well as marinas with services to St-Barthélemy and Saba.

Buses are infrequent, so rental cars or taxis are the best way to get around – but beware of heavy traffic. Trisport (p196) rents bicycles, while **Johnny's Scooter Rental** (☎587-0272; www.johnnysscooterrental.com; Juancho Yrausquin Blvd; scooter/ATV rental per day US$65/99; ⏰8am-5:30pm) rents scooters and ATV quad bikes.

Spice market, Marigot

Marigot, St-Martin

Marigot, the capital of French St-Martin, is a town dominated by a stone fort high up on the hill. A distinctive European flavor is palpable here, with a produce market and a handful of *boulangeries* (bakeries).

Virtually leveled by Hurricane Luis in 1995, Marigot was also hard-hit by subsequent hurricanes including Lenny in 1999 and Gonzalo in 2014, and most recently Hurricane Irma in 2017, which damaged 90 per cent of the island's structures.

Although Marigot is generally safe during the day, it's a no-go zone after dark.

SIGHTS

Fort Louis Ruins

(Rue du Fort Louis; ⌚24hr) FREE In 1767 three gun batteries were placed up on top of this hill. In 1789 Fort Louis was constructed by St-Martin's then-governor Jean Sebastian de Durat to protect Marigot's harbor warehouses storing rum, salt, coffee and sugarcane from marauding British and Dutch pirates. It's been abandoned for centuries and contains only remnants from bygone eras, but English and French interpretive panels detail its history and the view alone rewards the 50m climb from the road up to the ruins.

Musée de Saint Martin Antilles Museum

(St-Martin Archaeological Museum; http://musee-saintmartin.e-monsite.com; 7 Rue Fichot; ⌚9am-1pm & 3-5pm Mon-Fri) FREE Clay figurines from 550 BC (the oldest discovered in the Antilles), Arawak-sculpted gemstones and shells and period photography are among the historical displays that bring the island's history to life at this small but absorbing museum, which spans the Arawak period (from 3250 BC) to European colonization and island fashion in the 1930s. Interpretative panels are in English and French.

Produce Market Market

(Blvd de France; ⌚food 7am-3pm Wed & Sat, bric-a-brac & clothing 7am-3pm Mon, Tue, Thu & Fri) The twice-weekly produce market on Marigot's waterfront has tropical fruit such as passionfruit and bananas, root vegetables, goat's meat and chicken, and freshly caught fish from the surrounding waters. Local rums include Mauby (bark-infused rum) and Shrub (crushed-orange-peel-infused rum). There are also plenty of souvenir stalls.

On other days (except Sundays, when it's closed), you'll find jewelers selling garnet from Friar's Bay and other local arts and crafts (avoid coral and turtle-shell products, which are illegal), as well as clothing (mostly imported from China).

EATING

Port La Royale marina is lined with restaurants offering everything from pizza and burgers to seafood and French specialties.

Enoch's Place Caribbean $
(Front de Mer; mains €10-14; 11am-2pm & 5:30-9pm Mon-Sat) For a down-to-earth local experience, head to this bustling eatery handily positioned on a corner of Marigot's open-air market. Dishes are made fresh daily and might include spicy Creole shrimp, smoky grilled ribs, barbecued red snapper fillets, tangy goat curry, oxtail stew, conch salad and St-Martin's best johnnycakes. There's no seafood on Mondays when the fishing boats don't run.

La Croissanterie Bakery $
(Pont La Royale; dishes €6-16; 7am-3pm) In a breezy marina-side setting, La Croissanterie serves its namesake croissants along with crêpes, omelettes, croques monsieur and madame (toasted ham-and-cheese sandwiches, the latter with a fried egg on top), and quiches, plus international staples such as burgers, pizza and pasta. Cash only.

Ô Plongeoir International $$
(0590-87-94-71; Front de Mer; mains lunch €12-18, dinner €16-28, tapas €7-15; noon-9:30pm Mon-Sat;) Opposite the yacht club, this open-air eatery is a great place to gaze at Anguilla in the distance (and, often, visiting iguanas from the hillside above). Salmon gravlax, tempura tiger prawns, grilled calamari, blackened red snapper fillets, bavette steak with béarnaise sauce, honey-spiced roast duck and oven-baked Camembert are among the menu highlights. Tapas is served between 5pm and 6pm.

Le Tropicana Caribbean $$
(0590-87-79-07; Pont la Royale; mains €14-31.50; noon-9:30pm Mon-Sat) Right on the dock of the marina, this colorful spot's chairs and tablecloths are a mélange of sunny yellows and oranges. Poached salmon with raspberry-butter sauce, lobster-stuffed chicken breast with Jamaican pepper jus and sole meunière give it a strong local following, but the biggest winners are lush desserts like Grand Marnier soufflé and chocolate fondue.

INFORMATION

Tourist Office (0590-87-57-21; www.stmartinisland.org; Route de Sandy Ground; 8:30am-1pm & 2:30-5:30pm Mon-Fri, 8am-noon Sat) Has a limited range of brochures and maps. Look up to spot the glittering domed ceiling mosaic.

GETTING AROUND

Buses serve Marigot but schedules are highly unpredictable so you're better off taking a taxi.

JEFF GREENBERG/GETTY IMAGES ©

Cockburn Town (p208), Grand Turk

TURKS & CAICOS

In This Chapter

Turks & Caicos at a Glance

Grand Turk is a step back in time. At just 6.5 miles long, this tiny dot amid the sea is a sparsely populated, brush-covered paradise. Cockburn Town, the main settlement, has narrow streets frequented by wild donkeys and horses. Beaches rim the land and calm blue water invites you in for a refreshing swim. If you're not up for exploring the island, there is plenty to keep you occupied for the day at the Cruise Center, but we highly recommend a day of snorkeling, diving, or swimming on one of the impressive reefs that have made Grand Turk a well-known Atlantic diving destination.

With a Day in Port

- Join a tour to Gibbs Cay for snorkeling and swimming with stingrays. (p207)
- Trot along the seashore on horseback at East Side Beach. (p207)
- Dive the reef wall off Pillory Beach. (p206)

Best Places for...

Cocktails Sand Bar (p210)

Local cuisine Osprey (p211)

Pizza Turk's Head Inne (p211)

Grand Turk was significantly damaged by Hurricane Irma (p300) in September 2017. While we have endeavoured to keep the information in this chapter as up-to-date as possible, some places may still be affected while the community rebuilds.

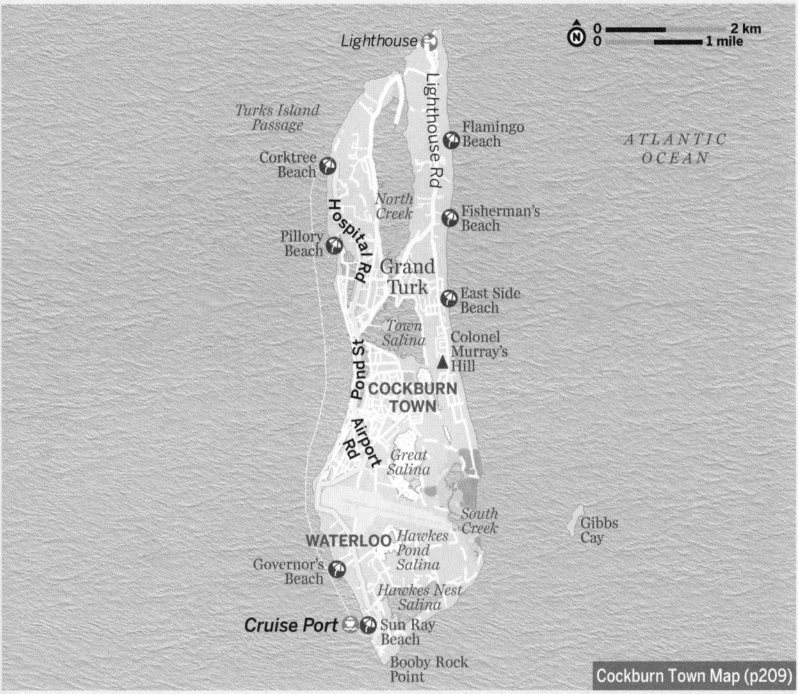

Lighthouse
Lighthouse Rd
Turks Island Passage
Flamingo Beach
ATLANTIC OCEAN
Corktree Beach
North Creek
Fisherman's Beach
Hospital Rd
Pillory Beach
Grand Turk
East Side Beach
Town Salina
Colonel Murray's Hill
Pond St
COCKBURN TOWN
Airport Rd
Great Salina
South Creek
Gibbs Cay
WATERLOO
Hawkes Pond Salina
Governor's Beach
Hawkes Nest Salina
Cruise Port
Sun Ray Beach
Booby Rock Point
0 2 km
0 1 mile

Cockburn Town Map (p209)

Getting from the Port

Ships dock at the Grand Turk Cruise Center on the central-west side of the island. It has a Margaritaville, a small beach, a pool, and a handful of other shops and restaurants.

Taxi Hiring a taxi is the best way to get around; expect to pay US$5 to US$10 to get anywhere on the island. It's also possible to rent a car or jeep for around US$90 per day.

Fast Facts

Currency US dollar (US$)

Language English, Spanish, Creole

Money ATMs are available at the Scotiabank, a short walk from the cruise port in Waterloo Plaza.

Visas Not required for citizens of the US, EU or Australia.

Best for free wi-fi Wi-fi is readily available at the shops and restaurants in the Grand Cruise Cruise Center where ships dock.

Cruise Center beach, Grand Turk

Grand Turk's Best Beaches

Grand Turk has beautiful beaches in abundance. While the beach at the Cruise Center stays pretty packed with passengers, the island is small enough that it's a cinch to hop in a taxi and whisk away to a more secluded, tropical strip of sand and sea.

Great For...

Don't Miss

Governor's Beach is one of the most beautiful beaches on the island, and only 3 miles from the cruise port.

Governor's Beach

Backed by the pines and low scrub of Columbus Landfall National Park and adorned by the picturesque iron hulk of a beached ship, Governor's Beach is a lovely place for a quiet dip. It's also a scene of celebration during events such October's Lobster Festival. At the back of the beach you'll find shade among the pines that hug this gorgeous stretch of sandy coast.

Pillory Beach

Head to the northwest side of the island for a quiet beach close to the shops, bars and restaurants in North Cockburn Town, including the beachfront Ike & Donkey Beach Bar at the Bohio Dive Resort. The white-sand beach stretches for more than 2 miles down the coast, often making it easy to find a secluded, quiet spot.

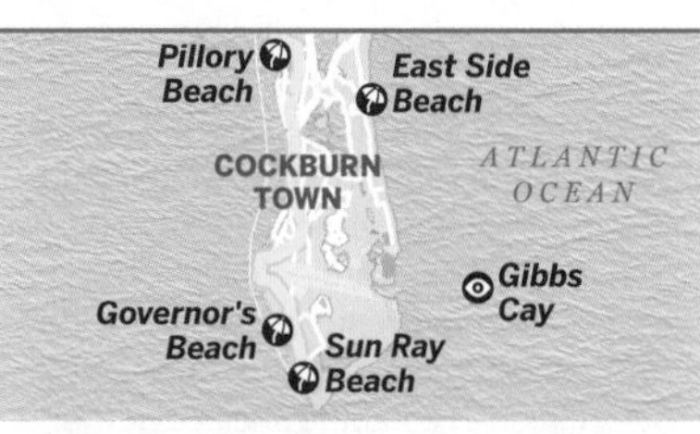

Explore Ashore

It takes about 10 minutes in a taxi to get to Governor's Beach from the Cruise Center, but allow at least three hours for this beach excursion.

Need to Know

A taxi from the Cruise Center costs US$4. There is a parking lot at Governor's Beach for rental cars and jeeps; we recommend taking all valuables out of your vehicle.

Sun Ray Beach

Also known as the Cruise Center Beach, this is the first stop for many. You'll find everything you need in a Caribbean beach here: free lounge chairs, drink service, a Margaritaville within a stone's throw. The beach gets super crowded in the afternoon, so it's best to hit the sand early and get a nice spot in the shade. If you're not into crowds rent a taxi and head to one of the less crowded beaches on the island. Snorkel gear is available for rent at several places along the shore.

Gibbs Cay

Take a tour to Gibbs Cay and swim or snorkel as stingrays glide past above the white-sand seafloor. It's a memorable adventure, the boat ride being as fun and beautiful as the time spent in the water. The 11-acre island is a mile off the coast of Grand Turk so you'll get an excellent distant view of the tropical coast as you swim with the docile stingrays.

East Side Beach

A bit windier and with more seaweed than the beaches on the more protected west coast of the island, East Side Beach is the longest beach on Grand Turk at 4 miles long. It's not the best beach for swimming and most cruise visitors venture here as part of a horseback-riding tour. Horseback tours can be arranged with one of the tour providers at the Cruise Ship Center or by setting up a horse holiday in advance of your Caribbean cruise. East Side Beach has poor road accessibility; it's best to visit with a tour or taxi driver and avoid searching for it with a rented car or jeep.

Cockburn Town

The legacy of Grand Turk's salt-raking past survives in the salt-rotted Bermudan and Victorian architecture along Front and Duke Sts. Some buildings are derelict, some have been lovingly restored, several survive as inns, and some have been replaced by ugly, unfinished concrete shells, but the overall impression is of collapsing colonial charm, fringed with tropical foliage. To the south lies the grand 1815 home Waterloo, residence of past governors. The best shopping to be found on the island is in the street stalls that open up on Duke St when the cruise ships are in port.

SIGHTS

Turks & Caicos National Museum Museum

(946-2160; www.tcmuseum.org; Front St; US$7; 9am-1pm Mon-Wed, 1-5pm Thu, also open for cruise ships) This great little museum has everything from shipwrecks to messages in bottles and crash-landed spacecraft. Artifacts from the Molasses Reef wreck, the oldest European wreck yet discovered in the Americas, are highlights.

General Post Office Historic Building

(946-1334; Front St; 8am-4pm Mon-Thu, to 3:30pm Fri) One of the most notable

Understand

Grand Turk Lighthouse

Standing on a bluff high above the notorious northeast reef, wrecker of many ships and nearly of the salt industry (cargo ships began to balk at the danger, demanding greater safety), this iron **lighthouse** (Northeast Point; US$3) was cast in England in 1852 and assembled in situ. The views out to sea are spectacular, and there's a high-rope course to add spice to your visit.

Chukka Caribbean Adventures (232-1339; www.chukkacaribbean.com; Lighthouse Rd) has an office near the lighthouse, organizing horseback rides in the sea, stingray-feeding trips to Gibbs Cay, ziplining and other activities.

CHUCK W WALKER/SHUTTERSTOCK ©

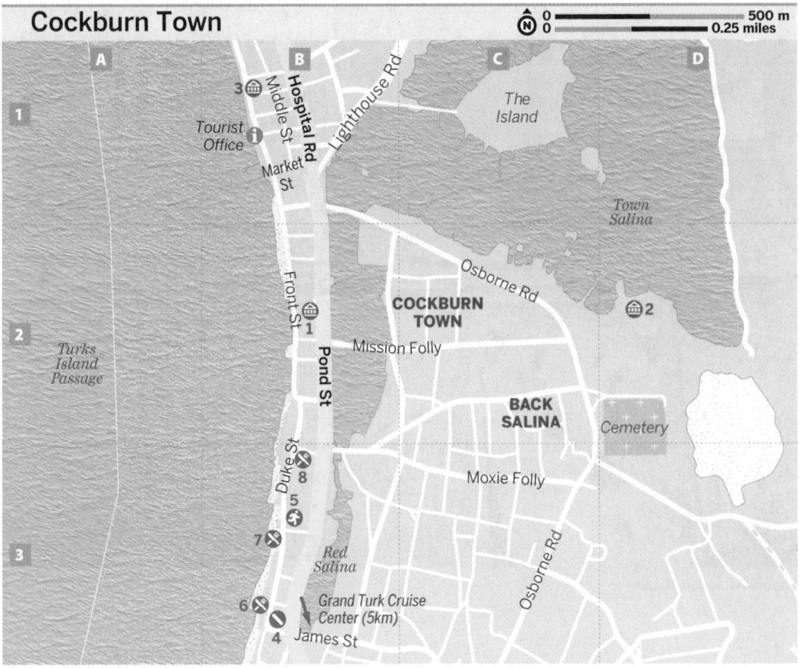

Cockburn Town

Cockburn Town

Sights

1 General Post Office B2
2 Salt House D2
3 Turks & Caicos National Museum B1

Activities, Courses & Tours

4 Grand Turk Diving Co B3
5 Oasis Divers B3

Eating

6 Osprey B3
7 Sand Bar B3
8 Turk's Head Inne B3

buildings on Front St is the handsome colonial post office, once a private home for one of Grand Turk's leading families, now a still-functioning post office. It also houses the Philatelic Bureau, where some of TCI's colorful stamps, beloved of collectors, can be seen.

Salt House Museum

(off Osbourne Rd; opens when cruise ships dock) FREE This modest museum, housed in an old whitewashed storehouse by the Town Salina, documents Grand Turk's great pre-cruise-ship industry: salt.

ACTIVITIES

Oasis Divers Water Sports

(946-1128; www.oasisdivers.com; Duke St; 8am-4pm) Runs a huge range of diving and snorkeling tours (two tanks for US$115, night dives for US$80). Also runs ecotours to swim with the stingrays on Gibbs Cay, spot humpback whales in February and March, and other memorable activities.

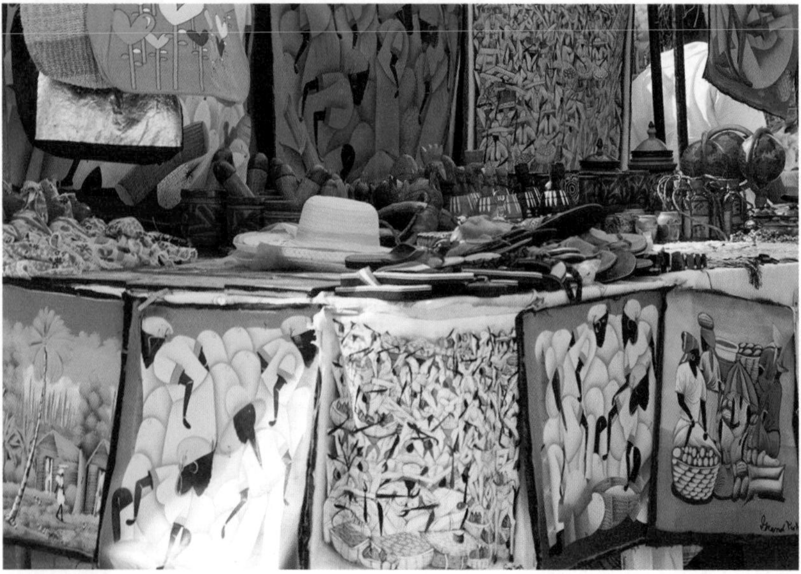

Marketplace, Grand Turk

Grand Turk Diving Co Diving

(946-1559; www.gtdiving.com; Duke St; 8am-4pm) Local legend Smitty runs this excellent outfit. There are two-tank dives for US$115, singles for US$80 and night dives for US$85. Full PADI courses are offered for US$450. You can also hire a bike for US$20 per day.

EATING

Front and Duke Sts boast the best and most atmospheric places to eat.

Sand Bar Pub Food $

(243-2666; www.grandturk-mantahouse.com; Duke St; mains US$13-18; 11am-1am;) With a convivial open-air bar and decking stretching out over the water, the Sand Bar

Whale-Watching

The annual migration of 2500 to 7000 Atlantic humpback whales through the Columbus Passage, the deep-water channel separating the Caicos and Turks islands, is one of the Caribbean's great sights. Moving through the channel (also known as Turks Islands Passage) between January and March, with the most reliable sightings in February and March, the mighty creatures are on their way to their breeding grounds in Silver Bank in the Dominican Republic, and Mouchoir Bank in TCI's southern waters. Scores of local boats take visitors close to the action. If you prefer terra firma, perhaps with a drink in hand, you can also watch from the shores of Grand Turk and Salt Cay, as they are close to the passage.

Understand

Early History of Turks & Caicos

Recent discoveries of Taíno artifacts on Grand Turk and Middle Caicos have shown that the islands originally had much the same indigenous culture as their northern neighbors. Known as the Lucayans, this branch of the Taíno people probably began arriving here around AD 750, permanently settling most islands by around AD 1300. Sadly, this young society soon came into contact with European rapacity. While the local claim that Columbus made his first New World landfall at Grand Turk in 1492 is unproven, what is certain is that within 30 years of that date the Lucayan civilization in these islands was gone, decimated by slavery and disease.

The island group remained virtually uninhabited for most of the 16th and 17th centuries, passing between the nominal control of Britain, France and Spain. Permanent populations only developed from the 1670s, when Bermudian salt rakers settled the Turks islands and used natural *salinas* (salt-drying pans, still prominent features of Grand Turk and Salt Cay) to produce sea salt. Captured by the French and Spanish in 1706, the islands were retaken by the Bermudans soon afterwards. It was also around this time that piracy in the islands enjoyed its heyday, with famous outlaws such as Mary Read, Anne Bonny, Calico Jack Rackham, Captain Kidd and Blackbeard preying on wrecked and gold-laden shipping from the many hiding places the islands offer.

is justifiably the most famous and popular spot in town for an evening rum punch. The food's good too, and the whale-watching, when the humpbacks pass by close to shore in February and March, can be amazing.

Turk's Head Inne International $$
(☎946-1830; www.turksheadinne.com; Duke St; mains US$26-28; ⏰6-9pm Wed-Sat) The in-house restaurant at this boutique hotel, housed in a lovely timber home dating to around 1830, is one of the best places to eat in Cockburn Town. Expect dishes such as seared tuna with ginger and soy, and lobster with heart-of-palm salad.

Osprey International $$
(☎946-2666; www.ospreybeachhotel.com; Duke St; mains US$18-25; ⏰7am-9pm; ) This terraced poolside restaurant is one of the most pleasant places to eat in Cockburn Town. There's a legendary BBQ on Wednesday and Sunday nights: amazing seafood, poultry and beef are grilled before your eyes, paired with salads and served up to a happy throng. There are great ocean views and the house band keeps the energy levels up.

INFORMATION

Tourist Office (☎946-2321; www.turksandcaicostourism.com; Front St; ⏰8am-4:30pm Mon-Fri) Located in the old shore-front customs house in Cockburn Town, this office is happy to dispense advice and historical knowledge to visitors.

GETTING AROUND

Cockburn Town is easily explored on foot. Taxis are available but can be quite expensive. Cars, scooters, buggies and golf carts are available to rent for exploring the rest of the island; the standard rental period is less than eight hours.

Cruise ship port, Oranjestad (p222)

In This Chapter

Aruba at a Glance

North Americans fleeing winter make Aruba the most visited tourist island in the southern Caribbean. The draws are obvious: miles of glorious beaches and a cute, compact capital, Oranjestad. Venture away from the resorts and you're in for a real treat. At the island's extreme ends are rugged, windswept vistas and uncrowded beaches. Crystal-clear waters are bursting with sea life and shipwrecks, providing incredible opportunities for snorkeling and diving. And if you're just searching for the perfect beach to put your toes in the sand and watch the sea sparkle, Aruba has some of the most beautiful beaches in the world.

With a Day in Port

- Explore the beautiful beaches dotted across the island. (p218)
- Go shopping at the Royal Plaza and then casino-hop in the capital or play a round of golf. (p222)
- Hire a tour operator to take you to Arikok National Wildlife Park and visit the natural pool, a circular body of water separated and protected by rocks from the ocean. (p216)

Best Places for...

Coffee Coffee Break (p227)

Local cuisine The West Deck (p226)

Ice cream Happy Spot (p225)

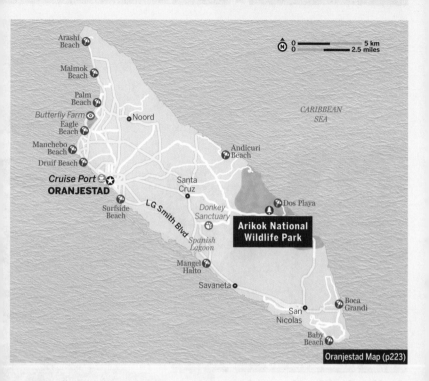

Arashi Beach
Malmok Beach
Palm Beach
Butterfly Farm
Eagle Beach
Noord
Manchebo Beach
Druif Beach
Andicuri Beach
CARIBBEAN SEA
Cruise Port
ORANJESTAD
Santa Cruz
Surfside Beach
LG Smith Blvd
Donkey Sanctuary
Dos Playa
Arikok National Wildlife Park
Spanish Lagoon
Mangel Halto
Savaneta
San Nicolas
Boca Grandi
Baby Beach
0 5 km
0 2.5 miles

Oranjestad Map (p223)

Getting from the Port

Most of the best beaches on the island are on the west coast,

Taxi Taxis cost US$10 to US$20 for up to five people to travel to any of the beaches on the island, around 20 minutes each way.

Bus Public buses (US$2.30) run between Oranjestad, Malmok and Arash, but taxis are much faster if you've only got several hours in port.

Fast Facts

Currency Arubin Florin (Afl), US dollars (US$) accepted

Language English, Spanish, Dutch, Papiamento

Money ATMs are available at the cruise port at the Caribbean Mercantile Bank.

Visas Not required for citizens of the US, EU or Australia.

Best for free wi-fi The cruise port, Eagle Beach and Mangel Halto.

Arikok's natural pool

Arikok National Wildlife Park

Arid and rugged, Arikok National Wildlife Park is a vast stretch of desert wilderness, covering much of the east coast (and 20% of the island's total area). Park highlights include swimming in the Natural Pool, glorious beaches and great hiking.

Great For...

Don't Miss

The native pictographs and ruins on the Cunuco Arikok trail.

The park is a fascinating contrast to the heavily developed and lushly landscaped west coast. Even the ocean is different over here. Midnight blue, it smashes against the rocky shore with a fury not evident on the west coast.

As you explore, you'll notice the peculiar flora: the iconic and bizarrely twisted divi-divi; the *kwihi*, with its tasty sweet-sour long yellow beans; and the *hubada*, which has sharp, tough thorns. Spiky aloe plants abound, as do some 70 varieties of cactus. Bring sun protection, money for snacks and souvenirs, hiking boots or good walking sneakers, and plenty of water.

Natural Pool

This pool is the park's highlight. Centuries of waves pounding the shoreline has worn a natural depression into the limestone

Rock formations, Arikok National Wildlife Park

GALINA SAVINA/SHUTTERSTOCK ©

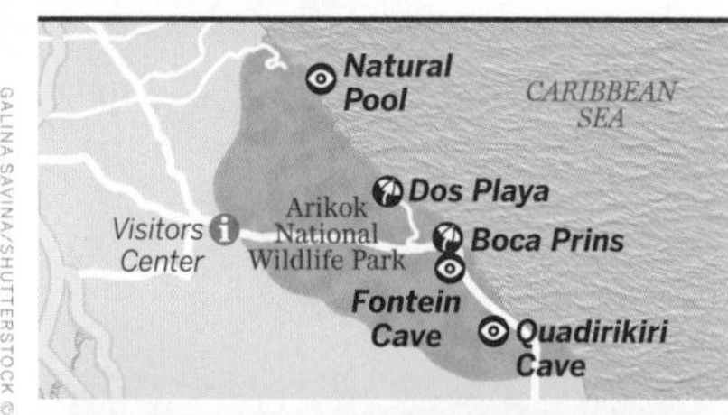

Explore Ashore

It is possible to navigate the poorly marked and rough non-paved roads with a rented jeep or van, but we highly recommend taking a 4WD tour to the park.

Need to Know

Stop at the **visitors center** (585-1234; www.arubanationalpark.org; adult/child US$11/free; ticket sales 8am-4pm) to pay your park admission fee, pick up a map and browse the displays on the park's flora and fauna.

coastal ridge. The surrounding rocks break the surf so, with waves crashing all around, you can take a peaceful, cooling dip. Bring your mask and snorkel and commune with the fish who are hiding out in there. Access is possible by 4WD or – better – a 3.5-mile walk from the visitors center.

Dos Playa

North of Boca Prins, there are two stunning beaches – known as Dos Playa – that have been carved out of the rocky coastline by the pounding surf. Dos Playa is an important nesting area for leatherback, hawksbill, green and loggerhead turtles.

Boca Prins

Along the wild, rocky east coast, the waves carved out a striking sandy cove that gets rocked with explosive surf. The constant winds continue to pound this coast, throwing up sand to create an ever-growing sea of dunes in the surrounding area.

Fontein Cave

This limestone cave is extensive, although only the entrance hall is open to visitors. Aside from the rock formations, the cave contains some well-preserved drawings from Caquetíos peoples (a branch of the Arawak), dating back about 1000 years.

Quadirikiri Cave

Lit by the 'window' that allows natural light to filter in, this large limestone cave is home to several species of bat. According to local legend, Quadirikiri was the beautiful daughter of an ancient Caquetío chief. When she fell in love with a foreign man known as White Feather, her father was incensed and held her captive in this cave.

Eagle Beach

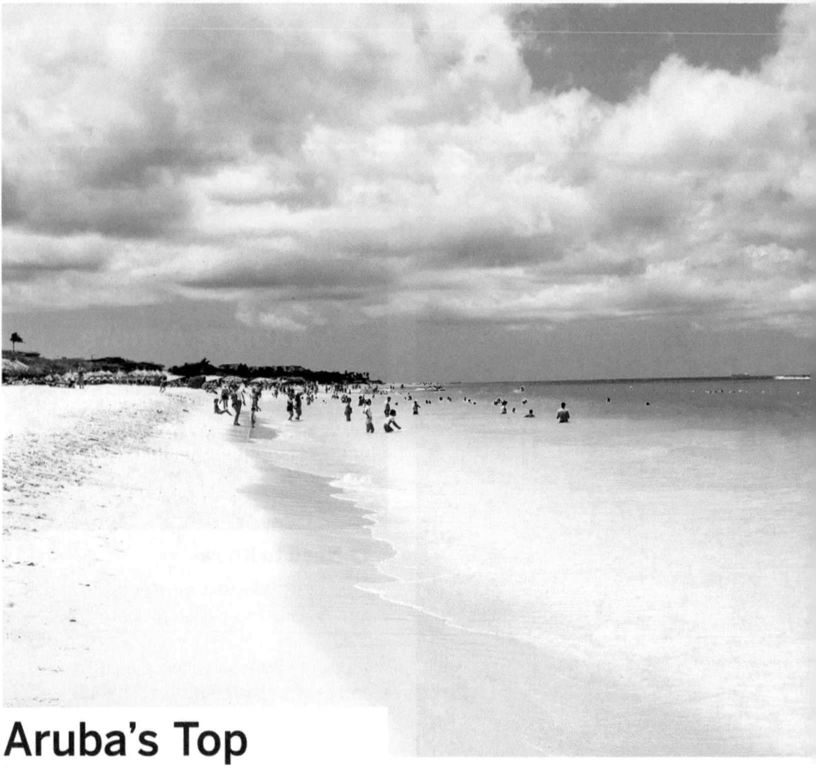

Aruba's Top Beaches

White sand, blue sea, bright sunny days most of the year, consistent and temperate warm weather, excellent shopping and amenities, and remarkably friendly locals make Aruba's beaches among the best in the Caribbean.

Great For...

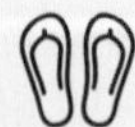

Don't Miss

Eagle Beach, one of the most beautiful stretches of sand on the island.

Druif Beach

The closest beach from the cruise port, Druif Beach is easily accessed from the parking lot on the south end of the Divi Dutch Village Beach Resort. Since it's close to the port, Druif can get rather crowded when cruise ships are in port, and souvenir peddlers are common on this long stretch of white sand. Downtown Oranjestad is nearby, making Druif an excellent stop before a day of shopping and exploring the sights in town.

Eagle Beach

Fronting a stretch of the low-rise resorts just northwest of Oranjestad, Eagle is a long stretch of white sand that regularly makes lists of the best beaches in the world. There

Druif Beach

Explore Ashore

Most of the best beaches are north of the cruise port on the west side of the island. Druif Beach is within walking distance, about a 30-minute walk from the cruise terminal. Allow at least three hours for Druif Beach; for beaches further afield allow more travel time and minimum of five hours.

Need to Know

There's free wi-fi at Eagle Beach, one of the several hot spots on the island installed by the Tourism Authority.

are shade trees in some areas and you can obtain every service you need here, from a lounger to a cold drink. Get cold tropical drinks at the Oasis, a little tiki hut centrally located on Eagle Beach. If you rent a chair with umbrella for US$20 to US$30, you'll enjoy drink service from your lounger.

Eagle Beach is a leatherback turtle nesting area, so parts of the beach may be closed from March to July.

Arashi Beach

Near the island's northwestern tip, this beach is a favorite with locals and popular with families. There's good bodysurfing, some shade and just a few rocks right offshore.

Palm Beach

Palm is a classic white-sand beauty, but only for those who enjoy the company of lots of people, as it fronts the high-rise resorts. During high season it can get jammed, but for some that's part of the scene.

Surfside Beach

Surfside may not be as spectacular as Palm Beach or Eagle Beach, but it is a pretty pleasant place to spend an afternoon if you're hankering for some sun, surf and sand. It's the best, most swimmable beach in Oranjestad proper, with plenty of shade and a handful of excellent beach bars. It's only steps from the airport, so planes taking off and landing will give you something to look at (for better or for worse).

Oranjestad Historic Walk

Cruise ships dock in the heart of the Oranjestad historic district, placing passengers within walking distance of many historical and noteworthy sights. Along with a rich history spanning from native history, through the colonial and modern era, downtown Oranjestad offers abundant shopping, casinos, excellent restaurants and lively bars.

Start Renaissance Mall
Distance 0.8-miles
Duration 20 minutes of walking, allow 3 hours

5 Walk north on Kazernestraat, and then veer left (west) onto Shelpstraat and visit the **Aruba Archaeological Museum** (p222), featuring relics of indigenous history.

6 Continue west on Kazernestraat, then turn left (south) onto Weststraat. You'll pass the **Royal Plaza Mall** (p225), a multistory colonial building filled with shops, restaurants, and bars that overlook the cruise port.

4 Continue west on Wilhelminastraat to **Plaza Daniel Leo**, a beautiful square surrounded by colonial-style buildings that now house shops and restaurants.

3 Continue north on Oranjestraat and turn left (west) onto Wilhelminastraat, stopping by the historic **City Hall** (p223), originally the private home of Eloy Arends and one of the most impressive historic homes on the island.

2 Return to Lloyd G Smith Blvd, turn right (north) onto Oranjestraat, and walk to the Willem III Tower, Aruba's first lighthouse. Take a moment to visit the **Historical Museum** (p222) nearby, housed in Fort Zoutman.

1 From the **Renaissance Mall** (p225) head east on Lloyd G Smith Blvd and then veer right onto the Linear Park Trail. Explore **Wilhelmina Park** (p223), built in honor of Queen Wilhemina in 1955.

Oranjestad

Oranjestad is a good city to explore on foot, with colonial-era architecture, shopping and waterside parks all within walking distance.

SIGHTS

Aruba Archaeological Museum Museum

(☎582-8979; www.namaruba.org; Schelpstraat 42; ⏰10am-5pm Tue-Fri, to 2pm Sat & Sun) FREE The capital's newest museum is housed in the beautifully restored colonial-era Ecury Complex, home to a successful merchant family throughout the 20th century. The engaging exhibits focus on Arawak life in the precolonial period, with a reproduction of a traditional home and multimedia presentations. Actual artifacts are few, though there are some stone tools and other relics dating from 4000 BC.

Fort Zoutman Fort

It's not much to look at, but it is an 18th-century fort built to defend the port against pirates. The attached Willem III Tower was added later, serving as both lighthouse and clock tower until 1963. The complex now houses the small **Aruba Historical Museum** (☎582-6099; $5; ⏰8:30am-4pm Mon-Fri) and the weekly **Bonbini Festival** (US$5; ⏰6:30-8:30pm Tue).

Understand

Caquetío People

Aruba's earliest inhabitants were the Caquetíos – a branch of the Arawak – who were hunter-gatherers (and fishers) along the northwest coast, as early as 2500 BC. Evidence of their civilization is still visible today in the piles of conch shells that were discarded around the salina (salt pan) near Malmok Beach. From AD 1000 to 1500, these natives settled in five different villages around the island, where they crafted pottery and practiced agriculture, growing corn and yucca. Artifacts from this so-called Ceramic Period are on display at the Aruba Archaeological Museum. The cave paintings in Fontein Cave (p217) also date to this period.

Spain claimed the island in 1499, but its inhospitable arid landscape provoked little colonial enthusiasm, even earning Aruba its status as *una isla inutíl* – or 'a useless island.' Eventually, most of the native population was enslaved and taken to work on the plantations in Hispaniola.

Cave paintings, Fontein Cave WWP/TRVL/ALAMY ©

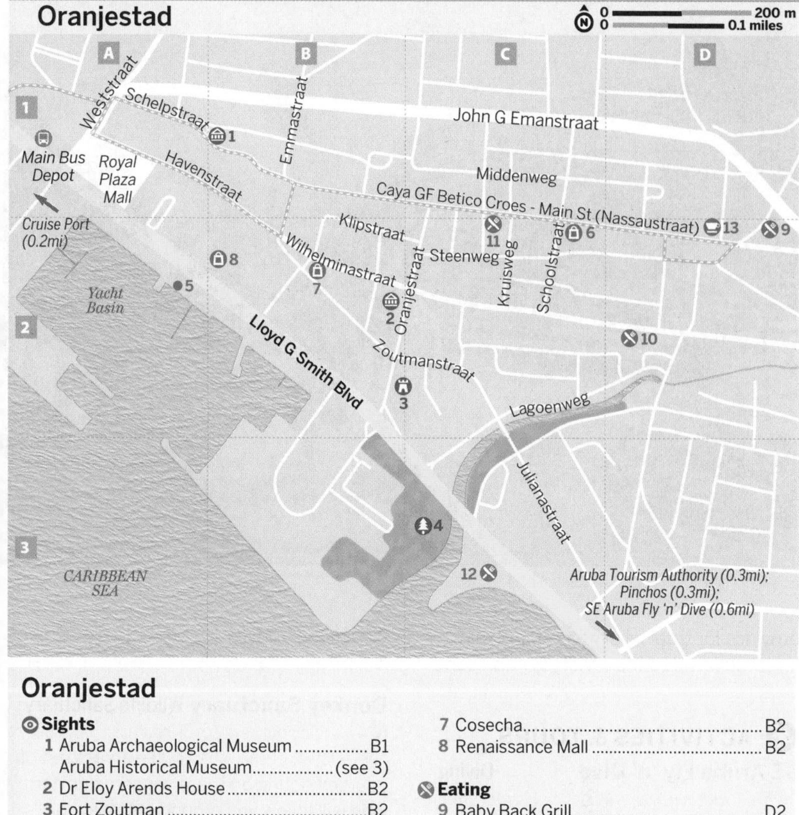

Oranjestad

Sights

1 Aruba Archaeological Museum B1
Aruba Historical Museum .... (see 3)
2 Dr Eloy Arends House B2
3 Fort Zoutman B2
4 Wilhelmina Park C3

Activities, Courses & Tours

5 Atlantis Adventures A2

Shopping

6 Aruba Aloe C2
7 Cosecha B2
8 Renaissance Mall B2

Eating

9 Baby Back Grill D2
10 De Suikertuin D2
11 Happy Spot C2
12 The West Deck C3

Drinking & Nightlife

13 Coffee Break D2

Dr Eloy Arends House — Historic Building

(Wilhelminastraat 8) A local landmark – and no wonder, it's a beauty. Dating to 1922, the elegant, emerald-green, white-trimmed house is now part of the council complex.

Wilhelmina Park — Park

This shady refuge is a tribute to Queen Wilhelmina, the longest-reigning Dutch monarch (1998–48).

Butterfly Farm — Gardens

(www.thebutterflyfarm.com; JE Irausquin Blvd; adult/child US$15/8; 8:30am-4:30pm) Tucked in between the low-rise and high-rise resort areas, this place will make your heart go aflutter, as the gorgeous gardens are teeming with butterflies and moths of all sizes and colors. Guided tours walk you through the lepidoptera life cycle. If you ever wanted to see butterflies mating or emerging from their pupa, here is your chance. The habitat

Shopping near Oranjestad cruise-ship port

provides for tropical dry forest and rainforest species, so the variety is impressive.

ACTIVITIES & TOURS

SE Aruba Fly 'n' Dive Diving
(☎588-1150; www.se-aruba.com; Lloyd G Smith Blvd 1a; 2-tank dive from US$90) This highly recommended dive shop is located just north of the airport, which explains the name. Trips to local dive sites depart every morning at 9am, with transportation available from area hotels or the cruise-ship terminal. Fly 'n' Dive is unique in that they cater to divers and snorkelers.

Atlantis Adventures Boating
(☎522-4500; www.depalmtours.com; LG Smith Blvd 82; adult/child US$105/80; ⌚departs 11am, noon & 1pm) See the creatures of the sea from the comfort of an air-conditioned passenger submarine. The vessel descends some 130ft to the ocean floor, allowing passengers to observe ample sea life, as well as a couple of shipwrecks, through the portals of the sub. The 100-minute tour includes the transfer to/from the sub, which is a pleasant ferry ride on top of the water.

Donkey Sanctuary Wildlife Sanctuary
(www.arubandonkey.org; Bringamosa; donations appreciated; ⌚9am-4pm) Make an ass out of yourself doting on these winsome critters, who will follow you around for attention and snacks. Originally brought to Aruba by the Spaniards, many donkeys went rogue when they were no longer needed on farms. The donkeys at the sanctuary are well taken care of: they are named, treated, fed, protected and loved. You won't be able to resist them!

SHOPPING

Numerous shopping malls cluster around Lloyd G Smith Blvd and the cruise-ship terminal. There are also vendor huts selling 'crafts' along Lloyd G Smith Blvd, but these knickknacks are mostly made in China. The best shopping is along the main drag, Caya GF Betico Croes, where there's a lively mix of international luxury brands and local shops. Bargaining is not encouraged.

Understand

Aruba's Economy

Prosperity came to the island in the form of the huge oil refinery built to refine Venezuelan crude oil in the 1920s. This large complex occupies the southeastern end of Aruba and still dominates the blue-collar town of San Nicolas. Jobs at the plant contributed to the development of a local middle class, and the island thrived.

Mid-century, the industry began to modernize and many oil workers lost their jobs. The Dutch government established a tourist commission to promote the nascent holiday sector as an alternative source of employment. In 1959, the first multistory hotel, the Caribbean Hotel, opened on the island and tourism has been booming ever since.

Aruba Aloe Cosmetics
(www.arubaaloe.com; Caya GF Betico Croes 78; ⏲9am-6pm Mon-Sat) Did you get too much sun? Swing by this little boutique to pick up some 'After Sun', made from the gel of the revered aloe plant, which grows prolifically on this island. There's a wide range of high-quality skin-care products – all made from local plants at the Aruba Aloe factory.

Cosecha Arts & Crafts
(www.arubacosecha.com; Zoutmanstraat 1; ⏲noon-6pm Mon, 10am-6pm Tue-Sat) If you're looking for a unique, locally made souvenir, look no further. Cosecha is the local artists' cooperative stocking a range of wonderful creations, from sea-glass jewellery to handwoven tote bags to driftwood and ceramic sculpture to fine arts and paintings.

Renaissance Mall Mall
(www.shoprenaissancearuba.com; Lloyd G Smith Blvd 82; ⏲10am-7pm Mon-Sat) Affiliated with the luxury resort, this upscale shopping center is replete with art galleries, designer boutiques and chain stores.

Royal Plaza Mall Mall
(Lloyd G Smith Blvd 94; ⏲9.30am-6pm Mon-Sat) Aruba's giant shopping mall opposite the cruise-ship port is an eye-opener with its ornate pink facade. Good for souvenirs and boutique brands.

EATING & DRINKING

In addition to the brick-and-mortar restaurants, snack trucks are an island institution, serving up a wide range of street food from sunset into the wee hours. Look for them in the parking lots near the Yacht Basin.

Baby Back Grill Barbecue $
(☎582-4410; Caya GF Betico Croes; mains US$6-8; ⏲11am-11pm; 📶) Like a snack truck but it doesn't go anywhere. This completely open-air restaurant grills up tender ribs, steaks, chicken and more for appreciative local masses. There are shady picnic tables where you can eat your barbecue.

Happy Spot Ice Cream $
(Caya GF Betico Croes; smoothies $3-4; ⏲11am-8pm) More than a dozen blenders are kept busy making milkshakes and fresh juice drinks at the open-air hut on the main shopping drag.

De Suikertuin Cafe $$
(☎582-6322; www.desuikertuin.com; Wilhelminastraat 64; mains US$8-20; ⏲8am-4pm; 📶🌶) This charming yellow house contains a sweet surprise: a delightful cafe filled with homemade goodness. (In fact, the name means 'sugar house'.) It's the perfect place to indulge in crêpes or quiche for breakfast, or nibble on salads and sandwiches for lunch. The interior is as cool as they come (in all senses of the word).

Understand

Aruba's Environment

Despite the lush landscaping that surrounds the resorts, Aruba has an arid climate, with less than 20i of rainfall per year. Its indigenous plants are hardy desert species, including some 70 kinds of cactus, as well as the ubiquitous aloe plant and the iconic divi-divi tree. Native animals are mostly reptiles, including a large variety of iguanas and lizards. Bird life abounds, including the ubiquitous banana quit and the striking troupial. Donkeys and goats run wild on the island's eastern side.

Aruba's most visible environmental woe is the puffing stacks of the oil refinery in San Nicolas. Smog also comes from the world's second-largest desalination plant, south of the airport, which roars away 24/7. (In fairness, water on the island is safe and delicious to drink.)

Meanwhile, the island has set a goal of using 100% renewable energy resources by the year 2020. Toward this goal, the Vader Piet Windmill Farm was constructed on the southeast coast, with a second wind farm in the works.

The need to balance the island's healthy economy with its limited water and energy resources has been a major point of discussion on the island, as locals have pressed for growth controls. This has slowed – but certainly not stopped – the rampant development of hotels and condos on the long strip to the north.

Eagle Beach (p218) MIKOLAJN/SHUTTERSTOCK ©

The West Deck Caribbean **$$**
(www.thewestdeck.com; Lloyd G Smith Blvd; mains $8-20; ⏲10:30am-11pm; 📶) At the water's edge, the West Deck is a casual, open-air beach bar with a friendly atmosphere and terrific food. Look for conch fritters, steak and plantain pinchos, fish sliders and barbecued ribs. Order up a tropical fruity cocktail and you'll know you're on vacation.

Pinchos Seafood **$$$**
(☎583-2666; www.pinchosaruba.com; Lloyd G Smith Blvd 7; mains US$24-36; ⏲5pm-midnight) Pinchos is surely one of Aruba's most romantic spots. Set on a pier jutting into the ocean, the restaurant is surrounded by twinkling stars and lapping waves. Local fish and hearty steaks show off a fusion of flavors, such as the pan-seared grouper

Trolley, Oranjestad

with apricot-ginger dipping sauce, or the maple bourbon barbecue skewer. Reservations recommended.

Coffee Break Coffee
(☎588-5569; www.arubacoffeeroasters.com; Caya GF Betico Croes; ⏰7am-6pm; 📶) With lots of metal and linoleum, it's not exactly the coziest of cafes, but as this is the headquarters of the Aruba Coffee Roasting Co, you can expect the most freshly roasted, richest, most delicious coffee on the island. Besides fresh-brewed coffee and espresso drinks, there's also homemade pastries and refreshing gelato. It's definitely worth a stop.

INFORMATION

Aruba Tourism Authority (☎800-862-7822; www.aruba.com; Lloyd G Smith Blvd 8; ⏰7:30am-noon & 1-4:30pm Mon-Fri)

GETTING AROUND

The easiest way to get around Oranjestad is to walk, as most of the sights and attractions are within an area of a few square miles. There is also a free, single-track, electric **trolley** (⏰10am-5pm) that runs from the cruise-ship terminal, through downtown Oranjestad and along Caya GF Betico Croes, before looping back to the port. It runs every 20 to 30 minutes.

BUS

Arubus (☎297-520-2300; www.arubus.com; single/day ticket US$2.60/5) operates several routes from the **main bus depot** (Lloyd G Smith Blvd) in Oranjestad to the airport and on to San Nicolas, with additional routes to the resort area (20 minutes), as well as Malmok and Arashi Beaches (30 minutes).

CAR

There are several car-rental providers at the cruise terminal. We recommend getting off the ship as early as possible and renting a jeep before the car rental services sell out. Many of the roads are rough on the island and the jeeps can navigate the terrain best. Most car or jeep rentals cost US$50 to US$100 per day.

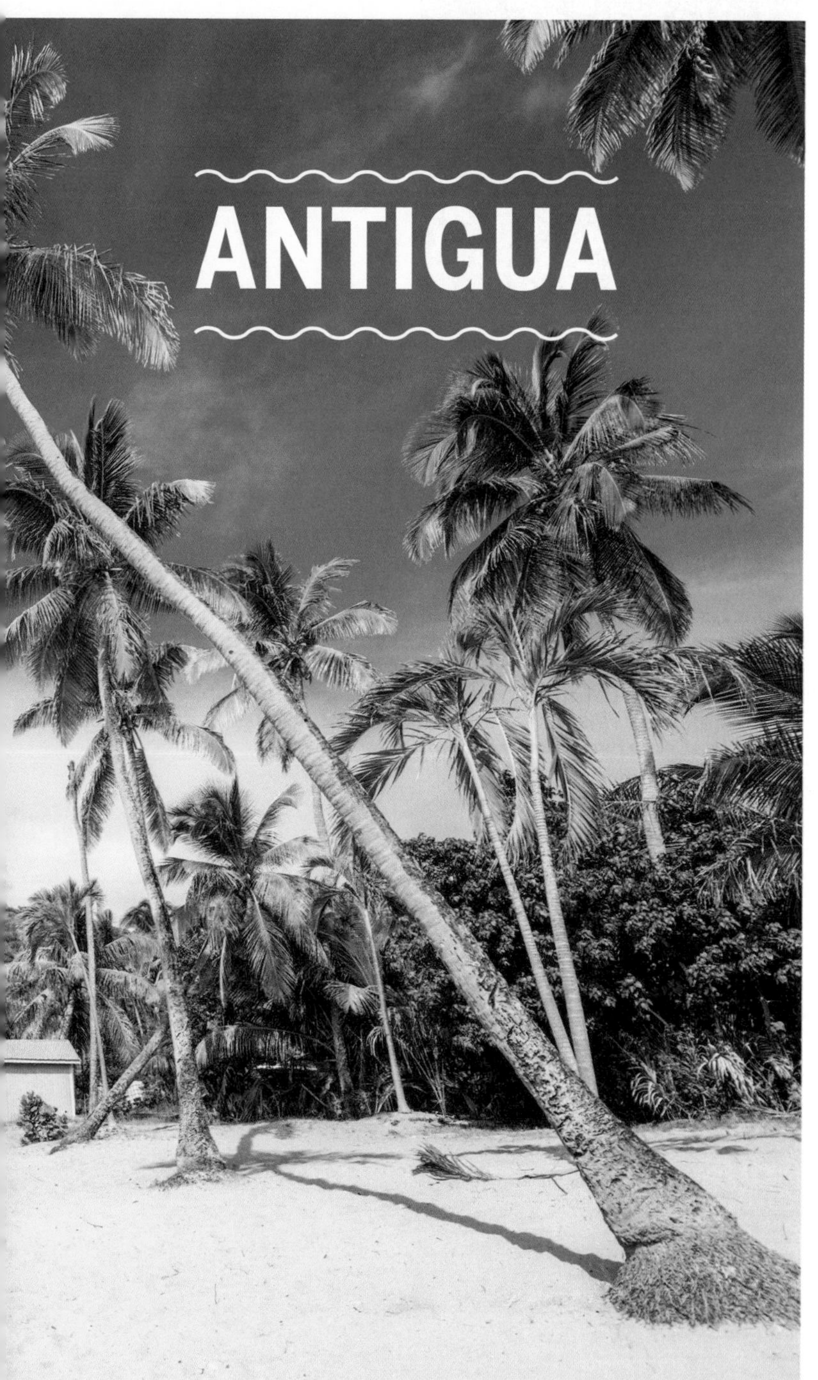
ANTIGUA

In This Chapter

Antigua at a Glance

On Antigua, life's a beach. Its corrugated coast cradles hundreds of perfect little strands lapped by beguiling enamel-blue water, while the sheltered bays have provided refuge for everyone from Admiral Nelson to buccaneers and yachties. There's a distinct English accent to this island: you'll find it in the bustling capital of St John's, in salty-glamorous English Harbour, and in the historic forts and other vestiges of the colonial past. Yet, Antigua is also quintessential Caribbean, full of candy-coloured villages, a rum-infused mellowness and bright-eyed locals that greet you with wide smiles.

With a Day in Port

- Visit the shops and art galleries at Nelson's Dockyard. (p232)
- Take a taxi to Jolly Harbour and relax on Valley Church Beach. (p234)

Best Places for...

Coffee Rituals Coffee House (p241)

Cocktails C&C Wine Bar (p240)

Local cuisine Roti King (p240)

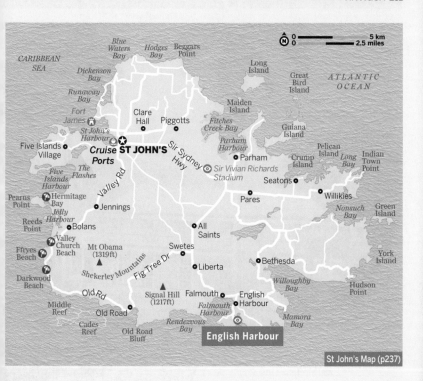

St John's Map (p237)

Getting from the Port

There are three cruise ports in St John's: Heritage Quay, nearby Redcliffe Quay and Deep Water Harbour (a 15-minute taxi ride from the two other ports). If you're docked at Heritage Quay or Redcliffe you'll be able to explore the capital city of St John's on foot. We do not recommend walking around the Deep Water Harbour port.

For destinations further afield, use a taxi or, if you want more independence, hire a car.

Fast Facts

Currency Eastern Caribbean dollar (EC$), US dollars (US$) accepted

Language English, Spanish

Money ATMs are available at the cruise port.

Visas Not required for citizens of the US, EU or Australia.

Best for free wi-fi Most restaurants and coffee shops near the cruise port offer free wi-fi.

Nelson's Dockyard

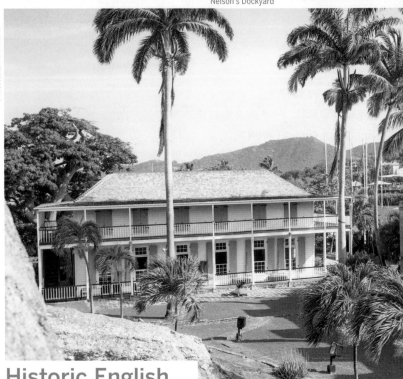

Historic English Harbour

Nowhere does Antigua flaunt its maritime heritage more than in English Harbour, a charming town with a rich past. Visit Nelson's Dockyard, where the famous English seaman was stationed during the Napoleonic Wars.

Great For...

Don't Miss

Carpenter's Rock Trail that leads from Galleon Beach to Shirley Heights.

The town sits on two sheltered bays, Falmouth Bay and English Harbour, where salty boats and ritzy yachts bob in the water. The era when the British Navy was based here is still encapsulated in the beautifully restored Nelson's Dockyards, home to shops, restaurants and bars that overlook a beautiful marina.

Nelson's Dockyard

Continuously in operation since 1745, this extensively restored Georgian-era marina was made a Unesco World Heritage site in 2016. Today its restored buildings house restaurants, hotels and businesses.

The Dockyard Museum relates tidbits about Antigua history, the dockyard and life at the forts. Among the many trinkets on display is a telescope once used by Nelson himself.

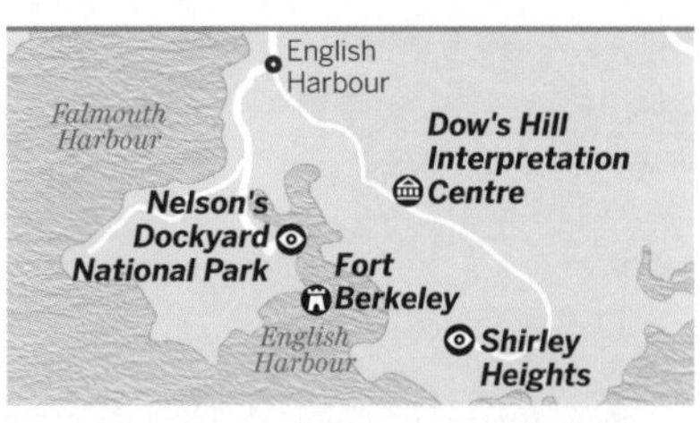

Explore Ashore

It's a 45-minute taxi ride (around US$24 for up to four people) from the cruise port in St John's. Public buses cost US$1; route 17 runs between West End and the Dockyard. Allow at least four hours for a trip to Historic English Harbour.

Need to Know

Admission to Nelson's Dockyard is US$8. The site is wheelchair accessible.

Fort Berkeley

Though ruined, this **fort** (Nelson's Dockyard) FREE, built in 1704 to protect English Harbour, still has enough walls and a cannon to evoke the challenges of the colonial era. It also offers a nice perspective of the harbor, Nelson's Dockyard and Galleon Beach.

Dow's Hill Interpretation Centre

For a primer on Antiguan history from the Amerindian era to the present, watch the 15-minute multimedia presentation at this **interpretative center** (268-481-5021; www.nationalparksantigua.com; Shirley Heights Rd, English Harbour; US$8; 9am-5pm) just past the entrance to Shirley Heights. Part of the Nelson's Dockyard National Park, it's low-tech and child-oriented but still informative.

Shirley Heights

This restored military lookout and gun **battery** was named after St Thomas Shirley (1727–1800), who became the first Governor of the Leeward Islands in 1781. Get some historical background at the small interpretive center, then continue uphill to explore the grounds for crumbling ruins and sweeping views.

As you head up the rise, the road forks with the left lane leading to the **Blockhouse**, where you can see the vestiges of officer's quarters and a powder magazine. If you turn right at the fork, the road dead ends at the **Shirley Heights Lookout**.

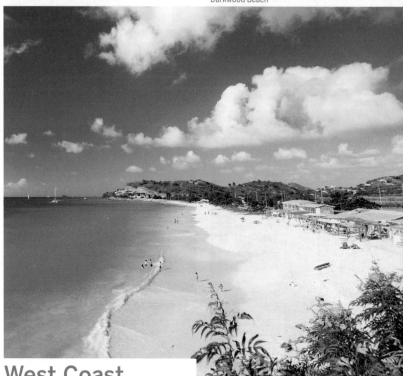

Darkwood Beach

West Coast Beaches

The coastal road south of Jolly Harbour wears a necklace of some of Antigua's best beaches, which are popular with cruise-ship passengers and locals alike.

Great For...

Don't Miss

Valley Church Beach, the best beach on this stretch of coast.

Hermitage Bay

This dreamy, secluded arc punctuates the end of a 2½-mile-long road (the last 2 miles are graded dirt road). Wave-tossed shells litter the white sand that remains largely crowd-free despite being next to the ultra-posh Hermitage Bay resort.

Valley Church Beach

This pretty palm-lined beach has calm and shallow aquamarine waters and powdery white sand, and is an obvious first-call for cruise-ship travelers. Most gather around the popular beach restaurant called the Nest, so if you're looking for a quiet spot, head to the south end of the beach. The gate to the beach is open from dawn to sunset. If it's closed, park on the street and walk in.

Valley Church Beach

DMITRI KOTCHETOV/SHUTTERSTOCK ©

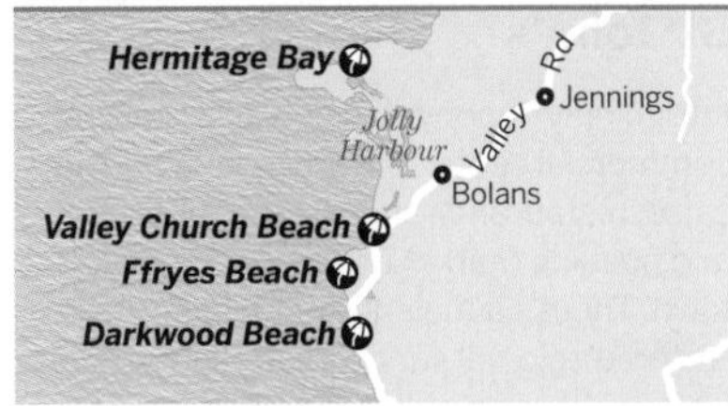

Explore Ashore

Allow at least three hours for a trip from the cruise port to the beaches in this area. We recommend taking a taxi rather than the bus if you are operating on a tight schedule.

Need to Know

A taxi ride is a half hour to Valley Bay and nearby beaches; it costs around US$25 for up to four people. The route 20 bus runs to Jolly Harbour.

Ffryes Beach

This long, sea-grape-shaded sandy ribbon has barbecue facilities, showers and toilets, and is popular with local families on weekends. Grab a cocktail in time for sunset from **Dennis Cocktail Bar & Restaurant** (268-462-6740; www.dennisantigua.com; mains EC$52-109; 10:30am-late, closed Mon Apr-Oct; P ;). Behind it is the gentle arc of Little Ffryes Beach, overlooked by the all-inclusive Cocobay Resort.

Darkwood Beach

This road-adjacent swath of beige sand makes for a convenient swimming and snorkeling spot. The eponymous **cafe** (cafe 10am-sunset) has a shower (US$1), changing rooms and also rents beach chairs. It's popular with locals on weekends.

Getting There & Away

Privately operated minivans offer services to and from the beaches, beginning and ending journeys in St John's. Buses heading down the west coast depart from the West bus station. There's no set timetable. Buses depart St John's when full and generally run from about 6am until 7pm, stopping at regular and requested stops along the way. It's also possible to flag down a bus. There are very few buses on Sunday. Fares cost EC$2.25 to EC$4. Bus Stop Antigua (www.busstopanu.com) has details.

St John's

Intriguingly shabby, Antigua's capital and commercial center is worth a spin for the cafes, restaurants, shops, cute museum and bustling market lining its compact town. There's a melange of buildings from restored colonial survivors to modern-day horrors. St John's all but shuts down at night and on Sundays. The town's sights and businesses are all within walking distance of the cruise-ship pier.

SIGHTS

Fort James Fort

(Fort Rd; P; 17) FREE Fort James, a small stronghold at the north side of St John's Harbour, dates back to 1706, but most of what you see today was built in 1739. Still sporting a few of its 36 cannons, a powder magazine and wall remnants, the site drips with atmosphere: it's moodily rundown and is rarely the scene of crowds.

A taxi from St John's costs US$12.

Public Market Market

(Market St; 6am-6pm Mon-Sat) Forage for exotic local produce such as sorrel, black pineapple and sugar apple alongside more familiar bananas, limes, mangoes and eggplant at St John's vibrant market, which spills out into surrounding streets on Friday and Saturday mornings. It's a fun place for browsing, snacking or people-watching. For fresh fish, follow your nose to the stalls next to the bus station, where vendors are happy to fillet your purchase.

Museum of Antigua & Barbuda Museum

(268-462-1469; www.antiguamuseums.net; cnr Market & Long Sts; adult/child under 12yr EC$8/free; 8:30am-4pm Mon-Fri, 10am-2pm Sat) In the stately 1750 courthouse, this modest museum traces the history of Antigua from its geological origins to its political independence in 1981. The hodgepodge of objects includes Arawak pottery, models of sugar plantations and the cricket bat of hometown hero Viv Richards. On display

Public market, St John's

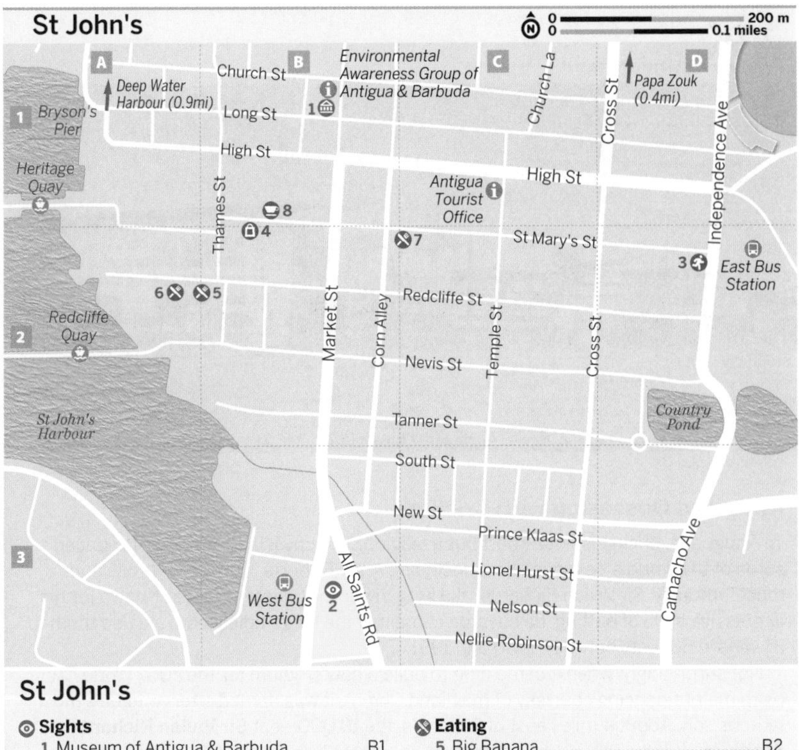

St John's

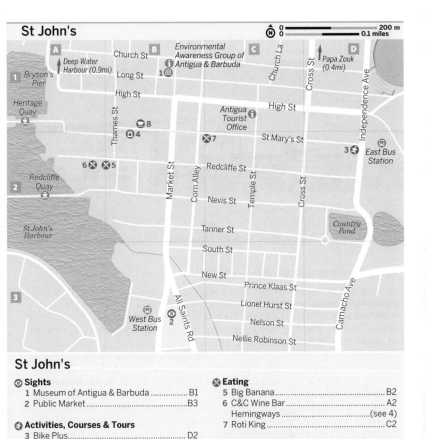

Sights
- 1 Museum of Antigua & Barbuda B1
- 2 Public Market B3

Activities, Courses & Tours
- 3 Bike Plus D2

Shopping
- 4 Natura B2

Eating
- 5 Big Banana B2
- 6 C&C Wine Bar A2
- Hemingways .... (see 4)
- 7 Roti King C2

Drinking & Nightlife
- 8 Rituals Coffee House B1

outside are four narrow-gauge locomotives from the early 20th century once used to transport sugarcane.

ACTIVITIES & TOURS

Adventure Antigua Adventure
(☎268-726-6355; www.adventureantigua.com) Eli Fuller, a former Olympian and third-generation Antiguan, offers educational and fun tours. His signature trip is the all-day Eco-Tour (US$115), which involves boating, swimming and snorkeling amid the pristine waters of North Sound National Park. The Xtreme Circumnav (US$170) aboard a 45ft speedboat includes a snorkel trip, a stop at a stingray marine park and a swim at remote Rendezvous Bay.

Book online for a 10% discount.

Antigua Rainforest Zip Line Tours Zip Lining
(☎268-562-6363; www.antiguarainforest.com; Fig Tree Dr, Wallings; adult/child from US$79/59; ⏰tours hourly 9am-noon Mon-Sat) Channel your inner Tarzan (or Jane) while roaring

Understand

Antigua's Obsession with Cricket

To Antiguans, cricket is not a sport but a religion. The tiny island state has produced some of the world's best cricketers, including Andy Roberts, Curtley Ambrose and, most famously, Sir Vivian Richards, aka King Viv or the 'Master-Blaster.' Known for his aggressive style of batting, he became captain of the West Indies team and led them to 27 wins in 50 tests between 1980 and 1991.

Not surprisingly, when it came time to build a new stadium for the 2007 World Cup (with major financing courtesy of mainland China), it was named after Antigua's most famous son. About 4 miles east of St John's, the 10,000-seat **Sir Vivian Richards Stadium** (☎268-481-2450; www.windiescricket.com; Sir Sydney Walling Hwy) ranks among the region's top cricket facilities yet has been dogged by difficulties from the start. The worst blow came in 2009 when the International Cricket Council imposed a one-year ban after a Test match between West Indies and England had to be called off due to unhealthy playing conditions. Play resumed in February 2010 and these days the new and improved stadium again hosts regional and international matches.

The cricket season runs from January to July with official matches usually played on Thursdays, Saturdays and Sundays. If you want to see local passion in action, check www.windiescricket.com or www.antigua-barbuda.org for the schedule.

Sir Vivian Richards Stadium INDUSTRYANDTRAVEL/SHUTTERSTOCK ©

through the treetops suspended on zip lines. The 2½-hour 'Full Course' includes 12 zips, short hikes between suspension bridges and a challenge course. Note that the park is usually only open when a cruise ship is in port and that reservations are a must.

Treasure Island Cruises Boating

(☎268-461-8675; www.facebook.com/TreasureIslandCruises) Denzil and Brian take small groups of people out on boat trips aboard a 70ft catamaran that combine sailing, snorkeling, entertainment and a barbecue. Options include the Circumnavigation tour (US$120), the Cades Reef tour (US$120) and the Bird Island tour (US$100).

View from Shirley Heights (p233)

Bike Plus Cycling

(☎268-462-2453; cnr Independence Ave & St Mary's St; bike rental per day from US$17.50) Well-respected bike shop has a sizeable fleet of bicycles for rent.

SHOPPING

Duty-free shops cluster in Heritage Quay just off the cruise-ship pier, but don't expect major bargains except on booze and cigarettes. It segues into the Vendors' Mall, a cacophonous maze of trinkets and T-shirts (bargaining advised). Adjacent Redcliffe Quay (the former site of St John's slave market) has more upscale galleries and boutiques. For local color, skip over a block or two to Market, Thames and St Mary's Sts.

Natura Cosmetics

(☎268-725-6402; www.facebook.com/pg/naturahealthandhealing; Lower Mary's St; ⏰9am-4pm Mon-Sat) This pretty store is the domain of Silvana and Jennifer, two local women who produce an entire range of herbal remedies and healing balms from organic ingredients grown on the island. Bestsellers include the Mosquito Cream, the Sunburn Soothe and the Bye Bye Bumps Acne Cream. There's also a line of edibles including honeys, jams and chutneys.

EATING & DRINKING

St John's has several excellent restaurants as well as plenty of street food in the downtown area and near the market, which is busiest on Saturday mornings.

Big Banana Pizza $

(☎268-480-6985; www.bigbanana-antigua.com; Redcliffe Quay; pizzas EC$25-81; ⏰10am-midnight Mon-Sat; 📶) Some patrons have been coming to this buzzy former rum warehouse (locally known simply as 'Pizzas') for more than 30 years, so irresistible are its pizzas that come in four sizes, on regular or thin crusts and with classic toppings. On weekends you may have to elbow your way inside. Thursdays from 5pm to 9pm is 'Ladies Night' with EC$5 cocktail specials.

Roti King Caribbean $

(☎268-462-2328; cnr St Mary's St & Corn Alley; roti EC$18-26; ⏰10am-midnight Sun-Thu, to 2:30am Fri & Sat) This little sibling-owned cottage does brisk business all day long with its mouthwatering roti – chicken, shrimp, pork, beef, veggies or conch swimming in a mildly spicy curry sauce and wrapped into a soft flatbread. Try them with a homemade passion-fruit or sorrel juice or ginger beer.

Papa Zouk Seafood $$

(☎268-464-6044; www.facebook.com/Papazouk; Hilda Davis Dr; mains EC$55-90; ⏰7pm-midnight Mon-Sat) This high-energy joint is a local institution, famous for its Antiguan-style bouillabaisse and fresh fish – mahi-mahi to butterfish – served grilled or fried. With zouk on the sound system, crazy murals, Christmas lights and a nautical decor, it's the kind of place that's downright trippy even before you've started sampling the vast rum selection. Reservations essential.

C&C Wine Bar International $$

(☎268-460-7025; www.ccwinehouse.com; Redcliffe Quay, Redcliffe St; dishes EC$25-68; ⏰noon-5pm Mon, to 10:30pm Tue-Sat) 'Eat, drink, socialize' is the tantalizing motto of this locally adored courtyard cafe where South African wines complement tasty pastas, burgers, paninis and mains such as fragrant shrimp coconut curry. Tables spill from the pint-sized wine shop–bar onto a romantic courtyard, and fill to capacity crowd during 'Lasagne Thursdays' and 'Karaoke Saturdays' – book ahead.

The name, by the way, stands for Cutie and Claudine, the charming hosts.

Hemingways Caribbean $$

(☎268-462-2763; www.hemingwaysantigua.com; Lower St Mary's St; mains lunch EC$24-65, dinner EC$50-85; ⏰9:30am-10pm Mon-Sat) No matter where the hands of the clock are, you can have a fine meal upstairs at this breezy 1820s Creole cottage with gingerbread trim. Skip the international choices and go for local flavors such as spicy chicken curry, coconut rum-flambéed lobster and

St John's marina

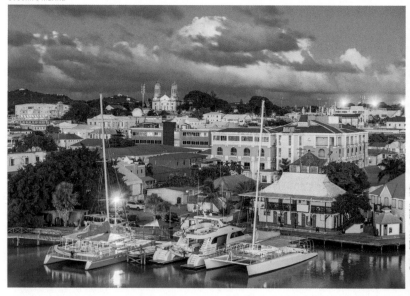

the off-menu blueberry bread pudding with rum-butter sauce. The veranda tables are great for people-watching.

Rituals Coffee House Cafe
(268-562-7870; Lower St Mary's St; 8am-7pm;) This local chain has good coffee drinks and fresh sandwiches and, thanks to free wi-fi, is a popular hangout among the island youth.

INFORMATION

Antigua Tourist Office (268-562-7600; www.visitantiguabarbuda.com; ACB Financial Centre, High St; 8am-4pm Mon-Fri)

Environmental Awareness Group of Antigua & Barbuda (www.eagantigua.org; cnr Market & Long Sts; 9am-4pm Mon-Fri) Upstairs from the Museum of Antigua & Barbuda, EAG works toward raising awareness about issues of conservation and sustainability, and also organizes workshops, turtle-watching trips and guided hikes. The website has information about upcoming events.

GETTING AROUND

Sights and eateries are easily accessible on foot, and taxis are also available.

BUS

Services depart when full and stop at regular and request stops en route. Be aware that buses can be very slow and often don't run on schedule, which can be bad for cruise passengers on a tight schedule. Fares cost EC$2.25 to EC$4.

West bus station (Market St) Minivans headed to points north, west and south (eg Jolly Harbour, the beaches and English Harbour) leave from this station next to the public market. There's a **taxi stand** (268-562-0262; www.unitedtaxiassociation.com; 8:30am-6pm) adjacent to the West bus station, and taxi drivers also hang around Heritage Quay.

East bus station (Independence Ave) For destinations east and southeast of town (eg Betty's Hope, Long Bay).

CAR

You can rent a car in St John's from well-known American car rental brands, but it is very expensive (often around US$200) and is not recommended. If you don't mind spending the money, we recommend Hertz in downtown St John's.

TAXI

Avoid the more expensive taxi stand directly in front of the port and walk to Thames Street where you'll find more affordable taxi service to the beaches and other sights. Unlike many of the other islands, there are no set rates for taxi service, so you'll need to haggle over the price. Most taxis are vans, and it's best to put a group together to save money before leaving the port. Standard rates are US$3 to US$7 per person to anywhere on the island if there are four or more passengers.

PAULO MIGUEL COSTA/SHUTTERSTOCK ©

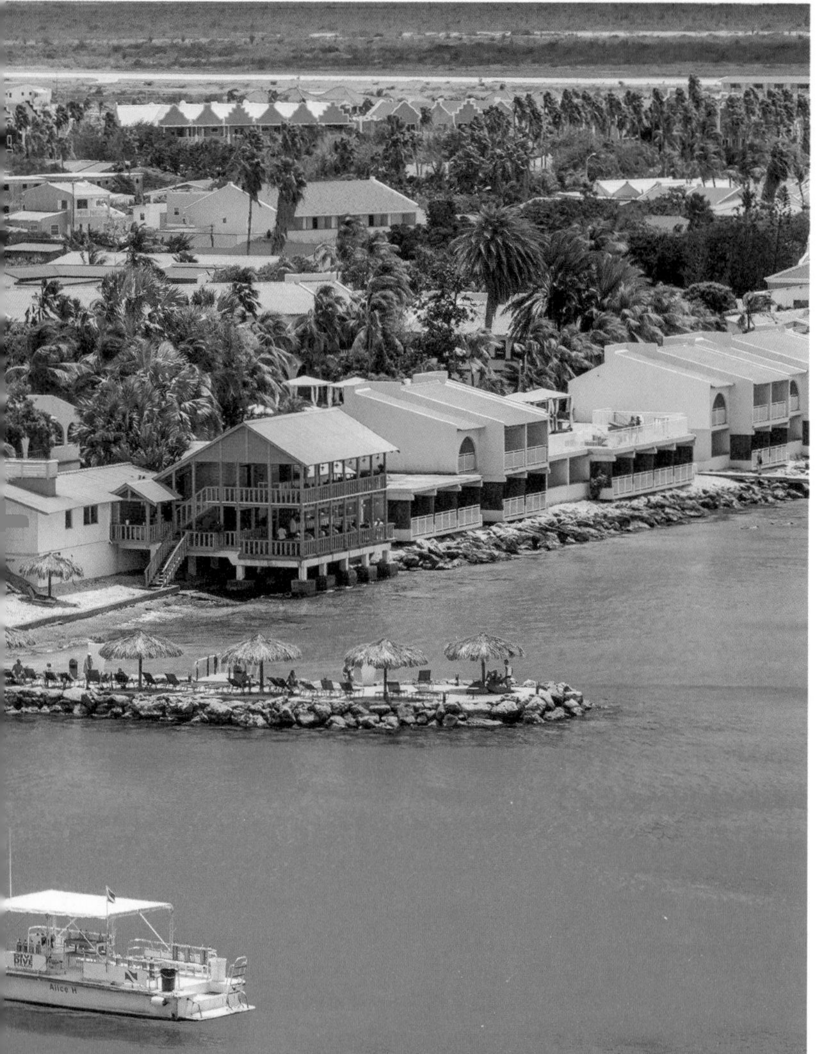

BONAIRE

In This Chapter

Bonaire at a Glance

A small island with a desert landscape, Bonaire is not for everyone – but it is for divers and snorkelers who want to immerse themselves in that vibrant world under the sea. The beauty of Bonaire is that the coral reef, designated a national park, is just a few feet from the shoreline. Dozens of exceptional dive sites are easily accessible from the shore and teeming with life, making this island an independent diver's (and snorkeler's) paradise. Above the surface, there is world-class windsurfing on Lac Bay and excellent kayaking among the mangroves. Biking trails wind through the arid hills, while driving routes show off the island's historical and natural sights.

With a Day in Port

- Dive or snorkel one of the many colorful reefs and dive sites near the island's coast.(p246)
- Kayak and snorkel at the Mangrove Info Center.(p247)

Best Places for...

Coffee Karel's Beach Bar (p252)

Cocktails Cuba Compagnie (p252)

Local cuisine Wil's Tropical Grill (p251)

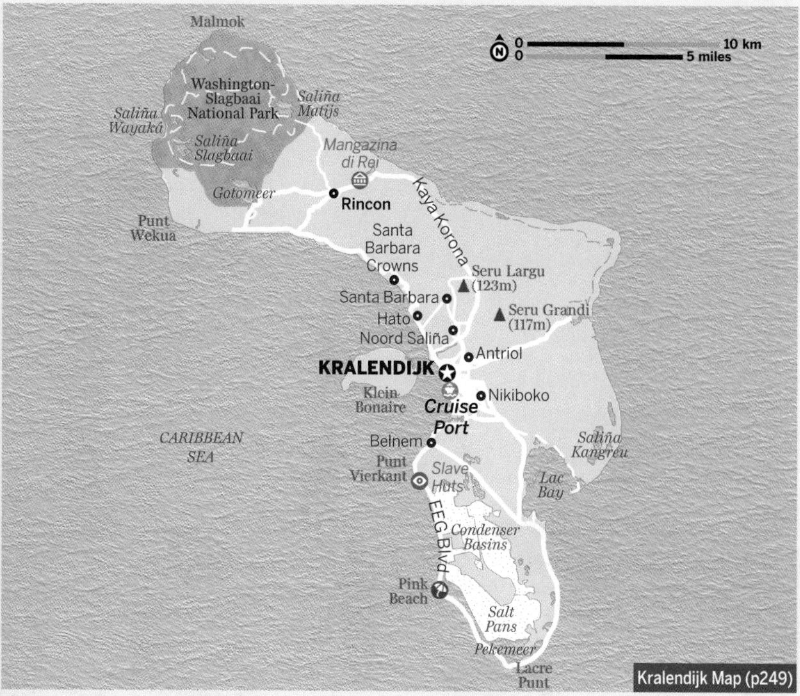

Kralendijk Map (p249)

Getting from the Port

Cruise ships dock in downtown Kralendijk, and passengers will find it easy and enjoyable to explore the port on foot. Taxis (US$5 to US$10 per person round trip to most places) are the best way to get around the island and to reach the beaches with snorkeling and diving sites. Most taxi drivers will also offer to give you a great hour-long tour of the island for around $40 for up to four people.

Fast Facts

Currency US dollar (US$)

Language English, Papiamento, Dutch

Money ATMs are available across the island, including at the Harborside Mall near the cruise port.

Visas Not required for citizens of the US, EU or Australia.

Best for free wi-fi Karel's Beach Bar (p252), a short walk north of the cruise port.

Washington Slagbaai National Park

Snorkeling & Kayaking

Even the license plates on Bonaire declare it a 'Diver's Paradise'. It's true that visitors are spoiled for choice when it comes to beautiful beaches, and diving and snorkeling opportunities.

Great For...

Don't Miss

Diving the colorful and stunning coral growths on the Salt Pier pilings.

There are 22 beaches on the island and 90 excellent dive sites, including several wrecks and some of the healthiest, most colorful reef formations that you'll find in the Caribbean. The vast majority of snorkel and dive sites are found on the west coast of the island, stretching out in both directions from the cruise port. One of the most popular dive sites is the *Hilma Hooker* wreck dive. Snorkelers will be very happy with the reefs at Pink Beach and Karpata.

Diving & Snorkeling

Bonaire's dive sites are strung along the western side of the island. The closeness of the reefs, the clarity of the waters and the system of marking the sites combine to make for unparalleled access for divers. You can reach more than half of the identified dive sites from shore.

BEAT J KORNER/SHUTTERSTOCK ©

The Bonaire National Marine Park, recognized by Unesco, covers the entire coast of the island, including Klein Bonaire, to a depth of 200ft (60m). Between the two islands, there are about 90 named dive sites; look for the painted yellow rocks. The sites vary greatly in terms of depth, currents and other factors, but there are plenty of sites that are ideal for beginners.

Kayaking Among Mangroves

On the island's southeastern side, Lac is a large inland bay that provides a critical habitat for green turtles, queen conchs – and windsurfers.

The northern side of Lac Bay is sheltered by mangrove forests, where wetland birds breed and reef creatures mature (which explains why the mangrove is sometimes called a 'coral reef nursery'). It's a gem for paddlers and snorkelers, who can spot young fish, sea stars and sponges in the crystal clear waters.

The **Mangrove Info Center** (780-5353; www.mangrovecenter.com; Kaminda Lac 140; 30min tour US$27/46; from 8:30am Mon-Sat) offers guided kayak trips, as well as excursions in a solar-powered boat. Stop by the information center (completely powered by wind and solar, by the way) for some informative displays about this unique ecosystem.

Dive Operators

Recommended dive operators include Bonaire Dive & Adventure (p249) and Wanna Dive (p249). They offer tank rental and refills, equipment rental, certification, boat dives to less accessible sites and guided shore dives.

Explore Ashore

Allow at least four hours for a two-tank diving trip, and allow at least three hours for a kayaking trip among the mangroves.

Need to Know

Before diving independently, all divers must pay the US$25 marine-park fee (US$10 for snorkelers) and do an orientation and check-out dive at a local dive shop, to get comfortable with weights, conditions and park rules.

Kralendijk

Kralendijk is a small island capital, with a long, strollable seafront and a smattering of colorful, colonial architecture. It lacks historic sites or beautiful beaches, but it's a pleasant place to stop, shop, lunch, dine or drink with sunset views.

Right around the cruise-ship terminal, the compact 'downtown' area is lined with shops and restaurants and shady plazas, all of which lend their tropical charm to the capital. Outside of this three-square-block area, the city spreads out in a less orderly sprawl, with marinas, resorts and artificial beaches hogging the waterfront.

SIGHTS

Terramar Museum Museum

(717-0423; www.terramarmuseum; Kaya JNE Craane 6; adult/child US$10/free; 9am-6pm Mon-Sat) Brand new in 2016, this small museum provides an overview of the history and archaeology of Bonaire. There's an assortment of artifacts, accompanied by audio clips that put a voice to the historical facts. In the front room, an impressive timeline and video demonstrate how peoples have moved around the Caribbean region over the course of history.

Legend of Captain Don

In 1962, Captain Don Stewart arrived in Bonaire from California aboard the *Valerie Queen* with just 63 cents to his name. He fell in love with the island, and devoted the next 50-plus years to protecting the reef and making it more accessible to divers and snorkelers. Although the good captain passed in 2014, his legacy lives on at the so-called 'home of diving freedom,' resort Captain Don's Habitat, and at the island's 90 dive sites, many of which he marked and named himself.

Klein Bonaire Island

About 1km off the coast of Kralendijk, this little deserted island is where you'll find the region's most attractive beach, aka No Name Beach. There are no facilities, aside from the marked dive sites. But this is a popular spot for cruisers and beach bums who come over to snorkel the turquoise waters and lounge on the white sands. The *Good Return* or *Kantika de Amor* water taxis (p253) can give you a lift across the sea.

Fort Oranje Fort

(museum 8am-noon & 1:30-4:30pm Mon-Fri) FREE Follow the cannons south along the waterfront to a small bastion that was built by the Dutch in 1639 and served as the governor's mansion until 1837. The defensive cannons were actually scavenged from a British warship that grounded on the south shore in the early 1800s. Although the British gained control of Bonaire several times during the Napoleonic Wars, the island (and thus the fort) never saw any action.

ACTIVITIES

Sea Turtle Conservation Bonaire Wildlife-Watching

(STCB; 717-2225; www.bonaireturtles.org; Kaya Korona 53; turtle tours US$40) Three mornings a week, travelers can accompany the STCB workers on their rounds monitoring the sea-turtle nests on Klein Bonaire. The organization maintains careful records of all new and existing nests, including counting the egg shells and looking for stragglers from any newly hatched nest. For travelers who can make a longer-term commitment, there are several cool volunteer opportunities.

Kralendijk

Sights
1 Fort Oranje C3
2 Terramar Museum B2

Shopping
3 Artisan Market C3
4 Bonaire Affair B2
5 Jan Art Gallery C3
6 Salt Shop C3

Eating
7 Bobbejan's Take-Away B1
8 Wil's Tropical Grill C2

Drinking & Nightlife
9 Cuba Compagnie C3
10 Karel's Beach Bar B2

Long-term volunteers undergo training to become independent 'beachkeepers' – monitoring beaches all around the island. From January to April, STCB recruits snorkelers to help out with its in-water survey to count, identify and record sea turtle species.

Bonaire Dive & Adventure Diving

(☎717-2229; www.bonairediveandadventure.com; Kaya Gobernador N Debrot 77a; shore/boat dive $33/52, 6 days unlimited air or nitrox US$195; ⊙8:30am-4:30pm) Offers a full menu of dive packages, including boat and shore dives, air and nitrox etc. Orientation and check-out dive take place every day. The 'adventure' part of Dive & Adventure refers to mountain biking, kayaking and cave explorations.

Wanna Dive Diving

(☎717-8884; www.wannadive.com; Kaya Gobernador N Debrot 73, Eden Beach Resort; boat dive US$42, night diving US$65; ⊙9am-5pm) Wanna dive? Of course you do! In addition to the regular range of equipment and air, this low-key operation also offers full-day boat trips (US$150), east-coast diving (US$45) and night diving.

SHOPPING

The city's shopping area is crammed into a few blocks on Kaya Grandi, just one block in from the cruise-ship terminal. It's a short strip, but there are plenty of interesting local shops (and no international chains). An **artisan market** (www.bonaireartandcraftmarket.com; Plaza Wilhelmina; hours vary) sets up when there's a cruise ship in port.

Salt Shop Cosmetics
(www.bonairesalt.com; Kaya Grandi 9; 8am-6pm Mon-Sat) What could be a better Bonaire souvenir than something made from sea salt? This little shop carries sea salt for cooking (plus grinders and shakers), as well as bath and body products.

Bonaire Affair Gifts & Souvenirs
(Terramar Mall) On the strip in front of the cruise-ship terminal, this little shop is packed with goodies, including jewelry, paintings, driftwood art and lots of other island-themed knickknacks. Check out the scuba-diver-crossing bumper stickers.

Jan Art Gallery Art
(www.janartbonaire.com; Kaya Grandi 14) Janice Huckaby's paintings capture the glorious colors of Bonaire's reef, sea and sky. Paintings and prints are available, as are various souvenirs.

EATING & DRINKING

Bonaire's top restaurants are mostly clustered along Kralendijk's waterfront or on the main drag Kaya Grandi. The larger resorts all have restaurants – some of which are counted among the island's culinary highlights.

Between 2 Buns Sandwiches $
(www.facebook.com/between2bunsbonaire; Kaya Gobernador N Debrot; sandwiches US$8-12; 7am-5pm Mon-Fri, 8am-4pm Sat;) The go-to spot for a hearty and wholesome breakfast

Understand

Bonaire's Landscape & Wildlife

Bonaire's landscape is arid and mostly flat, with a few notable hills and valleys in the northern part of the island. Vegetation consists of cactus and scrubby trees – nothing else can really grow due to the lack of water and the onslaught of goats, donkeys and other nibblers. The southern part of the island is characterized by its vast salt flats and the lush mangrove swamps around Lac Bay.

Despite the seeming desolation, the island is rich with bird life, including the iconic pink flamingo and the endangered yellow-shouldered Amazon parrot. Other species you're sure to spot include the banana quit, brown-throated parakeet, caracara, tropical mockingbird and troupial, not to mention many water birds.

Speaking of water, this is where Bonaire is truly rich in life. Coral reefs grow in profusion along the lee coast, often just a few meters from the shore. Hundreds of species of fish and dozens of corals thrive in the clear, warm waters. Sea turtles, dolphins and rays are among the larger creatures swimming about.

Bonaire has few major environmental problems, but there are always concerns. Development and overgrazing have caused deforestation on much of the island. The reef along the coastline is protected by the marine park, but the degree of independence granted to divers makes the regulations difficult to enforce.

Caribbean mockingbird JOHN A. ANDERSON/SHUTTERSTOCK ©

or lunch. A wide variety of sandwiches are served on fresh bread. It's a perfect lunch stop between dives.

Wil's Tropical Grill Caribbean **$$**
(Kaya LD Gerharts 9; mains US$18-25; ⌚5:30-9:30pm Mon-Sat) If you're in port for the evening, don't miss this place. With contemporary art inside and a blooming garden outside, this modern Caribbean bistro exudes the colors and flavors of the region. The menu changes daily, but look for favorites such as Thai coconut shrimp and a house-smoked marlin. Start things off with a signature cocktail and you're in for a good night.

Bobbejan's Take-Away Barbecue $$
(717-4783; Kaya Albert Engelhardt 2; mains US$10-12; 6-10pm Fri & Sat, noon-2pm & 6-10pm Sun) Don't let the name fool you: there are tables here out back under a nice tree. But getting one is a challenge as *everybody* comes here for the super-tender ribs and the velvety peanut sauce on the plate of Indonesian-style chicken satay.

Spice Beach Bar Caribbean $$
(www.spicebonaire.com; Kaya Gobernador N Debrot, Eden Beach Resort; mains US$15-25, prix fixe US$35; 7am-11pm Sun-Thu, to midnight Fri & Sat) On the sand at Eden Beach Resort, this is a recommended spot for classic, casual fare, such as barbecue, burgers, satay or steaks. If you're looking for something fancier, the more formal restaurant offers a set menu.

Karel's Beach Bar Bar
(www.karelsbeachbar.com; Kaya JNE Craane 12; 9am-1am Sun-Thu, to 3am Fri & Sat) It's not technically a beach bar, but it is set on a pier that juts into the water and promises happy-hour specials, sunset views and good vibes all around.

Cuba Compagnie Bar
(www.cubacompagniebonaire.nl; Kaya Grandi 1; 5pm-late) The island's hottest spot is this sultry Cuban cafe, especially on Thursday night, when salsa dancers show their stuff. Any night of the week, the place is packed with happy patrons sipping mojitos and feasting on fusion fare. The atmospheric interior is adorned with eclectic artwork and old photographs, but the outdoor seating area is the place to be.

INFORMATION

Bonaire Tourist Office (717-8322; www.tourismbonaire.com; Kaya Grandi 2; 8am-noon & 1:30-5pm Mon-Fri) Staff can answer questions about tours and more, as well as offer a good selection of brochures.

GETTING AROUND

The city is small enough that you can explore most of it on foot, though you'll want a vehicle to get around the island. Bicycles are available for

Understand

Bonaire's History

The Arawaks lived on Bonaire for thousands of years before Spain laid claim to it in 1499. A mere 20 years later there were none left, as the Spanish sent all the natives to work in mines elsewhere in the empire. The only remains of the Arawak civilization on Bonaire are a few inscriptions in remote caves and some artifacts at the Terramar Museum (p248).

The depopulated Bonaire stayed pretty quiet until 1634, when the Dutch took control, building Fort Oranje (p248) to protect the harbor. The Dutch looked to the flat land in the south and saw a future in salt production. Thousands of slaves were imported to work in horrific conditions. You can see a few surviving slave huts at the southern end of the island, and at the **Mangazina di Rei** (786-2101; www.bonaireculturetours.com; Blvd Miguel A Pourier; adult/child US$10/5; 9am-4pm Mon-Fri), where the slaves had to travel to get their provisions, in Rincon at the north of the island.

When slavery was abolished in the 19th century, the salt factories closed. The population – former slaves, Dutch landowners and South American transplants – lived pretty simple lives until after WWII, when the salt ponds reopened (this time with machines doing the hard work). The revived industry, coupled with the postwar booms in tourism and diving, gave a real boost to the economy.

Bonaire's salt pans

rent, and are best on the paths and roads outside of town; Kralendijk can get very crowded when cruise ships are docked.

Rental cars are available but not recommended. The roads are very narrow and some of the roads outside of the towns are unpaved and often cause costly damage to rental cars and jeeps. Golf carts are a fun way to see the island at your own pace, while 4WD tours are a good way to see the undeveloped areas of the island.

Bonaire Cruisers (777-8777; www.bonaire-cruisers) is good for golf cart rentals and tours.

Good Return Water Taxi (Karel's Water Taxi; 788-8501; www.goodreturnbonaire.com; adult/child US$15/10; departs 10am, noon & 2pm Mon-Sat) Shuttles passengers to No Name Beach on Klein Bonaire, and back again 2½ hours later. It departs from Karel's Beach Bar (p252).

Kantika de Amor (796-5399; www.watertaxikleinbonaire.com; round-trip US$20; departs 10am, noon & 2pm) This trusty catamaran transported Queen Beatrix when she was visiting the island. Fortunately, you don't have to be royalty to get a ride. The *Kantika de Amor* takes passengers to Klein Bonaire three times a day, and brings them back to the mainland 2½ hours later.

CURAÇAO

In This Chapter

Curaçao at a Glance

With its delightful Dutch colonial architecture, bustling commercial capital and excellent history museums, go-go Curaçao feels like a little piece of Europe on the edge of the Caribbean. That is, a little piece of Europe with glorious hidden beaches, amazing onshore snorkeling and diving, and a wild undeveloped windward coast. Curaçao has a surging economy beyond tourism, which means that Willemstad has factories, humdrum neighborhoods and sometimes bad traffic. Catering to visitors is not the primary aim here. But if you're looking for a Caribbean island that is busy setting its own pace, Curaçao is for you.

With a Day in Port

- Walk the streets of Willemstad, and experience a Caribbean culture intertwined with old-world charm. (p260)
- Spend the day at the beach, preferably Kenepa, Playa Porto Mari or Cas Abao. (p258)

Best Places for...

Cocktails Rainbow Lounge (p267)

Local cuisine Old Market (p266)

Fine dining Rozendaels (p267)

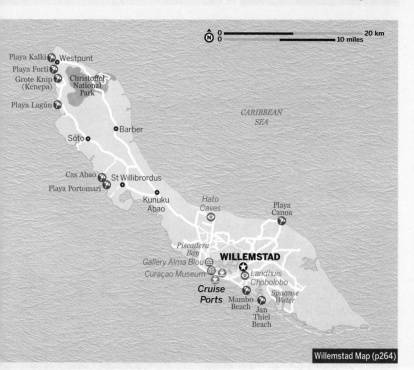

Willemstad Map (p264)

Getting from the Port

There are two ports in Willemstad. Ships that can make it under the bridge on Sint Anna Bay dock at the central Curaçao Cruise Terminal. The big behemoths of the cruise-ship industry dock at the Mega Cruise Terminal, a short walk south. They are both close to the main shopping and tourist district of Willemstad in Punda. If you're on foot, just cross the Queen Emma Bridge.

Fast Facts

Currency Netherlands Antillean guilder (NAf), US dollar (US$) is widely accepted.

Language English, Spanish, Papiamento, Dutch

Money ATMs are available across the bridge at the banks around Punda.

Visas Not required for citizens of the US, EU or Australia.

Best for free wi-fi Downtown Willemstad has free public wi-fi access.

Playa Porto Mari

SIMON DANNHAUER/SHUTTERSTOCK ©

Curaçao's Best Beaches

Most of the beaches dot the western side of the island, and with ships docking smack dab in the middle of them in Willemstad, passengers will have little problem finding a great beach to unwind. Pick your beach by your favorite activity.

Great For...

Don't Miss

Walking Kenepa Beach's beautiful shoreline.

The best beaches are scattered along the coast, so beach-hopping between them all isn't really feasible with the short amount of time passengers have in port.

Cas Abao

This mid-coast **beach** (www.casabaobeach.com; per car NAf10-12.50; ⌚8am-6pm) is an island favorite for its soft white sand, crystal-clear waters and surrounding scenery. It's a private beach with good facilities, including guarded parking lot, lockers, restaurant and massage hut. You can also rent snorkel gear, though you'll see more sea life further up the coast.

Cas Abao is almost due west of Sint Willibrordus, but you'll have to get here via the Kaminda Monica Kapel-Matheeuw. It's about 4km from the turn-off.

Playa Kalki
Westpunt
Grote Knip (Kenepa)
Christoffel National Park
CARIBBEAN SEA
Soto
Barber
Cas Abao
Playa Portomari
St Willibrordus

Explore Ashore

Allow three to four hours for a beach excursion, especially for the beaches on the north end of the island. A taxi to Kenepa or Playa Kalki will take about 45 minutes each way. A bus (US$2 each way, one hour) is the best option for budget travelers.

Need to Know

Bring your own drinks and snacks if you're heading to Kenepa Beach. The beach is undeveloped and the vendors that sell refreshments have high prices.

Grote Knip (Kenepa)

If you want to bask in the Caribbean glory of one of the most beautiful beaches on the island, head to Kenepa Beach – it's a real stunner. In fact, you've probably seen it on the cover of a Curaçao tourist brochure. A perfect crescent of brilliant white sand is framed by azure waters and verdant hills. There are a few snack shacks and places to rent snorkel gear, but it's much less cluttered than the island's private beaches.

Just south of this massive stretch of sand is Klein Knip (aka Kenepa Chiki), which is smaller but no less scenic. In both cases, avoid weekends, when half the island's population show up.

Playa Porto Mari

There's a lot to love about **Playa Porto Mari** (www.playaportomari.com; adult/child US$3.50/free; 9:30am-6:30pm), including the white coral sand and clear waters that shelter a unique double reef – excellent for snorkelers and divers alike. Look for the artificial 'reef balls' that were constructed to encourage new coral growth. Onshore, there are three hiking trails.

Playa Kalki

The westernmost beach, **Playa Kalki** (Sabana Westpunt) FREE is a small, secluded beach tucked into a cove near the island's far tip. It's not exactly a destination beach: the sea life is more vibrant at Playa Lagún and the scenery is more beautiful at Grote Knip, but crowds are fewer here.

Highlights of Old Willemstad

Explore the fascinating history and old-world charm of Willemstad on a walk through the historic district.

Start Mega Cruise Port or the Curaçao Cruise Terminal
Distance 2km
Duration One hour walking time, allow four hours minimum

Classic Photo Queen Emma Bridge

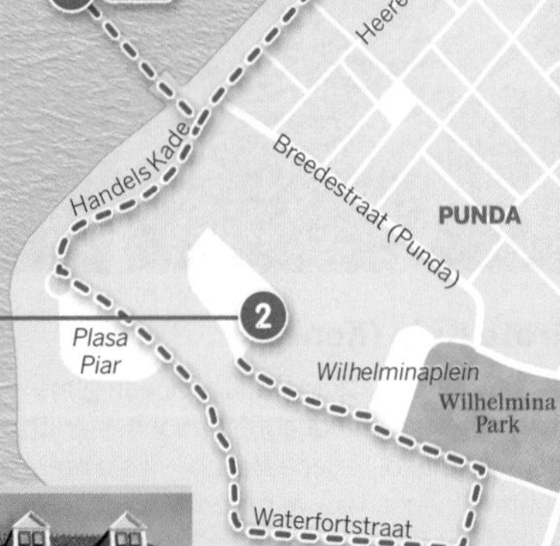

1 From the cruise terminal, head north and cross the **Queen Emma Bridge** (p262), which often opens on hinges to allow vessels cruising through Sint Annabai.

2 Walk to **Fort Amsterdam** (p262), via Plaza Piar, a fine example of colonial Dutch architecture. Explore the courtyard and church built in 1769.

3 Head back to Queen Emma Bridge and follow Handelskade, crossing the wooden walkway that spans the Waigaat waterway, leading to the **Curaçao Maritime Museum** (p263).

4 Cross back over the wooden walkway over the Waigaat, and follow Sha Caprileskade to the **Floating Market** (p263), a collection of charming and colorful sailboats that rope up along the Waigaat and sell mostly produce, fish, and souvenirs.

5 Continue east on Sha Caprileskade to the **Old Market** (p266), where you can stop for a bit of Caribbean food in a very casual, authentic restaurant. Follow the route back to the cruise ship.

Take a Break... Enjoy a drink and authentic Caribbean food at the Old Market.

Willemstad

The old town of Willemstad is split by Sint Annabaai, which is actually a channel to Schottegat, a large inland bay. On the western side is Otrobanda, an old workers' neighborhood that has a mixture of beautifully restored buildings and areas that are still rough around the edges. Follow Wan Lennepstraat uphill into a safe, historic neighborhood for great views of the city and harbor. East of the channel – and linked by the swinging Queen Emma Bridge – is Punda, the old commercial center. Just east of Punda is an equally historic colonial area, Pietermaai, which has a funky mix of decaying mansions, spiffy rehabs, oddball shops and quixotic cafes.

SIGHTS

Fort Amsterdam Fort

(www.fortchurchcuracao.com; Gouvernementsplein, Punda; grounds 8am-5pm Mon-Fri, church 10am-1:30pm Mon-Fri) FREE Dating from the 17th century, this much-modified fort is now home to government offices. Inside the large courtyard (enter through the gate on the western side), the rich colors of Dutch colonial architecture are on full display. The only building open to the public is the 1769 **Fortkirche**, the oldest church on the island. It contains the original pulpit and governor's pew, with other historic items on display in the small museum.

Queen Emma Bridge Bridge

Spanning the Sint Annabaai, this local landmark is sometimes called Our Swinging Old Lady. It's a pontoon bridge that swings open to make way for oceangoing ships. When the bridge is open, two free public ferries shuttle passengers back and forth between Punta and Otrobanda.

Museum Kura Hulanda Museum

(434-7701; www.kurahulanda.com; Klipstraat 9, Otrobanda; adult/child US$10/7; 9am-4:30pm Mon-Sat) Located in a 19th-century merchant's house and slave quarters, this excellent museum documents the brutal history of slavery in the New World, including the slave trade, slave culture and abolition. There is also a fantastic collection

Floating market, Willemstad

Understand

Curaçao's Landscape & Wildlife

Curaçao is a mix of lush areas near the coasts and more arid regions inland. (The contrast is on full display at Christoffel National Park.) Human development has meant that land-based wildlife is limited, though birdlife is rich. The National Underwater Park protects a 20km stretch of coastline along the island's southern tip, but the reef is rich with marine life all along the west coast, where there are dozens of dive and snorkel sites.

The main environmental threat in Curaçao is air and water pollution from the Venezuelan-run oil refinery and other industry on the inner harbor (Schottegat) of Willemstad. Given the importance of these installations to the local economy, efforts to control their negative effects are modest at best. The growing traffic problem (and exhaust-spewing diesels) means that getting stuck in a traffic jam is an unpleasant possibility.

of art and artifacts from West Africa showcasing the significant African influences on Caribbean culture.

Jewish Cultural-Historical Museum Museum

(☎461-1067; www.snoa.com; Hanchi Snoa 29, Punda; US$10; ⏰9am-4:30pm Mon-Fri) Since 1651, the Mikvé Israel Emanuel Synagogue is the oldest continuously operating Jewish congregation in the western hemisphere. Its small but fascinating museum occupies two 18th-century buildings, which originally housed the rabbi's residence and bathhouse. The museum's centerpiece is the original *mikveh* (bath), which was found during renovation. Also on display is a Torah scroll that was brought to Curaçao by the first Jewish settlers.

Floating Market Market

(Sha Caprileskade; dawn-dusk) A colorful place to see piles of papayas, melons, tomatoes and much more. The vendors sail 70km from Venezuela to set up shop here.

Curaçao Maritime Museum Museum

(☎465-2327; www.curacaomaritime.com; Van den Brandhofstraat 7, Scharloo; adult/child US$6.50/3, harbor tours US$10/5; ⏰9am-4pm Tue-Sat, harbor tours 2pm Wed & Sat) Engaging

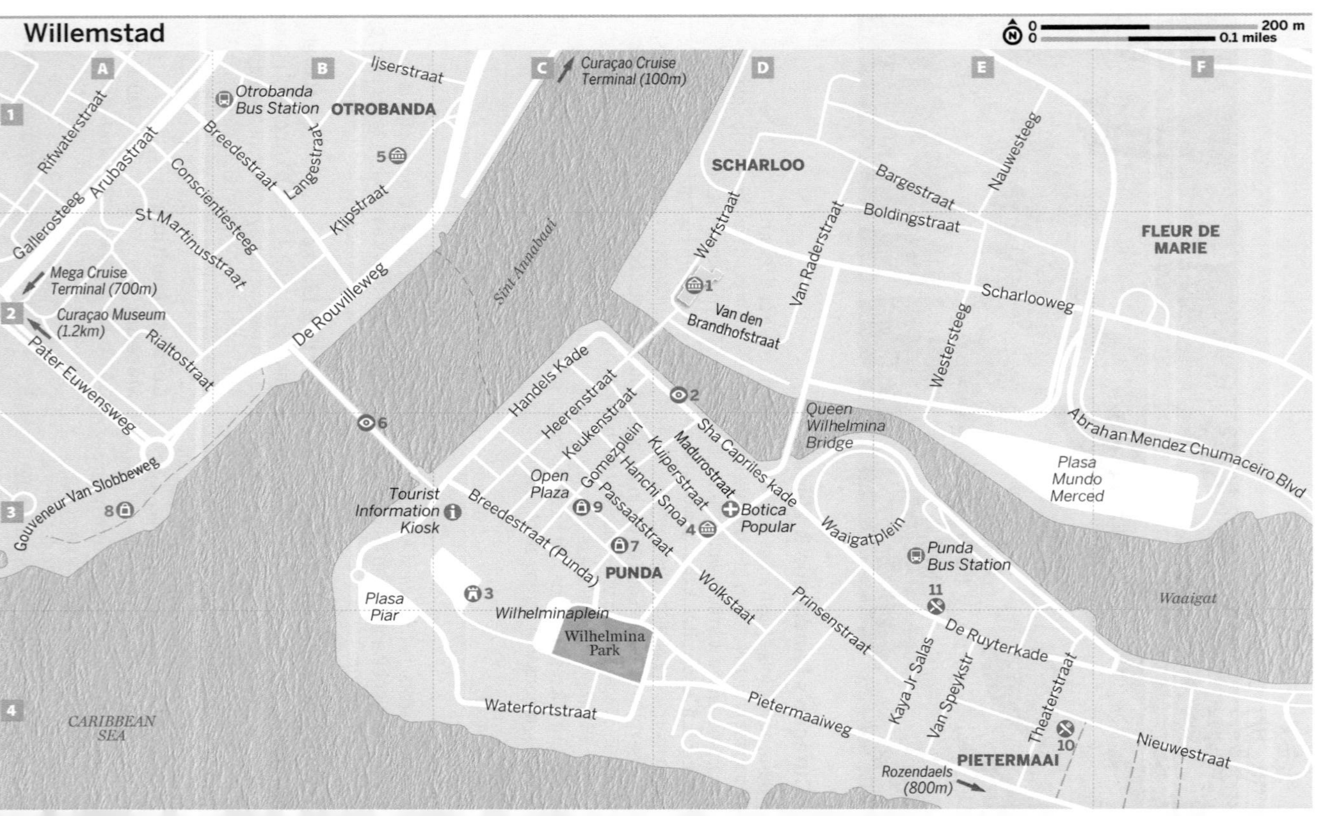
Willemstad
0 200 m
0 0.1 miles
OTROBANDA
SCHARLOO
FLEUR DE MARIE
PUNDA
PIETERMAAI
Otrobanda Bus Station
Punda Bus Station
Curaçao Cruise Terminal (100m)
Mega Cruise Terminal (700m)
Curaçao Museum (1.2km)
Rozendaels (800m)
Tourist Information Kiosk
Botica Popular
Sint Annabaai
Waaigat
CARIBBEAN SEA
Queen Wilhelmina Bridge
Plasa Mundo Merced
Plasa Piar
Wilhelmina Park
Wilhelminaplein
Open Plaza
Waaigatplein
Gomezplein
Abrahan Mendez Chumaceiro Blvd
Scharlooweg
Nauwesteeg
Westersteeg
Bargestraat
Boldingstraat
Van Raderstraat
Van den Brandhofstraat
Werfstraat
Sha Capriles kade
Madurostraat
Kuiperstraat
Hanchi Snoa
Passaatstraat
Keukenstraat
Heerenstraat
Handels Kade
Breedestraat (Punda)
Wolkstaat
Prinsenstraat
Pietermaaiweg
Waterfortstraat
Kaya Jr Salas
Van Speykstr
De Ruyterkade
Theaterstraat
Nieuwestraat
Ijserstraat
Klipstraat
Langestraat
Breedestraat
Conscientiesteeg
St Martinusstraat
Rialtostraat
De Rouvilleweg
Arubastraat
Rifwaterstraat
Gallerosteeg
Pater Euwensweg
Gouverneur Van Slobbeweg

Willemstad

Sights
1 Curaçao Maritime Museum D2
2 Floating Market D2
3 Fort Amsterdam C3
4 Jewish Cultural-Historical Museum D3
5 Museum Kura Hulanda B1
6 Queen Emma Bridge B3
Steam for Oil .... (see 1)

Shopping
7 Nena Sanchez Gallery C3
8 Rif Fort A3
9 Serena's Art Factory Store C3

Eating
10 Mundo Bizzarro E4
Museum Restaurant .... (see 5)
11 Old Market E3

displays trace the island's history, including exhibits on the Dutch West Indian Company the growth of Willemstad, the slave trade and more. A highlight is **Steam for Oil** (guided tour adult/child US$6.50/3, unguided US$2.50/free; 9am-4pm Tue-Sat, tour s1pm Wed & Sat), a working model of the oil refinery that has been a centerpiece of the island's economy.

Gallery Alma Blou Art Gallery

(462-8896; www.galleryalmablou.com; Frater Radulphusweg 4; 9:30am-5:30pm Mon-Fri, 9am-2pm Sat) FREE Housed in the 17th-century plantation house Landhuis Habaai, this cooperative gallery has the city's largest collection of works by local artists. The rotating exhibits usually feature one or two artists with local connections, but there's always a great variety of works on display, including whimsical sculptures in the courtyard and gardens about 3km northwest of Otrobanda. Also here is the Marshe di Artesania, the island's only handicraft market.

Curaçao Museum Museum

(www.thecuracaomuseum.com; Van Leeuwenhoekstraat; adult/child US$6/3; 8:30am-4:30pm Tue-Fri, 10am-4pm Sat & Sun) Small but worthwhile, this museum touches on art, history and society in its eclectic collections. Located in an unlikely residential location 1.6km west of the Otrabanda center, it's housed in a beautifully renovated military hospital. Highlights include the cockpit of the Snip (the first airplane to cross the ocean from Holland to Curaçao) and the impressive collection of contemporary sculptures in the garden.

Hato Caves Cave

(www.curacaohatocaves.com; FD Rooseveltweg; adult/child US$8/6; 9am-4pm) Near the airport, this is an impressive network of caves with the standard collection of faces and figures in the limestone walls (pirates, horses and, of course, the Virgin Mary), as well as a lovely indoor pool. One of the caves is home to a species of long-nose bats, which can be seen hanging from the ceiling. The trail through the caves is paved and illuminated, so there's nothing too daunting here.

TOURS

Old Willemstad Walking Tours Walking

(Anko van der Woude 461-3554, Gerda Gehlen 668-8579, Michael Newton 510-6978; www.otrobanda-pundatour.com; per person US$8; 5:15pm Mon, Wed & Thu) Each evening, a different architect takes to the streets to show off the highlights of historic Willemstad (Punda and Otrobanda).

SHOPPING

Most cruise-ship passengers do their shopping at the **Rif Fort** (www.shoprenaissancecuracao.com; Gouverneur van Slobbeweg, Otrobanda; 9am-7pm), which is filled with high-end shops selling clothing, jewelry and other fancy stuff. For something more interesting, there are a few boutiques and galleries tucked into Punda's narrow streets, as well as the monthly **Marshe di Artesania** (Handicraft Market; Frater Radulphusweg 4; 10am-2pm 2nd Sat of the month) on the outskirts of town.

Understand

The People of Curaçao

Historians do not believe that there are descendants of the island's original Caquetío inhabitants still living on the island. But the population of Curaçao is a rich mix of peoples. The majority have Afro-Caribbean roots (descended from the slaves who worked the plantations), but there is a sizable Dutch minority, as well as Latinos, Southeast Asians and other Europeans. Some 73% of the population are Roman Catholic, usually practiced with a healthy dose of Santería. Many other religions are represented, including a significant and long-standing Jewish presence.

DANIEL M ERNST/SHUTTERSTOCK ©

Serena's Art Factory Store Arts & Crafts
(www.chichi-curacao.com; cnr Windstraat & Gomezplein, Punda; ⏲10am-5pm Mon-Sat) Serena Janet Israel is the creative mind (and hands) behind Chichi, the vibrantly painted, big-bosomed lady sculptures that decorate the island's courtyards and alleyways.

Nena Sanchez Gallery Art
(Windstraat 15, Punda; ⏲10am-6pm Mon-Sat) Displays the vibrant and colorful works of the longtime local artist. Ms Sanchez has another, larger **outlet** (Landhuis Jan Kok; ☎864-0965; www.nenasanchez.com; Willibrordus) across from the flamingo lookout.

EATING & DRINKING

The most innovative cooking is happening in the kitchens of Pietermaai, where inviting restaurants and bars line the main streets. In Punda, keep your eyes open for humble backstreet eateries serving good traditional fare, but keep your wallet closed for most of the touristy places lining the Sint Annabaai.

Old Market Caribbean $
(Plasa Bieu; Sha Caprileskade, Punda; mains US$8-12; ⏲7am-2pm Mon-Sat) A local favorite. Folks of all stripes crowd into the vast barn-like structure to snag seats at the picnic tables and feast on down-home Curaçao cooking. The specialty here is local dishes such as goat stew, pumpkin pancakes, cactus stew and whole red snapper.

Rozendaels Caribbean $$
(461-8806; www.rozendaels.com; Penstraat 47, Pietermaai; meals US$15-25; 5-10pm Sun-Fri;) If you're able to fit in a visit before the ship leaves, Rozendaels will be a highlight of your trip. The secret garden setting and the personable service are a good start, but the food is near perfection. It's a fantastic place to try local delicacies such as *keshi yena* (cheese and chicken casserole) and grilled mahi-mahi.

Mundo Bizzarro Cuban $$
(461-6767; www.mundobizarrocuracao.com; Nieuwestraat 12, Pietermaai; mains US$8-20; 8am-10pm, bar till late;) The anchor of Pietermaai, this place evokes old Havana. The ground floor opens to the streets and alleys around; inside it's got a faux look of urban decay, which is countered by the fine food. Upstairs there's a bar with fab mojitos and live music on Saturday night.

Museum Restaurant Fusion $$
(Langestraat 8, Otrobanda; mains US$12-25; 11am-5pm Mon-Sat) An excellent casual restaurant in the grounds of the Kura Hulanda (p262); dine under a canopy of lush tropical trees amid historic buildings. The menu is eclectic with regional touches.

Rainbow Lounge Gay & Lesbian
(www.facebook.com/rainbowloungecuracao; Floris Suite Hotel, Piscadera Bay; 6pm-midnight) The Floris Suite Hotel bar is a gathering spot for gay and lesbian folks – and their friends – as well as anyone who wants to relax and drink in a welcoming, open atmosphere. Friday happy hours are a draw.

Blue Curaçao

Did you ever wonder why Blue Curaçao is blue? Find out at the **Landhuis Chobolobo** (461-3526; www.chobolobo.com; Elias RA Moreno Blvd; 8am-5pm Mon-Fri) FREE, where the liqueur is produced (in five different colors, actually) from the peels of Valencia oranges. Walk yourself through an informative tour of the history and production process, then hit the gift shop to sample the goods. Landhuis Chobolobo is located on the eastern side of the Schottegat.

MAXIMOV DENIS/SHUTTERSTOCK ©

INFORMATION

Tourist Information Kiosk (www.curacao.com; Breedestraat, Punda; 8am-4pm Mon-Sat) Has a wealth of information. It's by the Queen Emma Bridge on the Punda side.

GETTING AROUND

One highlight of a Curaçao visit is exploring the island, which is easiest to do with your own vehicle.

BUS

Public buses (NAf1.60 to NAf2.10) depart every two hours from **Otrobanda Bus Station** (Sebastopolstraat) for the West End (stopping in Willibrordus en route) and from **Punda Bus Station** (Waaigatplein) for the southeast (including Mambo Beach or Caracasbaai).

CAR

You won't need 4WD. Driving is on the right-hand side. We recommend Budget Rental service, which allows you to pick up your car and drop it off at the port for around US$50 per day.

TAXI

Taxis are more expensive on Curacao than many of the other islands. A typical taxi ride from the port to most of the beaches on the island is US$30 to US$50 each way for up to four people. Passengers can also hire a taxi for a tour of the island for around US$50.

Bathsheba Beach (p272)

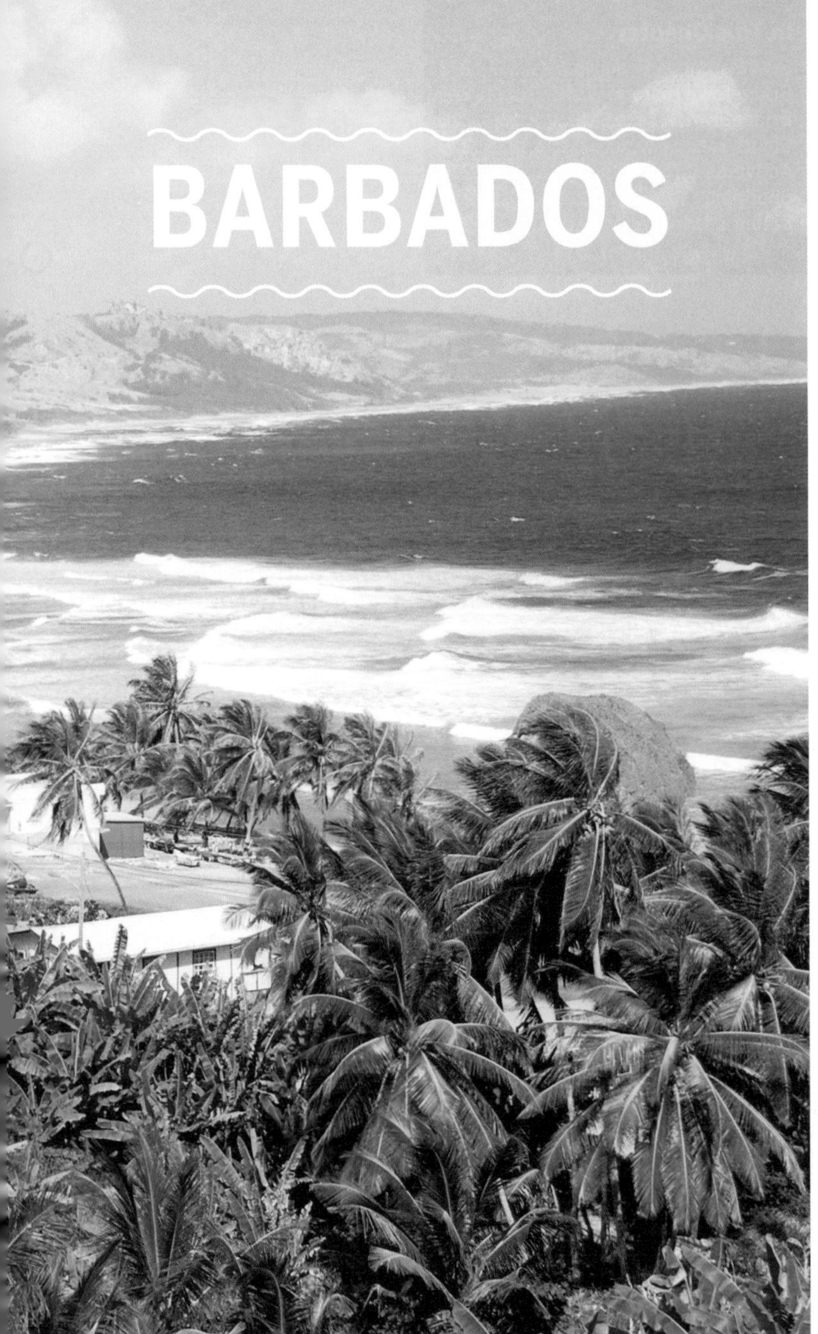

In This Chapter

Barbados at a Glance

While it's justifiably famed for its fantastic beaches, Barbados is an island that has it all. In addition to fine powdery sand and brilliant turquoise bays, you'll find smashing nightlife, a Unesco World Heritage–listed capital, a beautiful interior dotted with gardens, and wild surf on the lonely east coast, all inhabited by a proud and welcoming populace.

With a Day in Port

- Shop and tour the historic sights on a walking tour of Bridgetown.(p274)
- Do nothing but work on your tan all day at a Barbados beach.(p272)

Best Places for...

Coffee Waterfront Cafe (p281)

Cocktails Boatyard (p281)

Local cuisine Ideal Restaurant (p281)

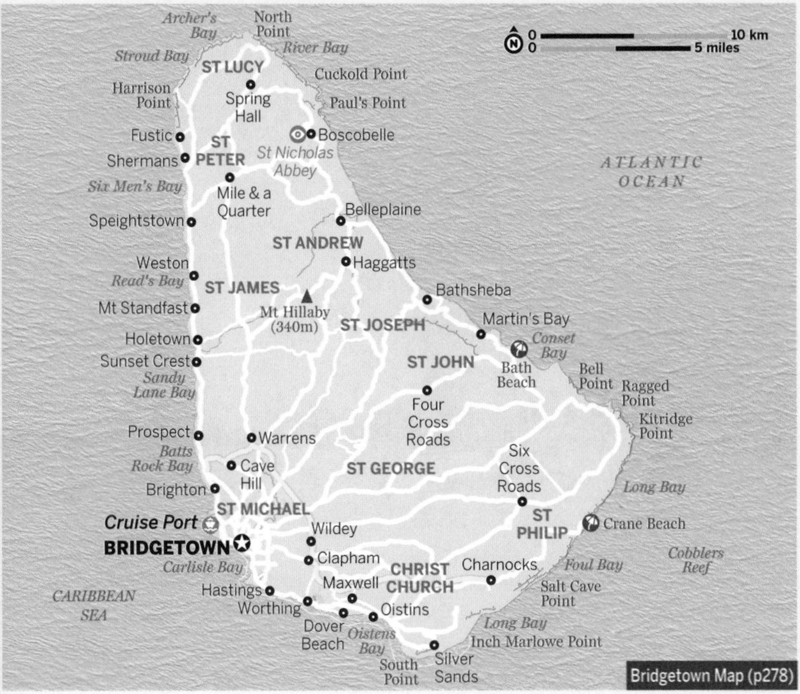

Bridgetown Map (p278)

Getting from the Port

Cruise ships dock in Bridgetown, and the shops and sights in downtown Bridgetown are a little more than a mile's walk away.

Bus There is a bus station two blocks from the cruise terminal. Bus services (B$2) run across the island and stop at most popular sights.

Taxi Taxis to downtown Bridgetown cost US$5, while getting to Crane Beach (about 45 minutes east of the cruise port) costs US$26.

Fast Facts

Currency Barbadian dollar (B$), US dollar (US$) widely accepted (bills, not coins)

Language English

Money ATMs are available across the island, with plenty of them downtown by the cruise port.

Visas Not required for citizens of the US, EU or Australia.

Best for free wi-fi Italia Coffee House in downtown Bridgetown.

Brownes Beach

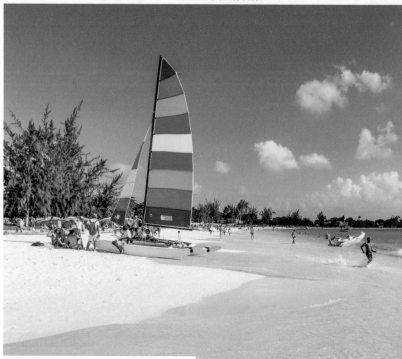

Best Barbados Beaches

You don't have to travel far from Bridgetown to reach good beaches. Carlisle Bay, just a 10-minute walk from town, has a couple of fine stretches of sand, while heading a little further up or down the coast will get you out of the crowds.

Great For...

Don't Miss

The natural pool and surfing at Bathsheba Beach on the east coast.

Brownes & Pebbles Beaches

A long white crescent of sand set against the brilliant waters of Carlisle Bay, Brownes Beach is a fine beach close to downtown Bridgetown (a 10-minute walk).

Running between two high-end hotels, Pebbles Beach is really just an extension of Brownes Beach. It has soft sands, calm waters and is home to water-sports outfitters. It offers a lively ambience rather than island tranquility and can get a bit crowded, but is a fine place to hang out. There are several shacks selling snacks, including great fish cutters.

Bathsheba

Drive northeast to the opposite side of the island and you'll discover Bathsheba Beach, a long, curving stretch of sandy shore lined with absolutely beautiful, large,

Bathsheba Beach sign

SABINE HORTEBUSCH/SHUTTERSTOCK ©

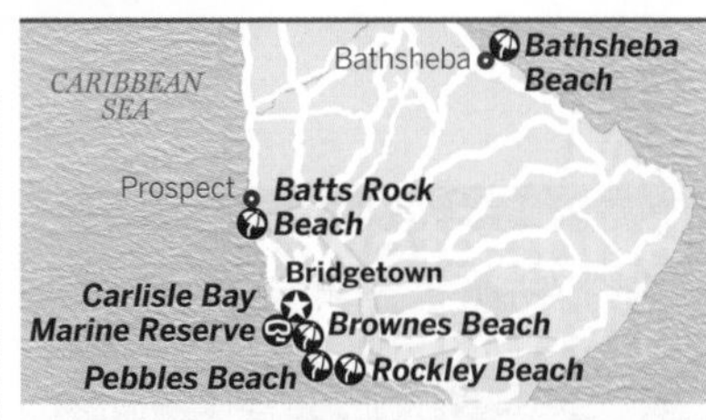

coral rock formations. The beach has several shallow pools for swimming, but the ocean beyond the natural bathing pools often has dangerous riptides that can make swimming hazardous. Nearby restaurants and bars provide an afternoon's worth of interest, making Bathsheba an excellent choice for the cruise passenger day trip.

Carlisle Bay Marine Reserve

If snorkeling's your thing, this reserve protects an area of calm and shallow water full of marine life just offshore from the city. In addition to marine turtles and schools of reef and predatory fish, there are five shipwrecks within the reserve boundaries.

Batts Rock Beach

Batts Rock Beach is next to Paradise Beach on the west coast, just a ten-minute taxi ride from the cruise port. In the small cluster of trees that separate the two beaches you'll find shaded picnic tables with an excellent ocean view. Passengers aren't the only creatures that enjoy Batts Rock Beach. Look out for the mischievous green monkeys that will steal your food if you don't keep a close eye on it. The beach is well protected and has calm water, good swimming and decent snorkeling in the rock clusters near the shore.

Explore Ashore

Beaches close to the cruise port take around 10 minutes to reach by taxi. Beaches on the eastern side of the island take 30 to 45 minute (US$50 for up to four people round-trip); allow at least four hours. Public buses (US$1 each way) are good but the trip will take more time, and you'll be locked into the bus schedule.

Take a Break

Visit the Boat Yard, a beach bar on Carlisle Beach, and have a rum punch made with Mount Gay Rum, the local label that has inspired many passengers to talk and drink like a pirate.

Rockley Beach

The largest beach in the area, **Rockley** (Accra Beach; Rockley Main Rd) is a picture-perfect crescent of sand backed by shade trees. The new boardwalk allows you to walk west for more than 3km to Hastings.

Bridgetown Historic Walk

Walk the historic city of Bridgetown for a journey through maritime and Caribbean history in a gorgeous waterfront city fit to explore on foot.

Start National Heroes Square
Distance 1 km
Duration 20 minutes walking, allow 3 hours total

5 Walk north on Spry St and then turn left (west) onto Magazine Lane and visit the **Nidhe Israel Museum** (p276).

3 Cross back to the north side of the river and continue to the **Parliament Buildings** (p276) on Broad St. The impressive tower with clock and bells was built in 1873, and the pendulum is 14ft long, with 7ft-long dials.

Take a Break Have a drink or meal at the Waterfront Cafe (p281), a short walk west of Independence Square.

2 Cross Chamberlain Bridge to **Independence Park**. Notice the pelican and flying fish on the front of Independence Arch, the national symbols of the island.

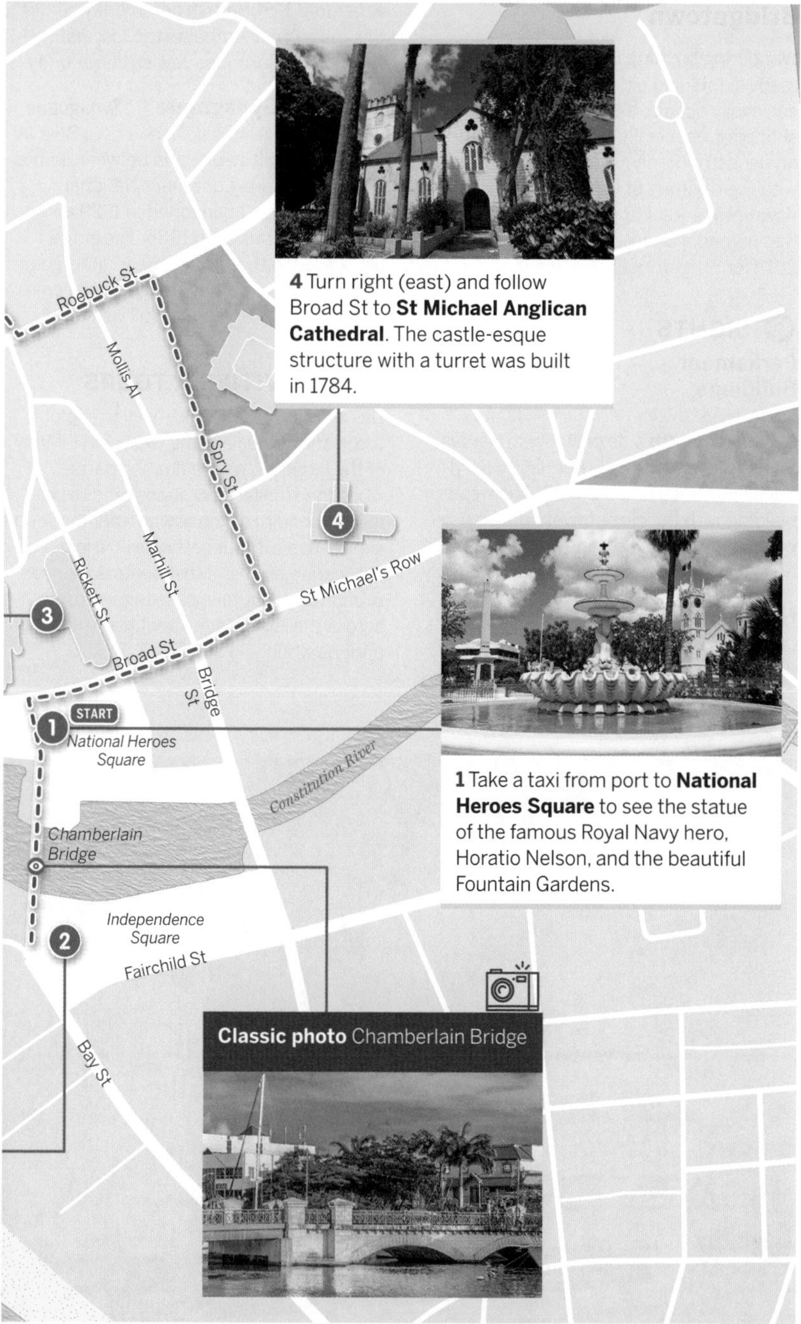

4 Turn right (east) and follow Broad St to **St Michael Anglican Cathedral**. The castle-esque structure with a turret was built in 1784.

1 Take a taxi from port to **National Heroes Square** to see the statue of the famous Royal Navy hero, Horatio Nelson, and the beautiful Fountain Gardens.

Roebuck St
Mollis Al
Spry St
Marhill St
Rickett St
St Michael's Row
Broad St
Bridge St
START
National Heroes Square
Constitution River
Chamberlain Bridge
Independence Square
Fairchild St
Bay St

Classic photo Chamberlain Bridge

Bridgetown

Wandering bustling Bridgetown, with its many sights and old colonial buildings, can easily occupy a day. There is good shopping, especially along Broad St and on pedestrian-only Swan St, which buzzes with the rhythms of local culture. The entire downtown area and south to the Garrison was named a Unesco World Heritage site in 2012 for its historical significance.

SIGHTS

Parliament Buildings Notable Building
(museum B$10; museum 9am-4pm Mon & Wed-Sat) On the north side of National Heroes Sq are two stone-block, neo-Gothic-style buildings constructed in 1871. The western building with the clock tower contains public offices; the building on the east side houses the Senate and House of Assembly.

Nidhe Israel Museum Museum
(822-5421; Synagogue Lane; adult/child B$25/12.50; 9am-4pm Mon-Fri) Housed in a restored 1750 Jewish community center, this museum documents the fascinating story of the Barbados Jewish community.

Barbados Synagogue Synagogue
(Synagogue Lane; 9am-4pm Mon-Fri) Built in 1833 this small synagogue between James St and Magazine Lane, near National Heroes Sq, was abandoned in 1929 and beautifully restored in 1986. The entire block around the synagogue is undergoing a major redevelopment to restore its colonial heritage, but you can still visit.

ACTIVITIES & TOURS

Day cruises are a popular way to explore the island, especially the west coast. Many of the larger boats are floating parties, while the smaller operations tend to be more tranquil. For those who want the scuba experience without getting wet, there are submarine cruises. Most boats dock near Bridgetown, but take passengers from across the island; ask about transportation options when you book.

Parliament buildings, Bridgetown

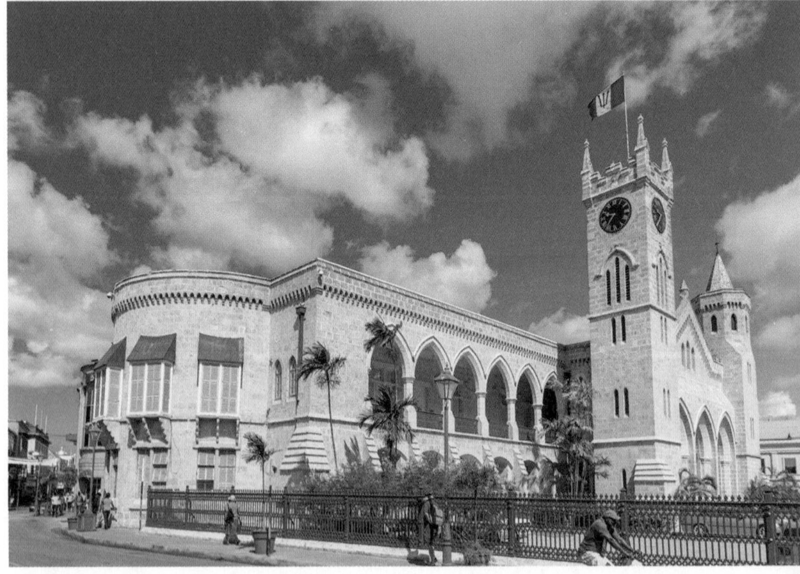

Understand

Surf's Up in Barbados

Barbados has gained international fame for its east-coast breaks. Ground zero is the **Soup Bowl**, off Bathsheba, and another spot called **Duppies**, up the coast. **South Point**, **Silver Sands** and **Rockley Beach** (p273) on the south coast are sometimes good, as is **Brandon's**, which is next to the Hilton Hotel at Needham's Point. There are some 30 other named breaks.

There are local guys renting out boards on the beach at most of the popular surf spots. Prices are negotiable depending on the quality of the board, but even the nicest board shouldn't be much more than B$20 per hour, or B$60 for daily rental. It's worth noting that the locals are generally nice and welcoming to outsiders.

Catching a wave at South Point JOHN SEATON CALLAHAN/GETTY IMAGES ©

Most tour companies offer a variety of half- and full-day options that either provide an overview with stops at key sights, or emphasize special interests such as nature and gardens. There is a huge range of choices, as you'll see from the brochure racks. Most, however, follow very set routes and you may well feel part of a herd. The various 4WD options are for those with Hummer envy.

The **Barbados Transport Board** (☎436-6820; www.transportboard.com) offers occasional scenic bus tours of the island. Check its website for upcoming itineraries.

The going rate for custom tours by taxi drivers is around B$80 an hour, but you can usually negotiate.

Calabaza Boating

(☎826-4048; www.sailcalabaza.com; Shallow Draught; adult/child from US$90/75; ⏰9:30am-2:30pm & 3-6:30pm) Professionally run sailing cruises with snorkeling stops at reefs and wrecks as well as turtle-watching. Groups are limited to 12 guests to ensure a more tranquil experience.

El Tigre Boating

(☎417-7245; www.eltigrecruises.com; Cavans Lane; adult/child from US$70/35) Offers a variety of cruises, including a three-hour option with snorkeling and turtle-watching.

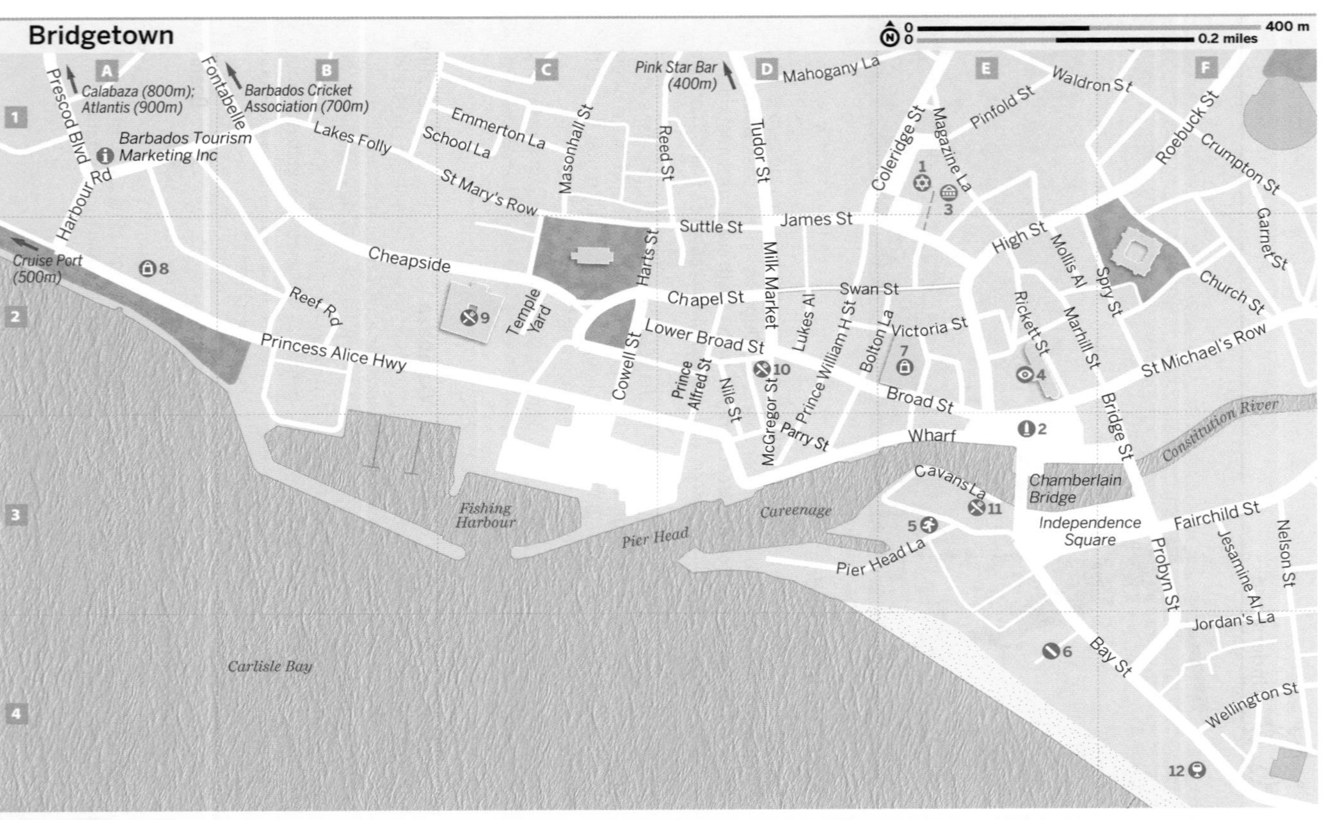
Bridgetown
0
0
400 m
0.2 miles
A
B
C
D
E
F
1
2
3
4
Calabaza (800m); Atlantis (900m)
Barbados Cricket Association (700m)
Pink Star Bar (400m)
Cruise Port (500m)
Barbados Tourism Marketing Inc
Prescod Blvd
Harbour Rd
Fontabelle
Lakes Folly
School La
Emmerton La
St Mary's Row
Masonhall St
Reed St
Mahogany La
Tudor St
Coleridge St
Magazine La
Pinfold St
Waldron St
Roebuck St
Crumpton St
Garnet St
Suttle St
James St
High St
Mollis Al
Spry St
Church St
Cheapside
Harts St
Chapel St
Swan St
Milk Market
Lukes Al
Prince William H St
Bolton La
Victoria St
Rickett St
Marhill St
St Michael's Row
Reef Rd
Temple Yard
Lower Broad St
Cowell St
Prince Alfred St
Nile St
McGregor St
Parry St
Broad St
Princess Alice Hwy
Wharf
Bridge St
Constitution River
Cavans La
Chamberlain Bridge
Independence Square
Fairchild St
Fishing Harbour
Careenage
Pier Head
Pier Head La
Probyn St
Jesamine Al
Nelson St
Jordan's La
Bay St
Wellington St
Carlisle Bay

Bridgetown

Sights
1 Barbados Synagogue E1
2 National Heroes Square E3
3 Nidhe Israel Museum E1
4 Parliament Buildings E2

Activities, Courses & Tours
5 El Tigre E3
6 The Dive Shop Barbados E4

Shopping
7 Cave Shepherd E2
8 Pelican Craft Village A2

Eating
9 Cheapside Market C2
Ideal Restaurant ..... (see 7)
10 Mustor's Restaurant D2
11 Waterfront Cafe E3

Drinking & Nightlife
12 Boatyard F4

The Dive Shop Barbados Diving
(☎422-3133; www.thediveshopbarbados.com; Ameys Alley, Upper Bay St; 1-/2-tank dive US$70/120) Well-established and reputable shop offering reef- and wreck-dive excursions to sites all over the island.

Atlantis Boating
(☎436-8929;www.barbados.atlantissubmarines.com; Shallow Draught; adult/child US$104/52; ⏰8am-4pm) The *Atlantis* is a 28-seat submarine lined with portholes. It departs from Bridgetown and tours the coral reef and shipwrecks off the coast.

SHOPPING

Pelican Craft Village Arts & Crafts
(Princess Alice Hwy; ⏰10am-5pm Mon-Sat) This ever-evolving complex of galleries and workshops, between downtown and the cruise-ship terminal, features the works of many local artists.

Cave Shepherd Department Store
(Broad St) The island's grand old department store has well-priced rum and a quality souvenir section.

EATING & DRINKING

Bridgetown is the best place to enjoy genuine local food and genuine local prices. You can find cheap eats at any of the markets.

Mustor's Restaurant Caribbean $
(McGregor St; lunch from B$14; ⏰10am-4pm Mon-Sat) Climb the stairs to a large, plain dining room. Choose from staples such as baked pork chops and flying fish. Then

Understand

It's All About Cricket

The national sport, if not national obsession, is cricket. Per capita, Bajans boast more world-class cricket players than any other nation. One of the world's top all-rounders, Bajan native Sir Garfield Sobers, was knighted by Queen Elizabeth II during her 1975 visit to Barbados, while another cricket hero, Sir Frank Worrell, appears on the B$5 bill.

In Barbados you can catch an international Test match, a heated local First Division match, or even just a friendly game on the beach or grassy field. Although international matches are less common here now that they are being spread more widely around the Caribbean, when it is Barbados' turn, thousands of Bajans and other West Indians pour into matches at Kensington Oval. For schedules and tickets, contact the **Barbados Cricket Association** (www.bcacricket.org).

select the sides – we love the macaroni pie. Finally, hope for an open balcony table.

Pink Star Bar Caribbean $

(Baxters Rd; cutters B$5; ⏲7pm-6am) Located on rough-and-ready Baxters Rd, Pink Star is famous among locals for being the cheapest place in town to fill your stomach. It opens in the evenings and runs through to dawn serving liver cutters, fried chicken necks and steppers (chicken feet) to the drunk and hungry masses. It's the Caribbean version of an all-night greasy-kebab spot.

Cheapside Market Market $

(Cheapside; ⏲7am-3pm Mon-Sat) Even if you're not intending to buy, this is a fascinating place to browse local produce in a grand old market hall recently restored by the Chinese government. It has some nice snack stands on the 2nd floor. The best times to visit are Friday and Saturday mornings. Southwest across Princess Alice Hwy, the open-air **public market** has all things briny fresh from the boats.

Understand

Essential Food & Drink

Bananas Local varieties are green even when ripe (look for them in markets).

Banks The island's crisp lager is refreshing after a day in the hot sun.

Barbadian rum Considered some of the finest in the Caribbean, with Mount Gay being the best-known label.

Conkies A mixture of cornmeal, coconut, pumpkin, sweet potato, raisins and spices, steamed in a plantain leaf.

Cou-cou A creamy cornmeal-and-okra mash.

Cutters Meat or fish sandwiches in a salt-bread roll.

Fish cakes There are myriad Bajan recipes, made from salt cod and deep-fried.

Flying fish Served fried in delicious sandwiches all over the country. It's a mild white fish that is great sautéed or deep-fried.

Jug-jug A mixture of cornmeal, green peas and salted meat.

Roti A curry filling rolled inside flat bread.

Bajan fish cakes FANFO/SHUTTERSTOCK ©

Ideal Restaurant Caribbean $

(Broad St; lunch from B$15; ⏲10am-4pm Mon-Sat) The main restaurant at the landmark Cave Shepherd Department Store food court has a small daily buffet of island favorites. It's very popular – the queues get long, but the service is fast. Ask a local where they go for lunch and they'll point here.

Waterfront Cafe Cafe $$

(☎427-0093; www.waterfrontcafe.com.bb; Careenage; sandwiches B$30-35, mains B$42-78; ⏲9am-6pm Mon-Wed, to 10pm Thu-Sat) Always packed, especially the breezy tables on the river. Lunches include a fine version of a flying-fish sandwich; dinners are more elaborate and have Mediterranean color and flair. There's live music ranging from steel pan to jazz – call to find out what's on.

Boatyard Bar

(www.theboatyard.com; Bay St; admission B$50; ⏲9am-8pm) An over-amped beach bar that pushes the sex-on-the-beach angle hard, the Boatyard gets visitors by the busload who come for the drinking contests and beach activities. By day there's a B$50 cover charge to use the many beach facilities, although B$40 is consumable at the bar restaurant. It also includes a boat trip onto the bay to see turtles.

Beasties of Barbados

The majority of Barbados' indigenous wildlife was overwhelmed by agriculture and competition with introduced species. Found only on Barbados is the harmless and elusive grass snake. The island also shelters a species of small (nonpoisonous) blind snake, plus whistling frogs, lizards, red-footed tortoises and eight species of bats.

Hawksbill turtles regularly come ashore to lay their eggs, as does the occasional leatherback turtle. As elsewhere, the turtles face numerous threats from pollution and human interference. The **Barbados Sea Turtle Project** (www.barbadosseaturtles.org; UWI, Bridgetown) is working to restore habitat and populations.

Most, if not all, mammals found in the wild on Barbados have been introduced. They include wild green monkeys, mongooses, European hares, mice and rats.

More than 180 species of birds have been sighted on Barbados. Most of them are migrating shorebirds and waders that breed in North America and stop over on Barbados en route to winter feeding grounds in South America.

Sea turtle STEVEN M LANG/SHUTTERSTOCK ©

INFORMATION

Barbados Tourism Marketing Inc (BTMI; ☎467-3600; www.visitbarbados.org; Warrens Office Complex, St Michael) Answers questions and offers brochures. A branch office at the cruise-ship terminal opens when ships are in port.

GETTING AROUND

Bridgetown is easily covered on foot, although taxis can be flagged on the street if necessary, or hailed from the waiting area. The set taxi fare from one end of town to the other is B$10.

The main bus stations are inconveniently located on opposite sides of town and there's no service between them, so if you're traveling from north to south, or vice versa, you'll either need to cross town on foot (15 minutes) or take a taxi (B$10).

Cars can be rented at the cruise port from several rental companies.

Local band, Philipsburg (p194), St-Martin/Sint Maarten

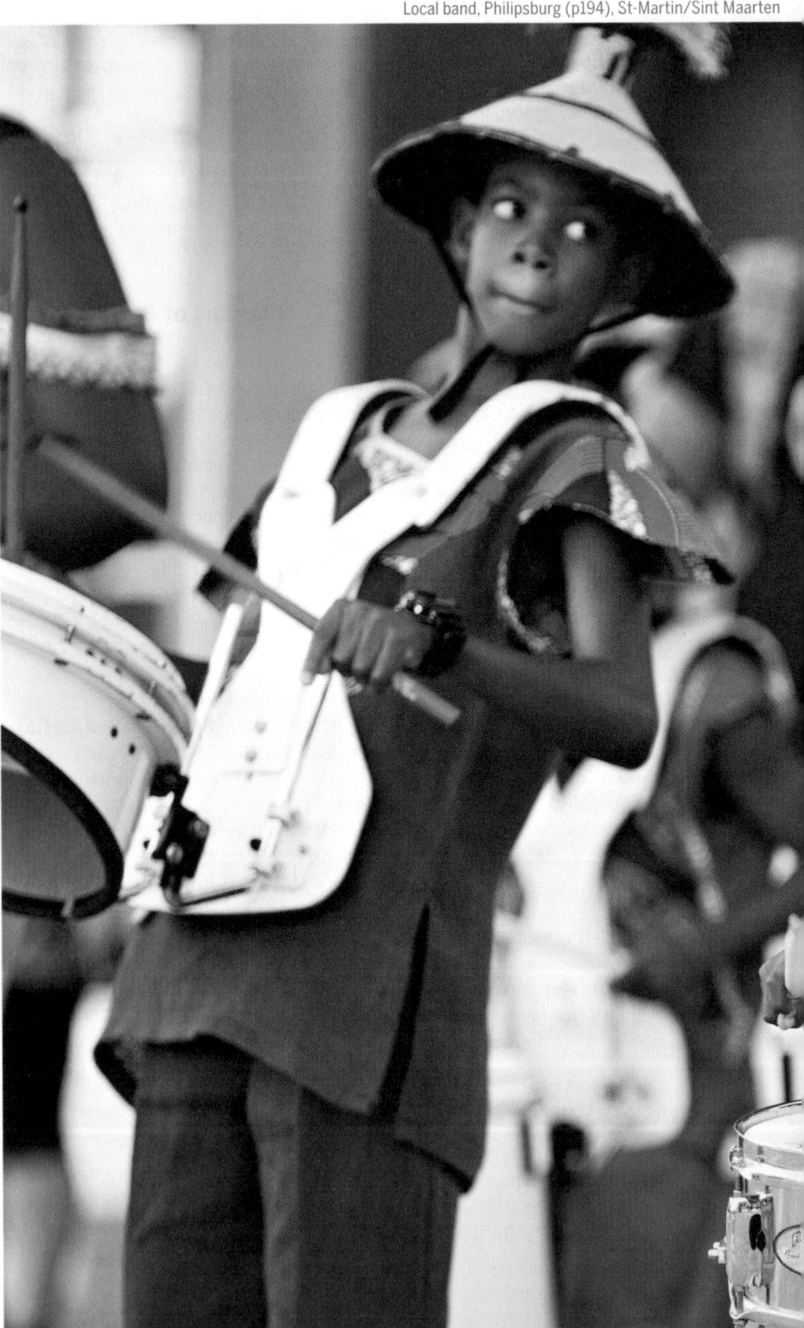

In Focus

Outdoor bar, Philipsburg (p194), St-Martin/Sint Maarten

Caribbean Today

With more than 700 islands in the Caribbean, there are a lot of beaches to lie back on and contemplate nothing more than your next rum cocktail. But this is also a region with a lively political mix, shaped by (and shaping) the currents of globalization. Look a little closer and you'll find today's Caribbean to be as interesting, complex and engaging as anywhere on the planet.

Climate challenges

The increased frequency of extreme weather events in the Caribbean, not least the stretching out of hurricane season, is proving challenging for many countries. The destruction of Category 5 Hurricane Irma (p300) and Hurricane Maria in 2017 was a sobering reminder of the power of nature for many island nations, leaving widespread flooding and damage to homes and agriculture. Hurricane Matthew impacted Haiti with its full force in 2016, while tiny Dominica is still recuperating from the wrath of 2015's Tropical Storm Erika.

Many islands are now turning to renewable energy, including wind power and geothermal energy, to provide a more sustainable future. The Caribbean has been through many storms – environmental, political and economic – but with luck and planning, its people should continue to weather them and build a more secure future.

Debts Old & New

The rise of East Asia has brought relief for some, with Taiwan and China vying for influence (and UN votes) through regional investments. While China has been splashing cash, Puerto Rico has been struggling with a huge ongoing financial crisis. The island has more than US$70 billion in debts, the result of a crisis triggered by the island's complicated tax and banking relationship with the mainland USA, and further exacerbated by high unemployment. Puerto Rico's need for a bail-out has added a new urgency to the island's perennial debate over independence versus seeking full statehood within the United States.

Slavery continues to be an issue in the Caribbean, and the seeking of reparations is now an official policy of the regional governmental grouping Caricom. The labor of enslaved Africans in the Caribbean once provided the economic spark that helped light Europe's Industrial Revolution, they argue, and these former colonies still suffer from the bad economic conditions they inherited at independence.

Moves on marijuana?

Cuban-US relations have put cigars back on the shopping list for many tourists, but it's another type of smoking that's made headlines in the region. In 2015 Jamaica decriminalized the possession of marijuana, more popularly known locally as *ganja*. Legalization is a trickier affair, as it requires the unpicking of international treaty obligations, but most observers assume it'll be on the cards before too long. The prime minister of St Vincent and the Grenadines has also anticipated more global moves for decriminalization and tied them to the need for economic diversification by proposing that marijuana should ultimately replace bananas as one of the Caribbean's main exports.

Cuba – the Caribbean's New Horizon

The Caribbean's biggest island is getting ready for a tourism-driven future. A relaxation of the US travel embargo has led to the resumption of direct flights between the two countries, and cruise companies flocking to add the island to their itineraries. Cuba helped invent the whole concept of Caribbean tourism back in the 1940s, and its return to the travel mainstream isn't to be underestimated.

The prospect of a huge new holiday market in the region has caused other Caribbean nations to glance nervously across the sea. The period since the global recession has been a tough one for many countries reliant on tourism. In Trinidad and Tobago, for example, visitor arrivals in 2016 were a quarter of what they were a decade previously, and the road back to growth is a tough one.

Mayan ruins at Tulum (p72), Mexico

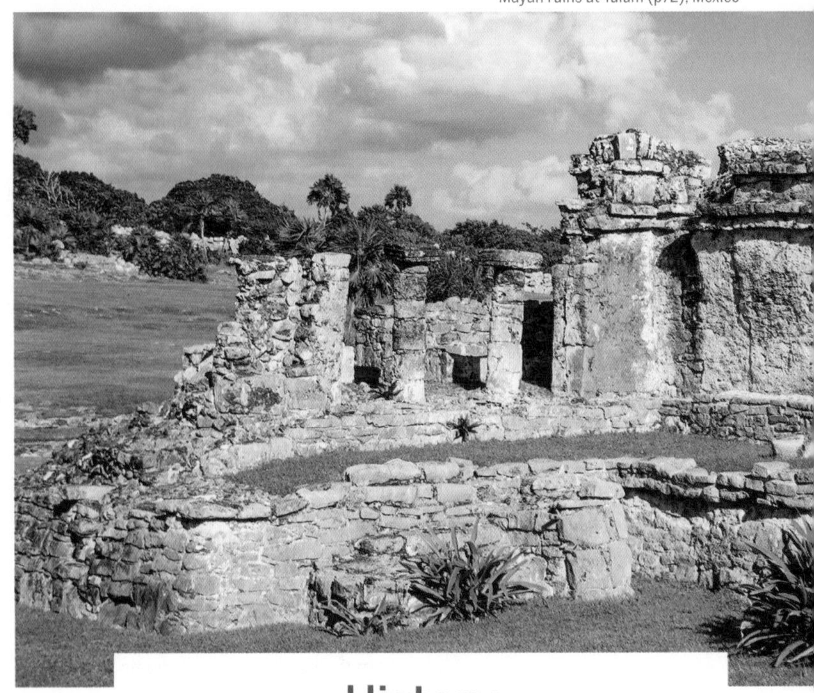

History

Murder, mayhem and bananas. The history of the Caribbean includes every kind of drama – from warring colonial powers to marauding pirates. The stain of slavery is ever-lasting and almost every aspect of life in the region today is a direct consequence of events through the centuries. Of course, where it was once a horrible playground for the ambitious, now it's simply a playground, a definite improvement.

4000 BC
First humans arrive in the Eastern Caribbean from South America.

AD 700–800
Taínos settle in Hispaniola, Cuba and Jamaica.

1492
Columbus becomes the first European to step foot in the Americas when he lands in the Bahamas.

SEAN PAVONE/SHUTTERSTOCK ©

Ahoy Arawaks

The first Caribbeans arrived on the islands closest to South America around 4000 BC. These nomadic hunter-gatherers were followed by waves of Arawaks (a collective term for the Amerindian people believed to be from the Orinoco River Delta around Venezuela and Guyana) who moved north and west, beginning the great tradition of Caribbean island-hopping. Indeed, one of the Caribbean's recurrent themes, from pre-Columbian times until right now, has been movement of peoples.

Around AD 1200 the peaceable Arawaks were minding their own business when the Caribs from South America started fanning out over the Caribbean. The Caribs killed the Arawak men and enslaved the women, triggering another wave of migration that sent the Arawaks fleeing as far west as Cuba and as far north as the Bahamas. When the Spanish explorers arrived, they dubbed the warfaring people they encountered 'cannibals' (a derivation of the word 'caribal' or Carib), for their reputed penchant for eating their victims.

1493
Columbus returns on his second voyage, sighting and naming much of the Eastern Caribbean.

1595
The famous English privateers Sir Francis Drake and John Hawkins use the Virgin Islands to attack Spanish shipping.

1651
Mass suicide by Caribs in Grenada who preferred to jump off a cliff than be subjugated by the Spanish.

Historic Reads

- For a comprehensive recent take on the region's history, check out Carrie Gibson's highly readable *Empire's Crossroads: A New History of the Caribbean.*
- *The Slave Ship: A Human History*, by Marcus Rediker, looks at the transportation of around 17 million Africans to the Caribbean and America during the era of the transatlantic slave trade.
- Alex Von Tunzelmann's *Red Heat: Conspiracy, Murder and the Cold War in the Caribbean* is a gripping account of a turbulent time in the region, from the Cuban Missile Crisis to Haiti's Papa Doc Duvalier.

While many traces of the Caribbean's first people, the Arawaks, were gone at the end of the 15th century, there were still Arawak-speaking people living in regions the Caribs had not yet conquered. These included the Taíno, the people whom Columbus first encountered and whose legacy lives on today in Puerto Rico.

And while the Arawak people were mostly gone, their way of life persisted, adopted by new arrivals, whether colonists or slaves. Crops and foods including tobacco, cotton, corn, sweet potatoes, pineapples, cassava (also called manioc or yucca) and tapioca are still island staples today.

Ahoy Columbus

Christopher Columbus led the European exploration of the region, making landfall at San Salvador in the Bahamas on October 12, 1492 – no matter that he thought he was in Asia. He too island-hopped, establishing the first European settlement in the Americas on Hispaniola, today shared by the Dominican Republic and Haiti. Columbus never fully realized that he hadn't discovered islands off the coast of East Asia (a misconception that lives on when an indigenous person is called an 'Indian'). But he did get around on his voyages. On his first voyage (1492–93) he visited Hispaniola, Cuba and the Bahamas; on his second voyage (1493–1494) he made it to much of the Eastern Caribbean starting with Dominica. He took hundreds of slaves, most of whom died before reaching Spain. His third voyage (1498) took him to Trinidad followed by Tobago and Grenada (which he considered part of China), and on his fourth voyage, after revisiting many islands, he ended up stranded in Jamaica for a year.

Discovering new lands gives glory, but what Columbus and subsequent explorers wanted was gold. Legions of Europeans prowled the Caribbean searching for treasure, but it turned out be much further west in Mexico.

That's not to say there weren't riches: the land was fertile, the seas bountiful and the native population, after initial resistance by the toughest of the remaining Caribs, forcibly pliant. The conquistadores set to exploiting it all, violently. Focusing on the biggest islands promising the highest returns, they grabbed land, pillaged and enslaved, settling towns in Cuba, the Dominican Republic, Puerto Rico and Jamaica.

1685
The French Code Noire gives slaves legal protection from murder but also allows for floggings.

1791
Slaves rise against their French masters, starting the 13-year Haitian Revolution and ending in Haitian independence in 1804.

1805
Beaten by the British in Dominica, the French burn Roseau to the ground and flee.

Except for mineral-rich Trinidad, taken early by the Spanish, the Eastern Caribbean was left largely to its own devices until the English washed up on St Kitts in 1623, sparking domino-effect colonization of Barbados, Nevis, Antigua and Montserrat. Not to be outdone, the French followed, settling Martinique and Guadeloupe, while the Dutch laid claim to Saba, Sint Eustatius and St-Martin/Sint Maarten. Over the next 200 years the Europeans fought like children over these islands, and possession changed hands so often that a sort of hybridized culture developed; some islands, like St-Martin/Sint Maarten and St Kitts, were split between two colonial powers.

Pirates & War

The Caribbean colonial story is largely one of giant agricultural interests – most notably sugar, but also tobacco, cattle and bananas – fueled by greed and slavery that promoted power struggles between landowners, politicians and the pirates who robbed them. The Bahamas, with hundreds of cays, complex shoals and channels, provided the perfect base for pirates such as Henry Jennings and 'Blackbeard' (Edward Teach), who ambushed treasure-laden boats headed for Europe. On the home front, Britain, Spain and France were embroiled in tiffs, scuffles and all-out war that allowed colonial holdings to change hands frequently. The English took Jamaica in 1655 and held Cuba momentarily in 1762, while the Spanish and French agreed to divide Hispaniola in 1697, creating today's Dominican Republic and Haiti. The legacies of this period – Santo Domingo's Fortaleza Ozama, the fortresses of Old San Juan and the vibrant mix of cultures – are among the most captivating attractions for travelers.

Sugar & Slavery

As piracy waned, the European powers looked to other ways to make the Caribbean profitable. Driven by a sweet tooth, they turned much of the region into a giant sugar plantation. And to labour in the fields they used African captives, brought into the Caribbean in terrifying numbers. The Atlantic slave trade had a scale so overwhelming that it depopulated vast tracts of western Africa. From its origins, starting with Portuguese and Spanish colonists in the 1500s, to the final abolition on Cuba in 1886, an estimated 17 million enslaved African people were brought to the Americas.

Upon arrival in the Caribbean, captives were marched to an auction block, exhibited and sold to the highest bidder. On the British and Dutch islands, families were deliberately broken up. Enslaved Africans were forced to learn the language of the plantation owners, but they blended their own use of it into hybrid Creole languages that were liberally spiced with African terms. Slave rebellions were common across the region, but only in Haiti were they ultimately successful, when a 13-year revolution led to the expulsion of the French and the establishment of the world's first black republic in 1804.

Slavery continued in the British empire until 1834, but the practice continued in Cuba until 1886, just 16 years before declaring independence from Spain.

1815
The Treaty of Vienna restores Guadeloupe and Martinique to France.

1834
Britain abolishes slavery throughout its empire; the Dutch follow suit in 1863.

1878
Sweden gives St-Barthélemy to France, ending its little-remembered colonial ambitions in the Caribbean.

★ Best for History

San Juan, Puerto Rico (p142)
Antigua (p229)
Curaçao (p255)
Tulum, Mexico (p72)
St-Martin/Sint Maarten (p185)

Loosening Colonial Ties

Some islands have opted to maintain strong neo-colonial ties to the parent country, as is the case with the French protectorates of St-Barthélemy, Martinique and Guadeloupe, and the commonwealth situation between Puerto Rico and the US. Independence on the one hand and statehood on the other has always had its champions in Puerto Rico, with statehood narrowly losing plebiscites in 1993 and 1998 but on tap for yet another vote in the near future.

In the post-WWII period, Britain moved to divest itself of its Caribbean colonies by attempting to create a single federated state that would incorporate all of the British-held Caribbean. One advantage of the federation was that it was expected to provide a mechanism for decolonizing smaller islands that the British felt would otherwise be too small to stand as separate entities.

After a decade of negotiation, Britain convinced its Caribbean colonies – Jamaica, Barbados, Trinidad and the British Windward and Leeward Islands – to join together as the West Indies Federation. The new association came into effect in 1958, with the intent that the federation work out the intricacies of self-government during a four-year probationary period before the islands emerged as a single new independent nation in 1962.

Although the West Indies Federation represented dozens of islands scattered across some 2000 miles of ocean, the British established Trinidad, at the southernmost end of the chain, to be the governing 'center' of the federation.

For centuries the islanders had related to each other via their British administrators, and the political and economic intercourse between the islands had been quite limited. In the end, the lack of a united identity among the islands, coupled with each island's desire for autonomy, proved much stronger than any perceived advantage in union.

Jamaica was the first to develop a rift with the new association and opted to leave the federation in 1961. Trinidad itself soon followed suit. Both islands were wary of getting stuck having to subsidize the federation's smaller islands, which had a history of being heavily dependent upon British aid. The concept of a smaller federation limped along for

1916–24
The US occupies the Dominican Republic; also occupies Haiti 1915–34.

1926
Holland America offers the first Caribbean cruise aboard the *Veendam*.

1937
Dominican dictator Rafael Trujillo orders Haitians be killed in retaliation for cattle rustling: 20,000 perish.

Caribbean Cruise-Ship History

In 1926, Holland America forever transformed cruise ship history by offering the first Caribbean cruise aboard the SS *Veendam II*. Cruise ships not only changed the business of tourism, they transformed the tiny islands south of the United States from mostly quiet, agriculture-based economies into booming, bustling vacation playgrounds visited by over 15 million cruise ship passengers a year. The *Veendam*, built in 1922, carried nearly 1900 passengers and around 300 crew. Today, ships such as Royal Caribbean's *Harmony of the Seas* can cruise the Caribbean with an astounding 6780 passengers on board. The economic and cultural impact the cruise-ship industry continues to have in the Caribbean is profound. As the cruise industry sails full steam ahead into an era of megaships that continue to grow larger with each inaugural breaking of the champagne bottle against their behemoth bows, the Caribbean continues to prosper and build into one of the most-visited vacation destinations in the world.

a few more years, but after Barbados broke rank and became an independent nation in 1966, the British were forced to go back to the drawing board.

The remaining islands continued to splinter. Dominica and St Lucia gained independence as single-island nations. Antigua, St Vincent, Grenada and St Kitts were each linked with smaller neighboring islands to form new nations.

Anguilla, which was connected with St Kitts and Nevis, rebelled three months after the new state's inauguration in 1967 and negotiated with the British to be reinstated as a Crown Colony. Montserrat also refused to be dispensed with so readily by the British and was allowed to continue as a Crown Colony.

The islands linked to St Vincent and to Grenada also initially grumbled, but they have managed to work out their differences well enough to maintain their unions.

The Dutch, like the British, also hoped to create a single federation of all their Caribbean possessions – Curaçao, Aruba, Bonaire, St-Martin/Sint Maarten, Sint Eustatius and Saba – collectively known as the Netherlands Antilles. In 1954 a charter was enacted that made these six islands an autonomous part of the Netherlands. Under the charter, island affairs were largely administered by elected officials, although the Dutch continued to hold the purse strings and maintain other controls. The islands were expected to develop the mechanisms for self-rule and move gradually, as a unit, toward full independence from the Netherlands. But that didn't work out. The islands never considered union as a single nation. Aruba was the first out in 1986 and became a single island state. The remaining five islands each followed over the next 24 years so that today, all six are independent of each other but still linked in some way to the Netherlands.

1959

Cuban Revolution triumphs, which ripples across the Caribbean. Puerto Rico welcomes many new casino owners.

1962

American, Soviet and Cuban leaders Kennedy, Kruschev and Castro go toe to toe in the nuclear Cuban Missile Crisis.

1967

Anguillans force the Royal St Kitts Police Force off the island for good, declaring independence.

A Rum-Punch Future

The last 100 years have been a mixed bag for the Caribbean. US intervention in countries seen as geostrategically important, particularly Haiti and Cuba, usually does more harm than good. Furthermore, monocrop agriculture – bananas in Jamaica, nutmeg in Grenada – means the islands are at the mercy of heavy weather and market fluctuations. At the same time, it polarizes societies into the rich who own the land and the poor who work it. The Cuban Revolution was the most enduring result of this. Economic instability, especially, has given rise to dictators such as Rafael Leonidas Trujillo who ruled the Dominican Republic for over 30 years, and the father-son dictators of Papa Doc and Baby Doc Duvalier who plundered Haiti for almost as long.

One thing all the islands have in common is tourism, which began taking hold when other sectors of the islands' economies began to crumble, particularly agriculture.

Jamaican History – Falmouth & Ocho Rios

The Jamaican port of Falmouth was laid out in 1769 and named for the English birthplace of Sir William Trelawny, then the governor of the island. The streets were planned as a grid and patriotically named after members of the royal family and English heroes. Planters erected their townhouses using Georgian elements adapted to Jamaican conditions. With its advantageous position, Falmouth became the busiest port on the north coast. Outbound trade consisted mainly of hogsheads (large casks) of wet sugar and puncheons (casks) of rum, while slaves were offloaded for sale in the slave market. The town's fortunes degenerated when the sugar industry went into decline during the 19th century and it was dealt a further blow with the advent of steamships, which the harbor was incapable of handling. By 1890 the port was essentially dead. The city has struggled along ever since. A cruise-ship dock was opened in Falmouth in March 2011 large enough to accommodate the world's second-biggest cruise liner, the 6000-passenger *Oasis of the Seas*. Contrary to local expectations, the cruise-ship dock has done little to boost Falmouth's economy, since passengers are typically whisked off to tour to other parts of the island and not encouraged to spend time in the town.

The name Ocho Rios is a corruption of the Spanish term *chorreros* (swift water) for the area's rivers. Not only was the area west of Ocho Rios the site of Columbus' first landing in Jamaica and of the first Spanish settlement, but Spain's last stand in Jamaica occurred at nearby Rio Nuevo. It was here that the British instituted huge slave-run sugar and pimento (allspice) plantations, crops that defined the region until the mid-20th century when bauxite mining and tourism took over.

1983
After president Ronald Reagan orders an invasion, 70 Cubans, 42 Americans and 170 Grenadians die.

1986
Aruba leaves the Netherlands Antilles and become an autonomous entity.

1994
in Antigua and Barbuda, Lester Bird continues the ruling dynasty started by his father, VC, in 1981.

Understand

History of Barbados

The original inhabitants of Barbados were Arawaks, who were driven off the island around AD 1200 by Caribs from South America. The Caribs, in turn, abandoned (or fled) Barbados close to the arrival of the first Europeans. The Portuguese visited the island in 1536, but Barbados was uninhabited by the time Captain John Powell claimed it for England in 1625. Two years later, a group of settlers established the island's first European settlement, Jamestown, in present-day Holetown. Within a few years the colonists had cleared much of the forest, planting tobacco and cotton fields. In the 1640s they switched to profitable sugarcane. and the landowners began to import large numbers of African slaves. England granted Barbados internal self-government in 1961 and it became an independent nation on November 30, 1966, with Errol Barrow as its first prime minister. While not flawless, Barbados has remained a stable democracy.

St-Martin/Sint Maarten is a good example. In 1930 the population stood at just 2000. But in 1943 the US Navy built large runways on the island to use as a base in the Caribbean. The French capitalized by using the runways to fly in tourists, by the 1950s bringing the population of St-Martin/Sint Maarten up to about 70,000 and making tourism the number one industry on both sides of the island. The US left similar infrastructure across the region, which proved useful for the cruise and package-holiday business as it got going in the 1950s.

Crop-leveling hurricanes (eg Gilbert in 1988, Hugo in 1989) spurred some islands to develop tourism industries, while others, such as Hurricane Matthew in 2016, damaged Haiti's nascent tourism industry, a hard blow in a country still recovering from the devastating earthquake six years earlier. In 2017, Hurricanes Irma and Maria were another massive blow to the region (see p300). Meanwhile, a 1997 World Trade Organization ruling favoring Central American bananas over Caribbean ones forced St Vincent and Martinique to look at diversifying. Unfettered tourism hasn't been without problems – not least in the environment – but overall the perception that tourism is a good source of jobs and revenue is widespread. Polls have shown that people in places as diverse as Trinidad and Barbados overwhelmingly say that the presence of tourists makes everybody's life better.

2004

Hurricane Ivan sweeps through the Caribbean, devastating Grenada.

2008

Presidential candidate Barrack Obama criticizes US companies using the Cayman Islands as a tax dodge.

2017

Hurricanes Irma and Maria cause devastation throughout the region.

Cricket match, Barbados

Caribbean Cultures

The Caribbean isn't just coconut palms and beach bars, it's a region of staggering cultural diversity. In many ways it's where the modern world was first born, where the peoples of the Americas, Europe and Africa first met – a product of globalization before the term was even invented. From Usain Bolt to Rihanna, the Caribbean is a place that still has an outsized impact on the wider world today.

People

The Caribbean's first human inhabitants were the Taíno and Arawak peoples, but aside from the Carib reserve (Kalinago Territory) on Dominica of some 3000 people, little vestige of the original inhabitants remains in the region. Instead, there is the complex swirl of cultures and colors from all the people who came after: English, Spanish, French and Dutch mixed with Africans brought over as slaves. When slavery was abolished, indentured laborers were imported from China, India and the Middle East, further blending islands' identities. Regional immigration also adds to the mix: in the 20th century Haitians have settled in the Dominican Republic and Cuba following work as sugarcane cutters, while expats from the US have altered the makeup of some islands like the Caymans.

The stereotypical island slacker, swinging in a hammock with joint in hand, couldn't be further from the truth in today's Caribbean. On most islands, economic necessity or outright hardship means working in the fields, factory or tourism industry in a constant effort to make ends meet. Family is the hub on which life turns and many rely heavily on the remittances sent home from relatives living abroad. Often casual with time and commitments, many islanders prefer to converse with a friend over one last beer than rush to catch a bus. In the villages away from big cities and on the small islands everyone knows each other.

Chivalrous at best, misogynistic at worst, machismo is a complex cultural phenomenon on many islands such as Trinidad. Far from the simple domination of women – indeed, some social scientists argue, convincingly, that it's really the women holding the reins in these societies – machismo embraces many facets of the human condition including emotional vulnerability and virility. It can also manifest itself in homophobia, which has reached alarming proportions on some islands. This is most notable in Jamaica, where 'traditional' masculine roles have butted up against an LGBT community increasingly asserting its rights to exist.

Religion

It's quite probable that every religion known to, well, God is practiced somewhere in the Caribbean. Nevertheless, Christian religions are still the classic forces on islands with a strong European heritage. Meanwhile, evangelical sects attract scores with the promise of a peaceful afterlife that appeals to those fed up with the tribulations of the here and now.

Many islands have uniquely Afro-Caribbean belief systems. Obeah in Jamaica, Santería in Cuba and especially Vodou in Haiti all trace their roots to Africa. Slaves brought their religions with them on the Middle Passage, which then became overlain and mixed with the Christian trappings of the European colonists. Masking tribal beliefs and traditions with those of the overseers ensured the survival of these religions. These roots still go deep – a popular saying has it that Haiti is 80% Catholic and 20% Protestant, but 100% Vodou.

Rastafari sprouted in Jamaica in the 1930s from Marcus Garvey's 'back to Africa' movement, but really took off in 1966 when Ethiopian emperor Haile Selassie, regarded as the religion's Messiah, made a state visit to Jamaica. Adherents – most famously Bob Marley – smoke ganja (marijuana) as a sacrament and believe that Africans are the 13th lost tribe of Israel who will be led from exile in Babylon (the West) to Zion or the 'Promised Land' (Ethiopia) by Jah (God).

Several islands have Jewish communities. The first Jews arrived in the Caribbean while fleeing persecution from the Spanish Inquisition in the 16th century. Curaçao's Jewish community dates from 1651, and has the oldest synagogue in the Americas.

Music

You're on a beach and you're listening to Bob Marley blaring out of the sound system of the bar that just sold you a cold one. You're in Jamaica, right? Maybe. In fact you could be on any warm beach on earth, so pervasive has Marley become around the world. Even though he died in 1981, at any given moment his songs must be playing in thousands of sandy-floored beach joints worldwide.

Although each island has its own musical style, all Caribbean music is percussion-based, born as a lingua franca from Africans confronting their new, nightmarish reality where music formed one of the few links to their mostly lost cultures (religion was the other). It's unsurprising that European and North American styles eventually began to infuse Caribbean rhythms. Thematically, sociopolitical commentary/criticism has always been a vital undercurrent but so too has sex – you'll hear lots of salacious rhythms and raunchy rhymes permeating the Caribbean airwaves.

★ Best Islands for Cultural Experiences

St-Martin/Sint Maarten (p185)

St Kitts & Nevis (p171)

Antigua (p229)

Cozumel (p69)

Puerto Rico (p131)

St-Martin/Sint Maarten

Art

You'll find a rich artistic culture on most of the islands, although you may have to peer past tourist-schlock to find it. Misunderstood Haiti is a perfect example. The Haitian Naive painters of the 1940s and 1950s (such as Hector Hyppolite) were internationally significant, changing Europe and America's idea of the Caribbean and art. The modern generation continues to build on those strong foundations with painters like Edouard Duval-Carrié. Some of the best works you'll find in galleries (and tourist shops) on islands are by Haitian artists.

Cuba is another artistic powerhouse, with Wilfredo Lam its most significant painter. Best known to the wider world perhaps is the photographer Korda, who shot the indelible image of Che Guevara. The Dominican Republic and Puerto Rico, both with arts schools, have a rich arts scene as well. One of the most celebrated Caribbean painters is impressionist Camille Pissarro, born on St Thomas in 1803 and known for his landscapes. In Jamaica, look for the expressive sculptures of Edna Manley, not least the statue *Negro Aroused* that's something of a national icon.

Four of the best museums for Caribbean art are the Museo de Arte de Puerto Rico in San Juan, the Dominican Museo de Arte Moderno in Santo Domingo, Havana's Colleción de Arte Cubano and the National Gallery of Jamaica in downtown Kingston.

In Print & Film

- Check out the extraordinary feature documentary *Fire in Babylon*, about the world-beating West Indies cricket team of the 1970s and '80s, to understand the importance of cricket to much of the Caribbean.
- Joshua Jelly-Schapiro's masterful *Island People: The Caribbean and the World* is the outstanding travelogue to come out of the region in recent years.
- Jamaica directly inspired Ian Fleming to create James Bond – he wrote all the novels there and lifted the spy's name from the author of a guidebook to Caribbean birds.

Literature

When the Jamaican writer Marlon James won the 2015 Booker Prize for *A Brief History of Seven Killings*, his epic novel spun out from the attempted assassination of Bob Marley, he was just the latest in a long line of great Caribbean authors. In fact, the list of Caribbean literary giants is so long your on-the-road reading could comprise only local writers.

The Caribbean has gifted the world two winners of the Nobel literature laureates, both of whom have firmly tackled the Caribbean's post-colonial world. Trinidad's VS Naipaul is the writer of witty novels such as *A House for Mister Biswas*, and a series

Understand

Caribbean Rhythms

Steel Pan & Calypso Hammered from oil barrels, the ringing drums of steel-pan bands are a testament to the adaptive ingenuity of Caribbean musicians. The drums play buoyant calypso, often punched up with braggadocio lyrics or laced with social commentary. Tobago-born Calypso Rose is the undisputed queen of Caribbean calypso. She recorded her first album in 1964 – and the most recent in 2016.

Reggae Born in the late '60s, reggae is the musical descendant of uniquely Jamaican genres ska and rocksteady. With a languid offbeat shuffle and an ambassador in Bob Marley, it's a cornerstone of island culture.

Merengue The blistering rhythms of this Dominican genre of music are inseparable from the highly stylized, passionate dance bearing the same name.

Ripsaw Played on the accordion, goatskin drum, guitar and sawblade, ripsaw is the national music of the Turks and Caicos Islands – also played in the Bahamas as 'rake & scrape'.

of acerbic travelogues. Meanwhile Derek Walcott, from St Lucia, was honored as one of the 20th-century's greatest poets, notably for his epic *Omeros*.

CLR James, from Trinidad, is another great of Caribbean letters, and author of *The Black Jacobins*, his epic retelling of the Haitian Revolution. That epochal event also inspired Cuban writer Alejo Carpentier to produce the first magic realist novel *The Kingdom of This World*, long before there was love in a time of cholera.

The voice of the Caribbean disapora is equally strong. Check out the work of Junot Diaz (Dominican Republic: *The Brief Wondrous Life of Oscar Wao*), Edwidge Danticat (Haiti; *The Dew Breaker*) and Andrea Levy (Jamaica; *Small Island*).

Understand

Go Local

You can't begin to experience the Caribbean until you get to know its people. And that doesn't just mean the person mixing the rum punch – although those folks are often fascinating in their own right. To meet the locals you need to join the locals. Here are some tips:

- Eat at lunch wagons or stalls. The food is cheap and you often get incredibly good local fare that hasn't been watered down for foreign palettes. Plus you can break the ice just by asking what's what.
- Drop by a local bar for a drink. It's perhaps not best for single women, but rum shops on places such as Aruba, Bonaire and Curaçao are the de facto community centers and you'll soon be part of the crowd.
- Look for community fish fries or barbecues. Typically held once a week, they're big street parties in the Eastern Caribbean, especially Barbados.
- Take the bus – locals love to show you their country and will go out of their way to show you things while you bounce down the road (and the jammed conditions of most buses mean you can't help but meet people).
- Be friendly, say hi. A no-brainer but why wait for others to welcome you? Icy resolve can melt when you make the first move.

Sports

You need only ask 'cricket or baseball?' to get your finger on the pulse. Closest to the US, baseball rules in Puerto Rico, the Dominican Republic and Cuba, with players by the dozens making the jump to the US big leagues. Catching a game in Cuba or the Dominican Republic is a window into the sport as a local passion.

Cricket is serious business in the Caribbean, where rivalries (and fans) are rabid and the sport attracts major dollars. Islands where cricket rules include Jamaica, the Leeward and Windward Islands, Barbados, and Trinidad and Tobago, and while there are no national clubs, the top players from these countries form the storied West Indies team. Antigua's Sir Viv Richards and Trinidad and Tobago's Brian Lara would sail into any cricketing all-time eleven. In recent years the rapid-fire Twenty20 game has become popular, with the formation of the Caribbean Premier League. Watch out for teams such as the Jamaican Tallawahs, Trinibago Knight Riders and Barbados Tridents.

Even more fast-paced than Twenty20 cricket has been the Caribbean's success in international athletics. Tour guides everywhere get visitors to make Usain Bolt's signature lightning pose, but behind him come a host of Jamaican runners including Shelly-Ann Fraser-Pryce, Elaine Thompson and Asafa Powell.

While volleyball (especially the beach variety) and soccer (football) are popular in the Caribbean, basketball just seems to grow in popularity. Puerto Rico and Cuba have leagues and players regularly make the jump to the NBA, following in the size-15 footsteps of superstars Kareem Abdul-Jabbar (Trinidadian descent), Patrick Ewing (Jamaica) and Tim Duncan (St Croix).

African tulip tree

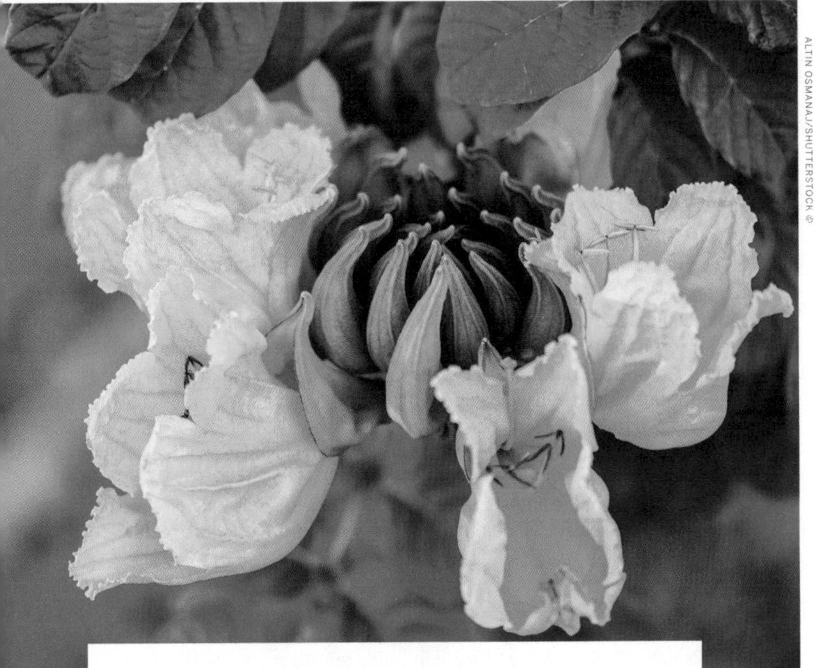

Environment

Viewed from space, the Caribbean islands form a string of green beads along a necklace that stretches across the blue from the Florida peninsula to the coast of South America. Biologically rich, both on land and below the waves, this once-pristine region is having to face up to the environmental challenges of the 21st century.

The Land

You will see two main types of islands in the Caribbean: limestone and volcanic. This can directly affect your traveling experience. Limestone islands were created by living coral forming layers of limestone that built up over millions of years. In fact, the islands look organic; one needs only see the Byzantine shapes of the Bahamas, the Virgin Islands, Anguilla, Antigua and Barbuda, Barbados, and Aruba, Bonaire and Curaçao to understand that these were formed by complex processes (St-Martin/Sint Maarten looks like something left by a bird). The islands have rolling interiors but their real allure is the crenellated coasts, which can provide ideal shelter for boats and are lined with countless beaches with brilliant white or even pinkish sand from the coral.

★ Best Places for Wildlife

Everglades National Park, Florida (p42)

El Yunque National Park, Puerto Rico (p136)

Nevis (p176)

St John Island (p156)

Curaçao (p263)

Alligator, Everglades National Park

Volcanic islands form a crescent from Saba to Grenada. Although most are dormant, there are still eruptions: Martinique (Mt Pelée, 1902), St Vincent (Soufrière volcano, 1979) and Montserrat, whose Soufrière Hills volcano has devastated much of the island in a series of eruptions since 1995. Volcanic islands typically have one or more tall cones that drop steeply down to flatter lands near the coast. The nearly perfect conical shape of Nevis is a good example. The upper reaches of the peaks often still have swaths of rainforest that proved too difficult to clear during the plantation era. The coasts generally lack the intricate curves and inlets of the limestone islands, which means natural ports are uncommon. Beaches can be dark volcanic sand but also bright white from offshore reefs.

Hurricanes

Caribbean hurricanes are born almost 2000mi (3200km) away off the west coast of Africa, where pockets of low pressure draw high winds toward them and the earth's rotation molds them into their familiar counterclockwise swirl. The storms start small but grow in strength as they cross the Atlantic, fed by warm moist air, as they bear down on the Caribbean and the North American eastern shore.

A low-level storm is called a 'tropical disturbance,' which may then grow into a 'tropical depression.' Faster winds upgrade the weather system to a 'tropical storm,' which is usually accompanied by heavy rains. The system is called a 'hurricane' when wind speeds exceed

Understand

Hurricane Irma's path through the Caribbean

In early September 2017, one of the largest hurricanes ever recorded charged through the northern Caribbean region, leaving flooding and wreckage in its wake. Hurricane Irma made landfall as a Category 5 storm the width of Texas, with wind speeds of 185 mph (300kmh) – its force sucked bays dry before creating storm surges that raced inland. The islands most strongly affected by the storm include Anguilla, Barbuda, Cuba, Puerto Rico, St-Barthélemy, St-Martin/Sint Maarten, Turks and Caicos, and the US and British Virgin Islands. The Bahamas, Haiti and the Dominican Republic also fielded some damage. Just a week later, Hurricane Maria formed in the Atlantic and increased from a Category 1 storm to a Category 5 in a mere 48 hours. This second superstorm closely followed the path of the first, making direct landfall and causing catastrophic damage in Dominica, St Croix and Puerto Rico. The Dominican Republic and Turks and Caicos were also impacted by the hurricane.

74mph and intensify around a low-pressure center, the so-called eye of the storm. Hurricane systems can range from 50 miles in diameter to several hundred miles across.

The strength of a hurricane is rated from one to five. The mildest, Category 1, has winds of at least 74mph. The strongest and rarest of hurricanes, Category 5, most typically build up in July and August and pack winds that exceed 155mph. Hurricane Katrina, which devastated New Orleans in 2005, was a Category 5 hurricane.

The Caribbean has often been hit hard by hurricanes. In 1988 Hurricane Gilbert tore through Jamaica, while in 1998 the destruction force of Hurricane Georges left around 340,000 people homeless in the Dominican Republic and Haiti. That country was again hit in 2016, when Hurricane Matthew wrecked buildings and agriculture across the southwest of the country. And in 2017, Hurricanes Irma and Maria tore through the region in quick succession, leaving a path of devastation in their wake.

The National Hurricane Center (www.nhc.noaa.gov), run by the US National Oceanic and Atmospheric Administration, is the place to head for current tropical storm information.

Manchineel Trees

Manchineel trees grow on beaches throughout the Caribbean. The fruit of the manchineel, which looks like a small green apple, is poisonous. The milky sap given off by the fruit and leaves can cause severe skin blisters, similar to the reaction caused by poison oak. If the sap gets in your eyes, it can result in temporary blindness. Never take shelter under the trees during a rainstorm, as the sap can be washed off the tree and onto anyone sitting below.

Manchineel trees can grow as high as 40ft (12m), with branches that spread widely. The leaves are green, shiny and elliptical in shape. On some of the more visited beaches, trees will be marked with warning signs or bands of red paint. Manchineel is called *mancenillier* on the French islands.

Wildlife

Animals

Except for large iguana populations and tree rats on certain islands, land animals have largely been hunted to extinction. Responsibility is shared between humans and other introduced species including mongooses, raccoons, cats, dogs and donkeys. Trinidad, home to a hundred species of mammal, is the exception to the rule.

If you're anxious to behold the Caribbean's richest fauna, you're going to get wet. One of the world's most complex ecosystems is coral, a diminutive animal that lives in giant colonies that form over millennia. Fish pecking away at nutritious tidbits or hiding out in the reef include the iridescent Creole wrasse, groupers, kingfish, sergeant majors and angelfish. Hang – or float – around and you might see inflatable porcupine fish, barracudas, nurse sharks, octopus, moray eels and manta rays.

Other species you may see include pilot, sperm, blue and humpback whales, famous for their acrobatic breaching from January to March. Spinner, spotted and bottlenosed dolphins, and loggerhead, green, hawksbill and leatherback turtles are common sights for divers. Manatees or sea cows, herbivorous marine mammals so ugly they're cute, are found in waters around Cuba, the Dominican Republic, Jamaica and Puerto Rico. All of these animals are on the threatened or endangered species list – part of the reason the Bahamas and other islands like Curaçao are criticized for their captive dolphin facilities.

Understand

Caribbean Fun Facts

- The Caribbean Sea is the world's fifth-largest body of water, just slightly bigger than the Mediterranean Sea.
- Several Caribbean islands, including Barbados, St Kitts and Nevis, and Grenada, have wild monkeys originally introduced from Africa by sailors during the slave-trade era.
- The sight of thousands of frigate birds puffing out their distinctive scarlet throat pouches in hopes of luring a mate on Barbuda is one of nature's great spectacles.
- If you see lionfish on the menu anywhere in the Caribbean, eat up! This invasive species feeds on local fish and has few predators, so let your dinner contribute to pest control.
- The breadfruit tree was first introduced to the Caribbean from Tahiti in 1793 by Captain William Bligh (of *Bounty* fame), as a source of cheap food for slave plantations.
- Dan Koeppel's *Banana: The Fate of the Fruit that Changed the World* explores the enormous impact of this ubiquitous fruit.

Frigate birds DON MAMMOSER/SHUTTERSTOCK ©

Hundreds of bird species, both endemic and migratory, frequent scores of islands. Look for iconic pink flamingos on the Bahamas and Bonaire. Common Caribbean seabirds include brown pelicans, white cattle egrets and herons. Hummingbirds and banana quits are always around, searching for something sweet.

Plants

The Caribbean has thousands of plant species. The tropics in bloom feel like an epiphany and you'll see flowering trees such as the orange flamboyant, the crimson African tulip, the white frangipani with its intoxicating scent, and the dark-blue blossoms of the lignum vitae, the hardest of all known woods. Hundreds of orchid species bejewel damper areas (best January to March), and vermilion bougainvillea, exotic birds of paradise, hibiscus of all colors and spiky crimson ginger pop up everywhere.

Environmental Issues

The sheer popularity of the region as a destination creates or aggravates environmental problems. Specific sites suffering from overexposure include the reef around Tobago Cays off St Vincent and the Grenadines, a popular anchorage for sailors, and the reefs around the Virgin Islands, which have been damaged by careless snorkelers and divers.

Overfishing is a major problem. The Bahamas outlawed long-line fishing in 1959, the first Caribbean island to do so, but now struggles with poachers; some communities have established marine preserves independently of the government to curb the abuse. More than half of the reefs in the Caribbean are dead or dying and the rest are severely threatened. Global warming is the biggest threat, as record sea temperatures kill beneficial types of algae that corals depend on symbiotically to survive, which results in the process called 'bleaching.'

Waste is also a big issue. Mountains of garbage crowd Havana, acrid refuse burns from Vieques to Puerto Plata, and sewage needs somewhere to go – too often into the sea, unfortunately. Larger islands, in particular, have had difficulty inculcating a culture of conservation. Deforestation is a problem in the Dominican Republic and Haiti alike. However, other islands have begun to take a lead in renewable energy, with increased solar generation in Barbados, the Dutch Antilles investing heavily in wind power, and Nevis, St Lucia and Dominica attempting to take advantage of their volcanic locations to try and develop geothermal energy.

Street vendor, Marigot (p200), St-Martin/Sint Maarten

Survival Guide

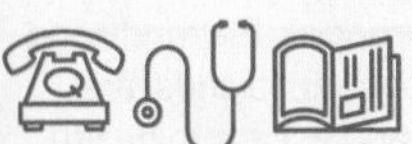

Directory A–Z

Customs Regulations

All the Caribbean islands allow a reasonable amount of personal items to be brought in duty free, as well as an allowance of liquor and tobacco. Determining what you can take home depends on where you're vacationing and your country of origin. Check with your country's customs agency for clarification.

Climate

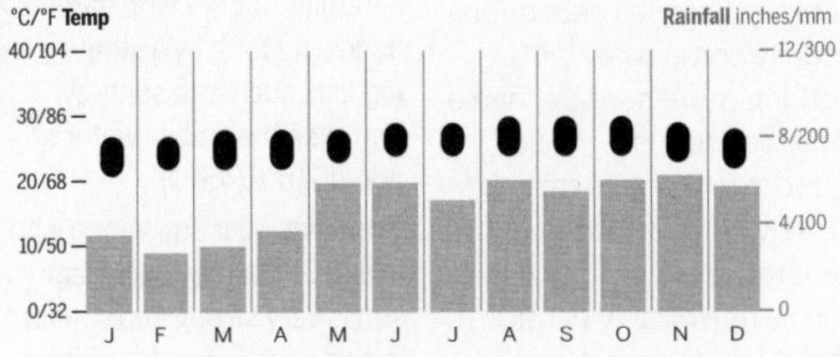

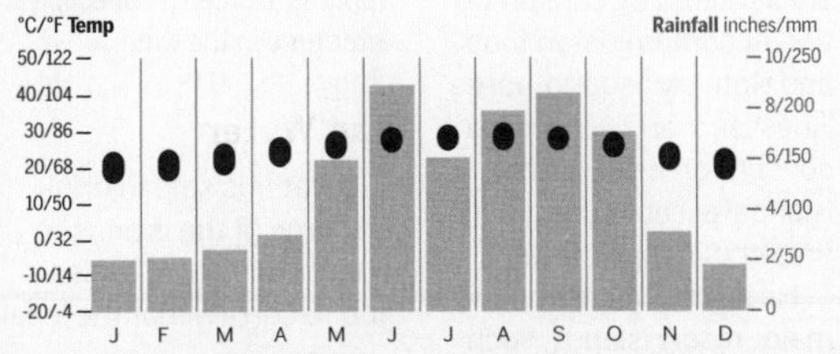

Dangers & Annoyances

In terms of individual safety and crime, the situation is quite varied in the Caribbean. Employ common sense.

- In big cities and tourist areas, take taxis at night.
- Avoid flashing your wealth, whether jewelry or blindly following your smartphone.
- Exercise extra caution in urban areas such as Pointe-à-Pitre (Guadeloupe), Fort-de-France (Martinique), some areas of Kingston (Jamaica), Port-au-Prince (Haiti) and downtown Port of Spain (Trinidad).

Also watch out for manchineel trees (see p301).

Electricity

Electrical current varies across the islands but most use 110V 50Hz with the standard North American two or three pin plug.

Embassies & Consulates

Nations such as Australia, Canada, New Zealand and the US have embassies and consulates in the largest Caribbean countries. Check your government's foreign affairs website for locations.

Etiquette

The Caribbean is famously laid-back, but it's also a place that insists on good manners.

Greetings Always greet people properly, and treat elders with extra respect. That said, don't be surprised at the directness of many conversations.

Dress Caribbean people dress smartly when they can (even more so when heading to a party or social event), and many government offices and banks have written dress codes on the

Practicalities

- **Smoking** Banned in public places and hotels and restaurants in many Caribbean destinations.
- **Weights & Measures** Some Caribbean countries use the metric system, others use the imperial system, and a few use a confusing combination of both.

door – beachwear should be confined to the beach.

Island time Even though locals may be relaxed about the clock, it's always wise to turn up to appointments at the stated hour (but be prepared to wait).

Gay & Lesbian Travelers

Parts of the Caribbean are not particularly gay-friendly destinations and on many of the islands overt homophobia and machismo is prevalent.

Gay men and lesbians generally keep a low profile, and public hand-holding, kissing and other outward signs of affection are not commonplace. Homosexuality remains illegal in some countries, most notably Jamaica and Barbados.

Still, there are several niches for gay travelers. Particularly friendly islands include Aruba, Bonaire, Curaçao, Dominican Republic, Guadeloupe, Martinique, Puerto Rico, Saba, St-Martin/Sint Maarten and the US Virgin Islands.

Useful links include the following:

Damron (www.damron.com) The USA's leading gay publisher offers guides to world cities.

Spartacus International Gay Guide (www.spartacusworld.com) A male-only directory of gay entertainment venues and hotels.

Health

Prevention is the key to remaining healthy while traveling abroad. Travelers who receive the recommended vaccinations for the destination and follow common-sense precautions usually come away with nothing more serious than a little diarrhea.

From a health point of view, the Caribbean is generally safe as long as you're reasonably careful about what you eat and drink. The most common travel-related diseases, such as dysentery and hepatitis, are acquired by consumption of contaminated food and water. Mosquito-borne illnesses aren't a significant concern on most of the islands, except during outbreaks of dengue fever.

Health standards on major resort islands, such as Barbados, Bermuda and the Cayman Islands, are high, and access to health care is good.

Environmental Hazards

A few things to watch out for:

Mosquito bites Caribbean mosquitoes and other biting/stinging insects come in all shapes and sizes, and are quite common. The biggest concern here, outside the few areas with malaria, is simply discomfort and hassle. Make certain you have a good insect repellent with at least 25% DEET.

Rabies Some islands do have rabies, so do as you would at home and avoid touching or petting strays.

Sea stingers Spiny sea urchins and coelenterates (coral and jellyfish) are a hazard in some areas. If stung by a coelenterate, apply diluted vinegar or baking soda. Remove tentacles carefully, but not with bare hands. If stung by a stinging fish, such as a stingray, immerse the limb in water at about 115°F (45°C).

Sunburn Wear sunscreen with a high SPF as the Caribbean sun is very strong and sunburn is common. Every day we see people who are as pink as lobsters and have their trips ruined because they didn't apply sunscreen – especially after time in the water.

Tap Water

Tap water is safe to drink on some of the islands, but not on others. Unless you're certain that the local water is safe, you shouldn't drink it.

Note: if tap water is safe to drink – as it is on the major destination islands except for Cuba – then avoiding bottled water reduces the significant environmental impact of plastic water containers.

Insurance

It's foolhardy to travel without insurance to cover theft, loss and medical problems. Check that your policy includes emergency medical evacuation costs, and any activities deemed risky by insurers, such as scuba diving or other adventure sports.

Worldwide travel insurance is available at www.lonelyplanet.com. You can buy, extend and claim online anytime – even if you're already on the road.

Internet Access

Internet access and wi-fi is generally easily found throughout most of the Caribbean. Check the Fast Facts box in each destination chapter for tips on finding free wi-fi.

Legal Matters

Due to the stereotype that pot-smoking is widespread in the Caribbean (it isn't), some visitors take a casual attitude about sampling island drugs.

Be forewarned that drug trafficking is a serious problem throughout the Caribbean and officials in most countries have little to no tolerance of visitors caught using. Penalties vary throughout the islands, but getting caught smoking or possessing marijuana (or any illegal drug) can result in stiff jail sentences. The exception is Jamaica, which has decriminalized possession of up to 2oz (56.7g; a fine still applies); the sale of marijuana is not legal.

Money

The US dollar is accepted almost everywhere, so it's not necessary to have local currency before you arrive. Carry smaller denominations to pay for taxis, street snacks or tips.

ATMs & Credit Cards

ATMs are generally common on all but small islands (and increasingly available in Cuba). Many give out US dollars in addition to the local currency. Credit cards are widely accepted but watch for surcharges.

Tipping

Restaurants Varies in the region although 15% is average. Watch for service charges added to bills.

Taxis Not usually tipped.

Exchange Rates

Caribbean currency	US$1	C$1	€1	UK£1
Aruban florin (Afl)	1.79	1.33	1.91	2.18
Barbadian dollar (B$)	2.00	1.49	2.13	2.44
Cayman Islands dollar (CI$)	0.82	0.61	0.87	1.00
Eastern Caribbean dollar (EC$)	2.70	2.01	2.88	3.29
Jamaican dollar (J$)	128.65	95.69	137.06	157.00
Trinidad & Tobago dollar (TT$)	6.74	5.01	7.18	8.23
US dollar (US$)	-	0.74	1.07	1.22

For current exchange rates, see www.xe.com.

The Art of Bargaining

Whether it's the beach vendor with the necklace you just have to have, the market stall owner with the cutest stuffed iguana or the slick jewelry store sales clerk, you will likely have a chance to try out your bargaining skills at some point in the Caribbean. Note, however, that fixed prices are also common, especially at large stores and duty-free malls. Know that 'no bargaining' can mean just that and isn't a ploy. Also note that it isn't just that bauble in the window that you can bargain for. Especially in the low season, almost everything, including accommodations, can be negotiated. Ask for a better room or a discount if you are staying for a few days. Although many people are put off at the prospect, bargaining can be an enjoyable part of shopping, so maintain your sense of humor and keep things in perspective. Try following these steps: Have some idea of what the item is worth. Why pay more than you would at home? Establish a starting price – ask the seller for their price rather than make an initial offer. Your first price can be from one-third to two-thirds of the asking price – assuming that the asking price is not outrageous. With offer and counter-offer, move closer to an acceptable price. If you don't get to an acceptable price, you're entitled to walk – the vendor may call you back with a lower price. Note that when you name a price, you're committed – you must buy if your offer is accepted. Keep things in perspective. Is it worth aggravation to save one last dollar in dealing with a vendor who may only make a few dollars a week?

Opening Hours

Opening hours vary across the region, although Sunday remains sacrosanct, with businesses and offices firmly shut throughout the Caribbean. Note that small and family-run businesses may close for a period between August and November.

Passports

All US citizens traveling to the Caribbean on a cruise ship will need a passport or a passport card to reenter the US. The latter is essentially a wallet-sized US passport that is only good for land and sea travel between the US and Canada, Mexico and the Caribbean. In some circumstances you may only need a valid driver's license but confirm this carefully with the cruise line.

The law does not affect the US state territories of Puerto Rico and the US Virgin Islands, which will continue to allow established forms of identification like valid driver's licenses.

Public Holidays

Regionwide public holidays:

New Year's Day January 1

Good Friday Late March/early April

Easter Monday Late March/early April

Whit Monday Eighth Monday after Easter

Christmas Day December 25

Boxing Day December 26

Taxes & Refunds

Value Added Tax is added on goods and services across the region. Rates vary from island to island. In some countries VAT is not included in menu prices, leading to unexpectedly inflated bills. Check whether quoted hotel rates include tax when booking.

It's sometimes possible for visitors to obtain VAT refunds on goods bought during a trip.

Telephone

Most cell phones work in the Caribbean; avoid roaming charges with easily bought local SIM cards. The biggest operators in the Caribbean are Digicel and Flow. Puerto Rico and US Virgin Islands are included in US plans.

Time

Eastern Standard Time (EST; five hours behind GMT/UTC) Turks and Caicos, Jamaica, the Cayman Islands, the Dominican Republic

Atlantic Standard Time (AST; four hours behind GMT/UTC) All other islands

Daylight Saving Time Only observed by Turks and Caicos.

Travelers with Disabilities

Travel in the Caribbean is not particularly easy for those with physical disabilities. Overall there is little or no awareness of the need for easier access onto planes, buses or rental vehicles. One exception is Puerto Rico, where good compliance with the Americans Disabilities Act (ADA) means many sights and hotels have wheelchair accessibility.

Visitors with special needs should inquire directly with prospective hotels for information on their facilities. The larger, more modern resorts are most likely to have the greatest accessibility, with elevators, wider doorways and wheelchair-accessible bathrooms.

While land travel may present some obstacles, cruises are often a good option for travelers with disabilities in the Caribbean. Many cruise lines can coordinate shore-based excursions in tour buses equipped for special needs.

The **Society for Accessible Travel & Hospitality** (www.sath.org) has useful information. Download Lonely Planet's free Accessible Travel guide from http://lp-travel.to/AccessibleTravel.

Telephone Codes

Island	Country code
Anguilla	+264
Antigua & Barbuda	+268
Aruba	+297
The Bahamas	+242
Barbados	+248
Bonaire	+599
British Virgin Islands	+284
Cayman Islands	+345
Cuba	+53
Curaçao	+599
Dominica	+767
Dominican Republic	+809 or +829
Grenada	+473
Guadeloupe	+590
Haiti	+509
Jamaica	+876
Martinique	+596
Montserrat	+664
Puerto Rico	+787
Saba	+599
Sint Eustatius	+599
St-Barthélemy	+590
St Kitts & Nevis	+869
St Lucia	+758
St-Martin/Sint Maarten	+599
St Vincent & the Grenadines	+784
Trinidad & Tobago	+868
Turks & Caicos	+649
US Virgin Islands	+340

Island Time

In the Caribbean life moves at a slow, loosely regimented pace. You'll often see signs in front of shops, bars and restaurants that say 'open all day, every day' and this can mean several things; the place could truly be open all day every day of the week, but don't count on it. If business is slow, a restaurant, shop or attraction might simply close. If a bar is hopping and the owner's having fun, it could stay open until the wee hours. If the rainy season is lasting too long, a hotel or restaurant might close for a month. In other words, hard and fast rules about opening times are hard to come by.

The only consistent rule is that Sundays are sacred and 'open every day' generally translates to 'open every day except Sunday.'

Visas

Requirements vary from island to island. Citizens of Canada, the EU and the US don't need visas for visits of under 90 days throughout the region.

Women Travelers

Although the situation varies between islands, machismo is alive and well. Men can get aggressive, especially with women traveling alone. On many islands local men have few qualms about catcalling, hissing, whistling, sucking their teeth or making kissy sounds to attract female attention. While much of this is simply annoying, it can make women feel unsafe.

Like it or not, women will generally feel much safer if traveling with a male companion. Women traveling alone need to be sensible and careful: avoid walking alone after dark, heading off into the wilderness alone, hitchhiking or picking up male hitchhikers. Generally try to avoid any situation where you're isolated and vulnerable. Don't wear skimpy clothing when you're not on the beach – it will just garner you a lot of unwanted attention. Also note that 'harmless flirtation' at home can be misconstrued as a serious come-on in the Caribbean.

Transport

Getting Around

Bicycle

The popularity of cycling in the Caribbean depends on where you go. Several islands are prohibitively hilly, with narrow roads that make cycling difficult. On others cycling is a great way to get around. Many of the islands have bicycles for rent.

Bus

Inexpensive bus service is available on most islands, although the word 'bus' has different meanings in different places. Some islands have full-size buses, while on others a 'bus' is simply a pickup truck with wooden benches in the back.

Whatever the vehicle, buses are a good environmental choice compared to rental cars and are an excellent way to meet locals. People are generally quite friendly and happy to talk to you about their island. Buses are also a good way to hear the most popular local music tracks, often at an amazingly loud volume.

Buses are often the primary means of commuting to work or school and thus are most frequent in the early mornings and from mid- to late afternoon. There's generally a good bus service on Saturday mornings, but Sunday service is often nonexistent.

Car & Motorcycle

Driving in the Caribbean islands can rock your world, rattle your brains and fray your nerves. At first. Soon, you'll get used to the often-poor road conditions, slow speeds and relaxed adherence to road rules and using your horn to punctuate any maneuver or passing thought on the road conditions.

Island Driving

Offer a lift It's common courtesy on many islands to slow down and offer pedestrians a lift (and is considered obligatory on some).

Beware of goats! Keep an eye out for stray dogs, iguanas, wild horses, chickens and goats, all of which meander aimlessly on the island roads.

Cede the right-of-way Drivers often stop to let others turn or pedestrians to cross even when you don't think it;s necessary.

Driver's License

You'll need your driver's license in order to rent a car, and frequently need to be over 21. On some of the former British islands, you may need to purchase a visitor's driver's license from your car-rental agent.

Rental

Car rentals are available on nearly all of the islands, with a few exceptions (usually because they lack roads). On most islands there are affiliates of the international chains, but local rental agencies may have better rates. Advance booking almost always attracts cheaper rates.

International rental agencies found across many islands in the Caribbean include:

Avis (www.avis.com)
Budget (www.budget.com),
Dollar (www.dollar.com)
Europcar (www.europcar.com)
Hertz (www.hertz.com).

Road Rules

Road rules vary by island. In general, note that driving conditions may be more relaxed than you are used to.

Many Caribbean countries drive on the left, but what side of the road to drive on depends on the island: this can be confusing if you're island-hopping and renting cars on each island. Adding to the confusion, some cars have steering columns on the opposite side of where you'd expect.

Taxi

Taxis gather outside cruise ports and are usually the quickest and easiest way to visit local sights while you're in port. Most taxis in the region don't have meters and some look like regular cars or minibuses. Check that the driver is a licensed taxi operator and ask for a rate card or agree on a fare (and currency) before getting in. A good taxi driver can also act as a local guide and ensure you get back to the ship on time!

Climate Change & Travel

Every form of transport that relies on carbon-based fuel generates CO_2, the main cause of human-induced climate change. Modern travel is dependent on aeroplanes, which might use less fuel per mile per person than most cars but travel much greater distances. The altitude at which aircraft emit gases (including CO_2) and particles also contributes to their climate change impact. Many websites offer 'carbon calculators' that allow people to estimate the carbon emissions generated by their journey and, for those who wish to do so, to offset the impact of the greenhouse gases emitted with contributions to portfolios of climate-friendly initiatives throughout the world. Lonely Planet offsets the carbon footprint of all staff and author travel.

Behind the Scenes

Acknowledgements

Climate map data adapted from Peel MC, Finlayson BL & McMahon TA (2007) 'Updated World Map of the Köppen-Geiger Climate Classification', Hydrology and Earth System Sciences, 11, 163344.

Cover photograph: Half Moon Cay, Bahamas, Richard Cummins, Getty©.

This Book

This 1st edition of Lonely Planet's *Cruise Ports Caribbean* guidebook was curated by Joshua Kinser and researched and written by Ray Bartlett, Paul Clammer, Alex Egerton, Anna Kaminski, Catherine Le Nevez, Hugh McNaughtan, Liza Prado, Andrea Schulte-Peevers, Regis St Louis, Mara Vorhees, Luke Waterson and Karla Zimmerman. This guidebook was produced by the following:

Destination Editor Bailey Freeman

Product Editors Paul Harding, Elizabeth Jones

Graphic Designer Campbell McKenzie

Senior Cartographer Corey Hutchison

Book Designers Virginia Moreno, Clara Monitto

Assisting Editors Gabrielle Stefanos, Ross Taylor

Assisting Book Designer Nicholas Colicchia

Thanks to Liz Heynes, Simon Hoskins, Valentina Kremenchutskaya, Kate Mathews, Lauren O'Connell, Trisha Ping, Tony Wheeler, Juan Winata

Send Us Your Feedback

We love to hear from travelers – your comments keep us on our toes and help make our books better. Our well-traveled team reads every word on what you loved or loathed about this book. Although we cannot reply individually to postal submissions, we always guarantee that your feedback goes straight to the appropriate authors, in time for the next edition. Each person who sends us information is thanked in the next edition, the most useful submissions are rewarded with a selection of digital PDF chapters.

Visit lonelyplanet.com/contact to submit your updates and suggestions or to ask for help. Our award-winning website also features inspirational travel stories, news and discussions.

Note: We may edit, reproduce and incorporate your comments in Lonely Planet products such as guidebooks, websites and digital products, so let us know if you don't want your comments reproduced or your name acknowledged. For a copy of our privacy policy visit lonelyplanet.com/privacy.

A–Z

Index

A

B

000 Map pages

000 Map pages

000 Map pages

T

U

V

W

Y

Z

000 Map pages

Symbols & Map Key

Look for these symbols to quickly identify listings:

- Sights
- Activities
- Courses
- Tours
- Festivals & Events
- Eating
- Drinking
- Entertainment
- Shopping
- Information & Transport

These symbols and abbreviations give vital information for each listing:

Sustainable or green recommendation

FREE No payment required

- Telephone number
- Opening hours
- Parking
- Nonsmoking
- Air-conditioning
- Internet access
- Wi-fi access
- Swimming pool
- Bus
- Ferry
- Tram
- Train
- English-language menu
- Vegetarian selection
- Family-friendly

Find your best experiences with these Great For... icons.

 Art & Culture

 Beaches

 Budget

 Cafe/Coffee

 Cycling

Detour

 Drinking

 Entertainment

Events

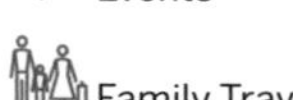 Family Travel

 Food & Drink

 History

Local Life

 Nature & Wildlife

Photo Op

Scenery

 Shopping

 Short Trip

Sport

 Walking

 Winter Travel

Sights

- Beach
- Bird Sanctuary
- Buddhist
- Castle/Palace
- Christian
- Confucian
- Hindu
- Islamic
- Jain
- Jewish
- Monument
- Museum/Gallery/ Historic Building
- Ruin
- Shinto
- Sikh
- Taoist
- Winery/Vineyard
- Zoo/Wildlife Sanctuary
- Other Sight

Points of Interest

- Bodysurfing
- Camping
- Cafe
- Canoeing/Kayaking
- Course/Tour
- Diving
- Drinking & Nightlife
- Eating
- Entertainment
- Sento Hot Baths/ Onsen
- Shopping
- Skiing
- Sleeping
- Snorkelling
- Surfing
- Swimming/Pool
- Walking
- Windsurfing
- Other Activity

Information

- Bank
- Embassy/Consulate
- Hospital/Medical
- Internet
- Police
- Post Office
- Telephone
- Toilet
- Tourist Information
- Other Information

Geographic

- Beach
- Gate
- Hut/Shelter
- Lighthouse
- Lookout
- Mountain/Volcano
- Oasis
- Park
- Pass
- Picnic Area
- Waterfall

Transport

- Airport
- BART station
- Border crossing
- Boston T station
- Bus
- Cable car/Funicular
- Cycling
- Ferry
- Metro/MRT station
- Monorail
- Parking
- Petrol station
- Subway/S-Bahn/ Skytrain station
- Taxi
- Train station/Railway
- Tram
- Tube Station
- Underground/ U-Bahn station
- Other Transport

Luke Waterson

Puerto Rico Raised in the remote Somerset countryside in southwest England, Luke quickly became addicted to exploring out-of-the-way places. While completing a Creative Writing degree at the University of East Anglia, he shouldered his backpack and vowed to see as much of the world as possible. Fast-forward a few years and he has traveled the Americas from Alaska to Tierra del Fuego and developed an obsession for Soviet architecture and pre-Columbian ruins in equal measure. He divides his time between Wales and Slovakia, where he keeps the world's leading English-language content site on Slovak travel and culture, www.englishman inslovakia.co.uk.

Karla Zimmerman

US Virgin Islands Karla lives in Chicago, where she eats doughnuts, yells at the Cubs, and writes stuff for books, magazines and websites when she's not doing the first two things. She has contributed to 40-plus guidebooks and travel anthologies covering destinations in Europe, Asia, Africa, North America and the Caribbean – all of which are a long way from the early days, when she wrote about gravel for a construction magazine and got to trek to places like Fredonia, Kansas. To learn more, follow her on Instagram and Twitter (@karlazimmerman).

musty newsrooms and the insatiable corporate appetite for superficial news, Alex decided to leap into travel writing in order to escape the mundane. He spends most of his time on the road checking under mattresses, sampling suspicious street food and chatting with locals as part of the research process for travel articles and guidebooks. A keen adventurer, Alex has hiked through remote jungles in Colombia, explored isolated tributaries of the mighty Mekong and taken part in the first kayak descent of a number of remote waterways in Nicaragua. When not on the road, you'll find him at home amongst the colonial splendor of Popayán in southern Colombia.

Anna Kaminski

Jamaica Having majored in Caribbean and Latin American history at university and having lived in Kingston and worked in Jamaica's prisons and ghettos in 2006, Anna was thrilled to research Jamaica for Lonely Planet a second time. On this occasion, she drove the scenic and often gnarly back roads of west Jamaica, visited numerous plantation houses, hiked through rugged Cockpit Country, attended the Maroon Festival and went to Boston Bay in search of Jamaica's best jerk pork. When not on the road for Lonely Planet, Anna calls London home.

Catherine Le Nevez

St-Martin/Sint Maarten Catherine's wanderlust kicked in when she roadtripped across Europe from her Parisian base aged four, and she's been hitting the road at every opportunity since, traveling to around 60 countries and completing her Doctorate of Creative Arts in Writing, Masters in Professional Writing, and postgrad qualifications in Editing and Publishing along the way. Over the past dozen-plus years she's written for scores of Lonely Planet guides and articles covering Paris, France, Europe and far beyond. Her work has also appeared in numerous online and print publications. Topping Catherine's list of travel tips is to travel without any expectations.

Hugh McNaughtan

Bahamas, Turks & Caicos A former English lecturer, Hugh swapped grant applications for visa applications, and turned his love of travel into a full-time thing. Having done a bit of restaurant-reviewing in his home town (Melbourne), he's now eaten his way across four continents. He's never happier than when on the road with his two daughters. Except perhaps on the cricket field.

Liza Prado

Puerto Rico Liza Prado has been a travel writer since 2003, when she made a move from corporate lawyering to travel writing (and never looked back). She's written dozens of guidebooks and articles as well as apps and blogs to destinations throughout the Americas. She takes decent photos too. Liza is a graduate of Brown University and Stanford Law School. She lives in Denver, Colorado, with her husband and fellow LP writer, Gary Chandler, and their two kids.

Andrea Schulte-Peevers

St Kitts & Nevis, Antigua Born and raised in Germany and educated in London and at UCLA, Andrea has traveled the distance to the moon and back in her visits to some 75 countries. She has earned her living as a professional travel writer for over two decades and authored or contributed to nearly 100 Lonely Planet titles as well as to newspapers, magazines and websites around the world. She also works as a travel consultant, translator and editor. Andrea's destination expertise is especially strong when it comes to Germany, Dubai and the UAE, Crete and the Caribbean Islands. She lives in Berlin.

Regis St Louis

Miami Regis grew up in a small town in the American Midwest – the kind of place that fuels big dreams of travel – and he developed an early fascination with foreign dialects and world cultures. He spent his formative years learning Russian and a handful of Romance languages, which served him well on journeys across much of the globe. Regis has contributed to more than 50 Lonely Planet titles, covering destinations across six continents. His travels have taken him from the mountains of Kamchatka to remote island villages in Melanesia, and to many grand urban landscapes. When not on the road, he lives in New Orleans. Follow him on www.instagram.com/regisstlouis.

Mara Vorhees

Cayman Islands, Aruba, Bonaire, Curaçao Mara Vorhees writes about food, travel and family fun around the world. Her work has been published by *BBC Travel*, *Boston Globe*, *Delta Sky*, *Vancouver Sun* and more. For Lonely Planet she regularly writes about destinations in Central America and Eastern Europe, as well as New England, where she lives. She often travels with her twin boys in tow, earning her an expertise in family travel. Follow their adventures and misadventures at www.havetwinswill travel.com.

Our Story

A beat-up old car, a few dollars in the pocket and a sense of adventure. In 1972 that's all Tony and Maureen Wheeler needed for the trip of a lifetime – across Europe and Asia overland to Australia. It took several months, and at the end – broke but inspired – they sat at their kitchen table writing and stapling together their first travel guide, *Across Asia on the Cheap*. Within a week they'd sold 1500 copies. Lonely Planet was born. Today, Lonely Planet has offices in Franklin, London, Melbourne, Oakland, Dublin, Beijing, and Delhi, with more than 600 staff and writers. We share Tony's belief that 'a great guidebook should do three things: inform, educate and amuse'.

Our Writers

Joshua Kinser

Curator, Plan Your Trip chapters Joshua Kinser is a writer, photographer and musician based out of Bat Cave, North Carolina, about 20 miles from Asheville. He spent more than five years working as a drummer on cruise ships, traveling throughout the Caribbean and repeatedly visiting nearly every cruise port in the region. He is the author of more than 16 books, including several travel guides to the southeast United States and a book series about what it's like to work aboard cruise ships.

Ray Bartlett

Cozumel Ray is a travel writer specializing in Japan, Korea, Mexico and the United States. He has worked on many different Lonely Planet titles, starting with Japan in 2004 and covering Cozumel and Tulum for this guide.

Paul Clammer

Jamaica Paul has worked as a molecular biologist, tour leader and travel writer. Since 2003 he has worked as a guidebook author for Lonely Planet, contributing to over 25 LP titles, covering swathes of South and Central Asia, West and North Africa, and the Caribbean. In recent years he's lived in Morocco, Jordan, Haiti and Fiji, as well as his native England. Find him online at paulclammer.com or on Twitter as @paulclammer. Paul also contributed to the Plan Your Trip and Survival Guide sections of this guidebook.

Alex Egerton

Barbados A news journalist by trade, Alex has worked for magazines, newspapers and media outlets on five continents. Having had his fill of

More Writers

STAY IN TOUCH LONELYPLANET.COM/CONTACT

AUSTRALIA The Malt Store, Level 3, 551 Swanston St, Carlton, Victoria 3053 ☎03 8379 8000, fax 03 8379 8111

IRELAND Digital Depot, Roe Lane (off Thomas St), Digital Hub, Dublin 8, D08 TCV4, Ireland

USA 124 Linden Street, Oakland, CA 94607 ☎510 250 6400, toll free 800 275 8555, fax 510 893 8572

UK 240 Blackfriars Road, London SE1 8NW ☎020 3771 5100, fax 020 3771 5101

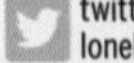 twitter.com/lonelyplanet
 facebook.com/lonelyplanet
 instagram.com/lonelyplanet
 youtube.com/lonelyplanet
 lonelyplanet.com/newsletter